After Roe

After Roe

THE LOST HISTORY OF
THE ABORTION DEBATE

MARY ZIEGLER

 Harvard University Press

Cambridge, Massachusetts
London, England
2015

Copyright © 2015 by the President and Fellows of Harvard College
All rights reserved
Printed in the United States of America

First Printing

Library of Congress Cataloging-in-Publication Data

Ziegler, Mary, 1982–
    After Roe : the lost history of the abortion debate / Mary Ziegler.
        pages cm
    Includes bibliographical references and index.
        ISBN 978-0-674-73677-1
    1. Abortion—United States—History—20th century. 2.   Abortion—
Law and legislation—United States—History—20th century. 3.   Pro-life
movement—United States—History—20th century. 4.   Reproductive
rights—United States—History—20th century.   I. Title.
    HQ767.5.U5Z54 2015
    362.1988'80973—dc23   2014039992

To my father,
who taught me
to look up.

Contents

Preface

The abortion debate in the decade after *Roe v. Wade* changed Thea Rossi Barron's life. Barron was a wife, a mother, and the second woman in her family to become an attorney. A self-described liberal Democrat, Barron became active in the pro-life movement when she agreed to debate doctors, attorneys, and social workers with different views. When running for the Kalamazoo, Michigan, City Commission, Barron had to answer questions about abortion, but in office she prioritized the rights of labor, the middle class, and the poor. She counted among her heroes Hubert Humphrey and Shirley Chisholm, and she saw herself as an advocate for the underdog.

In 1975, after her husband left the marriage and filed for divorce, Barron brought her family to Washington, DC. While looking for a new position practicing law, Barron offered her services as a speaker to Dr. Mildred F. Jefferson, then the president of the largest national antiabortion organization, the National Right to Life Committee (NRLC). Jefferson told Barron that her organization soon hoped to hire a lobbyist to work on Capitol Hill, and a year later she called Barron to offer a part-time position. Soon Barron gave up her job at a small litigation firm to become a full-time lobbyist for the NRLC.[1]

Working with both Democrats and Republicans, she played a key role in the passage of the Hyde Amendment, legislation outlawing federal funding for abortion. However, Barron never stopped defining her mission more broadly. She fiercely supported legislation banning pregnancy discrimination at work. Such legislation, Barron argued, represented only one example of the gender issues on which those on opposing sides of the abortion debate could find common ground.

With Eleanor Smeal of the National Organization for Women (NOW), she organized a 1979 summit designed to identify areas of agreement between those divided by the abortion wars. Larger political changes undermined Barron's quest for consensus. She had long urged her colleagues not to oppose the Equal Rights Amendment (ERA), a constitutional proposal prohibiting sex discrimination, since she believed her movement should "not work against an amendment that would bring equality to women."[2] Barron supported the amendment herself and believed that if the NRLC staked out a position in opposition, the organization would divide the ranks of the pro-life movement. However, in 1978 she discovered that her colleagues had gone behind her back to defeat the ERA, and when the NRLC leadership did not step up to stop it, Barron resigned. The road to common ground had come to seem infinitely harder to follow.[3]

Like Barron, Frances Kissling believed that those on opposing sides could find consensus on other important questions. Born into a Polish Catholic family, Kissling had joined a convent before realizing that she could not square her views with the Church's positions on birth control and divorce. She became the director of two abortion clinics in New York State and later helped to operate facilities in Mexico, Italy, and Austria. In 1977, she became the first president of the National Abortion Federation (NAF), a group uniting abortion providers.[4]

Kissling expressed deep concern about prohibitions on federal funding for abortion, helping to write the story of Rosie Jimenez, a twenty-seven-year-old college student and single mother. After learning she was pregnant, Jimenez sought out an abortion. Because Medicaid would no longer reimburse for abortion services, a local doctor turned her down, and Jimenez went to Mexico to get an abortion she could afford. Because of the illegal procedure, she died of septic shock. For Kissling, Jimenez's story demonstrated the unfairness of laws banning public funding for abortion. Just the same, Kissling believed that consensus was possible on gender issues beyond abortion. She enthusiastically attended the common-ground summit that Barron had helped to organize. Years later, however, other activists asked Kissling for proof that the event had taken place. It no longer seemed credible that so many had looked for shared solutions.[5]

The stories of activists like Kissling and Barron figure centrally in larger legal, historical, and sociological debates about everything from the defining traits of the pro-life and pro-choice movements to the proper role of the courts in American democracy. The conventional wisdom holds that the *Roe* opinion provoked a major grass-roots pro-life challenge to the legitimacy of the Supreme Court. For the abortion-rights movement, the story goes, *Roe* discouraged efforts to develop a broader and more equitable agenda that advanced all women's interest in accessing contraception, child care, and health care and in avoiding sterilization abuse.

Historians, Supreme Court justices, and legal scholars with disparate normative views on abortion have joined in their criticism of *Roe*'s broader societal impact: the opinion supposedly short-circuited a previously innovative dialogue between competing movements about what abortion rights ought to mean. *Roe* purportedly pushed American movement politics toward the "clash of absolutes" famously described by Laurence Tribe, as activists fought bitterly about the Equal Rights Amendment, contraception, and women's role in the American polity. By focusing so heavily on the effect of the Supreme Court's decision, however, scholars have exaggerated the importance of judicial intervention. In putting the Court at the center of the story, we have lost sight of equally important contributions made by the politicians, lobbyists, and grassroots activists who shaped the clash of absolutes Tribe discusses.[6]

Events and activism since 1973 have transformed and multiplied the meanings of "*Roe.*" Opposing activists deployed *Roe* in ways calculated to change the course of abortion politics. Within the abortion-rights movement, feminists used *Roe* as a reminder that abortion was a women's issue. At times, some movement members saw *Roe* as a symbol of the dangers of a single-issue agenda. In fundraising campaigns and efforts to mobilize new supporters, activists on opposing sides of the abortion wars reinterpreted the *Roe* decision in order to shape public consciousness of what the Court had said and whether its opinion deserved support.

These frequent movement reinterpretations of *Roe* remind us of its varied and often imprecise use in later scholarship. For supportive commentators, *Roe* represents the constitutionalization of reproductive rights or even the recognition of the relationship between fertility control and women's liberation. Other observers use *Roe* to refer to specific features of Justice Harry Blackmun's opinion: an emphasis on medical prerogatives, the neglect of the connection between abortion and sex equality, or the creation of a trimester framework governing access to the procedure. More generally, scholars, judges, and activists sometimes treat *Roe* as a stand-in for all "activist" judicial decision-making or its policy consequences. By using *Roe* in so many ways, we have contributed to misunderstandings of the opinion's impact. Carefully describing social movements' reinterpretations of the decision sets the stage for a deeper understanding of what "*Roe*" is and how it has made a difference.

As scholars and observers cast new values onto *Roe*, commentators swept away much of the history of how social movements actually responded to the decision. We have adopted a conventional account of post-*Roe* polarization that is fundamentally flawed, based upon assumptions about the aftermath of the Supreme Court decision rather than on systematic research. Despite the widely-recognized importance of social-movement reactions to the opinion, no one has written a comprehensive history of the decade after the Supreme Court's decision.

Drawing on over 100 oral histories and material housed at more than a dozen archives, this book tells that story, focusing on one of the most important periods in the evolution of American gender politics and constitutional law. By using *Roe* to refer to so many deeply-held beliefs and wider political shifts, we have attributed too much of what followed to the Supreme Court's decision. More importantly, as the book shows, we have missed many of the tactical decisions, ideological changes, and larger political transformations that helped to create the world of contemporary abortion politics.

The history presented here calls into question several core scholarly conclusions about abortion politics and the influence of the courts. Social movements did not react to the opinion in the sharply polarized way we have assumed. *Roe v. Wade* did not immediately create or even reveal a fault line in American gender politics, as the abortion-rights movement fought for sex equality against an antiabortion movement that defended a stereotyped vision of gender roles. The radicalization of the discussion came later and resulted from much more than the Court's opinion. Over the course of the 1970s and early 1980s, the Republican and Democratic parties took sides in the abortion conflict, and the newly mobilized New Right and Religious Right offered powerful strategic incentives for abortion opponents to join a larger conservative coalition. The much criticized single-issue, choice-based agenda deployed by abortion-rights leaders developed in response not just to the Supreme Court's decision but also to the popularization of neoliberalism (a policy vision of limited government, deregulation, and free markets), and the new emphasis within the abortion-rights movement on a message and agenda that would succeed in electoral politics. Americans often blame *Roe* for setting off the contemporary abortion wars. This book shows instead that the opinion played only one part in a much more complicated story.

Nor did the Supreme Court's intervention make movement dialogue about abortion rights any less rich—quite the contrary. Feminist women's health activists promoted the very kind of reproductive-freedom agenda that the *Roe* decision supposedly scuttled. Opposing advocates continued to debate not only the meaning of abortion rights but also the best understanding of the *Roe* Court's holding. And the pervasive belief that *Roe* immediately delegitimized the Court by circumventing the will of the majority ignores the actual social-movement reaction to the decision. In the decade after the ruling, pro-lifers did not blame the *Roe* Court for taking the abortion issue away from the American people. In fact, most leaders of the antiabortion movement believed that the Court had committed the opposite error, failing to protect a constitutional right to life from the uncertainties of democratic politics.

Movements involved in the abortion battle often serve as symbols of the bitterness of interest-group politics. Activists on each side supposedly share defining views about women's rights, sexual freedom, and fetal life. The book offers a much more nuanced picture. In the decade after the *Roe* decision, the members of the opposing movements were diverse. These activists often disagreed passionately with one another about a variety of gender issues. The meaning of the pro-life or pro-choice cause changed significantly over the course of the decade.

Furthermore, *Roe* supposedly put an end to productive social-movement experimentation with different constitutional norms. By imposing a single, national rule of law, the conventional wisdom holds, the opinion prematurely ended debate about the meaning or scope of abortion rights. As the book shows, however, activists on both sides used the decision and all it symbolized not merely to contest the legal right to abortion, but also to alter public understandings of sex equality, fetal life, and the role of the courts in American democracy.

Indeed, movement leaders viewed the Court's own holding as important raw material from which to forge new constitutional understandings. Competing activists popularized their own interpretations of the opinion, seeking to raise money, recruit new supporters, and shape the public's understanding of what "*Roe*" had said. It is now axiomatic that *Roe* protects women's decision-making freedom, but this interpretation departs from the text of the original opinion, with its emphasis on the interests of doctors and the privacy of the physician-patient relationship. Indeed, the contemporary view of *Roe* emerged as social-movement interactions informed the popular understanding of the Court's opinion, helping to produce the interpretation familiar to us today—that *Roe* protects women's abortion rights. The story of movement politics in the 1970s and early 1980s involves tremendous constitutional and political innovation as much as dysfunction and polarization.

Finally, these social-movement responses deserve study because key decision-makers—including sitting Supreme Court justices—look to this history in analyzing both abortion jurisprudence and the best general method of constitutional interpretation. Justice Antonin Scalia, one of the sharpest critics of the *Roe* decision, argues that anti-abortion backlash stemmed from the justices' willingness to substitute their own preferences for the result required by constitutional text or history. By contrast, Ruth Bader Ginsburg, one of the Court's strongest proponents of abortion rights, asserts that *Roe*'s unconvincing privacy rationale, as opposed to one based on sex equality, intensified pro-life opposition and undercut the progress previously made by abortion-rights activists.

Legal scholars use *Roe* as a case study of the problems with opinions that outpace popular opinion or reach unnecessarily far-reaching outcomes, but these debates rest partly on an inaccurate historical account. We should not treat *Roe* as a central example of the dangers of judicial review or of the problems with particular methods of constitutional interpretation until we better understand the aftermath of the Court's decision.

What is more, the Court's decision neither produced nor reflected worldviews we can identify today as pro-life and pro-choice. Throughout the 1970s and early 1980s, activists and politicians entered into an unpredictable set of negotiations about what it meant to support abortion rights. Our current understanding of the abortion wars took shape in response to the political changes in the decade after the *Roe* decision.[7]

If conventional narratives are flawed, how did *Roe v. Wade* alter American abortion politics? In the short term, on either side of the abortion question, the Supreme Court's decision helped to reorient movement priorities. Partly because of the legitimating effect of a Supreme Court decision, abortion-rights leaders tended to gravitate toward strategies and arguments that would build in some way on the Court's reasoning. Women of color and feminist health activists worked to re-define the idea of reproductive choice the Court embraced, advocating for protections against sterilization abuse and state support for family planning, health care, and child care. Within the mainstream abortion-rights movement, advocates concerned with women's legal rights—a group Serena Mayeri has called "legal feminists"—used *Roe* as a sym-bol of women's demand for reproductive autonomy.[8]

The Court's opinion affected pro-life activism as well. Before 1973, pro-lifers had believed (and argued) that the Constitution already protected a right to life. When the Court rejected arguments for fetal personhood, abortion opponents prioritized a constitutional amend-ment establishing a fetal right to life. In engineering this amendment campaign, the antiabortion movement became larger, more diverse, and more structured. Viewing the amendment as a priority, pro-lifers often sided with any politician or party that supported their consti-tutional vision. As importantly, an influential group of abortion op-ponents stepped up efforts to find common ground in response to the Supreme Court's decision. Since the justices had made abortion legal, these activists believed that pro-lifers had to do more to create mean-ingful alternatives to the procedure.

However, the Supreme Court's decision made the greatest differ-ence to abortion politics not because the justices issued an ambitious ruling but rather because so many social-movement members, politi-cians, and other actors used it to express important arguments and commitments. As a wide variety of commentators contested its mean-ing, *Roe* became a flash point for deeper struggles about the meaning of human life, sex roles, sexuality, and the role of the judiciary. To a much greater extent than any single Supreme Court ruling, *Roe* mat-ters because we have invested it with so much significance.

Tracing the changing meanings of *Roe* shows us that non-judicial actors contributed at least as significantly to the escalation of abor-tion conflict as did the justices themselves. Abortion-rights and pro-life activists confronted a rapidly changing social and cultural land-scape in the decade after the *Roe* decision. Both movements reacted to major shifts in the political terrain, including the mobilization of the New Right and the Religious Right, the decline of the population-control cause, and the continuing realignment of both major political parties. These developments profoundly—but gradually—shaped the abortion debate; polarization resulted neither immediately nor inevi-tably from the Supreme Court's ruling.

New antiabortion reform strategies stemmed from both tactical necessity and the changing beliefs of pro-lifers. Financial and political incentives made a turn to the Right attractive to the pro-life movement. With new allies within the Republican Party and the New Right and Religious Right, abortion opponents made arguments that intensified conflict. Moreover, by the beginning of the 1980s, with both the Democratic Party and the women's movement connecting abortion to sex equality, pro-lifers saw more value in antifeminist ideology.

Abortion-rights activists redefined their cause as they crafted a new relationship with the movements for civil rights, population control, and women's liberation. The ERA struggle of the 1970s pushed movement leaders to frame abortion as an issue of autonomy rather than equality. Shifting racial politics and a series of scandals about sterilization abuse raised the costs of population-control arguments for abortion.

More significantly, recapturing movements' redefinition of *Roe* reveals that activists did not primarily respond to forces beyond their control. Social-movement members made a series of decisions that raised the stakes of the abortion battle. Some of these choices resulted from short-term worries about fundraising, recruiting, or coalition-building. Pro-lifers pursued a partnership with the Right to guarantee financial stability and ensure political influence. Abortion-rights leaders found more merit in choice arguments when the movement zeroed in on electoral success. Other decisions tracked the beliefs of competing activists—such as feminists' conviction that all women had a right to control their own bodies or pro-lifers' views about the value of each unborn life. None of these choices came as an unavoidable or even predictable consequence of the Supreme Court's decision. Responsibility for the polarization of the abortion issue rests on the shoulders of a wide variety of actors outside the Court.

Do we still live in the world social movement members created in the decade after *Roe*? The story of the abortion battle between 1983 and the present falls outside the scope of this volume, but a few salient differences deserve mention. Antiabortion violence rose dramatically in the mid-1980s, aggravating hostilities between opposing movements, discouraging physicians from performing the procedure, and motivating remaining providers to become politically active. Beginning in the early 1990s, the Supreme Court radically revised abortion law, retaining *Roe*'s "essential holding" but developing a new test that many more abortion restrictions can pass.[9]

Just the same, the decade after *Roe* matters because the social-movement politics of the decade gave rise to several crucial features of the contemporary abortion battle. An abortion-rights movement that had showcased concern about population control and public health gave way to one focused on women's rights. The period marked the end of a capacious reproductive-rights agenda and witnessed the creation of a choice-based, single-issue strategy. A still-strong alliance between the pro-life movement and the political Right took hold. Battles within the antiabortion movement about the value and morality of incrementalism began in the decade after the Court's decision. The Supreme Court does not deserve so much of the praise or blame for the reality we now face. Both before and after 1983, politicians and movement members did at least as much as the justices to shape today's abortion struggle.

I entered into the world of the abortion debate of the 1970s and early 1980s through a wide-ranging and intensive reading of meeting minutes, strategy papers, personal correspondence, newspapers, speeches, pamphlets, and books. *The Lost History of the Abortion Debate* draws on personal papers and taped interviews, currently unavailable in any archive. The book also uses material housed at more than eighteen universities and libraries, including, among others, Harvard University, Smith College, the Dr. Joseph R. Stanton Human Life Issues Library and Resource Center, the University of Michigan, and the Concordia Seminary of the Lutheran Church-Missouri Synod. Along with secondary literature, the book benefits from over 100 oral histories taken from population activists, antiabortion luminaries, and leading abortion-rights advocates.

I chose to interview roughly fifty advocates on each side of the abortion struggle who worked in state or national organizations between 1970 and 1983. My goal was qualitative, not quantitative—that is, I did not seek to draw general conclusions about either movement but rather to relate the individual experiences of some of those who defined the abortion struggle in the decade after 1973. Given the passage of time, the death of influential participants, and the stigma surrounding abortion politics, I used a sampling method similar to what sociologists refer to as "snowball sampling," a technique often used with hard-to-locate populations. Drawing on secondary and primary sources, I identified a group of prominent activists in major national and state organizations. These interview subjects later referred me to other participants who played an influential role.[10]

Selecting activists in this way raises challenges. Volunteer bias—the idea that those willing to be interviewed differ systematically from those who do not—can pose a problem, since those veterans of the abortion wars willing to share their experiences may not resemble those who are more reticent. Activists are less likely to mention isolated individuals or those in small social networks than those who move in wider circles. Finally, given the stigma surrounding abortion, some possible subjects may wish not to discuss either their own involvement or that of their acquaintances, particularly when those individuals no longer participate in the abortion struggle.[11]

To overcome these challenges, I interviewed both influential decision-makers and those in lower levels of state and national movements. By sampling problems in different movement strata, I hoped to illuminate a wider range of experiences and understandings of the abortion wars in the decade after 1973. Within each movement, I also sought out a variety of opinions on controversial topics, working in this way to explore the wide range of ideological positions held by those on either side of the abortion question. Using this method to identify subjects allowed me to reach a diverse group of activists (for example, within the abortion-rights movement, speaking with those interested in women's rights, public health, and population control; and within the pro-life movement, talking to Catholics and Protestants, Republicans and Democrats, and men and women).[12]

In each interview, I asked a standard set of questions (for example, how an activist became involved in the abortion struggle, which political party that individual preferred before and after 1973, what that individual thought about contraception and the Equal Rights Amendment, and whether that individual found the *Roe* decision to be surprising), but I allowed my subjects to address other topics that I might have neglected.

Other scholars have documented the rewards and problems inherent in using oral histories. Many of the events documented in this book took place decades ago, and individuals' memory of those events, which may be incomplete or flawed at the outset, fades with time. Moreover, public history—the narratives set forth by institutions and the media—may warp individual recollections. By interacting with other members of small social groups, such as the abortion-rights or pro-life organizations studied in this volume, individuals also develop new historical interpretations. This process can be conscious, as social movements use history for instrumental purposes. Alternatively, the ideological commitments, gender, class, or ethnicity of the interview subject may change individual memory without any deliberate effort. Particularly in the abortion context, shared historical narratives serve to construct movement identity or to offer reasons for or against the overruling of *Roe v. Wade.* The book therefore shies away from using oral histories to establish the occurrence of events or broader historical trends.[13]

Nonetheless, the abortion struggle offers particularly profound reasons for recovering the stories of those who created post-*Roe* politics. Historians, legal academics, and sociologists convincingly describe the shared beliefs of activists in both movements. But these accounts often obscure how individuals had to adapt or even upend their priorities and identities to fit within the emerging pro-choice or pro-life categories. By weaving in individual experiences of the abortion wars, the book restores some of the complexity of post-*Roe* battles. Taken in isolation or collectively, oral histories can humanize activists, enrich our understanding of social-movement diversity, and reinforce evidence taken from primary or secondary sources. Most importantly, these individual voices remind us that those who defined post-*Roe* struggles resist generalization.

Archival research poses challenges of its own. Some advocates, particularly abortion opponents, have not preserved or donated relevant materials. The existing record may reflect the wish of donors to include or omit certain information, and collections can convey the distinct perspective of the individuals who contributed them. Because particular collections may be biased or incomplete, the book assembles material from a wide array of different sources, representing the work of organizations and individuals, supporters and opponents of abortion rights, and state and national figures. The book supplements these materials with relevant published materials, including secondary sources and contemporary newspapers, books, and magazines.

A good deal of important scholarship has traced the history of abortion and family planning in the United States prior to 1973 and the lead-up to *Roe* itself. Other work situates the abortion debate in the broader context of the politics of contraception and population control or fetal rights. The abortion wars also figure centrally in legal, sociological, and political science scholarship on social movements.

Many of these studies proceed chronologically. By contrast, I have structured this book around a series of major historical questions that preoccupy commentators across the ideological spectrum. Organizing the book in this way more clearly sheds light not only on the story of *Roe*'s aftermath but also on the stakes of that narrative for contemporary debates about law and social change, women's rights, reproductive freedom, and the courts' influence on American society. The book proceeds in three sections, taking up major historical issues surrounding the influence of the Supreme Court's opinion on the pro-life movement, the abortion-rights movement, and interactions between the two. Each section reclaims a lost chapter in the history of abortion politics. At the same time, each section responds directly to crucial historiographical questions that have shaped study of *Roe* and of judicial decision-making more generally. Finally, each chapter traces the varying interpretations of *Roe* used by different social movement members. At times, the book uses *Roe* to refer to the Supreme Court decision. For the most part, however, each section recaptures movement members' changing visions of *Roe* and what it represents.

The Introduction provides important context for the social-movement history that follows. Here, the book surveys the origins of the abortion battle, discussing the contributions to pre-*Roe* politics of eugenic legal reformers, family planning advocates, physicians, feminists, population controllers, Roman Catholic leaders, and political operatives. The Introduction briefly explores the Supreme Court's decision and then offers an overview of major social, political, and economic developments that influenced social-movement struggles in the decade after 1973. The clash of absolutes we now know took shape in response to the mobilization of the New Right and Religious Right in the later 1970s, to the gradual solidification of political party positions on abortion, to changing power dynamics within each movement, and to the shifting politics of the movements for women's liberation, civil rights, and population control. More importantly, with little input from the Court, social-movement members themselves reached strategic and ideological decisions that impacted the debate in years to come.

With this background in place, the book reconsiders the effect of the Supreme Court decision on the American political environment. Chapters 1 and 2 address the *Roe* opinion's influence on pro-life mobilization. Chapter 1 reconsiders claims that *Roe* prompted a popular crisis of faith in judicial legitimacy. Legal academics and judges contend that *Roe*'s unconvincing reasoning made judicial overreaching a preoccupation of both the pro-life movement and the political Right. By relating the story of pro-life constitutionalism from the 1960s to the early 1980s, Chapter 1 shows instead that abortion opponents responding to the decision in the mid- to late 1970s had little interest in the issue of judicial activism. Far from faulting the Court for taking the abortion issue away from the people, pro-lifers blamed the *Roe* majority primarily for failing to protect the unborn from the whims of democratic majorities.

Later, when abortion opponents began to voice concern about judicial review, they primarily did so for tactical reasons, expressing solidarity with their new socially conservative allies and offering new reasons for outlawing abortion. Over time, as pro-lifers worked more closely with the New Right, some abortion opponents came more sincerely to view judicial arrogance as a direct threat to the unborn.

Chapter 2 addresses the next phase of pro-life mobilization, focusing on the consequences of the movement's newfound interest in the courts beginning in the late 1970s. The chapter raises another question central to many concerns about *Roe*: whether the opinion produced a backlash that empowered extremists in the antiabortion movement. Chapter 2 questions conventional understandings of post-*Roe* extremism by documenting the emergence of pro-life incrementalism in the later 1970s. Heartened by Supreme Court victories, self-proclaimed incrementalists advanced a new, court-centered strategy. Movement members prioritized abortion restrictions thought likely to survive Supreme Court review.

In so doing, pro-lifers wanted to chip away at abortion rights, exposing the flaws in the *Roe* Court's reasoning and energizing the pro-life base. Although they faced criticism from other movement members, these incrementalists came to dominate the antiabortion movement. Their ascendancy complicates leading accounts of post-*Roe* backlash. Many incrementalists adopted the rhetoric of new allies in the Religious Right or New Right, but did so largely for strategic purposes. At the same time, incrementalists championed compromise on abortion itself, favoring restrictions over far-reaching bans that the Court would not yet tolerate. The rise of incrementalism exposes ongoing and ever-changing struggles about what it means to be pro-life.

Chapters 3 and 4 take up major historical questions involving *Roe*'s meaning to the abortion-rights movement. Chapter 3 challenges conventional narratives about the relationship between the abortion-rights and the women's movements. The chapter unearths intense internal disagreements about how best to frame abortion rights and whether to connect them to equality for women. In the late 1960s and early 1970s, over the strong objections of feminist members, organizations like NARAL (then, the National Association for the Repeal of Abortion Laws) and the Planned Parenthood Federation of America highlighted what some perceived as desirable consequences of legalizing abortion—improvements in health care for women, reductions in population growth, preservation of environmental resources, and decreases in welfare costs and illegitimacy rates.

After 1973, feminists used the Supreme Court's decision to reshape the argumentative strategies and identities of abortion-rights organizations. As used by feminists, *Roe* stood not so much for the decision issued by the Supreme Court as for the importance of women's rights—and constitutional concerns more broadly—to the politics of abortion. Feminists attributed to the Supreme Court decision a profound concern for women's interest in bodily integrity, equal citizenship, and autonomy.

As pro-lifers took aim at the 1973 opinion, feminists convincingly argued that supporters of abortion rights had to defend the opinion's constitutional rhetoric. Making *Roe* into a symbol of women's importance to the abortion struggle allowed feminists to remake abortion-rights advocacy. By the mid-1970s, the movement had substantially downplayed concerns about population control, prioritized claims about women's rights, and put feminists in new positions of leadership.

But how did abortion rights become so synonymous with choice? More importantly, did the Supreme Court leave the abortion-rights movement with a single-issue, privacy-based strategy that did not serve the needs of poor and minority women? In answering these questions, Chapter 4 documents the next stage in the evolution of abortion-rights advocacy, tracing the success in the late 1970s of arguments presenting abortion as a right to choose. Conventionally, scholars attribute the rise of choice-based arguments to the *Roe* decision. Since the Court presented abortion as a matter of decisional autonomy, as the conventional narrative maintains, abortion-rights activists adopted similar claims, defending the opinion's reasoning from frequent attack. Moreover, because abortion rights became perennially vulnerable, activists committed to keeping the procedure legal supposedly sacrificed a more comprehensive agenda. These strategic decisions proved particularly painful for poor and non-white women.

Chapter 4 calls into question the accuracy of this narrative. Focusing on the latter half of the 1970s, the chapter shows that choice-based contentions gained prominence not because of the Supreme Court decision but rather because of changing movement priorities. The first four years after *Roe v. Wade* proved disastrous for the abortion-rights movement. State legislatures passed a wide variety of restrictions, and Congress introduced a ban on Medicaid funding for abortion. The Supreme Court retreated from the protections set forth in *Roe.* Later in the decade, abortion-rights leaders blamed these defeats on pro-life electoral prowess. Mainstream organizations revamped their strategies to maximize the chances of electoral success. In this new environment, both a single-issue agenda and choice arguments gained support. As leading abortion-rights activists contended, Americans uncomfortable with the abortion procedure might favor a more abstract freedom to decide.

However, the Supreme Court's decision did not lead all supporters of reproductive rights to abandon a broader reform platform. The chapter chronicles the efforts of feminist women's health activists and women of color in the later 1970s to forge an agenda that would address not only abortion but also family planning, child care, sterilization abuse, workplace discrimination, health care, and a living wage. Often, these activists drew on the rhetoric of choice, emphasizing it in surprising and radical new ways.

By 1983, however, even movement dissenters had functionally adopted a single-issue agenda. These activists responded to the changing landscape of American politics rather than to the Court. With Ronald Reagan's meteoric rise, both abortion and the welfare state came under fire. A Republican majority stood ready to pass a law permitting the states or Congress to ban abortion. In response, abortion-rights activists championed individualism and freedom instead of demanding broader state support for women's reproductive choices. With abortion rights in imminent peril, a single-issue approach appeared to be the movement's only choice.

Chapters 5 and 6 focus on *Roe*'s impact on interactions between opposing movements: did the Supreme Court undermine popular experimentation with abortion rights, and did *Roe v. Wade* make it impossible for opposing activists to reach consensus on abortion or any other gender issue? Taking up the first of these questions, Chapter 5 brings to the surface the story of *Roe*'s reinterpretation in the 1970s. Conventionally, scholars suggest that the Supreme Court's 1973 opinion prematurely ended a vibrant public debate about abortion rights. While preempting state legislative experimentation, the Supreme Court also supposedly discouraged social-movement dialogue. By issuing a broad opinion, the justices theoretically sent the message that activists could no longer make a major contribution to public understanding of abortion rights. In this way, the *Roe* decision alienated abortion opponents, helping to create a less creative and productive abortion debate.

But as Chapter 5 demonstrates, the Court did not put a stop to efforts to redefine abortion rights; far from it. The chapter tells the story of another understanding of *Roe*—not as a decision made by the Supreme Court but as a canvas onto which activists could project different strategic aims. Those on both sides reinterpreted *Roe* as a way of winning new members, raising funds, remaking public views of what the Court had said, and preparing the ground for later law reform efforts. Competing groups drew on one another's understandings of the decision, ultimately settling on the version that predominates today—*Roe* protects a woman's right to choose.

Chapter 6 deals with another central question about the Court's influence on inter-movement dynamics: whether *Roe v. Wade* undermined promising compromises on abortion and other gender issues. Scholars assert that *Roe* polarized discussion, blocking otherwise viable alliances between women on either side of the abortion debate. The abortion conflict became a struggle to determine the proper role for women in American society.

As the chapter demonstrates, however, some abortion opponents pursued laws banning pregnancy discrimination at work, increasing contraceptive funding, and subsidizing day care or health care. In turn, at least in the context of fetal research and certain late-term abortions, some abortion-rights activists wished to recognize limited fetal protections. The Court's *Roe* decision did not reveal a stable set of beliefs about gender roles, nor did it eliminate interest in alliances between those in favor of abortion and those opposed to it. When a partnership between the New Right and the antiabortion movement became a defining feature of the abortion battle, a number of factors beyond the Supreme Court's decision, including political party realignment and the rise of the New Right and the Religious Right, contributed to the outcome.

The book concludes by asking how the history of *Roe*'s aftermath should reshape scholarly debate about abortion, the role of the courts in American democracy, and the relationship between law and social movements. A broader question runs throughout the book: how will our understanding of *Roe* and of the abortion wars change when we better understand the history of movement responses to the decision? To answer that question, the book recovers the lost history of movement debates and internal struggles. From this analysis emerges a more nuanced history of the world that *Roe* helped to create. As we begin to explore this world, I am reminded of one answer activists supplied to many of my questions: the truth is messy. It is that same messiness that makes the decade after *Roe* so fascinating and so deserving of study.

Abbreviations

ACCL	American Citizens Concerned for Life, Inc., Records, Gerald R. Ford Presidential Library and Museum, University of Michigan
ACLU	American Civil Liberties Union Records, Department of Rare Books and Special Collections, Seeley G. Mudd Manuscript Library, Princeton University
AUL	Americans United for Life Records, Concordia Seminary, Lutheran Church Missouri Synod, St. Louis, Missouri
BFP	Betty Friedan Papers, Schlesinger Library, Radcliffe Institute, Harvard University
BSP	Barbara Seaman Papers, Schlesinger Library, Radcliffe Institute, Harvard University
CEP	Catherine East Papers, Schlesinger Library, Radcliffe Institute, Harvard University
CKP	Claire Keyes Papers, David M. Rubenstein Rare Book and Manuscript Library, Duke University
COYOTE	Call Off Your Old Tired Ethics (COYOTE) Records, Schlesinger Library, Radcliffe Institute, Harvard University
CRP	Charles Rice Papers, on file with the author
EMP	Edwin Meese III Files, White House Staff and Office Files, 1981–1989, Ronald Reagan Presidential Library and Museum, Simi Valley, California
ERA	Equal Rights Amendment Papers, 1972–1984, St. Louis, Missouri, Collection, University of Missouri-St. Louis
FFL	Feminists For Life Pamphlet Collection, Schlesinger Library, Radcliffe Institute, Harvard University

GHW   George Huntston Williams Papers, Andover-Harvard Theological
Library, Harvard Divinity School

HBP   Harry A. Blackmun Papers, Library of Congress

HMP   Hugh Moore Fund Collection, Department of Rare Books and Special
Collections, Seeley G. Mudd Manuscript Library, Princeton University

JBP   Jane Bovard Papers, Institute for Regional Studies and University
Archives, North Dakota State University Libraries

JDR   John D. Rockefeller 3d Papers, Rockefeller Archive Center, Rockefeller University

JFP   Jerry Falwell Papers, Liberty University

JRS   The Dr. Joseph R. Stanton Human Life Issues Library and Resource
Center, Our Lady of New York Convent, Bronx, New York

KMP   Kate Millett Papers, David M. Rubenstein Rare Book and Manuscript
Library, Duke University

LEP   The Life and Equality, St. Louis, Missouri, Collection, University of
Missouri-St. Louis

LLP   Lawrence Lader Papers, Francis A. Countway Library of Medicine,
Harvard University

MCL   Missouri Citizens for Life Collection, St. Louis, Missouri, Collection,
University of Missouri-St. Louis

MMH   Moral Majority Collection, Hall-Hoag Collection of Extremist Literature in the United States, Brandeis University

MMP   Moral Majority Papers, Liberty University

MRL   Montana National Abortion Rights Action League Papers, Montana
Historical Society Research Center Archives

MTP   Meredith Tax Papers, David M. Rubenstein Rare Book and Manuscript Library, Duke University

NCAP   National Coalition of Abortion Providers Records, David M. Rubenstein Rare Book and Manuscript Library, Duke University

NDR   North Dakota Right to Life Association Records, State Historical
Society of North Dakota

NOW   National Organization for Women Records, Schlesinger Library,
Radcliffe Institute, Harvard University

NRL   National Abortion Rights Action League [NARAL] Records,
Schlesinger Library, Radcliffe Institute, Harvard University

PC   Population Council Archives, Rockefeller Archive Center, Rockefeller
University

PLN   Pro-Life Newsletter Collection, Schlesinger Library, Radcliffe Institute, Harvard University

PPFA I   Planned Parenthood Federation of America I Records, 1918–1974
(PPFA I), Sophia Smith Collection, Smith College

PPFA II Planned Parenthood Federation of America Records, 1928–2009 (PPFA II), Sophia Smith Collection, Smith College

PSR *The Phyllis Schlafly Report* Collection, Schlesinger Library, Radcliffe Institute, Harvard University

RHS Reproductive Health Services Papers, St. Louis, Missouri, Collection, University of Missouri-St. Louis

R2N2 Reproductive Rights National Network Records, David M. Rubenstein Rare Book and Manuscript Library, Duke University

TEP Thomas Irwin Emerson Papers, Manuscripts and Archives, Sterling Memorial Library, Yale University

WEAL Women's Equity Action League Records, Schlesinger Library, Radcliffe Institute, Harvard University

WC Wilcox Collection, University of Kansas

WSH Wilma Scott Heide Papers, Schlesinger Library, Radcliffe Institute, Harvard University

Timeline for Abortion History, 1965–1983

1965 The Supreme Court decides *Griswold v. Connecticut*, recognizing married couples' constitutional right to privacy.

1967 The National Organization for Women (NOW) endorses abortion law repeal.

The Family Life Bureau of the National Conference of Catholic Bishops forms the National Right to Life Committee (NRLC).

1968 Planned Parenthood-World Population calls for abortion repeal.

1969 NARAL (the National Association for the Repeal of Abortion Laws) is formed.

1971 Americans United for Life (AUL) is founded.

1972 In *Eisenstadt v. Baird*, the Supreme Court strikes down Massachusetts contraception ban for unmarried individuals.

1973 The Supreme Court decides *Roe v. Wade*.

The NRLC is formally incorporated as an independent organization.

American Citizens Concerned for Life (ACCL) is founded.

Involuntary sterilizations in Montgomery, Alabama, launch a sterilization-abuse scandal.

1974 First March for Life is held.

1975 Dr. Kenneth Edelin is convicted of manslaughter for performing an abortion.

The National Women's Health Network (NWHN) forms.

National Commission for the Protection of Human Subjects of Biomedical and Behavioral Research issues recommendations on fetal research.

1976   Congress passes the Hyde Amendment, a federal ban on Medicaid
        funding for abortion.

        The Supreme Court decides *Planned Parenthood of Central Missouri
        v. Danforth*, upholding parts of a multi-restriction statute.

1977   The Supreme Court upholds a state ban on publicly funded abortions
        in *Maher v. Roe*.

1978   The Reproductive Rights National Network (R2N2) is founded.

        In seeking greater political influence, NARAL launches "Impact '80,"
        a program centered on choice rhetoric.

        Akron, Ohio, City Council enacts antiabortion law that serves as
        model for incremental restrictions.

1979   With the assistance of New Right organizer Paul Weyrich, the Moral
        Majority is founded.

1980   The Republican platform endorses a fetal-protective constitutional
        amendment and restrictions on public abortion funding.

        In *Harris v. McRae*, the Supreme Court upholds the Hyde
        Amendment.

1981   The pro-life movement finds itself divided by constitutional amend-
        ment proposed by Senator Orrin Hatch (R-UT), allowing Congress
        and the states to restrict abortion. Pro-lifers fail to muster the votes to
        overcome a filibuster.

1983   When the Supreme Court decides *City of Akron v. Akron Center for
        Reproductive Health*, Reagan nominee Sandra Day O'Connor's dissent
        attacks the *Roe* decision, increasing pro-life interest in the Supreme
        Court nomination process.

        The Hatch-Eagleton Amendment, which would have declared that the
        Constitution does not recognize an abortion right, fails in Senate vote.

After Roe

Introduction

WE OFTEN THINK of *Roe v. Wade* as a turning point. Leading histories illuminate the twists and turns of pre-1973 reproductive politics—changing economic realities, the creation of new social movements, the evolution of American religion, and the remaking of ideas about sex roles. By contrast, we often view *Roe v. Wade* as a break in the story, an event that determined the future of gender wars in coming decades. Read against the long history of reproductive politics, however, the post-1973 period resembles the decades preceding it in salient ways. This Introduction situates the Supreme Court's decision and the years immediately following it in the broader context of reproductive politics. As this context makes clear, the post-1973 abortion wars, like the struggles of earlier periods, reflect both the influence of long-term trends and the choices made by politicians and movement members.

In the decades before the *Roe* decision, movements focused on family planning or abortion made room for individuals with very different tactical priorities and ideological visions. The aims associated with these movements changed as various factions within them gained or lost influence. Moreover, the relationship between different movements—movements for family planning, women's rights, eugenics, population control, environmental preservation, traditional sexual mores, or a right to life—remained contested. Consequently, what it meant to favor reproductive freedom varied a great deal over time.

Placing the decade after the *Roe* decision in historical context also makes apparent how opposing movements changed in response to larger political and social developments. These shifts created new opportunities for activists interested in building effective strategic partnerships, either with other social movements or with major political parties. At the same time, social changes cast old beliefs and practices in a new light.

The *Roe* decision made a substantial difference to reproductive politics. The opinion helped to nationalize antiabortion activism and made the passage of a fetal-protective constitutional amendment a pro-life preoccupation. *Roe* convinced other pro-lifers that efforts to seek common ground had become more important than ever before. For those supportive of reproductive rights, *Roe* fueled new discussions of how closely abortion should be tied to equality for women. Understood in context, however, the Court's decision represents only one of many social, legal, strategic, and ideological developments that gave rise to contemporary abortion politics.

The Family Planning Movement Emerges

On January 22, 1973, when Justice Harry Blackmun announced the Supreme Court's decision in *Roe v. Wade*, cultural fissures about abortion already ran deep. Debate about the place of fertility control in American culture exploded onto the scene in the second half of the nineteenth century, when sexual mores, American religious identity, and the medical profession all were changing dramatically. Earlier in the century, a majority of states permitted abortion before "quickening"—the time at which providers could detect fetal motion. By the 1850s, powerful new movements had organized to challenge the legal and moral status quo. Anti-vice crusaders turned to law as part of a battle against illicit sex. In a quest to protect American youth, these activists championed laws prohibiting devices, information, and preparations designed to end a pregnancy.[1]

In the same period, "regular" physicians competing with midwives and a variety of unconventional medical providers had financial motives for taking up the antiabortion cause. In the mid-nineteenth century, medical practice was extraordinarily democratic and under-regulated. When the recently formed American Medical Association (AMA) began promoting antiabortion laws in the 1850s, regular physicians had little more to offer patients than did their "irregular" competitors. The antiabortion crusade helped the regulars differentiate themselves from the competition. By condemning abortion, the regulars hoped to claim the moral high ground and demonstrate a superior medical understanding of fetal life. By the end of the century, because of the influence of anti-vice and pro-life activism, every state had introduced harsher laws, often allowing abortion only when necessary to save the life of the woman.[2]

By the early twentieth century, a complex family planning movement took shape to combat changes to the laws on contraception and abortion. Family planning champions drew on new ideas about the perfection of the human species, the size and power of government, and the role women should play in American society. Advocates like Margaret Sanger and Mary Ware Dennett contended that birth control would allow women to "take the first step in the assertion of freedom and self-respect."[3] At times, Sanger and her allies drew on the new ideas set forth by the Socialist movement, describing important links between poverty and a lack of fertility control. Birth controllers also borrowed from and reworked emerging arguments about a new social role for American women, one that separated biology and destiny.[4]

At the same time, Sanger and other birth controllers formed a troubled partnership with the eugenic legal reform movement. Coined by British scientist Francis Galton in 1883, the term eugenics described techniques designed to allow "the better races or strains of blood a better chance of prevailing speedily over the less suitable."[5] In the early twentieth century, researchers from Charles Davenport to Karl Pearson proposed patterns of heritability in traits including sexual immorality, alcoholism, criminality, and insanity. Building on these findings, eugenics supporters demanded new laws on everything from marriage to reproduction. The eugenics movement brought together sex radicals and moral purists, Progressives and racists, those interested in cutting welfare spending, and feminists. The movement had tremendous legal success, securing the passage of compulsory sterilization laws in thirty-three states and defending them before the Supreme Court.[6]

As was the case for feminist birth controllers, eugenicists' concerns arose partly because of a new political reality. The popularity of eugenics partly reflected Progressives' belief that scientific expertise could improve the law and that a muscular government could better the human condition. Eugenics supporters also responded to anxieties about masculinity and the loss of self-employment for men, tensions with new immigrants from Southern and Eastern Europe, and concerns about rising numbers of women working outside the home or attending college.[7]

The contemporary abortion wars have roots reaching back to reproductive conflicts over a century ago. A great deal has changed since eugenicists, feminists, purity crusaders, and physicians battled about reproductive freedom. Just the same, some of the central concerns of later reformers, such as the connection between sex equality and reproductive control or anxiety about sexual "promiscuity" and changing gender roles, appeared in the early twentieth century. As importantly, some of the forces contributing to the mutability of reproductive politics had already taken center stage. The movement for family planning redefined itself in response to the mobilization of new potential allies and to the evolution of medical practice. Because of the diversity of family planning advocates, the movement's goals remained difficult to pin down. The same unpredictability carried forward into the decades before and after the *Roe* decision. From the beginning, the conflict surrounding reproduction arose because of both the choices made by non-judicial actors and the political and social shifts those individuals confronted.

After World War II, Movements for Population Control and Women's Rights Mobilize

In the mid-twentieth century, reproductive politics evolved again. The new battles of mid-century reflected the influence of the Second World War, mounting concern about demographic growth, changing religious attitudes toward birth control, and persistent discontent about the narrow role assigned to American women. As had been the case in previous decades, political shifts, activists' tactical decisions, and changing perceptions all continued to transform the debate about fertility control.

World War II represented a crossroads for the family planning movement. The media documented an extensive Nazi program of compulsory sterilization that closely resembled the one at work in many American states. Before the War, mainstream support for eugenics had already declined, as researchers questioned the validity of eugenic science. Coverage of the Nazi sterilization regime helped to drive eugenics underground. With few exceptions, state use of compulsory sterilization laws plummeted. Even the leaders of the American Eugenics Society took care to avoid any discussion of race that could bring Nazism to mind.[8]

After 1945, some eugenicists found themselves drawn to a new social movement centered on the dangers of population growth. A postwar baby boom raised particular concern about growth rates in developing nations in Asia, the Middle East, Africa, and South America, as well as in poorer urban and rural communities in the United States. Early population-control organizations attracted many eugenicists. Building on earlier claims that the least genetically fit had the most children, eugenic supporters argued that lower growth rates would improve the overall genetic quality of the population. Influential population-control organizations, like the Population Council and the Association for Voluntary Sterilization (AVS), maintained close connections to the eugenic legal reform movement.[9]

Just the same, the population-control movement drew support from a diverse group of activists. From its inception, the Population Council appealed to those sincerely concerned about the impact of population growth on poor communities: a lack of adequate food, housing, sanitation, or health care. The movement also counted among its members Cold War hawks like Hugh Moore, who worried that unchecked growth would fuel the spread of Communism.[10]

The social undercurrents that gave rise to the population-control movement also helped to reshape religious attitudes about birth control. Starting in 1930, the leaders of several Protestant denominations revised their opposition to contraception. Notwithstanding the ongoing hostility of the Pope, many Catholics also took a more tolerant stance. Between 1965 and 1970, contraceptive use among the Catholic laity increased dramatically. In a 1968 Gallup poll, 76 percent of Catholics polled responded that birth control should be "available to anyone who wants it."[11]

Moreover, in the 1960s, changing attitudes toward birth control and sexual behavior helped to prompt a rethinking of women's role in American society. By 1966, an estimated six million women were using the birth control pill. By 1972, as the *New York Times* reported, nearly one half of unmarried women had been sexually active before age nineteen. An emerging women's movement used these changes as an entry point for discussing new ideas about the relationship between sexuality, sex, and equal citizenship. For feminists like the members of the National Organization for Women (NOW) or New York Radical Women, the reform of laws on birth control or abortion served as a necessary step in the expansion of opportunities for women.[12]

Family planning reform and calls for population control further tapped into developing worries about the environment. Concerns about limited resources, urban sprawl, growing pollution, and world hunger animated the efforts of new organizations formed on many college campuses. Crusaders in organizations like Zero Population Growth, Inc. (ZPG) asserted that the white middle class was populating itself to death. The organization united those concerned about abortion reform, the health of the environment, or the importance of sexual freedom.[13]

The future of reproductive politics remained up for grabs. The aftermath of World War II, the decline of eugenics, the creation of a population-control movement, and the emergence of feminism and environmentalism all marked the landscape in which lay actors pursued a new reproductive freedom.

In the 1960s and Early 1970s, A New Movement Challenges Abortion Bans

The highly contingent politics of reproductive freedom began to remake abortion policy in the second half of the twentieth century. New medical developments forced physicians to find new justifications for performing abortions. The emergence of social movements calling for women's liberation or demanding better environmental stewardship stoked demands for the repeal rather than the reform of existing laws. As would be the case after 1973, abortion reform created an intense opposition among activists concerned about fetal life, changing sexual norms, gender roles, or ethical standards. Marked by dynamic movement politics and different medical norms, the path taken by the abortion struggle was far from inevitable.

Before the 1940s, doctors inclined to perform the procedure could justify it as necessary to protect the life or the physical health of the woman. However, as obstetric and gynecological care improved, physicians had to reach for new explanations. Providers increasingly turned to mental-health exceptions in rationalizing use of the procedure. Partly for this reason, beginning in the 1940s and 1950s, a small group of medical professionals began demanding the reform of existing abortion laws. In 1959, the American Law Institute (ALI), an organization of legal experts, similarly proposed a model statute that would allow abortion in cases of rape, incest, fetal deformity, or threats to the physical or mental health of the mother. Some medical supporters of ALI-style laws, particularly psychiatrists, believed that existing statutes required doctors to participate in a medical fraud or to betray their patients' best interests. Aware of the ambiguity of existing legal exceptions to abortion bans, others joined the reform movement to put an end to the risk of looming legal liability.[14]

By the 1960s, public fears about fetal defects also strengthened the movement for new abortion laws. In 1962, Sherri Finkbine, a television presenter from Arizona, made the problem with abortion law real to millions of Americans. Finkbine had taken thalidomide, a popular drug used to treat morning sickness. Research revealed that the drug produced death or severe fetal defects, including phocomelia, a deformation of the limbs. Denied an abortion in the United States, Finkbine had to travel to Sweden to access the procedure. Her case touched off debate about whether women could justifiably have abortions in cases of fetal abnormality.[15]

So too did an early 1960s epidemic of German measles, a disease that led to the births of tens of thousands of children with deafness, blindness, heart defects, or mental handicaps. The German measles outbreak reframed abortion, which had appeared to be a choice made by minorities and the poor, as a procedure sought by respectable, white, middle-class women.[16]

For some supporters of reform, existing restrictions appeared inhumane and illogical. The laws most states applied seemed to constrain physicians, limit patients' access to the best care, and punish women facing cases of severe fetal abnormality. Introducing ALI-style statutes, as reform proponent Larry Lader explained, would allow "[d]octors to go about their medical business without the chaotic distraction of laws subject to varying interpretations."[17] In practice, though, ALI-style bills proved frustrating. In ALI states, doctors performing certain abortions still feared criminal charges and professional stigma. For many women, the procedure remained expensive and inaccessible. "You have to be rich, crazy, or a victim of rape to get an abortion legally in this state," a California resident told the *New York Times* in 1968.[18]

By the late 1960s, drawing on impatience with the reform regime, new social movements built support for the complete repeal of abortion restrictions. Early in the decade, as the women's movement took shape, abortion had not counted among the priorities of most feminist groups. By the end of the decade, however, feminists in organizations from the Radical Feminists to NOW connected abortion to women's quest for equal citizenship. As NOW leader Betty Friedan put it, these groups asserted that "[t]he right of woman to control her reproductive process must be established as a basic, inalienable, human, civil right."[19]

With the emergence of a branch of the environmental movement focused on sexual freedom and population control, the repeal cause won new supporters. While organizations like the Population Council took no formal position on abortion before 1973, recently formed groups like ZPG worked passionately for repeal. The newly energized movement scored victories in the late 1960s and early 1970s, as four states eliminated all meaningful legal restrictions on abortion access. As repeal made progress, some Americans voiced intense opposition to legal abortion. The opposition brought together leaders of the Catholic Church with professionals and homemakers committed to fetal rights.[20]

Before the intervention of the Supreme Court, the abortion battle had already become polarized. Across the country, opposing movements worked through the courts and state legislatures to advance their legal goals. Those on both sides claimed to have momentum on their side. New York repealed all laws limiting abortion access, but in 1970, the New York State Legislature voted to reinstitute certain abortion restrictions. Only a veto by Governor Nelson Rockefeller (R-NY) ensured that abortion-law repeal remained a reality. In Michigan, pro-lifers successfully defeated a 1972 resolution that would have liberalized abortion policy.[21]

At the national level, the Republican Party deliberately escalated abortion conflict in the early 1970s. Staffers working for Richard Nixon's 1972 presidential campaign viewed abortion as a promising wedge issue, one that would win the support of Catholics, Southerners, and others who had traditionally chosen the Democratic Party at the polls. In the states, tensions had already increased, as abortion opponents championed an absolute right to life.[22]

Before moving into the courts, the abortion struggle already divided the nation. The contest had no clear winners and losers. Changing medical indications for abortion exposed physicians to unprecedented liability, building support for reform. The mobilization of movements for women's liberation and environmentalism created new constituencies in favor of reproductive rights. Republican operatives and politicians brought abortion into party politics, intensifying conflict around the issue. From the moment states began introducing bans on contraception or abortion, reproductive politics developed in response to events in the larger society, including the formation of some social movements and the decline of others, the reconfiguration of party politics, and changes in medical practice.

Conventionally, historians and legal scholars suggest that the interference of the courts transformed the abortion wars. The Supreme Court forced on the American public a result not yet supported by popular opinion. The Court's intervention supposedly helped to launch the antiabortion movement, to eliminate possible compromises, to energize the Religious Right, and to cut off a productive debate about what reproductive rights ought to mean.

The *Roe* decision did influence the battle that followed, prompting a nationalization of antiabortion activities and creating a framework that supporters of abortion rights drew on and remade. But viewed in context, post-1973 abortion politics seem more complex than anything explained by the Supreme Court's intervention.

Activists Question the Constitutionality of Abortion Restrictions

Before the litigation of *Roe*, the abortion struggle had drawn attention to fundamental questions about the rights of women, the boundaries of medical authority, and the proper definition of personhood. However, *Roe v. Wade* emerged most directly from efforts to secure constitutional protection for reproductive rights.

Family planning champions began challenging the constitutionality of contraception restrictions in the 1960s, building a foundation for later litigation. In *Griswold v. Connecticut*, a seven to two majority struck down a Connecticut law banning the use of birth control by married couples. In a majority opinion written by Justice William O. Douglas, the Court suggested that the text of the Constitution implied the existence of a right to privacy. "Would we allow the police to search the sacred precincts of marital bedrooms for telltale signs of the use of contraceptives?" Douglas asked. "The very idea is repulsive to the notions of privacy surrounding the marital relationship."[23]

By 1971, the time seemed ripe for a federal constitutional challenge to abortion laws. Nonetheless, in *United States v. Vuitch*, the justices upheld a Washington, DC ordinance prohibiting all abortions except those "necessary for the preservation of the mother's life or health and under the direction of a competent licensed practitioner of medicine."[24] The Court rejected a due-process challenge to the law, concluding that it gave adequate notice that "health" encompassed both physical and mental well-being.[25]

Roe v. Wade came before the Court when the constitutional law of abortion and contraception seemed to be in flux. In 1972, a district court in Connecticut embraced feminist rhetoric in striking down an abortion law, stressing "the changed role of women in society and the changed attitudes toward them, [which] reflect the societal judgment that women can competently order their own lives."[26] Michigan appellate judges concluded that the abortion decision constitutionally belonged to the physician, rather than to the State. The Indiana State Supreme Court upheld an abortion ban after finding the State's interest in preserving fetal life to be compelling.[27]

In 1972, abortion-rights supporters took heart after the announcement of the Supreme Court's decision in *Eisenstadt v. Baird*, a case involving a Massachusetts law limiting the sale of contraceptives to unmarried persons. In a majority opinion written by Justice William Brennan, the Court used the Equal Protection Clause, rather than the Due Process Clause, to analyze the constitutionality of the Massachusetts law. Without directly addressing the scope of constitutional privacy, *Eisenstadt* concluded that any such right applied with the same force regardless of marital status. "If the right of privacy means anything," Brennan reasoned, "it is the right of the individual, married or single, to be free from unwarranted governmental intrusion into matters so fundamentally affecting a person as the decision whether to bear or beget a child."[28]

Eisenstadt raised new questions about the Court's views of abortion laws. Did the right to make childbearing decisions reach the termination of a pregnancy? On January 22, 1973, the day the Supreme Court decided *Roe v. Wade*, the public would know the Court's answer to both questions.

The Supreme Court Decides *Roe v. Wade*

In his case file on *Roe*, Justice Harry Blackmun kept a 1972 news story reporting that 64 percent of Americans polled by the Gallup Corporation agreed "that abortion should be a decision between a woman and her physician."[29] This idea—that the abortion right intersected with medical practice and belonged jointly to the woman and the doctor—defined Blackmun's opinion in *Roe*.[30]

In the lead-up to *Roe,* the Court considered the constitutionality of two laws. The first, a Texas regulation, prohibited abortion except when necessary to save the life of the woman. The second, a Georgia statute, echoed some of the ideas set forth by the ALI, requiring a woman seeking abortion to satisfy multiple physicians and a hospital committee.[31]

The Court's lead opinion, *Roe v. Wade,* began its substantive analysis by surveying the medical history of abortion, quite clearly treating abortion first and foremost as a question of medical authority and autonomy. The majority turned next to the justifications offered for the Texas abortion law. Since the State of Texas had not raised concerns about sexual promiscuity before the Supreme Court, the *Roe* decision dismissed out of hand the claim that abortion laws worked to discourage illicit sex.[32]

The Court next weighed the State's interests in protecting fetal life and women's health against a woman's ability to access abortion. Blackmun wrote that the right to privacy was "broad enough to encompass a woman's decision whether or not terminate her pregnancy." He explained the importance of the abortion decision by referring to the harms women experienced as the result of unwanted pregnancy, including "psychological harm" and the "continuing stigma of unwed motherhood." Nonetheless, for the *Roe* Court, the abortion right belonged at least partly to doctors. The choice, explained the majority, "must be left to the medical judgment of the pregnant woman's attending physician."[33]

Did the fetus count as a person under the Fourteenth Amendment? For the *Roe* majority, most relevant evidence weighed against fetal personhood. The constitutional text generally used "person" to refer to those who had already been born. The majority also rejected claims for a compelling state interest in protecting fetal life, stressing "the wide divergence of thinking on [the] sensitive and difficult question" of when life began.[34]

However, the Court did not entirely discount the State's interest in fetal life, working it into the trimester framework that would govern abortion law. In the first trimester, the government had to leave the abortion decision to the woman and her physician. In the second trimester, *Roe* permitted regulations that would safeguard the woman's health. After viability—the point at which a fetus could potentially live outside the mother's womb without medical aid—the State could legislate to protect potential life.[35]

We often view the Court's entry into the abortion wars as the moment when conflict intensified, compromise became impossible, and lay contributions to the constitutional debate about abortion declined, but the Supreme Court's decision did not dictate the course of the abortion wars in the decade to come. Instead, after 1973, a variety of shifting beliefs and strategic decisions continued to influence the struggle.[36]

Abortion Politics in the Decade after *Roe*

In the mid-1970s, those on opposing sides of the abortion issue found themselves in an unfamiliar political environment. The reorientation of political party positions on abortion, a dramatic new surge of rightwing activism, and the decline of population-control politics all substantially altered the world in which activists contested *Roe*'s meaning.

Before 1973, Richard Nixon's presidential campaign had identified abortion as an issue that could reorder American elections. The mid-1970s witnessed a striking acceleration of the process of party realignment. Over the course of the decade, social-conservative operatives worked to make pro-life positions synonymous with Republican politics.

These strategists, who later referred to themselves as the New Right, gathered in the aftermath of the Watergate scandal. The June 1972 break-in into Democratic Party headquarters in Washington, DC and the subsequent cover-up brought down the Nixon White House in the spring of 1973. The revelations of criminality surrounding the Watergate scandal crystallized grassroots conservatives' frustrations with the mainstream Republican Party. Nixon's replacement, Gerald Ford, selected a moderate Republican in favor of abortion rights, Nelson Rockefeller, as his vice president. For movement conservatives, Ford, Rockefeller, and Watergate stood as reminders of the lack of principle that defined the Republican Party.[37]

The chief architect of the New Right, Paul Weyrich, a veteran political operative and Roman Catholic, envisioned a conservative alternative to the liberal research institutes, fundraising infrastructure, and training centers set up in the 1960s. He went on to cofound the Heritage Institute, a conservative think tank, and the Committee for the Survival of a Free Congress (CSFC), a group that trained activists and raised funds to elect conservative congressional candidates.

Direct-mail guru Richard Viguerie joined Weyrich's efforts, founding *Conservative Digest* magazine in 1975 to serve as a mouthpiece for the New Right. Viguerie used his direct-mail company to raise between $35 million and $40 million for his conservative clients in 1980 alone. Beyond the groups formed by Viguerie and Weyrich, the New Right included organizations from the Conservative Caucus, a group specializing in recruiting new leaders and activists, to the National Conservative Political Action Committee, an organization focused on in-cash and in-kind contributions to political campaigns.[38]

Weyrich, Viguerie, and their allies wanted to create a social movement that could function independently from the mainstream Republican Party while forcing it to the right. In pursuing this goal, Weyrich borrowed from Nixon's strategy, using social issues like abortion to attract new supporters. Weyrich and the New Right took particular interest in the mobilization of evangelical Protestant voters, many of whom felt uneasy about abortion.[39]

The evangelical community Weyrich approached was diverse. Although sharing views on the inerrancy of the Bible, conservative fundamentalists, who more often read the Bible literally and more often favored separation from both other religions and from politics, stood apart from mainstream evangelicals attracted to the teachings of Billy Graham and the National Association of Evangelicals (NAE). Pentecostal and charismatic Protestants, like the followers of Pat Robertson, worshipped in different ways and, until the 1960s, remained more reluctant to enter the political fray than did other evangelicals. Before the 1970s, northern and southern evangelical Protestant groups had disagreed profoundly on issues from abortion to civil rights. For Weyrich, however, evangelicals appeared to be an untapped source of conservative votes. In a 1976 Gallup Poll, 34 percent of respondents claimed to have had a born-again religious experience, and nearly half of all Protestants polled agreed that the Bible "is to be taken literally."[40]

Weyrich and the New Right sponsored a number of well-funded organizations designed to activate evangelical voters and to unite them with similarly minded voters of different faiths. The best known effort of this kind gave rise to Jerry Falwell's Moral Majority in 1979—a fundraising behemoth, media giant, and political lobbying organization. The Religious Roundtable, a group that encouraged conservative Christians to become politically involved, commanded the attention of leading Republican politicians. Founded in 1978, a third group,

Christian Voice, quickly established its influence in conservative politics, gaining 100,000 members and a governing board that included fourteen members of Congress.[41]

The *Roe* decision did not create the New Right or the Religious Right. Certainly, even before 1973, some evangelicals strongly opposed abortion. However, both before and immediately after 1973, some influential evangelicals took more liberal stands on the issue. One year after *Roe*, for example, the Southern Baptist Convention reaffirmed its commitment to "a middle ground between the extreme of abortion on demand and the opposite extreme of all abortion as murder."[42]

Over the course of the 1970s, Weyrich and his allies redefined the abortion issue, describing it as one of several threats to the survival of the American family. The New Right made *Roe* into a symbol of sexual license, women's exit from the home, and the decline of religion. Citing Supreme Court decisions on school prayer, Weyrich also presented abortion as yet one more example of the Supreme Court's interference with religion.[43]

Most centrally, the New Right tied abortion to the proposed Equal Rights Amendment (ERA) to the federal Constitution. First proposed by feminist Alice Paul in 1923, the text of the ERA stated: "Equality of rights under the law shall not be denied or abridged by the United States or any state on account of sex."[44] In the early 1970s, feminists built momentum for the amendment. After Representative Martha Griffiths (D-MI) introduced the ERA in Congress, the 92nd Congress presented it in 1972 for ratification by the states.[45]

As soon as debate in the states began, Phyllis Schlafly, a veteran conservative activist, anti-communist, and former congressional candidate, wrote a newsletter condemning it. In asking "What's Wrong with Equal Rights for Women?" Schlafly called the ERA a fraud. "Why should we lower ourselves to 'equal rights,'" she asked, "when we already have the status of special privilege?" In the early 1970s, Schlafly's message resonated with evangelical Protestants, Mormons, Jews, and Roman Catholics troubled by feminism and women's changing roles.[46]

By making abortion a part of a more ambitious social-conservative agenda, the New Right convinced many of Schlafly's supporters that banning the procedure would protect the traditional family. Similarly, Schlafly and the New Right successfully persuaded pro-lifers that the ERA and the women's movement would strengthen abortion rights. By making *Roe* shorthand for a host of worries about sex equality and sexuality, Weyrich and Schlafly laid the groundwork for an alliance between pro-lifers and the Religious Right.[47]

In turn, a partnership with the New Right and the Religious Right promised economic stability and political relevance to what had been an isolated pro-life movement. At the same time, in working with the New Right, some pro-lifers revised their beliefs about the women's movement and the role of the courts in American politics.[48]

The New Right also reinforced each political party's position on the abortion issue. In the 1976 Republican primary, Ronald Reagan had departed from the conventional political script, taking a strongly pro-life stance on a fetal-protective amendment to the Constitution. Generally, however, both parties avoided taking a clear position on abortion.[49]

In the aftermath of Reagan's 1976 primary defeat, the New Right and Religious Right rallied around him, promising the Republican Party a loyal, fervent, and sizable group of voters. At the same time, Weyrich and his allies convinced pro-lifers that, if elected, Republicans would act forcefully to protect fetal life. By the 1980s, these efforts had paid off. Ronald Reagan, the Republican candidate in 1980, took pro-life positions on the campaign trail, and the party's platform endorsed a fetal-life amendment.

By 1980, the Democratic Party had also strengthened its support for legal abortion. Reframed as a symbol of women's liberation, abortion rights fit well in a Democratic agenda designed to help empower disenfranchised minorities and to secure civil rights. In 1980, the Democratic Party platform explicitly endorsed *Roe v. Wade* as the law of the land and opposed any fetal-protective constitutional amendment.[50]

Furthermore, those contesting the abortion wars identified a new set of allies, opponents, critics, and potential recruits. The once powerful population-control movement faced new resistance from the leaders of developing countries. A scandal about the forced sterilization of women of color portrayed population controllers as racist and exploitative. The 1973 Supreme Court decision also undermined population controllers' interest in the issue. Since the Court had already protected abortion rights, as some population controllers argued, those concerned about demographic growth should address other priorities, such as illegal immigration. At the same time, by angering the pro-life movement, the Court's decision made open support for abortion more controversial. An already overburdened population-control movement could ill afford to prioritize abortion rights.[51]

Similarly, opposing activists had to redefine their priorities to address an evolving racial politics. While men and women of color had expressed nationalist and separatist views well before the 1960s, the end of the decade witnessed the rise of a black-power movement that drew new attention to demands for self-defense and economic self-sufficiency. Leading members of groups like the Congress for Racial Equality (CORE) and the Student Non-Violent Coordinating Committee (SNCC) more forcefully articulated suspicions of the motives of the government, aid agencies, and interest groups championing abortion reform or family planning. At the same time, in the early 1970s, African-American, Chicana, and other minority feminists began to carve out a place in civil-rights organizations. Often working independently, feminists of color convinced their colleagues in black-power organizations that abortion could advance race as well as sex equality.[52]

With the black-power movement center stage, abortion-rights activists had reason to address concerns about the racial bias some saw embedded in their cause. Concern about racism partly reflected the disproportionately high rate of legal abortion in the African-American community. Moreover, the partnership of abortion-rights activists and population controllers raised the specter of racial bias. Some population controllers had historical ties to the movement for eugenic legal reform. Other advocates praised abortion reform as a strategy for cutting welfare costs and illegitimacy rates—an argument that some civil-rights activists found disturbing. At the same time, women of color created a distinctive vision of feminism and reproductive rights that abortion-rights supporters could popularize.

As feminists made abortion a priority, the women's movement became more mainstream, influential, and formally organized in the later 1970s. While the ERA campaign ultimately fell short, feminists managed to convince a majority in Congress and the states of the need for a sex-equality amendment. Feminist attorneys remade the constitutional law governing sex discrimination under the Fourteenth Amendment and the Civil Rights Act of 1964. With the mainstreaming of the legal wing of the women's movement, feminist leaders and arguments had greater standing in abortion-rights politics.[53]

While social and political shifts in the 1970s strengthened feminists' position in the abortion-rights movement, other economic and political forces contributed to the narrowing of the movement's aims. Ronald Reagan's triumph in 1980 built on public dissatisfaction with the American economy under Jimmy Carter. During the 1980 election season, Reagan blamed "stagflation"—a mix of high inflation, high unemployment, and low economic growth—on "big government." On the campaign trail, Reagan popularized neoliberalism, a policy vision based on the virtues of free markets, limited government, and deregulation. After 1980, Reagan arrived in office promising dramatic cuts to the size of government. Often, Democratic candidates offered their own ideas for cutting wasteful spending and reforming welfare. In the new, antigovernment climate, abortion-rights advocates had to change their claims and their substantive demands.[54]

The ERA battle further impacted the arguments and tactics of abortion-rights supporters. For many feminists, women required fertility control in order to participate equally in the political, economic, or social life of the United States. In spite of the apparent relationship between sex equality and abortion, feminists played down any connection between the two. As pro-lifers increasingly politicized the abortion issue, feminists dissociated it from the ERA. Given the stigma surrounding abortion, feminists worried that connecting the two issues—or tying equality arguments to abortion rights—would undermine support for the amendment.[55]

After 1973, the abortion fight continued to evolve in response to an ever-changing political climate. The mobilization of the New Right and the Religious Right, the decline of the population-control cause, the remaking of the civil-rights movement, the rise of neoliberalism, and the battle for the ERA all set the terms of the conflict. At the same time, movement members were not passive in the face of social changes they could not control. Like politicians and other nonjudicial actors, grassroots activists made choices that fundamentally changed the abortion debate.

The Stakes of *Roe* for Social-Movement Scholarship

Scholars offer a dramatically different perspective on the impact of the Supreme Court's decision. The conventional narrative suggests that *Roe* in no small part created the contentious battle we now know. First, social-movement scholars use the history of activists' reactions to the *Roe* decision to explore both the defining traits of pro-life and abortion-rights activists and the nature of social-movement mobilization. Kristin Luker's pioneering work contends that *Roe* helped to lay bare the basic worldviews held by those on either side of the abortion struggle. Luker argues that the Court's opinion "mobilized a new and much stronger opposition to abortion reform" and made debate about the procedure "increasingly emotional and passionate."[56] In part, the abortion battle intensified because it brought to the surface fundamental differences in the beliefs of Americans in favor of or opposed to abortion rights. It became clear that "[w]omen come to be pro-life and pro-choice activists as the end result of lives that center around different definitions of motherhood."[57]

Faye Ginsburg similarly sees *Roe* as "a catalyst to subsequent developments that Americans have come to identify as the current [abortion] controversy."[58] In Ginsburg's view, the Court's decision helped to clarify the values driving the abortion conflict. The abortion controversy, Ginsburg suggests, represents "the most recent manifestation of . . . struggles over the material, political, and symbolic definitions of gender."[59]

Scholars like Carol Maxwell and Suzanne Staggenborg agree that *Roe* helped to create a bigger, more radical, and more sophisticated pro-life movement. For example, Staggenborg views the 1973 opinion as bittersweet for the abortion-rights movement. On the one hand, *Roe* legitimated abortion rights, laying the foundation for the creation of more structured and sophisticated pro-choice organizations. At the same time, *Roe* escalated the conflict and limited the scope of abortion-rights advocacy. In response to the opinion, Staggenborg suggests that abortion-rights activists soon became "preoccupied with reactive tactics aimed at fending off countermovement attacks on *Roe v. Wade*."[60]

Recently, Ziad Munson has challenged the conventional view that *Roe* mobilized a majority of pro-life activists. While the opinion shocked pro-lifers, Munson suggests, it did "not mark the moment they first became involved in pro-life activism."[61] Nonetheless, Munson maintains that *Roe* represented "the beginning of the abortion debate in the United States," a debate defined by "increasing polarization of views and strident moralizing on both sides."[62]

For leading social-movement scholars, the aftermath of *Roe* illuminates the identity of the players in the abortion wars and the stakes of battle about the procedure. How would these accounts change if social-movement reactions to *Roe* defied our expectations? The book explores this question in later chapters.

The Supreme Court Debates the Fate of the *Roe* Decision

Current members of the Supreme Court draw on the history of social-movement responses in analyzing the need to overrule or rework *Roe*. Justice Antonin Scalia, a vocal critic of abortion rights, views movement responses to *Roe* as a signal of the opinion's lack of principle.

"As long as this Court thought (and the people thought) that we Justices were doing essentially lawyers' work up here," Scalia argues, "the public pretty much left us alone." The *Roe* Court's overreaching prompted a popular backlash. In Scalia's view, until the Court overrules the *Roe* decision, abortion politics will remain at an impasse. Worse, the Supreme Court's legitimacy will remain in question. "*Roe* fanned into life an issue that has inflamed our national politics in general," Scalia argues. "[K]eeping [the Court] in the abortion-umpiring business [will lead to] the perpetuation of that disruption."[63]

While strongly supporting sex equality, Justice Ruth Bader Ginsburg uses the history of social-movement reaction to *Roe* in justifying a new rationale for abortion rights. In Ginsburg's account, the *Roe* Court intensified backlash "by [virtue of] the opinion's concentration on a medically approved autonomy idea, to the exclusion of a constitutionally based sex-equality perspective."[64] The Court's reasoning proved to be both unconvincing and disconnected from established doctrine. More recently, Ginsburg has insisted that the *Roe* Court "had given the opponents [of access to abortion] a target to aim at relentlessly." In Ginsburg's opinion, the Court "seemed to stop the momentum" in favor of abortion rights.[65]

Both Scalia and Ginsburg use reaction to *Roe* in service of claims for legal change. For Ginsburg, *Roe*'s history points to the merits of an equality-based approach to abortion. Reaction to the opinion also sounds a cautionary note for justices who risk moving too far too fast, whether in the context of abortion or same-sex marriage. Scalia also draws on social-movement history in arguing for the overruling of *Roe* and for the more consistent adoption of interpretive methods limited to text, history, and original intent.

Understanding *Roe*'s history may make the difference between the decision's preservation, reworking, or undoing. If Scalia's account has merit, judicial opponents of the *Roe* Court's methodology or holding have additional ammunition for demanding the overruling of the decision. Conversely, if Ginsburg's historical analysis is correct, we would have more cause than ever to change the constitutional foundation for abortion rights.

Roe Serves as a Touchstone for Dialogue about the Best Method of Constitutional Interpretation

In the legal academy, scholars draw on *Roe*'s history in exploring the advantages and disadvantages of different approaches to constitutional interpretation. While sitting members of the Supreme Court focus partly on the evolution of abortion doctrine, legal scholars use responses to *Roe* in answering important questions about how judges should best interpret the Constitution and when, if at all, judges should consider the policy consequences of their decisions.

In praising minimalism, Cass Sunstein explains that the Court "should be very cautious about duplicating . . . *Roe*."[66] Minimalist decisions avoid broad holdings and philosophical rationales that spark controversy and undermine democratic deliberation. In analyzing *Roe*, Sunstein suggests that a more modest and minimalist decision "would not have caused so much destructive and unnecessary social upheaval."[67]

When describing the benefits of using statutes rather than judicial opinions to elaborate on important constitutional values, William Eskridge and John Ferejohn also invoke the aftermath of *Roe*. Eskridge and Ferejohn highlight the virtues of statutes as a method of enforcing fundamental values and addressing questions of constitutional structure. By contrast to judicial decisions, statutes allow for deliberation and consensus-building. Eskridge and Ferejohn contend: "[T]he Court should avoid the mistake of *Roe v. Wade*, which was to announce a Constitutional right . . . before [public consensus] had come to rest on an important norm."[68]

In defending pragmatism, his preferred interpretive method, Richard Posner also turns to the history of movement responses to *Roe*. Pragmatism requires judges to consider both the systemic and case-specific consequences of a particular decision. Pragmatism is forward-looking and empiricist, favoring narrow over broad decision-making. As Posner explains, "[p]ragmatism applied to law at most takes away from judges the claim to be engaged in a neutral scientific activity . . . rather than in a basically political activity of formulating and applying public policy."[69]

Posner sees *Roe* as an example of the consequences of rejecting (or at least misapplying) a pragmatic philosophy. In Posner's view, the Court erred by "prematurely nationaliz[ing] the issue of abortion rights"[70] and by ignoring "an important consequence—the stifling effect on democratic experimentation of establishing a constitutional right to abortion." Had a more pragmatic Court ducked the issue or decided the case narrowly, the justices might have arrived at "a sensible compromise, less likely to incite an anti-abortion movement."[71]

Reva Siegel and Robert Post have responded by identifying post-*Roe* conflict as a healthy part of a constitutional democracy. They

argue that courts must balance a respect for the rule of law with re-
sponsiveness to popular understandings of the Constitution. In this
analysis, movement reactions to *Roe* signal popular engagement with
important constitutional issues—a positive sign in any democracy.
Over time, the Court responded to competing demands by crafting an
abortion jurisprudence that resonated with the people but that also
satisfied the demands of rule-of-law values.[72]

For many legal scholars, *Roe* also serves as a prime example of
courts' inability to create meaningful social change. Legal academics
such as Jeffrey Rosen, Gerald Rosenberg, and Michael Klarman see
reaction to *Roe* as evidence of the limited effect of litigation on popular attitudes. In Rosen's view, *Roe* empowered extremists on either
side who rejected the idea of compromise out of hand. Rosen uses
the Court's decision as a case study of the ways in which most opinions track popular opinion and the consequences faced by the justices
when they fail to do so.[73]

Klarman describes *Roe* as an illustration of the way in which judicial decisions can undermine the cause that judges embrace. Speaking
of *Roe*, Klarman explains: "Naturally, a Court ruling that dictated
a result significantly different from the one that was simultaneously
being negotiated in legislatures generated a strong backlash."[74] In discussing reaction to *Roe*, Gerald Rosenberg also highlights the low
value of litigation as a tool for social change. In his view, the 1973
opinion reveals litigation to be a "strategy that produces little or no
change and induces backlash." For Rosenberg, *Roe* also exemplifies
the ways in which judicial decisions can encourage "reformers to re-
lax their efforts." In the abortion context, *Roe* seriously weakened the
"efficacy of pro-choice forces."[75]

For legal scholars, social-movement responses to *Roe* offer important lessons about the relationship between the courts and the larger
American society. The legal literature frames *Roe* as an example of
the dangers created by judicial review for the American polity, as
a case study on the limited value of litigation, or as a lens through
which judges can study the relative merits of different interpretive
methods. As do social-movement scholars, however, legal academics
use *Roe* as a symbol for many things, from the recognition of reproductive rights to the intervention of courts in divisive debates. The
many meanings of *Roe* have led to basic misunderstandings of social-
movement responses to the opinion. If we reclaim the history of the
abortion wars in the decade from 1973 to 1983, discussion of the role
of the courts will be more principled and informed.

Historical Scholarship Spotlights the *Roe* Decision

Histories of the abortion wars offer additional perspective on the consequences of *Roe v. Wade.* Some scholars describe the unintended costs of the Supreme Court's opinion. In exploring the creation of sexual civil liberties, Leigh Ann Wheeler contends that the abortion-rights movement's successes in *Roe* and *Doe* "inspired the emergence of a powerful antiabortion movement."[76] Donald Critchlow and Sara Dubow detail the bitter battle that *Roe* produced. In his work on the policy history of abortion and family planning, Critchlow writes that "*Roe v. Wade* only intensified growing polarization over the abortion issue."[77] Surveying the history of attitudes toward the fetus, Dubow argues that post-*Roe* debate became considerably more partisan. "Subsequent to the 1973 *Roe v. Wade* decision," she suggests, "disagreements over the status of the unborn would erupt and transform American culture in ways previously unimaginable."[78] Joining with legal academics, other scholars trace the substantial costs of the opinion for feminists, poor women, and women of color.[79]

Generally, scholars assign the Supreme Court tremendous influence. However, as the following chapters show, the abortion conflict turned on a number of events unrelated to the *Roe* decision. Moreover, activists on either side of the abortion issue did not merely react to major social changes. Often without focusing on the Supreme Court, members of both movements made choices that raised the stakes of the abortion wars. Activists sometimes reached these decisions for instrumental reasons, identifying ways to recruit new members, raise more money, or lay the groundwork for favorable legal changes. On other occasions, advocates acted to forward deeply-held beliefs about sex equality, the value of life, the importance of social justice, or the need for sexual freedom.

The *Roe* opinion notwithstanding, pro-lifers pursued a constitutional agenda having little to do with judicial overreaching. Preoccupation with the courts came later, in response to the movement's shifting political alliances and leadership. The Court's decision did not block feminist efforts to create a reproductive-rights agenda that would reflect the importance of abortion for women or the place of abortion in a more expansive agenda. Women on opposing sides of the abortion wars did not see the Supreme Court as standing in the way of efforts to build consensus. Even in defining *Roe* itself, activists proved to be surprisingly innovative and collaborative.

In considering the world of abortion politics in the decade after 1973, the book looks beyond the Supreme Court. Americans from across the ideological spectrum made the abortion battle a central part of their lives. If we recapture their stories, then we can better understand what *Roe v. Wade* has meant to American politics.

PART I

The Pro-Life Movement after *Roe*

CHAPTER ONE

Judicial Activism and
the Pro-Life Movement

ON THE NIGHT after the Court issued its decision in *Roe v. Wade*, Juan Ryan, a New Jersey attorney and leader of the National Right to Life Committee (NRLC), could not fall asleep. Pat Goltz, a feminist from Ohio, found herself unable to listen to music, thinking of all the babies who would never hear a song. Kenneth Vanderhoef, one of the attorneys who had represented antiabortion amici in *Roe* and *Doe v. Bolton*, felt "thunderstruck" by the decision, hardly hearing the syllabus of the opinion as it was read aloud in open court.[1]

In the days after January 22, 1973, pro-lifers debated how best to respond to the Court's decision. Like many abortion opponents, Dr. John Willke, a veteran pro-life activist, reacted by participating in a post-*Roe* campaign to restore what he believed to be long-recognized fetal rights. A devout Catholic and sex educator, Willke became famous for his slideshows on abortion. He told the story of fetal development in reverse, driving home what he believed to be the obviousness of fetal rights. The *Roe* decision did little to change Willke's commitments. He and many of his colleagues rejected proposals that would chastise the Court for its overreaching and return the abortion issue to the states. Willke's colleagues often believed that such a proposal would compound the Supreme Court's betrayal.[2]

How did the *Roe* decision impact the movement to which advocates like Willke belonged? Conventionally, we believe that antiabortion activists immediately protested the idea that unelected courts had imposed their views on the people. For these reasons, we think that *Roe* "prompted a crisis of constitutional legitimacy."[3] Pro-lifers supposedly led a revolt against perceived judicial overreaching.[4]

But did the Court's decision really produce a popular, pro-life movement against judicial activism? Some movement members did turn to arguments or strategies centered on judicial arrogance. However, for the better part of a decade after the Court's decision, the vast majority of lawyers, law professors, and grassroots activists in the antiabortion movement opposed efforts to strip the Court of its authority or to return the abortion question to democratic politics. Nor did most members of national or state antiabortion organizations stress arguments against judicial activism, either in criticizing the Court's abortion jurisprudence or in campaigning for a fetal-life amendment. Indeed, pro-lifers wanted the courts to act boldly to protect fetal rights not spelled out in the text of the Constitution. Abortion opponents asked the courts to rely on what could be seen as activist interpretive methods, taking the issue away from the people.[5]

The movement's shared vision of the role of the courts concealed deep internal disagreements about sexual mores and gender roles. In the 1960s, as state campaigns to liberalize abortion laws sprang up, local opposition groups varied a great deal from community to community, and by 1970, when organizers worked to build a national movement, a variety of groups contested the meaning of a right to life. One faction described the sexual revolution and the expansion of feminist activism as part of a more general, and deeply negative, cultural shift. Fighting the legalization of abortion required a war against recent social changes and a restoration of traditional norms— as one activist put it, a "total confrontation, a turning point in the moral history of this country."[6]

Other pro-lifers approved of, or at least did not oppose, some recent social and cultural changes. These abortion opponents tended to define themselves by their support for a particular vision of a caring society: fighting for an expanded social welfare net, broader rights for the poor and for vulnerable minorities, and certain reforms championed by legal feminists. Other movement members fell somewhere between these two extremes, viewing the women's movement, the sexual revolution, and contraception as being independent or even irrelevant issues. As ideological divisions in the movement became clear, members of this neutral party had to choose sides and often elected to define their cause narrowly, opposing abortion and nothing else.[7]

This deep division notwithstanding, pro-lifers shared an idea of the courts' constitutional and moral obligations. Judges had a duty to identify rights at best implicit in the constitutional text, particularly when those rights belonged to vulnerable classes. Pro-lifers articulated this vision at a time when conservative groups were beginning to attack perceived judicial overreaching, targeting decisions on busing, criminal procedure, and school prayer. Concerns about judicial tyranny reached from the streets to the legal academy. Beginning in the mid-1960s, scholars critical of Supreme Court decisions on sex equality and contraception argued that the Warren and Burger Courts had no principled basis for their decisions.[8]

Because of their disagreements about gender and sexual mores, many abortion opponents did not universally condemn recent Supreme Court decisions protecting rights to contraception or prohibiting sex discrimination. More importantly, in turning to arguments about equal protection and due process of law, pro-lifers asked the courts to use the doctrinal innovations condemned by many conservatives to recognize the unborn child's fundamental, implicit right to life.[9]

The Supreme Court's *Roe* decision intensified pro-lifers' commitment to a controversial constitutional agenda centered on expansive ideas of equal protection and implied fundamental rights. After 1973, in promoting a right to life, activists asked the courts to look to the Declaration of Independence, the Thirteenth and Fourteenth Amendments, international human rights law, and pre-*Roe* substantive due process cases recognizing rights implicit in the Constitution. Movement members preferred that such a right be protected by courts from the will of shifting majorities.[10]

What does this consensus tell us about the antiabortion movement in the decade after *Roe*? In spite of their ideological divisions, most movement members did not object to the *Roe* decision because the Court had removed the abortion question from the democratic process. Instead, as most leading abortion opponents saw it, the Court erred in leaving the unborn without the protection they deserved. As a post-*Roe* brief submitted by the United States Catholic Conference complained: "*Roe v. Wade* uniquely opens a protected constitutional right to the workings of the popular will."[11]

By the early 1980s, as movement tactics and beliefs shifted, leading pro-life activists more often turned to arguments about judicial activism. Over the course of the decade, a new breed of leader had come to influence the movement. Rejecting ideological purity, these advocates prioritized small, short-term successes. This strategy, although divisive, gradually attracted the support of a majority of movement members.[12]

For these new leaders, arguments against judicial overreaching offered obvious strategic advantages. In the late 1970s, important potential allies, including leaders of the Republican Party and the emerging Religious Right and New Right, often condemned judicial tyranny. In 1980, Republican candidate Ronald Reagan emphasized similar claims on the campaign trail.[13]

Partly by observing Reagan's campaign strategies firsthand, pro-life activists came to a new realization about the practical value of arguments against judicial activism. Since 1973, pro-lifers had worked to amend the federal Constitution. Failing to make significant progress, abortion opponents sought new ways to outlaw abortion. By joining an emerging conservative coalition opposed to judicial activism, pro-lifers believed they could more effectively pressure the Supreme Court. Belonging to a broad alliance also promised the movement greater influence over national elections and federal judicial nominations.[14]

In particular, pro-lifers' criticism of judicial overreaching resonated with members of the Religious Right, many of whom held deep concerns about the power of the Supreme Court. By condemning the Court, pro-lifers expressed solidarity with influential new allies. At the same time, in working closely with the New Right, some abortion opponents developed new beliefs about the judiciary. While contentions about judicial activism did not speak directly to the rights of the unborn, these arguments made sense to pro-lifers certain that the Supreme Court had done a great moral wrong.[15]

As this history suggests, the Supreme Court's decision did not dictate the politics of judicial review within the pro-life movement. Leading studies correctly highlight the importance of perceptions of judicial legitimacy within the antiabortion movement. Just the same, those who argue that the *Roe* decision undermined the Court's authority fail to account for how and why pro-lifers began stressing concern about judicial activism.

A Diverse and Divided Movement Forms, Championing the Right to Life

The pro-life movement began as a vibrant, fragmented, and flexible cluster of organizations. Beginning in the late 1960s, a number of private citizens mobilized to block laws repealing or reforming abortion bans. These early antiabortion groups brought together members of church discussion groups or bridge clubs, neighbors, close friends, colleagues, or even members of the same family. Although early pro-lifers differed considerably from one another, they tended to fall into two general groups. One included male and female professionals—physicians, lawyers, and law professors—some of whom became active to protest the positions on abortion taken by pro-reform colleagues or professional organizations. Others joined on the recommendation of coworkers or acquaintances already involved in the movement. These included physicians John Willke from Ohio, Fred Mecklenburg from Minnesota, and Mildred F. Jefferson from Massachusetts; attorneys like juvenile-court judge Robert Greene from Kentucky, attorneys Dolores and Dennis Horan from Illinois, and law professors like Charles Rice and Robert Byrn from New York.[16]

While pro-lifers were predominantly white, antiabortion organizers crafted groups that ignored or even subverted conventional hierarchies of class and gender. Many physicians and lawyers defined themselves first as grassroots activists and only secondarily as professionals. In state organizations in Minnesota, New York, Kentucky, and Michigan, for example, professionals took part in media appearances to highlight the respectability of their groups, but lay activists, many of them women and homemakers, held positions equal or superior to their professional colleagues.[17]

These homemakers formed the second major group of antiabortion leaders. For example, Randy Engel, a young mother living in Dayton, Ohio, became active after a friend pointed out an article in a local Catholic newspaper on efforts to control the growth of the Aleut-Indian population—an effort that Engel found deeply objectionable. She soon came to believe that the government showed disregard for human life in the context of both family planning and abortion. After moving to Pittsburgh with her family, Engel helped to form Women Concerned for the Unborn Child, a group of homemakers who lobbied against family planning funding and legal abortion.[18]

Influenced by various political climates and distinctive leadership styles, state groups adopted strikingly different visions of what it meant to be pro-life. An examination of two of the nation's leading state organizations, those based in New York and Minnesota, makes clear how differently abortion opponents viewed questions of strategy and identity. The New York organization emerged partly as a result of the efforts of Edward Golden. A self-described hard hat, Golden, a father of five and former Air Force officer, worked as a construction foreman near Albany, New York. Disturbed by the progress of abortion-reform bills in the states, Golden felt that "society was going downhill" and found three others who shared his view, forming a small pro-life organization in New York State. At first, his group prioritized writing letters to the state legislature. After 1970, when New York liberalized its abortion law, Golden and his colleagues changed tactics, focusing on lobbying and establishing a presence in the state legislature. As Golden explained: "[W]e knew we'd have to roll up our sleeves and really become political."[19]

A Methodist couple from Minnesota, Fred Mecklenburg and his wife, Marjory, headed a quite different pro-life organization, Minnesota Citizens Concerned for Life (MCCL). The group began almost by chance when Marjory, a home economics teacher, had a conversation with her neighbor Alice Hartle. A Catholic mother of nine, Hartle had recently heard that the Minnesota State Legislature was considering a bill that would permit abortions in cases where a child was likely to contract rubella and become blind. One of Hartle's children was blind, and she took offense at the idea that her daughter could be thought of as unwanted. In 1968, the two women drove to the Minnesota State Legislature, and after meeting a third concerned citizen, Kevin Powers, a Catholic and veteran Democratic Party activist, they decided to form an antiabortion organization.[20]

As Mecklenburg organized it, the MCCL worked quite differently than did Golden's New York organization. After 1970, Golden's group focused on direct confrontations and protests. By contrast, Mecklenburg and the MCCL did not permit protest or allow the use images of aborted fetuses. Instead, the group focused on public education, outreach programs in local schools, and involvement in local pregnancy-counseling offices. Whereas Golden's organization included more Republicans and Catholics, the MCCL involved a number of self-described or politically active Democrats, committed to "protection of the right to life of the mother and child."[21]

In the early 1970s, as the movement began to organize at the national level, the differences between state groups evolved into a more general ideological rift. In the late 1960s and early 1970s, national pro-life activities, such as they were, had begun to expand dramatically. Some of the early national groups took on traditionalist Catholic agendas that reached beyond the issue of abortion. For example, the Human Life Center, a group founded by Father Paul Marx at St. John's University in Minnesota, campaigned for traditional marriage and natural family planning. Founded by Catholic activists L.

Brent Bozell and Michael Lawrence, the Society for a Christian Commonwealth (SCC), a conservative lay Catholic organization, became known for its magazine, *Triumph*, and for its broad definition of "the attack on life," a definition that included "birth control, abortion, euthanasia, genetic manipulation, [and] the denigration of sex."[22]

Perhaps the best-known group active before 1973, the National Right to Life Committee (NRLC), served as an umbrella organization for affiliates and as a source of information on the struggles in individual states. Monsignor James McHugh, the head of the United States Catholic Conference's Family Life Division, recruited the leaders of state pro-life organizations, including Mecklenburg and Golden. NRLC leaders hoped that the organization would forge a single strategy and message for what had been a fragmented movement.[23]

A second major national organization, Americans United for Life (AUL), focused on the issue of education. Organization leaders believed, in the words of a September fundraising letter, that "if the American public at large can be educated to an understanding of the fundamental issue of abortion—what it really is—what really is done to that living being, the child in the womb, they will reject abortion on demand."[24]

The AUL and NRLC's tactics and limitations reveal a good deal about the national movement. Both organizations functioned primarily to coordinate the efforts of already active individuals or state groups. At the same time, by bringing together widely diverse organizations and individuals, the NRLC and AUL worked to identify beliefs and arguments shared by their constituents. In practice, this task proved to be difficult. Within the antiabortion community, activists realized that they disagreed quite strongly about what it meant to be pro-life.

Birth-Control and Sex-Discrimination Law Divide Pro-Lifers

In the early 1970s, ideological disagreements rocked the AUL and the NRLC. The first fight, concerning contraception and exceptions to abortion bans, erupted within the AUL. This battle stemmed from a deeper division within the early movement. Did the legalization of abortion follow naturally from what some activists viewed as damaging social changes that had begun in the 1960s? Or did the legalization of abortion represent, as an opposing faction believed, a betrayal of the noble principles underlying those changes?

These divisions also touched on explosive questions about the role the courts should play in American society. At the start of the abortion wars in the 1960s, conservative groups led an independent attack on the power of the judiciary. Letter-writing campaigns, constitutional amendment efforts, and street protests expressed popular anger about the Warren Court and Burger Court's decisions on school prayer, busing, and criminal procedure. Legal academics criticized the supposed activism represented by the *Griswold* decision, which identified a right to marital privacy without relying on the text or history of the Constitution. In 1971 and 1973, the Court relied on what some saw as an unconvincing analogy between sex and race discrimination to expand the reach of the Equal Protection Clause. Pointing to the Court's jurisprudence on reproduction and gender, academic critics and ordinary citizens identified what they saw as judicial overreaching.

In the late 1960s and early 1970s, when pro-lifers held profoundly different views of contraception and sex discrimination, claims about judicial tyranny had a less obvious appeal. Some pro-lifers saw the unborn as yet another minority—like people of color and women—deserving constitutional rights and social support. Viewed in this way, the best social changes of the 1960s and 1970s should be extended, making the country more compassionate about the plight of the vulnerable, the powerless, and the poor.

For traditionalists, abortion, the rise of the women's movement, and changing sexual mores reflected a "contraceptive mentality" that prized gratification and individual success over the responsibility owed to one's children, family, and community. Some proponents of this view certainly cited Catholic religious teachings in support of their position, particularly Pope Paul VI's 1968 anti-contraception encyclical *Humanae Vitae*. Still others, however, defined their cause as a moral rather than religious one. A number of leading activists fell at neither extreme, and some held no strong opinion on matters beyond the abortion question. When pushed to take a position, these advocates tended to oppose any effort to broaden the movement's ideological agenda.[25]

Within the AUL, Charles Rice, a professor of constitutional law, emerged as a leading traditionalist. A devout Catholic, a New York native, and a former Marine, Rice became involved in abortion politics while teaching at Fordham Law School. By the time he joined the AUL, Rice had published *The Vanishing Right to Live*, one of the first major antiabortion books. In it, Rice condemned not only abortion but also the "birth control fever" that had infected the women's movement and the larger American culture. Rice described birth control as "not a practice only but a new philosophy of man and sex. . . . It means the abandonment of self-control over sexual urges."[26] As part of the defense of a right to live, Rice demanded a campaign to restore a more selfless sexual politics. "Promiscuity," he wrote, "is the logic of birth control; but to have promiscuity with impunity there must also be abortion."[27]

Whereas Rice was a conservative and a deeply religious man, George Huntston Williams, the AUL Chairman, defined himself as an enthusiastic member of the ACLU and a strong opponent of the Vietnam War. The son of David Rhys Williams, a socialist and a champion of women's rights, Williams served as the Hollis Professor of Divinity at Harvard Divinity School, where he taught courses in Unitarian theology.[28]

Williams viewed the pro-life and civil-liberties movements as natural allies. In 1970, he published an elaboration of his theory on abortion in the widely-read antiabortion volume *The Morality of Abortion*. There, he called for "an integrated movement forward in the evolution of both fetal rights and the rights of women." While Rice had seen "birth control fever" as the root cause of the legalization of abortion, Williams believed that society could reconcile the rights of women and the unborn.[29]

In 1972, Rice discovered a book chapter written by Williams indicating that abortion should be legal under some circumstances, and at the second meeting of the AUL, Rice confronted him about it. Williams responded that he had joined the AUL with the understanding that the organization opposed only abortion on demand.[30]

Rice then pressed Williams on his view of contraception. Although mentioning that some contraceptives, including prostaglandins and IUDs, might be "abortifacients," Williams stated that he did not oppose contraception or believe that the organization should do so. Marjory Mecklenburg seconded this position.[31]

When the group met next, conflict flared again. This time, debate turned on the issue of exceptions to abortion bans. Rice and an ally presented a resolution committing the AUL to "opposition of all direct abortion without exception."[32] After a protracted discussion, AUL leaders voted seven to six to table the motion. Rice responded with an alternative resolution, stating that the "AUL condemns and

opposes, without exception" any abortion reform unless the procedure was necessary to save the life of the woman. After several hours
of argument, AUL leaders defeated the proposal by a vote of eight to
five.[33]

The March 10–11 meetings shook the AUL to its core. Some of its
most conservative members, including Rice, quit, joining the United
States Coalition for Life (USCL), an organization founded by Randy
Engel. Rice praised the group for focusing "not just opposition to
abortion, but [also on] opposition to all public involvement in contraception and sterilization."[34]

Not long after the March meetings, it became clear that the kind of
ideological disagreement revealed within the AUL cut across organizations. Rice and his former colleague, Robert Byrn, two of the movement's most influential theorists and strategists, carved out a place for
pro-life traditionalists. In 1963, Byrn, a professor of criminal law at
Fordham, became active in the pro-life movement. Since high school,
Byrn had been educated by Jesuits and considered himself a natural
"activist and perhaps non-conformist." He had spoken out against the
repeal of abortion restrictions in New York and served as the head of
the Metropolitan Right to Life Committee. In 1971, in an ultimately
unsuccessful suit, he petitioned to be appointed guardian ad litem for
all the fetuses scheduled to be aborted in New York City hospitals.
Byrn used the suit to publicize his movement's arguments about the
personhood of the fetus. While the two worked at Fordham, Byrn had
convinced Rice that support for abortion and support for contraception
could not be separated from one another. In the end, the two presented
a united front against both contraception and abortion, concluding
that many forms of birth control terminated existing pregnancies or
created a contraceptive mentality, making it inevitable that the nation
would turn to abortion.[35]

Inside and outside the AUL, abortion opponents on the other side
of this issue fell roughly into two camps. One, represented by Marjory Mecklenburg, supported contraception as an alternative to abortion. The MCCL even circulated materials insisting that there was
a "fundamental difference" between contraception and abortion:
"Birth control prevents conception—abortion destroys life once it is
created."[36] Partnering with Mecklenburg and her colleagues, other
pro-lifers generally downplayed the issue of contraception. Different
groups took this position in order to preserve organizational harmo-
ny, to focus resources on attacking abortion, or to attract a broader
group of recruits.[37]

The Equal Rights Amendment (ERA) created a similar schism within the movement. Some members of the antiabortion movement became active in fighting the ERA before 1973. For example, Margie Montgomery, the founder of Kentucky Right to Life and later a board member of the NRLC, concluded in 1973 that the amendment would expand rights to abortion. Montgomery, a mother and the head of the Louisville Parent-Teacher Association, drove to state legislative hearings on the ERA, where she and her daughter, still a high school student, testified against the amendment.[38]

On the opposite end of the spectrum, activists like Mecklenburg argued that both the ERA and the pro-life movement advanced equality for women. In Minnesota, pro-life activists like Mecklenburg and Darla St. Martin joined Women for Universal Human Rights, a group that favored a constitutional amendment that would ensure equal rights for both women and unborn children. Pro-life organizations committed to the ERA emerged in states like Missouri and California.[39]

In spite of these disagreements, movement members shared a belief in a right to life already protected by the Constitution—so much so that no formal amendment to that effect appeared necessary. This idea played a formative role in the early years of the AUL and the NRLC. The AUL's declaration of purpose, for example, cited the Declaration of Independence as evidence that the Constitution had always recognized a right to life. The NRLC also drew on rights-based rhetoric in describing its priorities and values.[40]

In defending the right to life, movement members stressed the humanity of the fetus. According to pro-life leaders, the common law had long recognized the legal standing of the unborn. Genetic and fetological studies established personhood as a scientific fact. As a person, the fetus would enjoy the same constitutional rights as anyone else.[41]

Significantly, pro-lifers argued that all Americans, including unborn ones, enjoyed a fundamental right to life. Although nothing in the constitutional text set forth such a right, abortion opponents believed that other provisions implied its existence. "The Declaration of Independence holds as self-evident the moral truths 'that all men are created equal, that they are endowed by their Creator with certain fundamental rights, that among these are Life, Liberty, and the Pursuit of Happiness,'" argued Robert Byrn in the early 1970s. "The fourteenth amendment institutionalized these principles . . . in the Constitution."[42]

Before 1973, in seeking protection for the unborn, pro-lifers looked first to the courts. Believing that the Constitution already protected a right to life, pro-lifers saw a fetal-protective amendment as counterproductive—a potential boon for an opposition insisting that the fetus had no existing constitutional rights. By contrast, the Supreme Court had already recognized rights only implied by the text of the Constitution, such as rights to contraception, and lower courts had identified the fetus as a person in property and tort cases. Why would the courts not recognize the right to life in a similar way?[43]

After the *Roe* Decision, Pro-Lifers Push a Fetal-Protective Amendment

What impact did the *Roe* decision have on pro-life activism? The Supreme Court's decision did not convince pro-lifers to resolve deep ideological disagreements on matters such as contraception and the ERA. Nonetheless, the *Roe* decision did help pro-lifers clarify their legal priorities. Far from sparking a crusade against judicial activism, the Court's decision strengthened activists' belief in a right to life that the courts should remove from popular politics.

Mobilizing to amend the Constitution and ban all abortions, pro-lifers took to the national stage and articulated a shared constitutional vision. The courts, they argued, had an obligation to restore the right to life negated by the *Roe* decision. Notwithstanding a lack of clear textual or historical evidence, as pro-lifers argued, the courts should infer the existence of that right by looking to the Thirteenth Amendment, the Fourteenth Amendment, the Declaration of Independence, or international human rights law. By securing a constitutional amendment, pro-lifers would force the courts to do what the *Roe* decision failed to do: protect the right to life from popular majorities. As one antiabortion law review article explained in 1973: "The Court with equal effort could have discovered the unborn's right to life, invested it with fundamental status, and clothed it in judicial protection."[44]

The struggle for a constitutional amendment both reinforced and spurred the nationalization of pro-life activities. First, the Court's decision prompted the formation of several new national groups, such as the Ad Hoc Committee in Defense of Life, a lobbying and education group founded by *National Review* editor J. P. McFadden. As importantly, the Court inspired the mobilization of new activists, many of whom assumed positions of leadership in the movement. As Kristin Luker has argued, some prominent national advocates recall the Court's intervention as the reason for their mobilization. For example, *Roe* supposedly motivated Elasah Drogin and Theo Stearns, the women who in 1974 founded Catholics United for Life (CUL), a California group focused on picketing abortion clinics.[45]

Nonetheless, consistent with sociologist Ziad Munson's findings, other leaders who joined the movement after the *Roe* decision did not describe it as a major factor in their mobilization. Consider the stories of two homemakers who went on to lead the post-1973 movement in Pennsylvania. Initially, when the *Roe* decision came down, Denise Neary believed that, while she personally could not imagine having an abortion, she had no right to impose her view on anyone else. Later, after speaking with other young mothers in her neighborhood and viewing an antiabortion slideshow, Neary underwent something of a conversion. Soon, the antiabortion movement defined much of her life. Similarly, Garnett Biviano, a young homemaker who converted to Catholicism after marrying her husband, became active not because of the Supreme Court decision but because of what she learned about abortion from her parents, family, and friends. Raised by a Methodist mother and a Presbyterian father, Biviano was raised to believe that life was an invaluable gift. After joining the antiabortion movement, both Biviano and Neary saw themselves as professional women, and sometimes their husbands and family members had to step up when pro-life work kept the two away from home. As Biviano would still put it years later, these activists viewed their cause as a "women's movement," pursued by and for women.[46]

A final dimension of the post-*Roe* nationalization involved a drive for a single set of arguments and reform priorities. After 1973, as part of this shift, movement attorneys elaborated further on their constitutional objectives. As the campaign for a fetal-life amendment to the Constitution suggested, abortion opponents did not fault the courts for straying from the text or history of the Constitution. Instead, abortion opponents often pointed to what the AUL called "natural law thinking." The AUL, for example, cited John Locke's *Second Treatise of Civil Government* as evidence that life and property were "natural rights." According to the AUL, the right to life "found [its] way into the Declaration of Independence." The AUL argued that in restoring the right to live, courts should interpret the Constitution in the spirit intended by the Declaration of Independence and international human rights law.[47]

As the AUL's advocacy suggested, abortion opponents urged the courts to protect rights not clearly set forth in the text of the Constitution. The Supreme Court had exposed the right to life to the will of the majority rather than removing control over that right "from the various branches of the United States government and from the states." By the mid-1970s, some abortion opponents asserted that the Court's arguably activist case law on privacy and contraception should lead logically to the recognition of a right to life. As the Court had recognized an implied right for married couples to use contraceptives, the United States Catholic Conference argued in 1976, "the granting of legal personhood is . . . properly the product of a constitutional analysis which recognizes the existence of rights which must be said to be implicit."[48]

Other pro-lifers invoked judicial opinions on sex and race discrimination derided as activist by some critics in the legal academy and popular politics. Pro-life law professor Robert Destro linked the right to life to judicial decisions on desegregation, sex discrimination, and the death penalty. Destro chastised the *Roe* Court for "reject[ing] the egalitarian tradition embodied in the Declaration of Independence and the Fourteenth Amendment." Influential antiabortion academic Joseph Witherspoon urged the courts to use still more novel interpretive tools to protect the unborn, such as the rarely used Privileges and Immunities Clause of the Fourteenth Amendment or the Thirteenth Amendment's prohibition of slavery. In spite of a lack of textual evidence, Witherspoon argued that the Thirteenth Amendment "sought to protect every human being, including unborn children . . . , in the fundamental human rights to life, liberty, and the pursuit of happiness." Rather than prompting a battle against judicial activism, the *Roe* decision motivated pro-lifers to find new ways to persuade the courts to protect the right to life from popular politics.[49]

At a major February 1973 strategy meeting, grassroots activists, pro-life attorneys, and other professionals articulated similar aspirations to change the Constitution. At the time, activists like Marjory Mecklenburg, attorneys like Kenneth Vanderhoef, and law professors like Robert Byrn hardly mentioned the issue of judicial activism. Discussion focused instead on the types of laws that might be constitutional under *Roe*: for example, proposed measures to make abortion legal only when performed by a certified physician or only when a spouse consented.[50]

Attendees returned time and again to one question: how could pro-lifers limit the impact of the Supreme Court's decision while claiming to defer to it? Or, as Marjory Mecklenburg expressed it, the group sought not so much to challenge the Court's authority as to "spell out at the local level . . . what the intention of the Supreme Court was as to ou[r] State laws." The group did agree on a "memorialization act" designed to express anger with the Court. However, the act did not question the Court's authority or even mention the justices, stating: "State Right to Life groups and people pro-life everywhere unanimously support an effort . . . that would guarantee the right to life for all humans."[51]

By the summer of 1973, some pro-lifers took aim at what they saw as judicial overreaching. That year, two influential New York groups, Women for the Unborn and the Celebrate Life Committee, circulated a pamphlet on the tyranny of the courts. Members of the groups stressed that "one does not have to be a trained lawyer to recognize that increasingly . . . 'the Constitution is what the judges say it is.'"[52] The pamphlet presented public protest as the best way to convince the Court to forsake the use of raw judicial power. The NRLC also experimented with such arguments. The organization passed a resolution censuring the Court for its "irresponsible exercise of raw judicial power" and labeled *Roe* a decision with no legal precedent other than "the tragic Dred Scott decision, which declared the black man to be virtually a chattel."[53]

After some consideration, leaders of the national movement chose not to emphasize claims about judicial activism. The movement's relative indifference to the issue of judicial overreaching became evident during the battle for a human life amendment. Before 1973, pro-lifers had largely opposed proposals to amend the Constitution, believing that the Fourteenth Amendment already protected the unborn. By contrast, after the *Roe* decision, pro-lifers concluded that the Supreme Court had destroyed fetal rights long recognized by both the Constitution and common law. In response, movement members backed a constitutional amendment designed to restore the right to life they favored. This fetal-protective amendment became a preoccupation for many pro-lifers—the issue by which most activists defined their place in the movement and chose among political candidates. For the most part, in discussing such an amendment, leaders of the national movement did not stake their claim on the tyranny of the courts. Instead, movement leaders promoted their own vision of a right to life that popular politics could not destroy.

If generally sharing views about the importance of constitutional change, abortion opponents disagreed intensely about what an ideal amendment would involve. These differences of opinion came to the surface in the months after *Roe*, when several members of Congress introduced fetal-protective constitutional amendments. In early 1973, for example, Representative Lawrence Hogan (R-MD) proposed an amendment that would protect a right to life "from the moment of conception," and Senator James Buckley (Conservative-NY) promoted an alternative proposal, stating: "With respect to the right to life, the word 'person' . . . applies to all human beings, including their unborn offspring at every stage of their biological development."[54]

Later in 1973, Congressman G. William Whitehurst (R-VA) offered a different approach. Whitehurst, a Methodist and former professor of history and political science, proposed a constitutional amendment that would overturn *Roe* by allowing the states and Congress to restrict or ban abortion. He made apparent that his was an amendment targeting judicial activism, arguing that the *Roe* "Court usurped authority properly belonging to the legislatures of the States." Whitehurst recognized that some states might vote for easy access to abortion, but he still insisted that "in a democratic society, the people should have the authority to decide issues as fundamental as what constitutes protectable life."[55]

Some influential pro-life academics did come out in support of Whitehurst's proposal. For example, Dr. Paul Ramsey, a prominent abortion opponent and professor at the Princeton Theological Seminary, testified in favor of the Whitehurst Amendment. He conceded that Whitehurst's approach could result in the "liberalization of abortion" or "its entire decriminalization."[56] In the name of democracy, however, Ramsey favored a so-called states-rights amendment. David Louisell, another prominent champion of the Whitehurst proposal, worked as a professor of law at the University of Virginia and later, at the University of California-Berkeley. Like Ramsey, Louisell objected to the *Roe* Court's overreaching, asking: "Can such judicial subjectivism justify withholding the issue from the people?"[57]

Nonetheless, the vast majority of pro-life professors, attorneys, strategists, and activists opposed an amendment attacking judicial activism and returning the abortion issue to popular politics. This consensus emerged partly through internal debates between law professors and attorneys like Byrn and Rice. The group included Witherspoon, a professor of constitutional law at the University of Texas Law School; Dennis Horan, a professor of law at the University of Chicago and a managing partner at the law firm Hinshaw, Culbertson, Moelman, Hoban, and Fuller; Kenneth Vanderhoef, a former prosecutor and graduate of the University of Gonzaga Law School;

and Nellie Gray, an attorney particularly well-known for having argued before the Supreme Court. A similar consensus took root among grassroots activists like Engel and Mecklenburg.[58]

Working with state activists, the attorneys' circle first identified ideological reasons for rejecting an amendment that would undo the Court's decision and return the abortion issue to Congress and the states. In a 1973 memo to Edward Golden, for example, Byrn argued that such an amendment did not reflect the moral principles or priorities of the movement. In testifying before Congress, Byrn further contended that the Whitehurst Amendment would be worse than the status quo created by *Roe*: it would put "the right to live at the perpetual mercy of shifting legislative majorities" and would signal that the unborn did "not possess a right to live."[59]

Grassroots antiabortion activists in states like Missouri and Pennsylvania shared Byrn's opposition to an amendment that would take the abortion issue from the courts. These advocates echoed Byrn's opinion that such an amendment would result in "the cheapening of human life."[60] A 1974 memo circulated between antiabortion attorneys, lobbyists, and state activists explained: "[W]e want to avoid implying that the Whitehurst people are our opponents. . . . Say little or nothing about Whitehurst."[61] Indeed, the NRLC as a whole passed a resolution stating: "a 'States Rights' amendment would not effectuate . . . rejection [of *Roe*] but would rather reaffirm the Court's decision."[62]

By 1974, the national antiabortion movement had achieved a broad, if general, consensus on many substantive and strategic questions. Instead of campaigning against judicial overreaching, abortion opponents prioritized constitutional proposals that would restore a fundamental right to life. Although divided about the details of an ideal amendment, pro-lifers generally opposed constitutional proposals that would merely overrule the *Roe* decision and allow the voters to decide on fetal rights.

The movement's shared constitutional commitments stood in sharp contrast to the divisions about gender and sexuality that had first cropped up in the late 1960s and early 1970s. The NRLC had replaced the AUL as the center of antiabortion conflicts. There had been signs of tension before *Roe*, when supporters of Marjory Mecklenburg and Edward Golden disagreed about the organization's structure. Whereas Mecklenburg favored a decentralized approach and a broad definition of the pro-life cause, Golden urged his colleagues to adopt a narrow focus and to create a hierarchical and highly formalized operation. The summer after *Roe* came down, conflict between the two factions intensified, much of it centering on Mecklenburg's role in ensuring that Warren Schaller, a Minneapolis rector, would become the organization's interim executive director.[63]

Tensions escalated in August 1973 when Schaller told the press about the organization's agenda. Schaller wished to define the right to life broadly—to argue in favor of a caring society that would bar euthanasia, guarantee child care and health care for women, and work to prevent unwanted pregnancies. In theory, NRLC traditionalists criticized Schaller for speaking without official authorization from the larger group. In reality, conflict about Schaller's statements reflected underlying disagreements about the organization's mission. Golden saw compromises on related issues, like contraception, as a waste of time. By contrast, the broad definition of a right to life advanced by Schaller and Mecklenburg reflected the importance they attached to coalition-building and consensus.[64]

Pro-Lifers Develop a Shared Set of Arguments

These disagreements notwithstanding, the NRLC and the broader movement managed to unite behind a single rhetorical strategy—the movement focused not on the court's abuse of power but on the constitutional right pro-lifers championed. Activists stressed their own religious, political, and economic diversity and cited the justifications for a constitutional right to life. Rather than drawing attention to their religious views, abortion opponents pointed to scientific fact and foundational constitutional principles.

These claims came to the fore in 1974, when a subcommittee of the Senate Judiciary Committee began hearings on a human life amendment to the Constitution. Warren Schaller played an influential role in the formulation of the movement's argumentative strategy. In February 1974, he first expressed concern about the organization's image: "Last week, many papers quoted Arlie Schardt of the Washington ACLU as stating that . . . the NRLC is Catholic dominated. . . . This kind of press will be hard for us to counteract." Schaller argued that the upcoming congressional hearings presented a perfect opportunity for the organization to redefine itself. He urged members and allies of the NRLC to stress pro-lifers' religious diversity.[65]

A wide variety of movement leaders responded to Schaller's request. In congressional testimony in support of the human life amendment, Pastor Robert Holbrook, the man who helped convince the Southern

Baptist Conference to oppose legal abortion, called attention to the religious diversity of the movement, as did David Bleich, an Orthodox Jewish rabbi. The same year, Dr. Mildred F. Jefferson, a rising star in the NRLC, emphasized that the movement included "many people from all walks of life, social conditions, religions or no formal belief, political parties or no partisan affiliation."[66]

It was one thing to describe and defend the movement's diversity and credentials. It was quite another to define and justify the movement's demands. In early 1974, Schaller argued that the movement should borrow from the scientific claims made in *Roe*. If the Supreme Court had relied on medical authority, so, too, should opponents of legal abortion. In his congressional testimony, Representative Hogan responded to Schaller's suggestion: "the question of when life begins is not difficult at all, because the answer has been established beyond reasonable doubt by modern science." In turn, as he asserted, the *Roe* Court's greatest mistake had little to do with judicial overreaching. Rather, as Hogan explained, "[t]he law acts improperly when it pretends to assert medical fact or ignores medical fact."[67] Senator Buckley also favored science-based claims, emphasizing "the genetic, biological, and physiological nature of the unborn child from conception onwards."[68]

During testimony in favor of a fetal-protective amendment, movement physicians, geneticists, and researchers also presented fetal rights as a matter of scientific fact. Dr. William Colliton, Jr., a movement veteran of almost a decade, criticized *Roe* primarily for "evad[ing] . . . the scientific answer to the question, When does life begin?"[69] Other doctors affiliated with the movement also offered evidence that "life begins at conception." Movement members hoped that such biological claims would force the Court and the American public to confront the humanity of the fetus.[70]

Movement members also drew an analogy between *Roe* and one of the Supreme Court's most infamous decisions, *Dred Scott v. Sandford*. In that case, the Court decided, among other things, that slaves were not citizens of the United States. A comparison to *Dred Scott* became an almost mandatory part of movement criticism of *Roe*. However, for pro-lifers, *Dred Scott* served mainly to highlight the moral errors made in *Roe*, not the overreaching of the Court. Both decisions, as the argument went, denied the personhood of vulnerable minorities. As Dr. John Willke and his wife Barbara testified before Congress: "One hundred years ago, the discrimination was on the basis of skin color[;] today it is on the basis of residence . . . [in] the womb."[71]

What do these claims tell us about the movement? It might be no surprise that pro-lifers would stress rights-based arguments when testifying in Congress or lobbying for a constitutional amendment. As historian Michael Cuneo has suggested, such claims might have presented the antiabortion movement as reasonable, law-oriented, and moderate. Nonetheless, leaders of groups like the NRLC and the AUL emphasized similar reasoning in internal debates, in materials designed to recruit new activists, and in press releases intended to shape public opinion. In a variety of institutional settings, movement leaders used constitutional rhetoric and outlined the same reform priorities. These contentions reflected the movement's suspicion of popular majorities. In opposing judicial activism, pro-lifers would have had to champion the will of the people. In reality, abortion opponents put little emphasis on the problems associated with judicial tyranny, since the movement did not wish to entrust the right to life to the democratic process.[72]

By 1975, the pro-life movement looked substantially different from the one shaken by the Supreme Court's decision in 1973. The AUL had created a legal defense fund that would later exert considerable influence over the antiabortion movement. In July 1974, Ray White, a Mormon and the NRLC's new executive director, unceremoniously fired Warren Schaller. In the same period, Randy Engel called on the NRLC to expel the Mecklenburgs because of their position on birth control. In the aftermath of conflicts with Engel and Golden, Marjory Mecklenburg resigned from the NLRC in the fall of 1974, relaunching the American Citizens Concerned for Life (ACCL), a national organization committed to finding some common ground with those on the other side of the abortion issue.[73]

Conflict within the NRLC also led to the formation of a conservative and absolutist group, March for Life. In January 1974, Nellie Gray had sponsored the first March for Life, a major protest in Washington, DC. A long-time employee of the federal government and an attorney, Gray had always considered herself a liberal. Later in life, she renewed her commitment to Catholicism, becoming one of the movement's hardliners. Gray believed that the constitutional proposals endorsed by the NRLC did not go far enough in protecting the unborn. Inspired by the success of the first March for Life, she helped to form and incorporate a new organization by the same name, one that supported only a human life amendment that barred all abortions, even those necessary to save the life of the woman.[74]

The NRLC witnessed a number of changes beyond the departure of Mecklenburg and Gray. Edward Golden had stepped down as president in 1974, tired of the seemingly endless disagreements that plagued both the NRLC and the AUL. Golden's successor, Kenneth Vanderhoef, another conservative Catholic, provided a good deal of continuity. Because of his experience with the United States Catholic Conference, Vanderhoef, like Golden, believed that the NRLC should have a fixed hierarchy and a centralized structure.[75]

A much larger change came with the 1975 election of his replacement, Dr. Mildred F. Jefferson. The daughter of a public school teacher and a Methodist minister, Jefferson was the first African-American woman to graduate from Harvard Medical School. She entered abortion politics in 1970 when the American Medical Association (AMA) considered a resolution liberalizing sanctions against members who performed abortions. After joining a group that tried unsuccessfully to block the new AMA resolution, Jefferson helped to found an anti-abortion organization in Massachusetts, and she quickly became one of the pro-life movement's most sought-after public speakers.[76]

From the outset, Jefferson pursued a strategy different from the one adopted by Golden or Vanderhoef. Jefferson had a gift for making the antiabortion movement a part of the daily news. If Jefferson represented a new kind of pro-life leader, the abortion debate had changed as well. As the chances for ratifying a fetal-protective amendment seemed to fade, pro-lifers pursued a broader range of reform goals. Just the same, arguments and strategies that focused on judicial activism did not figure centrally in the movement's agenda.[77]

The *Edelin* Trial Demonstrates the Potential of Incremental Change

In February 1975, a Boston jury convicted Dr. Kenneth Edelin of manslaughter for performing an abortion. The first African-American Chief Resident of Boston's City Hospital, he had established a reputation for providing reproductive health services to poorer Boston residents. During an investigation of fetal-tissue research at the hospital, witnesses accused Edelin of murder. While performing a late-term abortion, Edelin reportedly crossed a line. The witnesses claimed that the fetus had drawn breath outside of the mother's body before Edelin completed the abortion procedure. Acting on this allegation, Boston prosecutors charged Edelin with manslaughter.[78]

Unlike *Edelin*, many of the other criminal prosecutions pursued in the period clearly passed muster under the Court's *Roe* decision. Since the Court ruled that "the State . . . may proscribe any abortion by a person who is not a physician,"[79] prosecutors pursued charges against unlicensed doctors, midwives, and laypersons. The *Edelin* trial was considerably more ambitious. Dr. Edelin was not only a certified physician but also an obstetrician and gynecologist. The fetus at issue was about twenty-one weeks old, while the Court considered fetuses to be viable at twenty-three weeks at the earliest. *Edelin* represented a more direct effort to reshape abortion law. Consequently, a wide range of antiabortion activists participated in the *Edelin* trial. Fred Mecklenburg, a leading member of the ACCL, agreed to testify for the prosecution, as did Mildred Jefferson of the NRLC.[80]

Early on, prosecutors and antiabortion witnesses played up their respect for the supremacy of the Supreme Court. Jefferson did so by claiming that the *Roe* decision protected only abortions, which she defined as including procedures performed before the twenty-first week of pregnancy. She viewed any other procedure as a killing without constitutional protection. The Commonwealth of Massachusetts took an even stronger position: "In *Roe v. Wade*, the Court held inter alia that 'the right to privacy . . . is broad enough to encompass a woman's decision to terminate her pregnancy.' . . . Nowhere did the Court state or imply [that] this right of privacy extended to permit anyone to terminate the life of the child."[81]

The Boston jury convicted Edelin of manslaughter in February 1975, although he received no prison time as part of his sentence. Pro-lifers saw the conviction as a sign of hopeful things to come: for example, antiabortion leaders in Illinois predicted that *Edelin* would open an era of physician prosecutions and of judicial recognition of fetal rights.[82]

That prediction proved to be premature. Media coverage of Edelin's conviction focused not on the rights of fetuses but on the issues of racial and sectarian bias. The press made a good deal of the fact that Edelin's trial took place in Boston, thought to be the most Catholic city in the United States. The tone of television coverage was generally similar. In 1975, for example, Edelin appeared on the *Mike Douglas Show*. No abortion opponent participated in the program. When Edelin addressed his reasons for appearing on the show, Flip Wilson, a well-known African-American comedian, spoke up, saying that Edelin had come on the program because he was "black, beautiful, and innocent."[83] Studio employees then cued the audience to cheer. For abortion opponents, the press generated by the case did so much damage that, following Edelin's successful appeal, NRLC leaders claimed to have had little to do with the trial.[84]

The NRLC's disclaimers aside, pro-lifers' involvement in Edelin's trial represented the first step in a new, more deferential strategy. First, and most significantly, *Edelin* marked one of the movement's first major attempts to redefine the right set out in the *Roe* decision. Rather than urging the Court to overrule its prior holding, pro-lifers would convince the Court to reinterpret *Roe* until it no longer meaningfully protected access to abortion.

As importantly, *Edelin* taught some movement members about the importance of small victories. The late 1970s witnessed the rise of a new style of antiabortion leader. These strategists, later known as incrementalists, promoted regulations thought likely to succeed in the Supreme Court and defended them before the justices. Their strategy stemmed from a conviction that the Court of the 1970s would not overrule the *Roe* decision but could be made aware of its shortcomings. If the Court narrowed abortion rights further and further over time, as one incrementalist later put it, the decision would fall under its own weight.[85]

Why did a more robust attack on judicial activism emerge as these incrementalists—who worked so often in the courts and who insisted on deferring to their authority—gradually established themselves in the antiabortion movement? Analyzing this issue requires a consideration of the effort to ban the public funding of abortion.

From the beginning of the abortion wars, pro-lifers had worked to establish restrictions on public funding. Movement interest in such laws increased in the mid-1970s. After 1973, a wide variety of states, cities, and hospitals passed bans on the use of government monies or facilities for abortion. These laws sometimes fared badly in the federal courts. Some lower courts concluded that funding bans violated the Supremacy Clause of the federal Constitution. Generally, under the Supremacy Clause, Congress may preempt a state law by "express language in a congressional enactment, by implication from the breadth and depth of a congressional scheme that occupies the legislative field, or by implication because of a conflict with an express congressional enactment."[86] According to some lower courts, state funding bans added a new eligibility requirement—that a woman not be seeking abortion—to the criteria set forth by the federal Social Security Act. For this reason, some courts concluded that state bans implicitly conflicted with the federal law. If the constitutionality of state bans remained in question, abortion opponents desperately wanted Congress to pass a law explaining that it approved of funding bans.[87]

In 1974, Representative Angelo Roncallo (R-NJ) introduced the first federal Medicaid ban, and after the defeat of his proposal, Representative Dewey Bartlett (R-OK), a former governor of Oklahoma, tried to push through a similar bill. Funding bans, however, became associated with a different legislator, Representative Henry Hyde (R-IL). Because of his influence on abortion law, Hyde became a larger-than-life figure for groups on either side of the abortion debate. For organizations like NARAL, Hyde appeared to be a storybook villain, described in political cartoons as "The Infamous Mr. Hyde." By contrast, pro-lifers admired Hyde's tactical mastery. While criticizing the Supreme Court's decision and abhorring abortion, Hyde began to highlight his compliance with the Supreme Court's decision.[88]

At first, in a June 1976 "Dear Colleague" letter in support of the bill he cosponsored with Representative James Oberstar (D-MN), Hyde stressed that taxpayers should not have to fund "the killing of innocent preborn human life." Later, however, Hyde began to emphasize the pragmatism and likely constitutionality of his proposal. In a floor speech in defense of his bill the same month, for example, Hyde focused on the "constitutional issue that is involved in this question." As he explained: "Conceding that under *Roe* against *Wade* a woman has a constitutional right to seek abortion, the question here is whether it is mandatory that tax payers pay for that abortion."[89]

Similarly, during debate about his proposal, Hyde did not even directly respond to arguments that his bill discriminated against the poor. For example, during the 1976 debate, Representative Millicent Fenwick (D-NJ) accused Hyde of targeting the poor. Hyde responded: "I would certainly like to prevent, if I could legally, anybody from having an abortion, a rich woman, a middle class woman, or a poor woman. Unfortunately, the only vehicle available is the HEW Medicaid bill." Hyde's defense of the funding ban resembled the strategy deployed in *Edelin*. Instead of primarily emphasizing a right to life, Hyde stressed his own narrow understanding of the *Roe* decision.[90]

A similar strategy gradually became central to antiabortion lobbying and litigation in the later 1970s. Paradoxically, as incrementalists came to exercise a greater influence over the national movement, antiabortion organizations more often condemned judicial activism. Why did incrementalists, who focused so much on litigation and so clearly assumed that the Court was legitimate, come to emphasize the issue of judicial overreaching?

The same pragmatism that led incrementalists to claim deference to the Court increased the appeal of arguments against judicial activism. Later in the 1970s, as the progress of a fetal-protective constitutional amendment stalled, movement pragmatists began to see protests against judicial tyranny in a different light. After the 1976 election of Jimmy Carter, prominent movement members concluded that the opposition had blocked the nomination of pro-life judges to the federal bench. Believing that the courts responded to public pressure, abortion opponents thought they could more easily reshape the federal judiciary if they made a major impact on national elections. As importantly, influencing presidential politics could give pro-lifers a greater hand in the selection of judicial nominees.

In the late 1970s, as the New Right worked to unite groups angry about recent Supreme Court decisions, pro-life leaders slowly saw reason to present their demands in a way that spoke to powerful potential partners. Joining a coalition opposed to judicial activism would afford pro-lifers greater influence in the judicial nomination process. By participating in a broad alliance, pro-lifers also hoped to convince the Supreme Court that popular opinion was on the side of the unborn.

Finally, in the late 1970s and early 1980s, the emergence of Ronald Reagan as a strong ally of the pro-life movement reinforced activists' interest in arguments against judicial activism. After the 1980 election, adopting similar claims about the judiciary allowed pro-lifers to express solidarity with both the Republican Party and the Reagan White House.

Incrementalists Find New Value in Arguments About Judicial Overreaching

The war against judicial tyranny reached back several decades before the start of the abortion wars. In 1954 in *Brown v. Board of Education*, the Supreme Court struck down Jim Crow laws mandating the segregation of public schools. Writing in 1959, Professor Herbert Wechsler claimed that he could find no neutral legal principle explaining the Court's decision. Absent such a neutral principle, as Wechsler reasoned, the Court "function[ed] . . . as a naked power organ."[91] As other academics responded to Wechsler's criticism, segregationists mounted "massive resistance" to *Brown*, justifying their protests partly by reference to the Supreme Court's activism.[92]

Wechsler's vision of neutral principles resurfaced in debate about the judicial activism of the Warren Court. In 1962 in *Engel v. Vitale*, the Court ruled some forms of prayer in public schools unconstitutional. *Engel* and its progeny prompted protesters to bombard Congress with letters and to demand a constitutional amendment restoring school prayer across the nation. As the Warren Court expanded the procedural protections available to criminal defendants, popular anger grew. Critics concluded that the Court's decisions would lead to the release of obviously guilty criminals. Protesters even demanded the impeachment of Chief Justice Earl Warren.[93]

In the late 1960s and early 1970s, popular protest against judicial activism had a new target. After the *Brown* decision, the Supreme Court had not initially mandated a clear remedy for de jure school segregation. By the late 1960s, frustrated with stable rates of school segregation, the courts ordered the busing of students within and sometimes between districts. Parents, white ethnics, and racists mobilized to protest the new remedial orders. Anti-busing protests erupted in Boston and other American cities, and protestors marshalled familiar arguments about judicial tyranny. In the academy, commentators from Raoul Berger to Robert Bork targeted recent Supreme Court Fourteenth Amendment jurisprudence. After 1973, influential academics like John Hart Ely questioned the constitutional underpinnings of the *Roe* decision itself.[94]

Throughout the mid- and late 1970s, however, pro-lifers mostly kept their distance from attacks on judicial tyranny. The majority of state and national pro-life organizations continued to push some version of an ideal fetal-rights amendment. The so-called National Right to Life Amendment, a proposal with broad pro-life support, still required the courts to protect the right to life from the will of the majority.[95]

Pro-life commentators and grassroots activists maintained their allegiance to a right to life removed from popular politics, expressing ambivalence about the battle against judicial activism. In 1977 Robert Byrn argued that abortion opponents "do not need to take sides . . . [on] the question of how the judiciary may better function—with activism or restraint."[96] Similarly, in 1979, Harold O. J. Brown, the leader of a prominent evangelical Protestant antiabortion organization, the Christian Action Council, argued not against judicial activism but for the application of divine and natural law in American courts. As Massachusetts abortion opponent Dr. Joseph

Stanton explained to George Huntston Williams as late as 1979: "I have pained feelings about . . . diminishing respect for the courts."[97]

However, in the late 1970s, as the campaign for a fetal-protective amendment stalled, some pro-lifers gradually began to see greater value in arguments against judicial activism. In 1975, after five days of hearings, a Senate Judiciary Subcommittee defeated all eight proposals for a fetal-rights amendment that pro-lifers had proposed. In 1976 when Senator Jesse Helms (R-NC) proposed another fetal-rights amendment, the full Senate voted to table it, and after 1976, pro-lifers failed to bring it before Congress for a vote. Intent on advancing the rights of the unborn, movement pragmatists began looking for new arguments and strategies.[98]

If pro-lifers could not amend the Constitution, as a growing group of activists argued, perhaps the movement could change the composition of the courts. In 1974, however, when Richard Nixon nominated Connecticut Governor Thomas Meskill, a staunchly pro-life Catholic, to a vacant seat on the Second Circuit Court of Appeals, Meskill's public opposition to abortion provoked controversy. Later, according to rumors circulating in the pro-life movement, the judicial-selection commissions created by the Carter Administration supposedly screened out any candidate opposed to abortion. As pro-life activist Dennis Horan wrote in a letter to President Carter, movement members believed that sympathetic judges had been the victims of discrimination.[99]

In the face of perceived bias, some pro-lifers proposed strategies for reshaping the courts. First, as prominent New York activist Ellen McCormack explained in 1978: "when . . . it would not be pragmatically convenient for the Court to support abortion—then the judges may well lean in the other direction."[100] If the courts bowed to popular pressure, pro-lifers could influence abortion jurisprudence by flexing their political muscle. Swinging national elections and mounting major protests would create an impression of political power. In 1977, Illinois activist Joseph Scheidler similarly reasoned that abortion opponents could change "the very bad and arbitrary abortion decisions of the Court" by "altering the nation's mood so the Court will ultimately hand down a new ruling."[101] Second, the movement could make its mark on presidential politics, helping to elect a candidate who would nominate pro-life judges. The movement needed to ensure that "[p]ro-abortion forces" no longer had "more impact than pro-life forces in the judicial selection process."[102]

In the late 1970s, as pro-lifers became more concerned about the composition of the judiciary, the New Right used the idea of judicial overreaching to help forge a coalition of right-leaning groups. Activists protesting decisions on busing, school prayer, abortion, or *Miranda* warnings at first appeared to pursue substantially different goals. In the late 1970s, however, Paul Weyrich, Richard Viguerie, and their colleagues presented all of these judicial decisions as examples of the tyranny of the federal government. By targeting judicial activism, the New Right could transform fragmented, single-issue groups into a powerful united front.[103]

Influential pro-lifers gradually became convinced that they could achieve more in joining the new anti-Court coalition than they could on their own. As pro-life activist Peter Gemma later explained: "There was a sudden growing awareness on the part of all of us working in various single issues that if we pitched in together, we could get a lot more accomplished."[104] Weyrich and Viguerie's access to funding and political influence lent credence to this claim. Weyrich's allies provided meeting space for groups dedicated to the protection of the family and funded the formation of new pro-life organizations. The political action committee Weyrich and Viguerie backed claimed to have scored victories in prominent 1978 and 1980 congressional races.[105]

The New Right helped a variety of groups concerned about the Supreme Court to create a coherent political message and an effective political strategy. Pro-lifers had long believed that the justices had forsaken their duty to protect the unborn and other vulnerable classes. By 1980, however, pro-lifers began expressing their views in language endorsed by the New Right. Adopting the rhetoric of judicial activism allowed abortion opponents to air their outrage about the Court's betrayal. At the same time, for strategic reasons, pro-lifers began channeling their concerns about the judiciary into language that powerful allies endorsed.

In the early 1980s, as Ronald Reagan expressed his sympathy for abortion opponents, pro-life pragmatists used arguments against judicial activism as a way to build influence in the White House and the Republican Party. Beginning with Richard Nixon, Republican candidates had called for judicial restraint as an alternative to the activism embodied by certain Warren or Burger Court decisions. During the 1980 presidential campaign, the Republican Party platform went a step further, proposing "the appointment of judges at all levels of the judiciary who respect traditional family values and the value of human life."[106] By October 1980, the judicial-selection plank had drawn criticism from lawyers in both political parties, as well as from the American Bar Association House of Delegates. That November, Reagan advisor William French Smith responded by insisting that Reagan opposed only judicial activism. As Smith explained: "In a nutshell, [Reagan's] political philosophy is the laws of this country should be interpreted by the legislature and construed by the judiciary, and to the extent possible, not made by the judiciary."[107]

Reagan's success mattered tremendously to pro-life leaders. As early as 1976, he had made his opposition to abortion public. In 1980, when his campaign stressed arguments about judicial activism, abortion opponents began to do the same. Harold O. J. Brown's Christian Action Council stressed the importance of "send[ing] a political message to a clearly political Judiciary."[108] The Ad Hoc Committee in Defense of Life circulated fundraising materials stressing that "the Supreme Court . . . has been the prime mover for the whole anti-family movement."[109]

Arguments against judicial activism also played a crucial role in the movement's summer 1981 campaign to oppose the nomination of Sandra Day O'Connor to the Supreme Court. During her time in the Arizona State Legislature, O'Connor had reportedly voted in favor of an abortion liberalization bill. Consequently, pro-lifers reacted to her nomination with outrage.[110]

The O'Connor nomination had put considerable strain on the White House's alliance with the pro-life movement. Publicly, before the confirmation hearings began, the Reagan Administration paid little attention to the antiabortion attacks. An anonymous aide told the New York Times: "there's going to be a lot of sound and fury, but in the end, it's going to end up signifying little or nothing."[111]

Less publicly, staff working for Edwin Meese III, then-counselor to the president, argued to Reagan and to the rest of the Administration that more had to be done to appease the antiabortion movement. In a memorandum to Meese, a staffer suggested that arguments against judicial activism could placate pro-lifers: "It does follow, I think, that the nominee's record on the [abortion] issue be examined with special interest and that the nominee regard Roe v. Wade and its progeny as most unwise assertions of judicial power." As the memorandum suggested, the Reagan Administration had channeled opposition to Roe into objections to judicial activism.[112]

For abortion opponents, arguments against judicial activism seemed likely to strengthen political ties between the movement and the White House while increasing support for the campaign to undo the *Roe* decision. Consider, for example, the congressional testimony of Dr. John Willke, then the president of the NRLC. Throughout the 1970s, Willke had opposed an amendment returning the abortion issue to popular politics. By 1980 Willke wanted to get something done—to build pro-life momentum. In opposing O'Connor's nomination, he used arguments against judicial overreaching in pursuing this kind of pragmatic change, stating: "The Supreme Court's 1973 abortion decision had no authentic basis in the Constitution. Rather, it constituted the most extreme example of 'judicial activism' in this century."[113]

New Movement, New Politics

In June 1984, the NRLC held its annual national conference in Kansas City, Missouri. The highlight of the conference was the organization's endorsement for the 1984 presidential race. "The choice is very clear-cut," said then-NRLC president Dr. Willke. "It is Mr. Reagan."[114]

According to the conventional historical account, a conviction that *Roe* was undemocratic and illegitimate defined the national antiabortion movement and motivated activists like Willke. When Willke was speaking, the pro-life movement had drawn greater attention to claims about judicial activism. But for ideological and strategic reasons, the antiabortion movement did not, for the better part of a decade after *Roe*, much concern itself with the Court's authority or legitimacy.

Pro-lifers had long defined their cause in large part as a constitutional one—the preservation of a longstanding tradition involving the Declaration of Independence and the Fourteenth Amendment of the Constitution. This constitutional agenda drew on the reasoning of Warren and Burger Court decisions that many had attacked as activist. Pro-life academics and attorneys urged courts to use the Due Process Clause to recognize new fundamental rights—a move made in Supreme Court decisions on contraception that had won the praise of left-leaning commentators and activists. Pro-lifers also presented abortion as an act of discrimination that violated the Equal Protection Clause, comparing the unborn to illegitimate children, women, and other minorities recently protected by the courts. This constitutional agenda assumed that the courts should act boldly to protect implied constitutional rights from the will of the majority—a position some associated with judicial overreaching.

When the movement later emphasized arguments about judicial activism, it did so in response to changing political opportunities as much as to *Roe*. We cannot attribute antiabortion arguments about or interest in judicial activism so exclusively to *Roe* itself.

What mattered more, reining in the Court or protecting unborn children? If one asked national antiabortion leaders this question in the decade after the *Roe* decision, the answer would likely have seemed as obvious as John Willke's when he framed his spoke in Kansas City in 1984. The answer was clear-cut. And it had nothing to do with the legitimacy or the power of the Court.

The Incrementalist Ascendancy

IN THE LATE 1970s and early 1980s, the rise of arguments about judicial overreaching augured a larger shift in pro-life activism. John Willke's interest in condemning the tyranny of the courts stemmed from a growing belief in the value of pragmatism. Willke became a champion of incrementalism, arguing for compromise regulations that would restrict abortion without banning it altogether.[1]

Within the National Right to Life Committee (NLRC), incrementalism initially appeared uncontroversial. Judie Brown, the executive director of the organization in the mid-1970s, appreciated the victories achieved by incrementalist litigators. The pro-life movement had transformed Brown. A lapsed Catholic and career woman, Brown had worked at the Kmart Corporation and even had herself fitted for an intrauterine device before coming back to the Church in the late 1960s. After fighting a Washington State referendum liberalizing abortion, Brown and her husband joined pro-life organizations each time they moved from state to state, selling Christmas cards, raising money, and talking to their neighbors about the unborn. At first, when incrementalists began to score victories in the Supreme Court, Brown saw their efforts as a healthy complement to the pro-life movement's real work: a total, constitutional ban on abortion.[2]

For James Bopp Jr., incrementalism had even greater promise. A conservative Catholic, Bopp grew up in a strongly pro-life home. His father, a physician, viewed the procedure as unethical. Bopp went to law school and soon began working for the pro-life movement in Indiana. By 1978, he had become NRLC General Counsel. Bopp saw in incrementalist litigation the seeds of a strategy that could transform the abortion wars. If the movement prioritized statutes that could survive constitutional scrutiny, he believed that pro-lifers could build momentum, motivate new activists, limit access to abortion, and gradually convince the public of the humanity of the unborn.[3]

By the late 1970s, in spite of the vigorous objections of a minority of pro-life activists, incrementalism began to define the mainstream movement. Advocates embracing an incrementalist agenda led the NRLC and Americans United for Life (AUL). The leaders of the United States Catholic Conference proved receptive to such tactics. In many states, the kinds of legal reforms pursued by state antiabortion affiliates reflected the influence of incrementalist thought and strategy.[4]

While incrementalism prevailed as a guiding strategy for the pro-life movement, its triumph created a bitter and lasting schism within the pro-life community. After incrementalist litigation debuted in the mid-1970s, pro-lifers across the ideological spectrum generally viewed it as a useful tool for limiting access to abortion. However, by the end of the decade, movement absolutists, Judie Brown among them, argued that incrementalism had taken the place of efforts to ban abortion outright. At that time, incrementalism had moved outside the courtroom, becoming an overarching strategy for the pro-life movement. Incrementalists lobbied state legislatures to pass laws that the Supreme Court might actually uphold. "With professional help from nationally known pro-life attorneys," the *National Right to Life News* explained in 1979, "right to lifers have a reasonable hope that state abortion regulations will be upheld in court."[5] Incrementalists' focus on middle-ground restrictions stemmed from a belief that the pro-life movement had to achieve something concrete in order to remain a viable political force. By getting something done, pro-lifers could hollow out any abortion right the Supreme Court still recognized.[6]

The turn to incrementalism may seem inevitable, given the movement's lack of progress in securing a fetal-protective amendment. Perhaps pro-lifers faced a choice between settling for incremental restrictions the Supreme Court would sustain and abandoning hope altogether. In the later 1970s, however, some influential pro-lifers came to a radically different conclusion.

An ambitious group of hardliners blamed the failures of mid-decade on pro-lifers' cautiousness and preoccupation with respectability.

Absolutists like Judie Brown contended that the movement would never win over the American people if abortion opponents sacrificed the lives of unborn babies to achieve short-term political success. Brown and her allies pledged to "continue our support for only that legislation which recognizes the need for personhood to be extended to the preborn child."[7] At the same time that incrementalists narrowed their goals and turned to compromise measures, absolutists, most of them holding more conservative positions on social issues, demanded not just an absolute right to life but also a fight against contraception, sexual promiscuity, and secular humanism. Absolutists viewed a no-compromise approach as both ideologically principled and more likely to succeed than the modest solutions championed by incrementalists. In the absolutists' view, pro-lifers could succeed only by changing the hearts and minds of the public and by demanding more of politicians who claimed to be pro-life.[8]

By the early 1980s, the differences between incrementalists and absolutists had become striking. Absolutists began framing the pro-life struggle as a quest to protect the traditional family and vanquish any organization promoting secularism and immoral sex. Incrementalists saw these goals as both overly ambitious and distracting. Perhaps most importantly, incrementalists viewed compromise restrictions differently than did their absolutist counterparts. Incrementalists reasoned that compromise regulations could save the lives of unborn children, stoke the enthusiasm of the grassroots movement, and expose the flaws of the *Roe* Court's reasoning. For absolutists, the same incremental regulations represented a waste of scarce movement resources. As activists like Judie Brown believed, compromise regulations undermined the commitment of grassroots activists, betrayed the movement's core beliefs, and allowed politicians an easy way "to forever duck the issue of dealing . . . with an abortion amendment" or any other strong pro-life measures.[9] With the rise of incrementalism in the late 1970s came a lasting disagreement about what it took to be pro-life.[10]

What does the incrementalist ascendancy tell us about the backlash produced by *Roe*? Generally, scholars studying *Roe*'s impact point to the lasting empowerment of pro-life extremists in the wake of the decision. Some leading studies define pro-life extremism by the ever more absolute positions taken by movement leaders. For example, in drawing on his landmark study of backlash and civil-rights jurisprudence, Michael Klarman identifies extremists by their political positions, their rhetoric, and their willingness to use violence. Elizabeth Mensch and Alan Freeman criticize the *Roe* Court for conferring authority on pro-lifers unwilling to entertain any reasonable middle-ground solution. As they explain, "*Roe* triggered an opposition that would become increasingly absolutist in theologically defending the pro-life position."[11] Similarly, Jeffrey Rosen argues that the Supreme Court's decision strengthened the hand of fringe actors who had "lost the hearts and minds of a majority in the country."[12] Social-movement scholar Ziad Munson also highlights the "polarization of views" common among pro-life leaders after 1973.[13]

Scholars also identify pro-life extremism by the generally right-wing ideology abortion opponents endorsed. Rosen describes pro-lifers empowered by the *Roe* decision as "social conservatives."[14] Cass Sunstein indicates that the *Roe* Court mobilized "the strongest opponents" of the women's movement.[15] Some social-movement scholars also incorporate ideology into their understandings of pro-life absolutism. For example, Kristin Luker contends that a new wave of traditionalist and even extremist activists mobilized in response to *Roe*—activists "upset that motherhood [had] been demoted from a sacred calling to job." Irrespective of their understanding of extremism, however, commentators agree that the Supreme Court helped to embolden a new kind of pro-life leader: one more committed to absolute abortion bans, polarizing arguments, or right-wing politics.[16]

As this chapter suggests, the story was not nearly so straightforward. Even a decade after *Roe*, abortion opponents had not united behind a single platform. Instead, the movement remained internally divided, this time about the issue of compromise on abortion itself. Was it better to achieve something concrete, even if that meant allowing some abortions? Or were regulations of this kind a betrayal of what it meant to be pro-life? For leaders of the national movement, these questions created a conflict that was personal and enduring.

An understanding of the incrementalists' strategy complicates what it means to characterize an abortion opponent as an extremist. On the one hand, incrementalists did tend more often to adopt conservative positions on some issues, particularly those related to the women's movement. Incrementalist advocates also forged relationships with the New Right and the Religious Right. On the other hand, incrementalists championed compromise solutions that restricted but did not ban abortion. These activists shared a focus on achievable goals. To define these activists as extremists oversimplifies how and why they came to reshape the antiabortion movement. Studying incrementalist abortion opponents makes clear the need to rethink the categories used to analyze post-*Roe* backlash.[17]

The story of incrementalism also raises important questions about the degree to which the Court's decision transformed the antiabortion movement. The Court's intervention had an undeniable impact. However, as the incrementalists' story suggests, movement identity did not form in response to the Supreme Court but instead emerged over time from a hotly contested fight between those committed to undoing the decision. Our understanding of the abortion wars changes when we assign more agency to abortion opponents and examine more closely the conflicts between them.

Pro-Life Attorneys Identify Incrementalism as a New Litigation Tactic

In the mid-1970s, incrementalist litigation strategies evolved in parallel to the fight for constitutional change. The circle of pro-life attorneys tasked with crafting the perfect amendment had mostly assumed that merely changing the Constitution would adequately protect the unborn. Chicago attorney Dennis Horan was not so sure.[18]

The marriage of Dennis and Dolores Horan would have an important influence on the emergence of an incrementalist litigation strategy. As the Horans had envisioned, incrementalist litigators would not challenge the basic premises of the *Roe* decision, as so many pro-life attorneys did in the 1970s. Instead, litigators would assert that *Roe* allowed the states to restrict abortion. In the process, pro-lifers could gut the protections that the Supreme Court had created for abortion rights. As importantly, antiabortion attorneys hoped to reveal to the public that *Roe v. Wade* was an incoherent decision undeserving of public support.

The Horans helped to pioneer the incrementalist litigation model that would help to transform pro-life advocacy. Dennis emerged as the more influential spouse, becoming the head of his law firm and a leading member of the antiabortion movement. While operating a general law practice, Dolores signed many of the amicus briefs her husband helped to draft, maintained a successful legal career, and continued working on antiabortion amicus briefs after he passed away in 1988. Dennis Horan's influence on the incrementalist ascendancy was the story of a marriage as well as one of individual achievement.[19]

The two became involved in antiabortion activism through the efforts of Dolores's sister, Dr. Gloria Volini Heffernan, and her husband, Dr. Bart Heffernan. The Heffernans and a colleague, Dr. Eugene Diamond, an obstetrician/gynecologist, had been working to form an antiabortion organization in Illinois. Dennis and Dolores Horan joined them in founding what became the Illinois Right to Life Committee (IRLC), establishing its reputation as a respectable, professional organization.[20]

In the immediate aftermath of the Supreme Court decision, the NRLC leadership asked Horan to chair the NRLC's new Legal Advisory Committee (LAC), the body charged with crafting an ideal fetal-protective amendment. Horan shared many of his colleagues' commitments: a belief that the Constitution had always protected the unborn, and a dedication to a fetal-rights, rather than state-rights, amendment. Nonetheless, he argued that a constitutional amendment would not be self-executing. The Supreme Court would interpret it, and pro-lifers would have to convince the justices to do so correctly. More fundamentally, Horan argued for the value of "a National Public Interest law firm, which would . . . spearhead litigation toward the ultimate goal of reversing *Roe v. Wade*." While many movement members described their cause as an effort to ban all abortions from conception until natural death, Horan focused on convincing the Supreme Court to overrule its 1973 decision.[21]

As the constitutional amendment campaign began to grind to a halt, the Horans assembled a team of attorneys who shared their beliefs about the value of litigation. One of these attorneys, John Gorby, had a longstanding relationship with Horan. Whereas Horan was a Catholic and a trial lawyer, Gorby did not have strong religious convictions. Instead, Gorby's interest in human rights law sparked his involvement in abortion politics. After graduating from law school, he took a German exchange fellowship and worked as an assistant to Judge Hermann Mosler of the European Court of Human Rights. During his assistantship, Gorby read the lower court's opinion in *Doe v. Bolton* and concluded that the court had dodged the question of fetal personhood. He worked with Horan after joining the faculty of the John Marshall Law School in Chicago.[22]

Patrick Trueman, another member of Horan's team, had studied under Gorby at John Marshall, and he began working with Horan and Gorby over the summer while he was still in school. A devout Catholic, Trueman had wanted to do something to undo *Roe* since its decision in 1973, and after working under Horan and Gorby, Trueman took a leading role in pro-life litigation.[23]

Another influential colleague, Victor Rosenblum, was a prominent professor of law and political science at Northwestern University. A Reform Jew, Rosenblum defined himself as a civil libertarian and served on the executive committee of a regional chapter of the Anti-Defamation League. A self-described liberal Democrat, Rosenblum acted as the Vice Chairman of the AUL throughout the 1970s, and he participated in the strategy discussions of what became the AUL Legal Defense Fund (AUL LDF).[24]

The group found its first case in the mid-1970s, after the Chicago media covered the assault prosecution of Melvin Moore. Outraged that his pregnant girlfriend refused to let him into her apartment, Moore fired a gun at her closed door. Bullets struck Moore's girlfriend, injuring her and terminating her pregnancy. Learning that prosecutors had charged Moore only with assault, Horan encouraged Gorby and Trueman to argue for homicide charges in the death of the fetus. The two attorneys drafted a forty-five-page memorandum justifying homicide charges, and in 1975, prosecutors did charge Moore in the fetal killing. Although a jury ultimately acquitted Moore, the AUL memorandum offered the blueprint for a new strategy. The AUL LDF it seemed, stood to gain more from similar, indirect challenges to the Court's decision. In theory, a fetal homicide conviction would not represent a direct challenge to the decision, but a successful prosecution would create a precedent recognizing some kind of right to life for the unborn.[25]

In the latter half of the 1970s, as the AUL endorsed the new legal approach formulated by Horan, Gorby, and Trueman, Horan headed the group's efforts to craft an amicus brief in *Planned Parenthood of Central Missouri v. Danforth*, the first major abortion case to come before the Court since *Roe*. *Danforth* involved a multi-restriction Missouri statute passed in the immediate aftermath of the decision. The law required women to sign a form setting forth their informed consent to an abortion procedure. Other statutory provisions required spousal or parental consent before an abortion could be performed.[26]

The AUL *Danforth* brief echoed many of the movement's classic constitutional claims, invoking the Declaration of Independence and the Fourteenth Amendment. Nonetheless, the brief broke new ground, insisting that the challenged abortion restrictions were constitutional, even under *Roe*. For example, the *Danforth* brief argued that the *Roe* decision allowed for informed-consent restrictions on abortion, since the Court had recognized the importance of the abortion decision and the physical and psychological challenges confronted by a pregnant woman.[27]

The *Danforth* brief illustrated a valuable new incrementalist tactic. The *Moore* case had offered an opportunity to establish fetal rights outside the abortion context. In *Danforth*, by contrast, the AUL LDF defended a number of restrictions while claiming to defer to the Court's earlier decisions on abortion.

The Court's opinion in *Danforth* appeared to vindicate the strategy AUL attorneys had developed. Although striking down different parts of the statute, the Court did reject challenges to some provisions. Under part of the law, in the first twelve weeks of pregnancy, a woman seeking an abortion had to sign a written form certifying that her consent was free and informed. The Court upheld this requirement, reasoning that "the decision to abort, indeed, is an important, and often a stressful one, and it is desirable and imperative that it be made with full knowledge of its nature and consequences."[28]

Abortion opponents also took comfort from parts of the *Danforth* opinion that struck down parental-consultation and spousal-consent restrictions. The Court highlighted the breadth of the challenged restrictions. The spousal-consent measure, for example, gave husbands a functional veto over a woman's abortion decision. The parental-consultation restriction made no provision for minors capable of mature decision-making. To some within the AUL, the Court's opinion left open the possibility that narrower restrictions might be constitutional.[29]

While Henry Hyde had stressed the constitutionality of his proposed restriction to convince allies in Congress, AUL attorneys paid lip service to the legitimacy of the *Roe* decision to narrow judicial protections for abortion. Pro-life leaders adapted to a variety of institutional settings, offering different arguments to state legislatures, Congress, and the courts. In pushing a constitutional amendment, for example, abortion opponents often highlighted the constitutional and scientific arguments for fetal rights many movement members believed that the courts had decisively rejected. Nonetheless, as Hyde had recognized, claiming deference to the Court gave pro-lifers more room to maneuver in the courts as well as in Congress. Tangible victories could motivate a dispirited base and save precious unborn lives.

In the later 1970s, *Danforth* accelerated the transformation of the AUL's identity and priorities. Leading litigators took on positions of leadership on the AUL Board of Directors, as did Dr. Eugene Diamond, the physician who petitioned to serve as a guardian ad litem in cases brought by the AUL LDF. Patrick Trueman, a young AUL attorney, headed a separately financed legal initiative overseen by Dennis Horan and his colleagues. Trueman spoke on behalf of many in the organization when he asserted: "The need for a full-time public interest law firm for the right to life movement has become very apparent to all involved in our cause."[30]

In mounting an incrementalist litigation campaign, the AUL LDF created its own guidelines for pursuing cases. The LDF prioritized involvement in cases in which no other party took a strong antiabortion stand and built relationships with sympathetic local attorneys who agreed to step in if anyone challenged an abortion restriction. For example, in *Wynn v. Scott*, an Illinois case, the AUL intervened when the Illinois Attorney General refused to defend an abortion restriction. The group also focused on high-profile cases, especially those that reached the Supreme Court. In such cases, as Trueman explained in 1977, AUL attorneys found it useful to display the organization's "particular pro-life legal expertise" as a way of reinforcing perceptions that it was powerful, respectable, and sophisticated.[31]

As part of this effort, the organization submitted an amicus brief in one of three consolidated cases on abortion funding decided by the Supreme Court in 1977. *Poelker v. Doe*, *Beal v. Doe*, and *Maher v. Roe* all dealt with state or local laws barring the use of public money, employees, or facilities for abortion. The AUL submitted a brief in *Poelker*, a case involving a St. Louis, Missouri, law that prevented publicly funded hospitals from performing abortions. The *Poelker* brief elaborated on an incrementalist strategy used in *Danforth*, seeking primarily to narrow the privacy right recognized in *Roe*.[32]

How could AUL attorneys undermine the protections *Roe* provided? In a brief signed by Dennis and Dolores Horan and Victor Rosenblum, the AUL tried two different approaches. First, the brief argued that the Court had assigned the abortion right partly to the physician, who could refuse to perform the procedure for personal, medical, or financial reasons. Under *Roe*, the *Poelker* brief argued: "the abortion decision is a medical decision that cannot be effectuated unless it is arrived at in consultation and in agreement with a physician." Women had no right to access abortion. Rather, *Roe* gave women nothing more than the right to request the procedure. As the brief framed it, the Court had recognized a right belonging to a "woman in consultation with her physician, not the woman alone demanding of her physician."[33]

A second and ultimately more successful argument exploited the idea that abortion rights protected only a woman's right to be left alone. As the AUL LDF brief explained: "If the abortion decision is so private . . . it follows that government shall not itself be compelled to respond to the demand of the exercise of that right." If a woman could not afford an abortion or required the services of a public hospital, the State had no constitutional obligation to help her.[34]

Like its companion cases, *Poelker* did not appear to be a likely win for abortion opponents. The lower courts had sometimes struck down bans on the use of public monies or facilities. One constitutional concern, as we have seen, involved the compatibility of these local or state laws with federal Medicaid policy, a question that the Court would decide under the Supremacy Clause of the Constitution. According to some lower court opinions, the federal Social Security Act implicitly conflicted with state laws prohibiting abortion funding.[35]

Second, many lower courts had concluded that funding and facilities bans violated the Equal Protection Clause of the Fourteenth Amendment. Rather than holding that the Constitution guaranteed a right to funding, the lower courts focused on the differing treatment of childbirth and abortion. If women enjoyed a fundamental abortion right, as many lower courts reasoned, states and cities could not deny funding for it while financing the choices of women who carried their children to term.[36]

Given the success of equal-protection arguments in the lower courts, the outcome of *Maher* and its companion cases provided considerable validation for the incrementalist strategy developed by the AUL LDF. In *Maher*, the lead case, the Court concluded that *Roe* "implies no limitation on the authority of a state to make a judgment favoring childbirth over abortion, and to implement that judgment by the allocation of public funds." As the AUL LDF had argued in its *Poelker* brief, the Court defined the abortion right as a freedom from state interference. The only obstacle for poor women seeking abortion, the Court suggested, was poverty itself. Since the government "neither created nor in any way affected" women's financial struggles, the challenged law did not unconstitutionally burden the decision to choose abortion.[37]

Within the antiabortion community, *Poelker*, *Maher*, and *Beal* drew unprecedented attention to the AUL LDF and to incrementalist litigation strategies more generally. The AUL reminded other pro-lifers that the LDF had offered "substantial argumentation which the Supreme Court followed in its resolution of the *Maher*, *Beal*, and *Poelker* decisions."[38] The NRLC, which had played no part in the litigation, used the victories in the 1977 cases in its own fundraising materials.[39]

By October 1977, as an AUL meeting made clear, the LDF's litigation strategies had begun to influence the broader antiabortion movement. At that time, Patrick Trueman noted that NRLC fundraising letters had "credit[ed] [that organization's] lawyers with what AUL has produced," raising $30,000 in the process. At the meeting, Trueman forced Mildred Jefferson, a member of both the AUL and the NRLC, to admit that the latter organization's fundraising strategy needed to give due credit to AUL lawyers. Later on in the meeting, the AUL asked David Mall, the longstanding executive director of the organization, to step down and selected Trueman to replace him. Even Mall admitted that there had been a "change in the thrust of the organization": what had been an educational organization now focused on incremental legal change.[40]

In several ways, the October 1977 meeting signaled the increasing influence of incrementalism. For the first time, lawyers officially led the AUL and dictated its priorities. Moreover, some in the movement concluded that *Poelker*, *Maher*, and *Beal* had vindicated the strategy devised by Dennis Horan and his colleagues. By contrast, efforts to secure a constitutional right to life had not yet paid off. As Jefferson's actions had suggested, many movement members had desperately wanted a win, and incrementalism seemed best able to supply one. As John Gorby would still put it years later, the movement could ultimately get rid of abortion rights only if it was willing to "chip away [at] and erode" the *Roe* decision.[41]

Pro-Life Leaders Transform Incrementalism into an Overarching Strategy

In the later 1970s, in studying *Maher* and its companion cases, NRLC attorney James Bopp Jr. realized the potential of incrementalism for his movement. Bopp viewed incrementalism not just as a litigation tactic but also as a general plan of attack.[42]

In the late 1970s, as Bopp's ideas suggested, what had started as a litigation strategy became, for many in the movement, a promising philosophy and a tactic applicable in the political arena and the media as well as in the courts. Incrementalists still saw themselves as heirs to a longstanding civil-rights tradition, since they defended a right to life and preferred a constitutional amendment as the ideal legal solution. Incrementalists like Bopp, however, privileged success in the near term over these values. What other activists might view as compromises became necessary steps in undoing *Roe*. And if the movement aimed for middle-ground restrictions, the work of the pro-life movement would actually accomplish something, giving the "states . . . considerable latitude to regulate abortions short of prohibition."[43]

Apart from their adherence to a particular strategy, incrementalists differed in their views of gender roles, their party affiliations, and their economic backgrounds, especially when compared to absolutists, who tended to hold similar views on social issues like sex-discrimination law and contraception. Consider the differences between leading incrementalists on the NRLC Board in the late 1970s. Geline B. Williams, the co-founder of an antiabortion group in Virginia, became more prominent in the national movement later in the decade. Williams came from an influential family—her grandfather had served in the Virginia State Legislature, and her mother had been active in the national Democratic Party, speaking on behalf of President Franklin Delano Roosevelt and campaigning for equality for women. In the mid-1960s, Geline had helped to found an antiabortion group in Virginia, and by the early 1970s, she had become active in the fight to stop the Equal Rights Amendment. She admired Phyllis Schlafly, believing that second-wave feminism was as dangerous to society as abortion. By the late 1970s, Williams became a champion of incrementalism. She argued for step-by-step efforts to pass legislation and defend it in court. As Williams still puts it, "winning a little at a time, we were going to win more people."[44]

Sandra Faucher, another leading incrementalist board member, held dramatically different views about Phyllis Schlafly and the women's movement. A veteran of Democratic Party politics in Maine, Faucher helped to found an antiabortion organization in the state. Like Williams, Faucher campaigned against ratification of the ERA in Maine, believing that the amendment would forever entrench fetal killing. Unlike Williams, though, Faucher agreed with almost nothing Phyllis Schlafly said. Faucher believed that sex discrimination in the workplace remained an intractable problem. When she worked as a secretary, for example, Faucher resented having to call her male employers

"Mr." when they used her first name. Faucher also disagreed with Schlafly's anti-lesbian rhetoric and would years later count a lesbian couple among her closest friends.[45]

In spite of her differences with Williams, Faucher also became a leading proponent of incrementalism. In lobbying in the state legislature, Faucher felt disrespected by elected officials dismissive of her position on abortion. Instead of changing the minds of those already in the state legislature, Faucher became convinced of the need to replace them. In the late 1970s, after her election to the NRLC Board of Directors, she pushed for the creation of a political action committee. She also promoted model restrictions on abortion, as well as any effort that served as another way of chipping away at the *Roe* decision. As Faucher later explained, "if we can get something, it's better than nothing."[46]

In the late 1970s, the incrementalism endorsed by advocates like Williams and Faucher manifested itself in two primary ways. First, a wide variety of state and national organizations began prioritizing a standard set of abortion restrictions. These regulations no longer represented a second-best, controversial complement to the struggle for a fetal-protective amendment. Instead, movement leaders presented these restrictions as a priority. For example, in 1978, the NRLC listed the push for a perfect fetal-life amendment as only one of several equally important goals. As much as demanding an ideal amendment, NRLC leader John Willke argued that pro-lifers had to "increase [their] activities at the state level, making sure that state and local laws are designed to protect and defend life rather than destroy it."[47] By the early 1980s, some incrementalists even became convinced that pro-lifers should wait to push a fetal-rights amendment until victory was in sight. As these activists claimed, moving too fast and failing could demoralize the movement and undercut the chances for later ratification of a fetal-protective amendment.[48]

Second, incrementalists compromised in order to exert more influence in national elections. In the late 1970s, a number of antiabortion political action committees formed, including the National Right to Life Committee PAC. For the most part, these organizations worked for candidates who supported any of the antiabortion movement's major positions. In practice, a legislator could qualify as "pro-life" even if his votes fell far short of what abortion opponents wanted.[49]

Why did the movement sometimes require so little of its political allies? First, incrementalists attached considerable importance to popular perceptions of pro-life influence. Leaders in Congress, state legislatures, and the White House would more likely cater to the pro-life movement if they believed that a majority of Americans opposed legal abortion. Creating the appearance of a pro-life majority would convince the public and politicians of the movement's political punch. For example, in 1977, Dr. John Willke argued that only a show of political strength would "give Congressmen and Senators pause if they still contemplate opposing this civil rights issue."[50] Under these circumstances, it became less important precisely how committed to the cause members of that majority were.[51]

At the same time, incrementalists argued that electoral politics involved compromises with less-than-perfect politicians. Antiabortion PACs promised to swing elections to legislators in return for anti-abortion votes on important legislation. In order to pass the kind of incremental legislation favored by the movement, activists had to count on the support of men and women who did not share many of their beliefs.[52]

The McCormack Campaign Reshapes the Pro-Life Approach to Electoral Politics

Of course, pro-lifers had been involved with electoral politics as early as the late 1960s. Before the mid- to late 1970s, however, the movement had been studiously non-partisan. The 1976 election marked a turning point for antiabortion involvement in electoral politics. That year, Ellen McCormack, a homemaker from suburban New York, mounted a high-profile and surprisingly productive presidential campaign. McCormack ran as a Democrat, but she consistently presented herself as a single-issue candidate for whom conservatives and liberals alike could vote. Her success convinced a number of abortion opponents that the movement could have more influence over electoral politics, albeit not in the way McCormack herself had envisioned. Her campaign identified a core group of committed pro-life voters who could, under certain circumstances, swing an election. In the aftermath of the election, pro-lifers created political action committees intended to exploit a new strategy. Rather than running single-issue candidates, the new PACs worked to make mainstream candidates cater to antiabortion voters.[53]

McCormack borrowed from strategies pioneered earlier in the decade, when abortion opponent Barbara Keating had run a largely symbolic campaign for Senate against New York Republican Jacob

Javits (R-NY). While Keating posed no real threat to Javits, her television advertisements had reportedly reached forty-six million people. Even in losing, a prominent pro-life candidate could seemingly educate the public and reach new potential supporters. McCormack's own organization, Women for the Unborn, decided to experiment with Keating's strategy at the national level. Women for the Unborn had unsuccessfully pursued March for Life founder Nellie Gray before settling on McCormack herself—a founding member, a mother of four, and the author of a weekly antiabortion newsletter published in New York State. McCormack's inevitable loss made little difference to her sponsors. As Women for the Unborn argued in a strategy memorandum: "The lives of thousands of unborn babies would be saved [by the McCormack campaign], since many people change their minds on abortion—including many women contemplating it—when they receive the pro-life information that is now generally kept from them by the national press."[54]

Initially, McCormack's backers trained their fire on the Democratic Party. "A major issue we want to raise," her supporters explained, "is the reluctance of the Democratic Party to act favorably on the human life amendment."[55] In truth, McCormack's campaign reflected anxiety within the antiabortion movement about the realignment of both major political parties. When Gerald Ford, the Republican presidential candidate, refused to endorse a personhood amendment, Fran Watson, McCormack's campaign manager, fired back that "the pro-life movement will accept no compromise when it comes to protecting unborn children."[56] Those backing McCormack's campaign hoped to force more politicians to take sides on the abortion issue.[57]

Over the course of the 1976 primary season, the McCormack campaign had come to mean something more substantial to the antiabortion movement. In the New Hampshire primary, McCormack won 1 percent of the vote, approximately 4 percent in Massachusetts, and almost 10 percent in Vermont. McCormack's performance seemed to open new political opportunities. "If we can demonstrate that there is a swing vote of 3% among Democrats across the country," McCormack's campaign manager concluded, "this should cause Congressional Democrats to reconsider the present policy of blocking action on Right to Life." The McCormack Campaign appeared to establish the political relevance of single-issue, pro-life voters.[58]

In some ways, McCormack failed to deliver on the stated promise of her campaign—forcing the Democratic Party back into the pro-life camp. As Fran Watson explained in McCormack's nominating speech at the Democratic National Convention, McCormack had not been successful "in preventing the Democratic Party from becoming the party of abortion." For some observers, the 1976 campaign nonetheless made apparent a new strategy for influencing abortion politics that differed significantly from McCormack's own. Instead of running single-issue candidates, the movement could build on McCormack's success in identifying influential swing voters. Major party candidates might not have had fully satisfactory positions on abortion, but if they owed their election partly to antiabortion swing voters, they might deliver some of the policy changes the movement desired.[59]

The shift in electoral strategy apparent after the McCormack campaign became a signature feature of incrementalism in the antiabortion movement. Major movement political action committees enlisted support for the candidates who took the strongest pro-life positions, even if those politicians did not favor all of the legal changes the movement championed. Siding with winners made sense, since those politicians would repay antiabortion supporters while in office.

In the aftermath of McCormack's run, three activists who elaborated on this new electoral strategy, Paul Brown, Sean Morton Downey Jr., and Robert Sassone, formed one of the first antiabortion political action committees. Downey belonged to a show business family. He attended law school before becoming an entertainer, singing on a few records, writing songs, and recording the hit single "Boulevard of Broken Dreams" in 1958. Later, Downey campaigned for John and Robert Kennedy, protested the war in Vietnam, and marched on Washington with Martin Luther King Jr. He opposed abortion, however, and became active in the pro-life movement in 1970.[60]

Like Downey, Brown came from an Irish Catholic family that viewed John, Robert, and Ted Kennedy as "the father, the son, and the holy ghost."[61] Brown had built a career with the Kmart Corporation, and had not been particularly politically engaged for years. When his wife, Judie, rededicated herself to the Catholic Church, Paul attended with her, but he did not immediately form strong opinions about contraception, the welfare state, the Vietnam War, or the Equal Rights Amendment.[62]

Seeing himself as a champion of the working man, Sassone, an author and attorney, had worked at a bakery, an automobile factory, and an aerospace plant. He defined himself as both a committed pro-lifer and a union Democrat, and he expressed particular concern about abortion as a method of population control, since he believed that overpopulation was a myth, at least in the United States. He viewed abortion as dangerous to the security of the nation.[63]

In 1977 the three men founded the Life Amendment PAC (LAPAC) for pragmatic reasons. Brown concluded that pro-lifers needed a victory that showed that something could be done about abortion. LAPAC began targeting vulnerable incumbents who had supported abortion rights, focusing particularly on elections in which a 3 to 5 percent swing could change the outcome. LAPAC leaders believed, as Brown would still put it years later, that "[t]here is no difference between show business and politics."[64] In South Dakota, for example, in targeting Democratic Senator George McGovern, LAPAC sponsored a debate that virtually no one expected McGovern to attend. The organization recruited a little-known local school teacher to oppose McGovern in the Democratic primary and invited him to confront the absent McGovern in the debate. LAPAC then printed McGovern's voting record on abortion and placed it on his empty seat.[65]

Theatrics aside, LAPAC made a name for itself in the 1978 midterm elections. The group announced that it had successfully targeted prominent liberals, particularly Senators Dick Clark (D-IA) and Thomas McIntyre (D-NH), who lost to abortion opponents Roger Jepsen (R-IA) and Gordon Humphrey (R-NH).[66]

LAPAC's performance in the 1978 election inspired newly influential incrementalists in the NRLC. Earlier that year, in the contest for the NRLC presidency, Arizona activist Dr. Carolyn Gerster had defeated Mildred Jefferson in a bitterly emotional vote. Following the election, both Jefferson and her Executive Director, Judie Brown, resigned. The reasons for Jefferson's ouster remain somewhat obscure. The messy finances of the organization—including reported debts of $25,000, according to some accounts—likely played a part, as did Jefferson's conflict with other abortion opponents in Massachusetts. That year, veteran activist and attorney Philip Moran successfully challenged Jefferson for the Massachusetts spot on the NRLC Board.[67]

If the NRLC's evolution in the years to come offers any indication, Jefferson's expulsion might have been a vote for an incrementalist strategy. In 1978 the NRLC increased its involvement in national elections, and by 1979 the group had created a political action committee with Maine activist Sandra Faucher as project director. The National Right to Life PAC chose candidates based not just on the recommendation of state leaders or the past voting record of a candidate but also on the existence of "a broad base of political support." Winning mattered more than did choosing an ideal candidate.[68]

In practice, for both the NRLC and LAPAC, electoral politics required compromise. First, in the late 1970s, movement leaders generally believed that they could have the most significant impact if they worked to defeat established liberal Democrats supportive of abortion rights. With the mobilization of the New Right and the Religious Right, the NRLC highlighted the victories of Republicans sympathetic to the pro-life position. In 1978, when selecting politicians to target, LAPAC named the "dirty dozen," twelve mostly left-leaning members of Congress. Throughout 1979, Carolyn Gerster and Paul Brown maintained that they wanted to work more often with Democrats but could not find many real allies among them. For many abortion opponents like Sassone, Downey, or Marjory Mecklenburg, electoral success might require an alliance with a political party that represented only some of their core beliefs. Nonetheless, as the *National Right to Life News* explained in 1979: "[l]everage is key." The best way to create leverage, the *National Right to Life News* suggested, was to "approach a candidate with an organized political force."[69]

Moreover, achieving electoral success would require the support of imperfect candidates. By June 1980, Faucher, the head of the NRLC PAC, reported that forty-four Senators and two thirds of the members of the House opposed abortion. Of course, not all of these legislators took equally pro-life positions. In September 1980, for example, the Senate voted forty-seven to thirty-seven to permit states to fund abortions in cases of rape, incest, or threat to the life of the mother. In October, the House voted 292–100 to approve another compromise version of the Hyde Amendment, permitting federal Medicaid funding in cases in which the mother's life was at risk or in which women reported rape or incest within a two-month period. In 1978, when abortion opponents made no claim to control either house of Congress, the Medicaid funding bill was virtually identical to the 1980 version, with only the reporting requirement as a new addition.[70]

The Medicaid compromise of 1980 reflected the pragmatism embodied in the new antiabortion politics. This kind of political deal-making made strategic sense to a movement keen on making legislative progress and on convincing legislators of the movement's strength in numbers. Willke, a leading incrementalist, explained the importance of "the steadily increasing size, strength, and broad base of support that is present and is increasing for the Right to Life movement."[71]

Nonetheless, as the Medicaid battle indicated, the number of anti-abortion members of Congress increased, but the definition of "pro-life" became looser. Now, movement members counted among their supporters legislators willing to settle for far less than the antiabortion movement wished. Dr. Joseph Stanton, a leading Massachusetts activist, summarized this position in 1978 correspondence with Nellie Gray: "[I]f we do not work with those who maybe have not been given the grace to understand the issue fully, then I fear this movement will atrophy."[72]

Pro-Lifers Use an Akron Ordinance as a Model for Incremental Attacks

In 1978, when the NRLC announced its interest in electoral politics, the antiabortion movement worked on the passage of a multi-restriction ordinance introduced in the town of Akron, Ohio. Building on the AUL's *Danforth* victory, the law required the "informed consent" of women having abortions. Among other things, the ordinance also mandated spousal consent for married women and parental consent for minors. On February 28, 1978, the city of Akron approved the ordinance by a vote of seven to six.[73]

Somewhat unexpectedly, the Akron statute created a national controversy. The ordinance did not appear likely to impact a particularly large number of women. Just the same, it meant something different to an emerging group of movement incrementalists: a symbol of a revised strategy for attacking legal abortion. Rather than focusing as heavily on a constitutional amendment, the movement honed in on the strongest restrictions that the Supreme Court would likely enforce. Increasingly, incrementalists privileged political realism over the immediate passage of an ideal fetal-rights amendment.[74]

The public campaign to build on the Akron statute offers some insight into the workings of the new incrementalism. Beginning in 1978, pro-lifers began pushing for similar laws in other cities and states. In March, abortion opponents explained that the Akron law would serve as a model for measures in Cincinnati, Cleveland, and Chicago. That August, Michael Connelly, an attorney and activist at Baton Rouge Right to Life, proudly claimed that he followed the Akron law "right down the line."[75] Over time, pro-life attorneys revised Akron-style statutes, anticipating constitutional concerns about the wording of the original informed-consent provisions.[76]

Those defending the Akron model also used a different kind of argument. Rather than stressing the unborn's right to life, proponents of the Akron model defended its individual provisions. The Akron group behind the ordinance called itself Citizens for Informed Consent, and members of the group highlighted their compliance with the *Roe* decision. One member told the local and national media that Akron-style laws would help prevent women from choosing to terminate a pregnancy without "really knowing what an abortion is all about."[77]

A new unifying strategy fueled the Akron campaign. In the mid-1970s, Horan and his allies had forged an effective approach to litigation, and later, Bopp, Willke, and the NRLC joined other pro-life leaders in turning this tactic into a broad, new incrementalist philosophy. From start to finish, the movement would pursue restrictions with the "reasonable hope" that the Court would uphold them.[78]

As incrementalism reshaped the movement's political strategies and ultimate objectives, a divide within the antiabortion movement appeared. Absolutists and incrementalists disagreed first about which tactical approach would work the best. Absolutists, as Judie Brown explained, rejected the idea that incremental statutes had become the "only avenue open to [the pro-life movement] at the time 'politically.'"[79] If incrementalism prevailed, politicians could claim to be pro-life without ever delivering the kinds of legal protections the movement truly demanded. Moreover, absolutists argued that incrementalism caused grassroots activists to question their movement's commitments. As an ally of Brown's explained, if legislators defeated compromise laws, "it would be easy to say that nothing is 'possible' so we must accept defeat and 'get on' to other things."[80] By contrast, incrementalists believed that a direct attack on abortion rights would result in failure. In the meantime, they argued, a string of defeats would demoralize abortion opponents and cause them to abandon their cause. Small, concrete victories, the argument went, would improve recruitment, frighten politicians into compliance, and reduce the number of abortions performed.[81]

Second, incrementalists and absolutists defined their goals and values in somewhat different ways. Absolutists tended to be more ideologically homogenous and socially conservative than incrementalists, demanding a perfect constitutional amendment and often refusing to "support weak measures."[82] This agenda required dramatic social change—the reversal of achievements made by the women's movement and the sexual revolution. By contrast, incrementalists increasingly focused on restrictions that the Supreme Court would uphold. These victories, as the NRLC's ally, the Christian Action Council, explained, would make the Court "aware that it miscalculated the depth and breadth of public opposition to abortion."[83] To a beleaguered Court, upholding a growing array of restrictions might appear "a way out of the abortion controversy." In the short term, for strategic reasons, some incrementalists eventually came to prefer compromise proposals to a comprehensive fetal-rights amendment, believing that any failure would devastate the movement. These conflicting goals reflected different priorities held by those who gravitated toward each camp.[84]

Absolutists Mount an Attack on Incrementalism

Absolutism emerged as the result of frustration with the stalling of the campaign for a fetal-protective amendment in the mid-1970s. While many pro-lifers turned to a more practical strategy designed to achieve concrete and immediate results, a group of conservatives adopted an ambitious, social-conservative agenda. Over time, absolutists came to believe that a focus on incremental laws would make the pro-life movement look weak. By becoming more principled, as movement hardliners claimed, pro-lifers would become more politically powerful. Absolutists believed that only a no-compromise approach could "effectively take the continued killing of preborn children off the agenda."[85]

Often before forming organizations of their own, absolutists found themselves attracted to a different constitutional strategy, known in movement circles as "con-con" (short for constitutional convention). Rather than asking Congress first to pass a fetal-protective amendment by the required supermajority vote, activists in the later 1970s argued that the movement could convince two thirds of the states to pass legislation asking Congress for a constitutional convention. If thirty-four states made a request of this kind, the antiabortion movement could make progress in ratifying a human life amendment. While incrementalists increasingly worked outside of the constitutional amendment process, absolutists found themselves less willing to settle for anything less than total victory.[86]

The campaign for a constitutional convention began in New York, where antiabortion attorney Gene McMahon proposed the idea in

1973 as "a way of prodding Congress into action."[87] The proposal divided New York State Right to Life, with the organization's board of directors opposing an idea that a majority of rank-and-file members endorsed. In the later 1970s, as pro-life frustrations mounted, the con-con campaign spread rapidly. The movement for a constitutional convention represented a different response to the trends that inspired the campaign for Akron-style statutes. Like incrementalists, absolutists recognized that the campaign for a fetal-protective amendment was foundering, and absolutists had witnessed firsthand the progress of incremental restrictions in state legislatures. Hoping to capitalize on support in the states, con-con advocates argued that a purely constitutional strategy could still succeed, albeit not in the way the movement had proposed in 1973.[88]

Notwithstanding disagreements about the con-con strategy, its proponents scored some victories in the states. By 1977 nine states had joined the call for a convention, and in the next two years, pro-lifers counted five more states in favor of the convention. These successes did not end conflict about the wisdom of the strategy. The NRLC publicly opposed the idea. As Mildred F. Jefferson told the *New York Times* in 1977, "We expect to work through Congress to get them to nullify the effects of the Supreme Court decision."[89]

Even without the official support of the NRLC, a number of abortion opponents (including some NRLC members) endorsed the con-con campaign. Supporters of the strategy included Ellen McCormack, traditionalists like Randy Engel and Charles Rice, and Dan Buckley, the founder of a pro-life organization called Americans for a Constitutional Convention.[90]

The campaign for a constitutional convention came during a period in the later 1970s when stand-alone absolutist groups began to organize and flourish. After stepping down from her position in the NRLC, Judie Brown had accepted seed money from New Right leader Richard Viguerie to form a new antiabortion organization. As Viguerie designed it, this new group, the American Life League/American Life Lobby (ALL), would take part in a broader right-wing coalition, rejecting the neutral positions the NRLC still took on issues like contraception.[91]

In launching the ALL, Brown went further than Viguerie had perhaps imagined. Founded in 1979, the ALL set out an ambitious agenda, put out a newsletter, *ALL About Issues,* and defined itself by its differences with the mainstream movement. Whereas the

NRLC prized its religious diversity, Brown's ALL presented itself as a Catholic organization. While the NRLC took no official position on birth control, the ALL made the fight against contraception central to its law reform efforts.[92]

By the end of the 1970s, the ALL had built relationships with 4,250 affiliates. Its publication reached an audience of 56,000. The organization undertook a campaign to end the funding of family planning programs under the federal Social Security Act. The ALL also argued for teenage abstinence-education programs, attributing "sexual experimentation" to "peer pressure, coercion, disturbed family situations, . . . or internal psychological problems."[93] The ALL took on not just abortion but also non-marital sex. As an April 1981 ALL newsletter explained: "There is no such moral standard as 'responsible sexuality' outside of marriage."[94]

Joseph Scheidler, another player in the debate of the late 1970s, had worked as a journalism professor and considered joining a Catholic religious order before entering the abortion wars. In the early 1970s, he had served as the Executive Director of Dennis Horan's Illinois Right to Life Committee before being asked to step down. In 1978 Scheidler co-founded another organization, Friends for Life, in order to pursue what he felt to be the only strategy that would succeed in challenging the Court's decision. In 1980, however, after deep tactical disagreements with his colleagues, Scheidler again left to form his own organization, the Pro-Life Action League.[95]

Since the early 1970s, Scheidler had criticized the tactical choices made by many abortion opponents. These frustrations began during his time in the IRLC, when he watched a film made by the organization. The movie told the story of a woman who deliberated about abortion and ultimately decided against it. Scheidler, who advocated controversial tactics that would be the most likely to attract media attention, found the film to be too apologetic and called for activists to protest outside clinics. He promoted "sidewalk counseling," a set of techniques for approaching and talking to women entering abortion facilities. He believed that the movement should use the most graphic images of abortion to promote its cause. The point, in Scheidler's view, was to be memorable. As he still put it years later: "People will have an easier time remembering names than an organization. I wanted them to know Joe Scheidler."[96]

Scheidler and Brown represented an emerging absolutist wing of the antiabortion movement. Although members of this faction had been active throughout the decade, by the late 1970s they increasingly formed organizations of their own. Historian Michael Cuneo has suggested that these hardliners organized because of mounting frustrations with the mainstream movement's secular message and focus on a human life amendment. But contrary to what Cuneo's thesis suggests, after forming their own organizations, absolutists continued to promote a constitutional amendment and to prioritize the idea of a fundamental right to life. Moreover, if absolutists took issue with the secular message offered by the mainstream movement, they picked a strange time to form organizations of their own. In the late 1970s, more than ever before, prominent antiabortion organizations adopted religious rhetoric, held prayer breakfasts, and focused on recruiting devout evangelical Protestants. Incrementalists allied with the Religious Right in the late 1970s identified strategic reasons for using religious rhetoric.[97]

The creation of independent absolutist groups seems to have come instead as the result of a number of factors. Paul Brown and Joseph Scheidler, like many abortion opponents, expressed concern about their movement's lack of progress in the quest to secure a fetal-protective amendment. Potentially controversial tactics—picketing clinics, vandalizing property, or engaging in sidewalk counseling—became more attractive when other strategies failed to deliver the desired result. "How would you dispose of an arrogant humanist on the highest Court in the land?" Joseph Scheidler had asked in detailing his strategy. "You turn him over to the people."[98]

To some extent, absolutists also responded to the creation of new political opportunities. Religious Right organizations, although primarily Protestant, championed views on contraception, secularism, and feminism with which conservative Catholics like Judie Brown or Scheidler agreed. Groups like the Moral Majority mobilized a new political cohort that shared many of absolutists' core beliefs. Abortion opponents like Judie Brown or Joseph Scheidler similarly saw their campaign as a crusade for the moral future of the United States, or, as Moral Majority fundraising materials put it in 1980, "fighting for a moral America."[99] The Religious Right convinced absolutists that, as Paul Brown explained, "secular humanism [was] the real enemy."[100] The emergence of the Religious Right created an important opportunity for Catholic activists like Brown or Scheidler seeking allies with similar views.[101]

Activists like Judie Brown and Joseph Scheidler cannot be easily categorized, however. Scheidler, for example, still maintains that the women's movement of the 1960s and 1970s accomplished some laudable goals, especially promoting equal pay for equal work. At the same time, he would become known for the emotionally charged and hardly feminist rhetoric used in the clinic protests he led. Brown similarly remained a complex figure. Committed to motherhood, she claimed in the late 1970s that she had subordinated her own career to the needs of her children and husband. At the same time, between 1979 and 1981, Brown made herself into a force in American politics, arguably more influential and intimidating than her husband.[102]

By 1980 the absolutists formed something of a united front. In January 1980 absolutists held the First Annual Respect Life Leadership Conference. Fifty leaders, including Scheidler and the Browns, attended. Like members of the NRLC, conference participants voted to endorse Ronald Reagan and to prioritize a fetal-protective amendment. Some differences with the mainstream movement did become apparent. For example, Scheidler urged attendees to focus on sit-ins and pickets, tactics with which the NRLC remained uncomfortable. The agenda set forth at the conference linked abortion to euthanasia, divorce rates, and secularism.[103]

A number of Catholic and evangelical Protestant antiabortion groups took up similar arguments against secular humanism, linking legal abortion to rising divorce rates, the emergence of a gay-rights campaign, and the visibility of the women's movement. In October 1980, for example, the Ad Hoc Committee in Defense of Life described abortion as part of a broader effort to destroy the family. "Check out the divorce, drug and crime rates," the committee argued. "Try not to see 'the gays' who have suddenly tumbled out of more closets than we ever knew existed."[104] In the early 1980s, LAPAC identified secular humanism, not the abortion-rights movement, as its true enemy. In a June 1981 edition of *ALL About Issues*, the ALL similarly called for sit-ins in order to help "the victim[s] of secular humanism."[105]

Incrementalists generally rejected this view of the antiabortion cause. Americans United for Life, for example, pushed neither outright bans on abortion nor any broader attack on secular humanism. In 1979 Thomas Marzen of the AUL explained the central importance of informed-consent regulations: "Many abortion clinics have told women seeking abortions that the unborn is 'just a blob of tissue.' If women are aware that abortion is a painful procedure for the fetus, they may come to understand that the child is human."[106] The

AUL, like the NRLC, focused on realistic goals. As an AUL newsletter explained: "The challenge, therefore, to the Right to Life movement is to enact carefully drawn legislation and to present sound legal argumentation in the courts in support of these laws." To incrementalists, an attack on secular humanism seemed counterproductive.[107]

Before 1980, conflicts between incrementalists and absolutists nonetheless remained muted. The election of Ronald Reagan and a nominally antiabortion Congress also united the movement. Indeed, the 1980 election season inspired profound optimism. As a December 1980 column in *The Moral Majority Report* proclaimed, "Now, as never before, the passage of a human life amendment to the U.S. Constitution in the next session of Congress is within grasp."[108] The *National Right to Life News*, the flagship publication of the NRLC, boasted that "the pro-abortionists were left in shambles."[109] "It was Fantasy Island come true," Dr. John Willke said of the 1980 election with obvious delight.[110]

The 1980 election obscured differences between incrementalists and absolutists. Well into the 1980s, both groups described a fetal-protective amendment as the movement's ultimate goal. While leading pro-lifers had taken an interest in federal judicial nominations in the late 1970s, the movement preoccupation with judicial selections came later. During the 1980 election, Ronald Reagan had promised to nominate antiabortion judges to the federal bench. By the mid-1980s, efforts to change the composition of the courts became a centerpiece of movement strategy, particularly among incrementalists. Remaking the courts represented a new way of achieving the slow but meaningful changes incrementalists pursued. With the Republican Party committed to the antiabortion movement in the mid-1980s, activists for the first time could realistically demand nominees opposed to *Roe*.[111]

In the early 1980s, however, absolutists and incrementalists believed that they would not need to change the composition of the Court in order to undo *Roe*. With support in the executive and legislative branches, pro-lifers believed they could pass a human life amendment in the near term. The issues that had divided the movement faded temporarily from view when a fetal-protective amendment seemed within reach. In the early 1980s the NRLC, by then a torchbearer for incrementalism, even brought together scholars and attorneys to draft a "pro-life unity amendment" subsequently endorsed by the organization.[112]

Just the same, the conflict between incrementalists and absolutists was real, and over the course of the early 1980s, it intensified. While those on both sides still endorsed the idea of a fetal-protective amendment, pro-lifers disagreed about how it could be obtained. On the surface, the conflict about incrementalism centered on a tactical question—how most effectively to undermine abortion rights. Over time, it seemed that something deeper was at stake. Absolutists maintained the original mission pro-lifers had endorsed: the creation, by constitutional amendment, of a right to life that banned all abortions, reaching further than the bans on the books before 1973. Increasingly, incrementalists indefinitely postponed the quest for a perfect amendment, instead prioritizing what the movement could achieve in the present political moment.

The Hatch Amendment Deepens the Incrementalist/Absolutist Divide

The conflict between incrementalists and absolutists remained mostly below the surface until Senator Jesse Helms (R-NC) introduced a new tactic for protecting the right to life. The human life bill, as it was called, recognized the personhood of the fetus from the moment of conception and declared that no person, fetuses included, could be deprived of life without due process of law. First introduced in January 1981, the bill denied the lower courts of jurisdiction in abortion cases, forcing the Supreme Court to quickly confront the constitutionality of the law.[113]

The proposal promised to undo a crucial part of the *Roe* decision—its conclusions about the personhood of the fetus—without the expense and difficulty involved in the ratification of a constitutional amendment. The bill, as explained by Senator John East (R-NC), would vitiate abortion rights by defining the fetus as a person under the Fourteenth Amendment. Under the human life bill, any law permitting abortion, it seemed, would run afoul of the Fourteenth Amendment.[114]

In early 1981, law professors in favor of abortion rights attacked the constitutionality of the bill (as did some critics of the Court's 1973 opinion). The bill raised fundamental questions about who had the power to interpret the Constitution. For centuries, the Supreme Court had claimed a power of judicial review—that is, the final authority in determining the constitutionality of a law and a related power to strike down laws that violated the Constitution. By contrast, Congress could legislate only if it had specific constitutional authorization.[115]

The framers of the human life bill had relied on Section Five of the Fourteenth Amendment. That provision gave Congress the power to enforce the equality- and due process-based protections set forth in the amendment. But what did this enforcement power involve? Proponents of the human life bill, such as Senator East, argued that Congress could proclaim new rights and redefine old ones. A series of Supreme Court decisions dating from the 1950s and 1960s suggested that Congress had "a major role in defining the substantive content of the Constitution."[116] Opponents of the bill responded that Congress could only remedy violations of the rights already defined by the courts.[117]

At the same time, pro-lifers hotly debated the merits of the bill. Paul and Judie Brown initially argued that the bill would distract the movement from its quest for a perfect constitutional amendment. Professor Charles Rice, who testified that the bill was constitutional, privately concluded that it did not do enough to protect the fetus, permitting abortion between the time of fertilization and implantation. Leaders of the NRLC more strongly favored the bill. In testifying in favor of the proposal, for example, Dr. John Willke, sought to allay concerns that the bill would ban common forms of contraception.[118]

The debate took a turn when then-executive director of Minnesota Citizens Concerned for Life, David N. O'Steen, called on movement members to reject the bill. O'Steen had joined the antiabortion movement after leaving a position teaching mathematics at the University of Houston. He built a highly effective political action committee for Minnesota Citizens Concerned for Life and played an influential role on the NRLC Board of Directors. After having taught himself the basics of constitutional law, he concluded that the human life bill was "ultimately doomed to fail before the Supreme Court."[119]

O'Steen circulated a confidential memorandum that proposed a classically incrementalist, two-amendment strategy as an alternative. First, the movement would promote an amendment allowing the states and Congress to ban abortion. O'Steen believed that Congress and the states would easily ratify such an amendment. With a states' rights amendment in place, Congress could pass a human life bill, and the American people would get used to life without abortion. After the movement achieved these goals, it could easily pass a fetal-rights amendment.[120]

The O'Steen memorandum caught the attention of Senator Orrin Hatch (R-UT). When he joined Congress in 1976, Hatch became one of the most vocal opponents of legal abortion. He portrayed himself as a defender of the traditional family but worried that the Supreme Court would strike down the human life bill. Hatch viewed the two-amendment strategy as a strategically and constitutionally superior option. In September 1981, he asked the staff of the Senate Judiciary Committee to study the "federal rights" amendment that O'Steen had proposed—one that would give Congress and the states joint jurisdiction over abortion. Later, Hatch would become the most visible champion of the O'Steen approach.[121]

By contrast, Judie Brown viewed the O'Steen memorandum with skepticism. She wrote Charles Rice about her concerns, and he agreed that her fears were justified. In June 1981, he wrote Brown that a permissive amendment—one allowing but not requiring the states to ban abortion—would "legitimize . . . early abortions and insulate . . . them from any legislative restriction."[122] Worse, such an amendment would end any hope of ratifying a perfect amendment. As Rice asserted: "It is unrealistic to think we will be able to adopt more than one constitutional amendment on the abortion issue."[123]

At the same time, movement incrementalists moved to support the Hatch Amendment. James Bopp viewed the proposal as the most promising development in years. Incrementalists on the NRLC Board shared his opinion. Willke also defended the proposed strategy, explaining that "once the nation becomes used to living without the freedom to abort, then we will be able to come back with 'the human life amendment' and lock it in."[124] As Geline Williams would state years later, incrementalists believed that "the overturning of *Roe v. Wade* was the best effort we [the movement] could make."[125]

In September 1981, Judie Brown responded by declaring war on the Hatch Amendment and anyone who supported it. In *ALL About Issues*, she called the Hatch Amendment "a betrayal of all of our principles."[126] Voting for the Hatch Amendment, Brown argued, would allow legislators to identify as pro-life without lifting a finger to protect the unborn. She explained: "It is my personal conviction that we cannot pick and choose which babies to save—not by states, not by geographical location."[127] Other absolutists answered the call to oppose the Hatch Amendment. Joseph Scheidler's Pro-Life Action League came out against Hatch's proposal. The evangelical Protestant Christian Action Council argued that politicians would use the Hatch

Amendment "to solve their own political problems, not the abortion problem."[128]

All the while, incrementalists worked behind the scenes to build movement support for the Hatch Amendment. The National Conference of Catholic Bishops endorsed it in early November. In testifying before Congress, Archbishop John Roach explained the rationale for the bishops' decision. "There is a strong urgency to get something," he explained. "The Hatch Amendment has a real possibility of passing."[129]

NRLC incrementalists also managed to win a vote on Hatch's proposal. In an emergency meeting called in December 1981, incrementalists on the board narrowly pushed through a resolution supporting the amendment, winning by a vote of thirty-one to twenty-four. Unsurprisingly, supporters of the resolution focused on the chances of winning. As John Willke told the *New York Times*: "It [was] a question of strategy, not of the conviction of the people here, that we were deciding today."[130]

If the disagreement between incrementalists and absolutists had been fierce before, the NRLC vote made it explosive. Absolutists on the NRLC Board began calling for Willke to resign from his position as NRLC President. Early in 1982, Judie Brown released a statement on the absolutist position, explaining: "[w]e cannot join any group of individuals who believe that regulation of abortion is an acceptable path for the pro-life movement to follow." Led by Brown, the absolutists attacked the basic premise of incrementalism—that the movement should prioritize realistic restrictions on abortion.[131]

The Hatch Amendment debate exposed profound disagreements between movement incrementalists and their opponents. In the late 1970s Judie Brown, Joseph Scheidler, Father Paul Marx, and their allies had worked to redefine the antiabortion cause. *The Human Life Review*, the journal published by J. P. McFadden's Ad Hoc Committee in Defense of Life, ran a series of anti-gay articles that linked support for extramarital or homosexual sex to abortion. Brown's allies held conferences criticizing sex education, praising natural family planning, and damning contraception. These activists described a social decline much broader than that symbolized by the legalization of abortion: the creation of "a sexist society in which the ego surmounts all else, removing the loving . . . aspects of the marriage act and turning all human beings into animals that cannot live without sex."[132]

Incrementalists campaigned only for abortion restrictions, taking no position on contraception, sex education, or secular humanism. Some, like Sandra Faucher, did not agree with Brown's opinions on those subjects. Others believed that Brown's strategy could not work at any point in the foreseeable future.

Incrementalists and absolutists also disagreed about the issue of compromise. In criticizing the Hatch Amendment, absolutists argued for an all-or-nothing approach. Moreover, anything less would allow legislators to benefit from being called pro-life without ever seeking to ban abortion. Nor, absolutists predicted, would grassroots activists work hard for anything less than an ideal human life amendment. Volunteers had left jobs and sacrificed time for a sacred principle. Incremental restrictions would not command the same loyalty. By contrast, incrementalists believed that successful compromise regulations would energize the movement and reduce the number of abortions performed. At the same time, by chipping away at *Roe*, incrementalists wanted to expose its flaws, preparing the way for the eventual overruling of the decision.

In early 1982, the battle between absolutists and incrementalists had damaged the chances of passing either the human life bill or the Hatch Amendment. In March, Senator Helms offered a modified version of the human life bill, and President Reagan intervened, calling on abortion opponents to stop fighting and pass one of the proposals. In the same month, the full Senate Judiciary Committee voted ten to seven in favor of Hatch's proposal. The vote represented the first time that an antiabortion amendment had made it out of committee. Incrementalists greeted the news with enthusiasm. Willke called the vote a "milestone" and a "major victory."[133] Hatch spoke in favor of the idea of compromise, stating that his amendment "puts us in the middle [between] the two extremes dominating the debate."[134]

However, the divisions between abortion opponents helped to doom Hatch's proposal. When the amendment came up for a vote before the full Senate, Senator Robert Packwood (R-OR), a longstanding supporter of abortion rights, led efforts to filibuster the measure. With abortion opponents divided about Hatch's proposal, the full Senate killed it by a vote of forty-seven to forty-six. In September 1982, Hatch withdrew the amendment from consideration. In the 1982 midterm elections, the Democratic Party retook the House, decreasing the chances that any major antiabortion legislation would pass at the federal level. In 1983 as a measure of last resort, Senator Thomas Eagleton (D-MO) proposed a modification of the Hatch

Amendment—one that would state only that the Constitution did not protect an abortion right. However, with pro-lifers still in deep disagreement, the Hatch-Eagleton Amendment failed in June 1983, defeated in a Senate vote of forty-nine to fifty, with one abstaining.[135]

In spite of the failure of the Hatch Amendment, other events in the early 1980s accelerated the shift toward incrementalism. First, Ronald Reagan's Supreme Court nominees began delivering the results pro-lifers had expected during the 1980 election. Initially, some movement members discounted the importance of judicial selections, since Reagan nominated Sandra Day O'Connor, a judge believed to favor abortion rights. However, in June 1983, when the Supreme Court finally decided a case involving the constitutionality of the Akron statute, O'Connor criticized the reasoning of the *Roe* decision. Although the Court voted six to three that the statute was unconstitutional, O'Connor wrote a dissent describing *Roe*'s trimester framework as "on a collision course with itself."[136]

O'Connor's opinion in *City of Akron v. Akron Center for Reproductive Health (Akron I)* offered new hope for incrementalists. Throughout the 1970s, even pro-life pragmatists had argued that only a fetal-protective amendment would outlaw abortion. *Akron I* convinced more pro-lifers that the Supreme Court itself might overrule the *Roe* decision. In the years to come, the movement would invest more in the Supreme Court nomination process.[137]

Nonetheless, the conflict between absolutists and incrementalists surrounding the Hatch Amendment continues at the time of this writing. Starting in 2011, the movement again found itself divided by the issue of personhood amendments. Founded in 2008, a Colorado-based group called Personhood USA began fighting to put a state constitutional ban of abortion on the ballot. In 2011 and 2012 the organization pushed for similar measures in states like Mississippi, California, Montana, Nevada, Arkansas, Ohio, and Florida. In discussing these proposals, movement members divided along familiar lines. James Bopp Jr., still the general counsel for the NRLC, condemned the personhood movement. "There has always been a division," he asserted, "between those who want to concentrate on what will make a difference, and those who are interested in making a statement that makes them feel better."[138] Judie Brown also maintained her absolutist stance, calling Bopp's position "political [and] gutless."[139] "As a Catholic," she said, "it's the most scandalous thing I've ever heard."[140]

Backlash in Context

What does the incrementalist ascendancy tell us about the nature of post-*Roe* extremism? Certainly, the late 1970s witnessed the mobilization of conservative evangelical Protestants and fundamentalist Christians, many of whom opposed *Roe*. The antiabortion movement partnered with the New Right and Religious Right and sometimes adopted the rhetoric used by its new allies.

Just the same, defining many pro-lifers in the period as extremists obscures as much as it reveals. For the most part, the antiabortion movement has favored political and legal realism, concrete victories, and efforts to decrease the number of abortions performed. The absolutists who opposed any such compromise did become more vocal in the late 1970s, intensifying clinic protests and capturing substantial media attention. Nonetheless, in the debates of the late 1970s and 1980s, absolutists often found themselves on the losing side. The voices of compromise tended to prevail.

We should not overstate the interest in compromise expressed by incrementalists. For the most part, these activists embraced the idea of a fetal-protective amendment and did not believe that abortion should be legal under any circumstances. Instead, incrementalists' interest in compromise measures stemmed from their realism. If the movement could not do any better than middle-ground restrictions, then such restrictions became activists' priority.

Nonetheless, the incrementalist ascendancy offers a new perspective on antiabortion extremism and backlash. Incrementalists defy easy categorization. They attacked the women's movement and changes to the nuclear family, but often did so for reasons of political expediency. They wished to ban all abortions but gradually came to oppose efforts to achieve that goal. In analyzing post-*Roe* backlash, we should acknowledge these nuances.

The incrementalists' story also offers a different sense of the process by which movements form an identity. The very idea of backlash suggests that antiabortion activists primarily reacted to events beyond their control. As the materials assembled here suggest, the prevailing definition of the pro-life cause reflected more than the influence of the Supreme Court. Activists forged an identity for their movement in a series of intensely contested debates, many of which continue at the time of this writing.

Judie Brown and James Bopp Jr. experienced these battles first-hand. Former colleagues, allies, and co-workers, Bopp and Brown had shared a vision of a constitutional amendment that would protect the unborn for all time. Well into the 1970s, Bopp and Brown had opposed an amendment that would return the abortion issue to the states. Emerging from a series of experiments and internal battles, incrementalist strategies made Bopp and Brown into bitter adversaries. Regardless of whether or not we identify it as backlash, the type of struggle Bopp and Brown witnessed—one negotiated and shaped by activists themselves—deserves greater study.

PART II

The Abortion-Rights Movement after *Roe*

CHAPTER THREE

Women's Rights versus Population Control: Abortion and Racial Politics

IN FEBRUARY 1973, Reverend Jesse Jackson saw pro-life politics as a natural extension of his work in the civil-rights movement. In the aftermath of the *Roe* decision, Jackson contacted the NRLC to express his interest. He had found his calling directing Operation Breadbasket in Chicago, a program introduced by Dr. Martin Luther King Jr.'s Southern Christian Leadership Conference. In 1971 Jackson founded Operation PUSH (People United to Save Humanity), a group focused on civil rights and economic self-help for people of color. He responded to the *Roe* decision by denouncing legal abortion. Jackson highlighted his religious convictions, explaining his belief that "life [was] the most sacred possession a man can claim."[1] He also worried that racism drove the campaign to legalize abortion. As Jackson explained, "there [were] indisputable traces of genocide in the possible uses of [the Court's] ruling."[2]

A decade later, he described abortion in radically different terms. In the early 1980s, Jackson had launched a promising political career. Mounting a presidential campaign against the incumbent, Ronald Reagan, Jackson defended legal abortion, describing it not as an issue of population control but as one of autonomy for women. As Jackson explained during a 1984 presidential debate: "My position is: I'm not for abortion. I'm for freedom of choice."[3]

Jackson's changing rhetoric forms part of the history of the relationship between the abortion-rights and women's movements. In the view of influential feminist legal scholars, *Roe v. Wade* weakened the ability of both movements to campaign effectively for the rights of the poor and women of color for whom Jackson spoke. Scholars and advocates such as Catharine MacKinnon, Rhonda Copelon, and Martha Minow have suggested that *Roe*'s privacy framework paved the way for laws and judicial decisions denying access to public facilities or funding for abortions, constraining "the emerging jurisprudence of privacy within a framework that produced inequalities."[4] Viewed in this way, *Roe* is supposed to have "undercut . . . arguments . . . for the rights of caretakers"[5] and served "to siphon off deeper challenges to our scientist, capitalist society."[6]

We often equate the abortion-rights movement too easily with the women's movement, assuming a strong and stable relationship between the two. For this reason, it is easy to believe that *Roe v. Wade* exacerbated tensions between the women's movement and people of color. To the extent that the *Roe* Court talked about women, the justices focused on privacy from the State. In defending the decision, then, feminists supposedly deemphasized the needs of poor, often non-white women, privileging freedom over government support.[7]

However, by not adequately capturing movement redefinitions of *Roe*, scholars have often oversimplified the relationship between feminism and abortion-rights activism. Before the decision came down, pragmatists within the abortion-rights movement played a dominant role in defining the movement's message, identity, and agenda. Some movement members embraced the women's movement and its substantive agenda. Other activists—many of whom had connections to the medical community or to the movement for population control—advanced the arguments thought most likely to succeed in court or in the political arena. In either case, instead of linking abortion to rights for women, leading advocates primarily described the procedure as a means to an end: the prevention of deaths suffered during dangerous illegal abortions or the reduction of domestic population growth.

In the mid-1970s, however, feminists gradually made *Roe* a symbol of the relationship between the abortion-rights and women's movements. Far from constraining feminists, the Supreme Court's decision helped them to renegotiate the racial and gender politics of abortion. Beginning in the later 1960s, diverse supporters of abortion rights contested the meaning of legal abortion and its relationship to race and sex equality. The Supreme Court did not dictate the terms of this battle. In part, abortion-rights leaders responded to the changing politics of civil rights in the late 1960s and early 1970s—the rise of the black-power movement, the mobilization of feminists of color, and growing controversy about population control. As pro-lifers championed bans on abortion funding, feminists could more easily present the opposition as indifferent to the well-being of poor and non-white women.

Nonetheless, feminist activists deliberately used the Supreme Court decision to gain the upper hand in internal struggles. Projecting new meaning onto the Court's decision, feminists convincingly argued that legal abortion reflected the importance of equality on the basis of race and sex. As the abortion-rights and women's movements grew closer, activists redefined their cause and its relationship to racial justice.

Population Control Reshapes the Racial Politics of Abortion

In 1973 when the Supreme Court decided *Roe v. Wade,* the racial politics of abortion had come to a crossroads. Earlier, abortion opponents had played on racial and racialist biases in limiting access to the procedure. In the later nineteenth century, physicians and anti-vice crusaders had connected legal abortion to fears of a growing immigrant population, describing abortion as a symptom of the immorality of the foreign-born.[8]

While not coming out in favor of abortion, some birth controllers also drew on racist beliefs in the early twentieth century. Eugenic legal reformers spoke to concerns about the genetic stock of racial minorities, immigrants, and the poor. Later, after scientists discredited once-popular eugenic theories, a race-specific narrative about unwed motherhood shaped policy on illegitimacy, welfare, and sterilization from the 1940s to the 1970s. Believing that "unfit" women could not make wise reproductive decisions, segregationists, conservatives, and traditionalists favored "permanent" solutions, such as the nominally voluntary sterilizations championed by groups like the Association for Voluntary Sterilization (AVS). Often mobilizing in the 1940s and 1950s, first-generation population controllers generally focused on contraception and sterilization, leaving aside the abortion question.[9]

By the late 1960s, as the abortion issue came to the fore, the abortion-rights and pro-life movements found themselves immersed in a new racial politics. Influential population controllers began endorsing abortion as a tool for curbing birth rates. At the same time, the population-control movement enjoyed unprecedented popular support, public funding, and congressional influence. The basis for an alliance between population controllers and abortion-rights leaders fell into place.

Some movement members, including prominent feminists, found value in the demands for sexual freedom and environmental steward-ship often articulated by younger population controllers. More often, abortion-rights leaders wanted to draw on the popularity of popula-tion control in building support for their own cause. In turn, some population controllers believed that legal abortion would help defuse a pending demographic crisis.

However, the alliance with population controllers heightened the racial tensions surrounding abortion. Often for strategic reasons, sup-porters of abortion rights emphasized the policy benefits of legalizing abortion, including lower welfare expenses, a downturn in the num-ber of illegitimate births, and a slower pace of population growth. These arguments understandably concerned civil-rights leaders, who believed that the abortion-rights movement had effectively promised a decrease in the number of minority children born in the United States.

Conversely, with civil-rights politics in flux, pro-lifers found new opportunities to appeal to racial minorities. Black nationalism had deep roots in civil-rights politics. But beginning in the late 1960s, the mainstream civil-rights movement took on a new identity, center-ing on a militant rejection of the racial status quo. Some prominent black-power activists took aim at the movement for abortion reform. Pointing to the rhetoric of population controllers, black-power ac-tivists questioned whether the white majority would use abortion to wipe out people of color. Pro-lifers fueled these fears, arguing that legal abortion would be a "'white man's' solution to the problems of poverty and race."[10]

For those seeking to make abortion-rights activism synonymous with feminism, the influence of population politics proved disturbing. Time and again, feminists—who played a crucial role in efforts to le-galize abortion—urged their colleagues to build a closer relationship with the women's movement. Treating abortion as a method of pop-ulation control seemed to grant women reproductive freedom only when doing so would benefit the larger society. Believing that women could not enjoy equal citizenship without fertility control, feminists argued instead that all women had a right to abortion irrespective of its consequences.

The battles of the pre-*Roe* period testify to the complexity of the rela-tionship between the movements for women's liberation and abortion rights. Before 1973, partly because of the ascendancy of population politics, that relationship remained fluid and less close than we might believe.

Nonetheless, it would be a mistake to draw too close a connection between abortion-rights activists and population controllers. Abortion reformers made a variety of arguments unrelated to out-of-control birth rates. For their part, population controllers rarely prioritized abortion, instead focusing on voluntary-sterilization initiatives, maternal-health programs, and domestic or international contraception measures. Some population groups never endorsed abortion reform.[11]

Before 1973, however, claims about population control, like contentions about public health, became a prominent part of the abortion-rights arsenal. Many of the older leaders of abortion-rights organizations had ties to the population controllers. Moreover, Congress viewed uncurbed demographic growth as a serious problem, and major donors like the Scaife Foundation made population control a priority. Leading figures in the movement, like Hugh Moore and John D. Rockefeller III, provided financial support to state-level campaigns to legalize abortion. Nor did abortion-legalization groups discount the political appeal of population arguments. Similar claims found favor with a broad spectrum of politicians, judges, and members of the public.[12]

In the late 1960s, as a new generation of population controllers rose to prominence, the movements to curb birth rates and legalize abortion grew closer than ever before. Earlier, in the 1940s and 1950s, the population-control movement had focused primarily on growth in what activists called "underdeveloped" countries in Asia, Africa, South America, and the Middle East. The first generation of population controllers prioritized research into new reproductive technologies. Some prominent groups, like the Association for Voluntary Sterilization and the Population Council, maintained ties to the eugenic reform movement. As late as 1962, Hugh Moore, who would soon become the AVS president, believed that the organization "favored legal sterilization of imbeciles and the like."[13] Similarly, a preliminary draft of the Population Council Charter set forth eugenic aims, particularly initiatives to reverse "a downward trend in the genetic quality of [the] population."[14]

Other population controllers focused on the international instability they believed could result from skyrocketing birthrates. Cold War hawks like Moore viewed uncurbed growth as a threat to American democracy—a potential tool for Communist operatives. In Moore's view, "population pressures [were] already contributing to the conditions that can lead to social unrest and war."[15] Other activists expressed genuine concern about the impact that unchecked growth could have on poor communities. Population controllers organized groups with deeply different objectives, tactics, and philosophies. While the Population Council prioritized research on better contraceptive methods, Moore's Population Crisis Committee (PCC), founded in 1963, worked primarily "to direct legislative action and influence in favor of more vigorous federal population programs."[16]

By the late 1960s, however, when some population controllers endorsed legal abortion, a new generation of activists linked their cause to the sexual revolution, the women's movement, and better environmental stewardship. Some demographic experts began to conclude that, as a *Chicago Tribune* column put it, "[t]he population explosion [was] largely a white middle class problem."[17] At a 1968 conference on world population held by Planned Parenthood (then called Planned Parenthood-World Population), commentators agreed that the "population problem in the United States [was] being caused by well-educated, middle-to-upper-income families, [who were] predominantly white."[18]

A prominent new group, Zero Population Growth, Inc. (ZPG), organized to combat the supposed sexual irresponsibility of the white middle class. Founded in 1968 by Stanford Professor Paul Ehrlich, Connecticut attorney Richard Bowers, and Cornell Professor Thomas Eisner, ZPG, alone among major population-control groups, campaigned heavily for legal abortion before 1973. The inspiration for the organization came many years before, when as a graduate student studying evolution and population dynamics, Ehrlich concluded that nothing was being done about ballooning birth rates in the developed world. He believed that overpopulation would harm human beings as much as it had the butterflies he studied. After taking a position at Stanford, he began speaking about the dangers of overpopulation, and this project led to the formation of ZPG.[19]

Initially, some ZPG hardliners remained convinced that voluntary contraception would not be enough to end the overpopulation crisis. However, its founders intended the group to have a broad, grassroots membership, focusing not so much on lobbying or research as on public education efforts designed to "get the word out that there were too many Americans."[20]

Unsurprisingly, younger ZPG recruits—often self-described environmentalists or feminists—had a different vision for their movement. In particular, these ZPG members favored only voluntary means of curbing population growth and viewing population control as a vehicle for environmental preservation, sexual liberation, and equality for women. Consider the example of Judith Senderowitz, a woman who went on to lead both the New York chapter of ZPG and the national organization. While pursuing graduate studies at Columbia University, she happened to see an advertisement for a two-dollar, semi-annual membership in ZPG. One of the first students to attend the group's inaugural meeting, she rose rapidly through the ranks of ZPG, becoming the chairperson of the New York City branch and, later, the head of the state-wide organization. In New York, Senderowitz shaped ZPG into an organization that favored abortion rights as well as measures to combat overpopulation.[21]

ZPG leaders described sexual liberation as an important benefit of curbing population growth. In his influential 1968 book *The Population Bomb*, Ehrlich had argued that controlling birth rates would allow Americans to free themselves from "a sexually repressed and repressive society."[22] Thomas Eisner, another ZPG founder, suggested that sterilization and other means of family planning represented "a lovely kind of solution that has given us a nice, relaxed attitude toward making love."[23]

ZPG pamphlets and advertising materials also praised the sexual revolution while demanding personal responsibility. Particularly on college campuses, slogans like "Love . . . Carefully" and "Make Love, Not Babies" defined ZPG as a champion of sexual liberation. ZPG justified population control partly by seeking to disconnect sex from reproduction. At least for some ZPG members, legalizing abortion made sense as part of this broader agenda. As activists like Senderowitz concluded, sexually active, middle-class people should have all methods of fertility control, including abortion, at their disposal. Indeed, when the *Chicago Tribune* asked a group of concerned college students what would be "the first and most feasible step" that could be taken to curb overpopulation, many respondents identified legal abortion as a promising solution.[24]

ZPG leaders also believed that Americans could not save the environment unless birth rates dropped. Other population controllers had strategic reasons for linking their cause to environmentalism. For example, Hugh Moore used anxieties about pollution and urban sprawl to build youth support for population control, and he sponsored the first Earth Day celebration in 1970. By contrast, younger ZPG members sincerely worried that unchecked birth rates would lead to a future of declining resources and dangerous pollution. As a leader of New York ZPG explained, "It doesn't make any difference whether the family can support all those children or not. . . . [T]he food and water supply [will diminish]. And I hate to think about all that pollution."[25]

ZPG members—often younger, more progressive, and more activist—tended to be more involved in the movement to legalize abortion. In 1969 ZPG co-founder Richard Bowers took a leading role in the National Association for the Repeal of Abortion Laws (NARAL), presenting legal abortion as a crucial step in the control of birth rates. State-level ZPG affiliates also participated in pro-repeal rallies in Connecticut and Illinois and worked as part of the national pro-repeal effort.[26]

However, as Judith Senderowitz still recalls, ZPG remained divided about the abortion issue after she became the president of the national organization in the early 1970s. The disagreement about abortion did not turn on whether it should be legal, a subject on which virtually everyone agreed. Instead, ZPG board members held conflicting views about whether women's abortion rights should be viewed as a population issue or as a priority for the organization. While feminist members described rights for women as an integral part of their cause, older leaders did not see the connection between recognizing a right to abortion, expanding autonomy for women, and reducing population growth. These disagreements tended to break down along generational lines. As Senderowitz and Ehrlich recall, older members of ZPG—generally, professors, environmentalists, and biologists—took one side, while younger, more activist members took the other.[27]

Inside and outside of ZPG, more and more population controllers began to view legal abortion as an indispensable reform. Hugh Moore had a close relationship with Larry Lader, a former member of the Population Crisis Committee, and Moore provided substantial financial support to organizations like NARAL. John D. Rockefeller III, the leader of the research-oriented Population Council, also made significant donations to NARAL and other pro-reform groups. In 1970 Richard Nixon appointed Rockefeller to lead a new commission on population policy. In early 1972, with the release of The Report of the Commission on Population Control and the American

Future, reporters highlighted the commission's call for the repeal of all criminal abortion laws.[28]

Generally, however, support for legal abortion defined a younger, more environmentalist wing of the population-control movement. Even within groups like the Population Council, younger, often female members were more likely to endorse legal abortion. For example, at the July 1971 Women's National Conference on Abortion, Emily Campbell Moore of the Council spoke up on the best strategy for abortion reform. At the conference, feminists stressed the importance of sex equality and gay rights. Moore called such arguments strategically "counterproductive." She believed that population rhetoric would remove obstacles to abortion reform. "We have to be single-minded," Moore asserted. "We have to go before gray-haired legislators all over this country."[29]

Protecting the environment appealed to some members of organizations like NARAL, the Planned Parenthood Federation of America (Planned Parenthood), or the National Organization for Women (NOW), as did calls to end sexual oppression. Groups like NARAL and ZPG shared members and even leaders. As importantly, abortion reformers hoped to draw on the popularity of population control. Population policies promised something to a broad variety of constituencies: eugenics supporters and feminists, environmentalists and fiscal conservatives, anti-communists, sexual liberationists, and those concerned with humanitarian aid. In June 1969, when Nixon was considering the creation of a population commission, bipartisan support grew for a bill establishing a National Center for Population and Family Planning in the Department of Health, Education, and Welfare. The bill won the support of twenty-three senators and sixty representatives from both major parties, including Representatives George H. W. Bush (R-TX) and James Scheuer (D-NY). Voters' concerns about the issue seemed to match those of leading politicians. A 1972 poll found that 65 percent of respondents agreed that rising birthrates were a serious problem, and more than half felt that population growth was forcing the nation to exhaust its natural resources. If legalizing abortion fit within this broader program, the abortion-rights cause would appear more mainstream, less controversial, and more likely to succeed.[30]

Abortion-rights groups often adopted population-control arguments as an alternative to those involving liberty and equality for women. Some supporters of abortion rights had no independent interest in the women's movement or its demands. Many other activists, however, sympathized with or even focused on the struggle for women's liberation. For movement pragmatists, however, women's-rights claims seemed risky. In the early 1970s the women's movement remained poorly understood and, in some cases, unpopular. For example, the 1971 Virginia Slims American Women's Opinion Poll found that only 42 percent of respondents favored a movement to "strengthen or change women's status in society." Moreover, the women's movement pushed not only for abortion but also for equal employment, changes in the portrayal of women in the media, and publicly funded child care. Invoking women's liberation appeared likely to create the kind of controversy the movement could ill afford.[31]

Just the same, overpopulation rhetoric made the politics of abortion more racially charged. Civil-rights activists took issue with some population controllers' ties to segregationists or eugenic legal reformers. The focus of international overpopulation and domestic family planning programs—many of which applied primarily to poor, non-white individuals—caused further alarm. When New York repealed its abortion laws, a disproportionate number of African-American women sought out the procedure, reinforcing arguments that abortion would decimate non-white populations.[32]

For this reason, some abortion-rights activists took a strong stand against their movement's emphasis on population control. Some feminists found such claims objectionable in principle. Still other activists worried that population-control claims would alienate people of color, especially given past connections between supporters of eugenics and some population-control programs. Before 1973, because of these conflicts, the members of leading abortion-rights organizations sometimes found themselves deeply at odds with one another.

Abortion-Rights Organizations Use Population Politics to Build Support for Change

In the late 1960s, when its members first considered an endorsement of legal abortion, Planned Parenthood played a central part in the population-control movement. In 1942 Planned Parenthood had succeeded Margaret Sanger's earlier organization, the American Birth Control Federation. In 1952, Hugh Moore helped to fund International Planned Parenthood Federation (IPPF), the international arm of Planned Parenthood, and Sanger served as the organization's first leader. Moore also formed the World Population Emergency Campaign, a source of financial support for Planned Parenthood that joined with the latter organization in 1961 to become Planned Parenthood-World Population (PP-WP). In the 1960s, PP-WP set its sights on foreign aid programs, seeking federal support for cheaper contraceptives, easier access, and incentives that would encourage the use of birth control. The organization worked closely with the Population Council, the United Nations, and the Ford and Rockefeller Foundations, presenting voluntary family planning and population control as essentially the same thing.[33]

The move to legalize abortion formed one part of PP-WP's domestic agenda. Since 1965, Planned Parenthood workers provided birth control services in poor neighborhoods, often working under the auspices of the Office of Economic Opportunity. Earlier in the twentieth century, Sanger had consistently worked to separate birth control and abortion, presenting the former as a way to prevent the evils of the latter. By the late 1960s, however, organization leaders reconsidered this position. Prominent members of the organization, including Dr. Alan Guttmacher, worked with the Association for the Study of Abortion (ASA), a group that had led the call for abortion reform. Mary S. Calderone, a leading Planned Parenthood member and sex educator, argued that illegal abortion had created a major public health crisis. Citing "the cold shoulders" women confronted when seeking an abortion, she criticized "the social ostracism and punitive attitude toward those who are greatly in need of concrete help and sympathetic understanding."[34] Feminist-leaning members, including Harriet Pilpel, asserted that "in order to insure a complete and thorough birth control program, abortion must be made available as a legal right to all women who request it."[35]

At a 1968 meeting, 650 representatives of Planned Parenthood affiliates across the nation endorsed the repeal of all abortion restrictions. The organization's medical advisory committee had initially presented abortion as a matter of women's rights, suggesting that every woman had "the right and responsibility" to "decide when and whether to have a child." Later, however, the group's 100-member board of directors stressed that the physician, more than the woman, should have the final say, taking into account the woman's "social, economic, and cultural environment."[36] When Planned Parenthood issued its final statement, the organization presented abortion primarily as a "medical procedure." While insisting that abortion constituted a "right for every patient," the statement mostly stayed away from feminist rhetoric.[37]

The racial politics of the Planned Parenthood endorsement proved to be tricky, particularly given the organization's ties to the population-control movement. Planned Parenthood made its announcement in the wake of comments by a Pittsburgh branch of the National Association for the Advancement of Colored Persons (NAACP), suggesting that abortion reformers intended "to keep the Negro birth rate as low as possible." At the 1968 meeting, to counter accusations of racism, the group selected Dr. Jerome Holland, an African-American sociologist, as its new chairman. Holland insisted that anyone drawing a close connection between racism and abortion repeal was "not aware of the real meaning of family planning and its uses."[38]

In spite of emerging concerns about "black genocide," the influence, funding, and popularity of the population-control movement proved alluring to Planned Parenthood leaders working for abortion rights. Dr. Alan Guttmacher, the leader of PP-WP from 1962 until his death in 1974, had ties to the population movement. Guttmacher had served as the vice president of the American Eugenics Society and held leadership positions at AVS. A practicing obstetrician-gynecologist, Guttmacher viewed abortion as an urgent public health issue, and he believed that women had a right to abortion.[39]

He nonetheless encouraged PP-WP to use what many saw as uncontroversial arguments that would reach the largest number of potential supporters. In 1970, for example, Guttmacher attributed the movement's recent success in New York and Hawaii to "the realization of the population problem." "We're now concerned more with quality of population than with the quantity," he said in commenting on the two repeal laws.[40]

Consequence-based claims also figured centrally in the organization's campaign to preserve legal abortion in New York. In defending the repeal of all abortion restrictions, Robin Elliott, Planned Parenthood's Director of Information and Education, primarily stressed arguments that he thought would work the best. He put out materials claiming that illegal abortion posed an intolerable risk to women's health. Other pamphlets prominently displayed images of women who had died because of botched operations. Elliott's brochures contended that legal abortion had resulted in lower rates of child abuse and illegitimacy and lower welfare costs.[41]

Even those interested in abortion as a matter of women's rights used population rhetoric to further their cause. One particularly telling incident involved Dorothy Millstone, a feminist member of PP-WP and member of the Socialist Party. As Elliott still recalls, Millstone had hoped to introduce a "Population Education" program in public schools. Since she had little interest in the population-control cause, Elliott expressed surprise when told of her plan. Millstone retorted that she was simply teaching about what interested her—sex education, contraception, and access to abortion—in a way that the schools would accept.[42]

In the early 1970s, population-control arguments also redefined NARAL's agenda. NARAL emerged as the result of activists' frustrations with the unpredictability and unfairness of the reform laws on the books in states like California and Colorado. At a meeting in February 1969, 300 representatives formed a single-issue organization committed to the repeal of all restrictions on abortion. NARAL's founding members included feminists, civil libertarians, doctors, public health advocates, and population controllers who agreed that, in the words of the organization's first resolution, "the abortion decision should be made without all legal encumbrances, so that women and physicians are able to exercise their best judgments."[43]

A group of self-identified radicals believed that NARAL should model itself on the civil- rights movement, prioritizing direct action protest. A leader of the radicals, Larry Lader, had begun writing on family planning during his career as a freelance magazine contributor. By the time he published a book on abortion in 1966, he had become a central figure in the abortion-legalization movement. A colleague still remembers Lader as being exceedingly polite, hardly the prototypical angry activist. The same advocate recalls that no one questioned Lader's commitment. As she remembers: "Abortion was his life."[44] Lader's closest ally among the radicals, Betty Friedan, had arguably become the most famous feminist in the nation, the author of *The Feminine Mystique*, and a living symbol of women's liberation.[45]

A second faction, led by Lonny Myers, an Illinois activist and anesthesiologist, believed that NARAL should focus on repeal bills in state legislatures. In particular, the two sides clashed about whether NARAL should endorse abortion referral services or conduct protests. Myers and her allies insisted that NARAL could not afford to appear too radical. Myers joined Ruth Proskauer Smith, the former executive director of AVS and a Planned Parenthood leader, and New

York lobbyist Ruth Cusack in insisting that protests mattered less than lobbying influential policymakers.[46]

The compromise reached on September 27, 1969 committed NARAL to both lobbying and grassroots protest. The organization struck this balance by encouraging other groups—student groups, women's liberation organizations, or conservation groups—to conduct protests for which NARAL would have no formal responsibility. At the same time, by establishing itself as reasonable and respectable, NARAL would lobby for repeal bills, educate the public, and secure the support of prominent donors and supporters.

Over time, the September 1969 compromise would create a rift among the radicals who came to lead NARAL. Lader's former ally, Betty Friedan, led a group of NARAL members committed to arguments presenting abortion as a woman's right. Lader broke with Friedan to lead a second group concerned about the tactical disadvantages of women's-rights arguments. NARAL, in Lader's view, had to find a way to win.[47]

In particular, Lader and other NARAL pragmatists called for a greater emphasis on population control. The subject first came up for discussion that September when feminist Lucinda Cisler proposed a resolution redefining the organization's mission. She insisted that NARAL would achieve its goals much sooner if it described abortion as something that "Planned Parenthood, the Association for Voluntary Sterilization, and ZPG could all support."[48] Cisler argued that NARAL should endorse access to sterilization and birth control as well as abortion—part of an effort to "appeal to groups concerned about population and conservation," groups she counted as "important potential allies."[49] On September 27, 1969, the NARAL Board of Directors defined their cause using the language Cisler had suggested, calling for "all public hospitals [to] offer contraception, sterilization, and abortion to anyone requesting these services."[50]

By January 1970, NARAL leaders began to clash about whether to prioritize arguments about women's rights or population control. Betty Friedan and Carol Greitzer, a feminist city councilor from New York City, encouraged their colleagues to link NARAL's cause more closely to the women's movement. Friedan and Greitzer rejected a proposed title for NARAL's 1970 protest event, "Children by Choice," "because of its population implications."[51]

As an alternative, Friedan and Greitzer promised to identify support among women's groups for the proposed protest. ZPG leader and NARAL Executive Committee member Richard Bowers responded that "NARAL should see that [abortion] repeal is closely tied in with the growing ecology movement."[52] Bowers continued his fight through February, at least temporarily convincing Friedan that NARAL should emphasize population-control arguments.[53]

The following September, however, feminists again objected to NARAL's emphasis on population control. At a meeting of the organization's board of directors, Friedan proposed a resolution stating that "NARAL should support political groups working toward the basic purpose of the right of a woman to decide whether or not to have children." At a meeting of the group's board of directors, the motion died for lack of a second. In response, Lader proposed a resolution stating: "to prevent increasing overpopulation, American parents in general . . . should adopt as a social and family ideal the principle of the two-child family." The board of directors voted twenty-six to eighteen to table the motion. Greitzer led the charge against the resolution, arguing that too close a relationship with population controllers could "hurt [NARAL's] position with legislatures."[54]

Notwithstanding Greitzer's concerns, NARAL increasingly joined forces with population controllers. In the early 1970s, NARAL, Planned Parenthood, and Zero Population Growth held joint media strategy sessions and campaigned together for legal abortion in Washington State and Colorado. In 1971, NARAL Executive Director Lee Gidding urged the Rockefeller Commission on Population and the American Future to recognize "abortion as an essential method of birth control," and in 1972, the NARAL Executive Committee passed a resolution calling for an increase in federal funding for population research.[55]

Moreover, in the early 1970s, NARAL often stressed that abortion would put a stop to spiraling birth rates. Certainly, NARAL connected abortion to constitutional privacy and equality for women. However, the organization's official debate handbook included a whole category of arguments related to overpopulation. When pro-lifers argued that legal abortion would have prevented the birth of many talented Americans, the handbook emphasized that with legal abortion, "possibly Hitler wouldn't have been born either." NARAL's debate handbook highlighted that "[l]egal abortion [would] decrease the number of unwanted children, battered children, child abuse cases, and possibly subsequent delinquency, drug addiction, and a host of social ills," as well as ensuring "a reduction in welfare rolls." "Since contraception alone seems insufficient to reduce fertility to the point of no-growth," the debate handbook explained, "we should permit all voluntary means of birth control (including abortion)."[56]

Why did NARAL decide to downplay women's-rights claims? Possibly, abortion-rights proponents anticipated that a backlash would follow if the courts or legislatures adopted what then might have appeared to be a radically egalitarian, feminist framing of the abortion issue. There is little in the archival record to support this theory. Some members of the abortion-rights coalition did worry about trying to accomplish too much too soon, but these anxieties surrounded the question of whether restrictions should be modified or repealed outright. As late as 1969, Alan Guttmacher and Planned Parenthood still worried about the repercussions of moving too fast toward total repeal of restrictions on abortion.[57]

For the most part, those seeking to de-emphasize women's rights claims seemed less concerned about backlash than they were about identifying the fastest path to victory. Within NARAL, for example, Lucinda Cisler recorded the reasons for the organization's rejection of women's-rights resolutions. In her notes, Cisler suggested that more pragmatic claims would make the organization seem moderate, practical, and responsible. She also drew attention to the alliances with population control or physicians' groups that might be available if the organization framed abortion in the right way. To some activists, downplaying women's-rights claims appeared to maximize the movement's chances of winning in state legislatures, the media, and even in court.[58]

By 1973, even Friedan's National Organization for Women (NOW) had formed a partnership with population controllers. In 1966 during the annual national conference of the State Commissions on the Status of Women, leading feminists organized NOW in order to "bring women into full participation in the mainstream of American society now."[59] At its founding, NOW was small enough, in the words of one of its members, to "fit in someone's living room."[60] From the beginning, NOW aspired to create a pragmatic women's organization focused on law reform. For example, its original task forces took on the issues of sex stereotypes in employment, education, the media, and politics while addressing the interplay of race, poverty, and sex biases that made women victims of "double discrimination."[61]

On November 18–19, 1967, NOW leaders met to decide whether the organization should endorse abortion rights. Some members worried that a pro-repeal position would make the organization seem too radical. One attendee wondered aloud about whether "[p]eople [would] not join" if NOW endorsed abortion. This prompted a debate about whether or not abortion, as a method of population control, advanced a racist agenda. One member asserted that "Negro women are forced to get abortions so they will not lose their welfare checks."[62]

But did abortion rights fit within NOW's core program? Some present asserted that "Catholic members of NOW [would] quit" if the organization came out in favor of abortion rights. Prominent feminist Marguerite Rawalt hesitated to support a proposed resolution favoring abortion rights, believing that members had the organization's "newspaper image to think of." Future NOW president Wilma Scott Heide saw the abortion issue as largely unrelated to NOW's priorities, asserting: "We want social change—this is institutional change." Those who supported a proposed resolution on abortion rights felt equally strongly, suggesting that it spelled out a necessary component of the sexual revolution. As one member insisted: "So far, not a thought has been given to women, who are the most concerned on the question of abortion."[63]

A sizeable faction pushed for a compromise resolution, one calling only for "the reappraisal of existing abortion laws." Several members, including Friedan, opposed the new proposal, insisting that the "question of abortion can only be answered yes or no." Finally, after hours of debate, the board voted for the endorsement, fifty-seven to fourteen. Several of those opposed to the measure left the organization, founding the Women's Equity Action League (WEAL), a group focused only on employment and education.[64]

After the vote, between 1967 and 1970 NOW advanced the kind of women's-rights arguments made by pioneering California feminists Lana Clarke Phelan and Pat Maginnis, both of whom served for a time on the NOW Abortion Committee. As Friedan elaborated in a speech given at the 1969 NOW National Convention, NOW described abortion not as a medical matter directed by physicians but rather as a "civil right for women," a decision that women should make free from the control of either doctors or the government.[65] As she explained: "there is no freedom, no equality, no full human dignity and personhood possible for women until they . . . demand . . . control over their own reproductive process."[66]

When Pittsburgh native Wilma Scott Heide, a nursing professor, became the president of NOW in 1970, population-control arguments played a more vital part in the organization's advocacy. A leading figure in a NOW Pennsylvania affiliate, Heide joined the women's movement while her husband served as the president of an extension campus of Penn State University. She later challenged sex-segregated want ads, litigated to force United Airlines to hire older women as flight attendants, and worked for the ratification of the Equal Rights Amendment in Pennsylvania. She also adopted population-control rhetoric in arguing for the legalization of abortion and the guarantee of women's rights.[67]

Heide turned to population-control arguments in November 1970, when Christopher Tietze, the Associate Director of the Population Council's Biomedical Division, asked NOW members to participate in a study on the effects of abortion on women's health. In writing to the leaders of NOW state affiliates, Heide recommended a partnership with population controllers, suggesting that "[t]he request from the Population Council represents the fact [that] we are viewed as responsible and stable."[68] Heide also spoke on behalf of NOW before the Rockefeller Commission and asserted that women's rights and overpopulation were inextricably linked. As Heide later explained to a colleague at ZPG: "[U]nless girls and women [have] . . . alternatives to motherhood as their chief adult occupation, women [will] continue to value and be valued for their reproductive capacity more highly than their productive ability to be leaders . . . in our public life."[69]

NOW's use of population-control rhetoric did create controversy within the organization. When Heide solicited feedback about working with the Population Council, the leaders of a plurality of state affiliates opposed the move. Within a few years, however, NOW had created a working relationship with population organizations. By early 1971, NOW's national conference featured programs on "population control and reproduction control." Before 1973, over the strong objection of some members, NOW established strong relationships with organizations like ZPG and the Ford Foundation.[70]

As NOW's experience suggests, before 1973, abortion-rights leaders often justified abortion as a means to many ends, including population control. Even in the amicus briefs submitted in *Roe* by Planned Parenthood, NOW, and NARAL, such consequence-based arguments played an important part. Why legalize abortion? The social costs of unwanted children, leading organizations stressed, provided one compelling justification. In particular, citing a study published in Sweden on the social problems caused by unwanted children, several amicus briefs argued that unplanned births had a "direct cost in alcoholism, crime, and welfare."[71]

In the mid-1970s, feminists strengthened the relationship between the abortion-rights and women's movements. The Court's *Roe* decision did not determine the actions taken by feminists or limit the decisions available to them; far from it. In part, feminists reacted to the changing politics of civil rights and population control in the mid-1970s.

Controversy about forced sterilization at home and abroad brought population controllers under scrutiny. With so many scandals to address, population advocates felt it wise to distance themselves from the abortion controversy.

At the same time, pro-lifers worked harder than ever to stoke fears of abortion as a means of "black genocide." The NRLC sought to cultivate a partnership with Reverend Jesse Jackson. Thea Rossi Barron, the Legislative Counsel and lobbyist for the NRLC, met with Jackson and sent a telegram he had drafted to every member of Congress, calling for a ban on federal funding for abortion. Abortion opponents worked to blur the distinction between abortion-rights activism, population control, and eugenics. Dr. Joseph Stanton, a leading pro-lifer, called John D. Rockefeller III of the Population Council "the Grandfather of Liberalized Abortion."[72] For some within the abortion-rights movement, the opposition's accusations offered another reason to downplay population-based claims for abortion.[73]

Moreover, in the mid-1970s, while working in a variety of civil-rights organizations, women of color began to speak out in favor of fertility control for women. These activists asserted that many non-white women required more than mere freedom from state interference. Gradually, feminists of color helped to bridge the gap between the abortion-rights and civil-rights movements, reinforcing the perception that legal abortion truly involved women's rights.[74]

Feminists also benefited from the Supreme Court decision itself. Drawing on the Court's authority, feminists insisted that the justices saw abortion as an indispensable tool for women seeking equal treatment. Later, as pro-lifers built momentum in state legislatures and the courts, feminists could more convincingly urge their colleagues to turn away from consequence-based arguments. Previously prominent arguments based on public health or population control had done little to stop the progress of the antiabortion movement. Feminists insisted that the movement needed fresh claims and new leadership. Moreover, as pro-lifers focused on restrictions that disproportionately affected low-income families, feminists could more easily present themselves as advocates for poor women of color. Feminists within the abortion-rights movement made *Roe* a symbol of women's need for fertility control. In the process, movement leaders began to present reproductive rights in a way that more women of color could respect.

Pro-Life Pressure and Civil Rights Politics Undercut the Appeal of Population Claims

Starting in the late 1960s and early 1970s, a new relationship between abortion-rights activism and women's liberation began to form in the crucible of American racial politics. At a 1966 rally in Mississippi, Stokely Carmichael of the Student Non-Violent Coordinating Committee (SNCC) called for a new era in civil-rights politics: "We been saying freedom for six years and we ain't got nothing. What we gonna start saying now is Black Power!"[75] To many, Carmichael's slogan announced a fresh start for civil-rights politics. SNCC and the Congress for Racial Equality (CORE) had played crucial roles in the civil-rights movement of the 1950s and early 1960s, leading freedom rides and efforts to register African-American voters during the Freedom Summer of 1964. By the late 1960s, however, these organizations joined an evolving black-power movement defined by a commitment to self-defense, community empowerment, economic self-sufficiency, interest in separatism and nationalism, and a new cultural politics. Established organizations like SNCC and CORE joined with new groups like the Black Panther Party to "harness the anger, frustration, and energy of black ghettos outside the South."[76]

In the North, black-power and civil-rights organizations formulated a new platform. In the South, groups like the Deacons for Defense and Justice made public demands for self-defense, defying local authorities and white supremacists. As Carmichael explained, black power involved "pride rather than a shame in blackness, and an attitude of brotherly, communal responsibility among all black people toward one another."[77]

While Carmichael's call to arms appeared to usher in a new era in racial politics, the black-power movement drew on deeply-rooted ideas about African-American separatism, nationalism, and self-defense that reached back to the mid-nineteenth century. Revived in the late nineteenth century by the African Methodist Church and in the 1920s by Marcus Garvey's *Negro World*, nationalist ideas gained adherents in the mid-1950s with the rapid expansion of the Nation of Islam. Nonetheless, in the late 1960s and early 1970s, leaders of the black-power movement brought these ideas more forcefully to the surface of American culture.[78]

The explosion of black-power politics in the mid- to late 1960s reflected frustration with entrenched white supremacy in both the North and South. Although Congress had passed the Civil Rights Act of 1964 and the Voting Rights Act of 1965, African-American migrants to the North still experienced persistent de facto segregation and limited opportunity. These setbacks prompted some civil-rights leaders to ask whether people of color "could achieve lasting improvements in their lives while continuing to ask for white liberal support and intervention" and while "remaining tied to the rhetoric of interracialism and nonviolent direct action."[79] Although Martin Luther King Jr. and other movement leaders questioned the value of violent rhetoric or separatism, even King drew on the ideas set forth by black-power activists, arguing: "We must not be ashamed of being black. We must believe with all our hearts that black is beautiful as any other color."[80]

Black-power politics gave new force to attacks on the movement for legal abortion. Leaders like H. Rap Brown of SNCC rejected abortion as "black genocide." Brown's critique resonated with some of those seeking to forge a distinctive African-American culture. Viewing small families and birth control as white values, some activists expressed skepticism about what they saw as the imposition of alien ideas about reproduction and sexuality. Worse, arguments linking overpopulation to crime, juvenile delinquency, and child abuse attributed the problems confronted by African-Americans to unwanted children rather than racial bias. As Jesse Jackson argued: "[p]oliticians argue for abortion largely because they do not want to spend the necessary money to feed, clothe and educate more people."[81] Finally, the black-genocide argument touched on fears within the African-American community about persistent white bias. "Back in the slavery days, black folks couldn't grow kids fast enough for white folks to harvest," explained prominent African-American comedian Dick Gregory in 1971. "Now that we've got a little taste of power, white folks want us to call a moratorium on having babies."[82]

Many African-Americans, particularly physicians and feminists, found black-genocide arguments utterly unconvincing. Dr. Jerome

Holland of Planned Parenthood emphasized that legalized abortion would prevent the unnecessary deaths of black mothers and babies. An African-American physician, Edward Keemer, worked with NARAL in a Michigan abortion test case pursued in 1971. Shirley Chisholm of NARAL called the black-genocide argument "male rhetoric, for male ears."[83] In the early 1970s, popular advice columns in the *Chicago Defender* advised African-American women about how and why to seek contraception or support the repeal of abortion bans. Yet many African-American women appeared afraid that abortion or even contraception would be used against them. For example, one Planned Parenthood worker reported: "Many Negro women have told us, 'There are two kinds of [birth control] pill—one for white women, and one for us . . . and the one for us causes sterilization."[84]

As pro-lifers stoked fears about the supposed connections between abortion, birth control, and racism, certain arguments made by groups like NARAL took on uncomfortable undertones. Following a disappointing televised debate with pro-lifers, Larry Lader urged his colleagues to bring attention to "horror of bringing a deformed child into the world with half a head, no arms, etc." or to "the tragedy of the unwanted child, possibly leading to the battered child and infanticide."[85] NARAL's official debate handbook also included claims attributing the problems of poverty, child abuse, overcrowding, and violence to overpopulation rather than to racial discrimination. Such arguments angered African-Americans already suspicious of the motives of abortion reformers and population controllers.[86]

The spread of abortion-reform statutes in the American South aggravated worries about racism in the abortion-rights movement. There might have been nothing inherently suspicious in these developments: in North Carolina and Georgia, for example, a small and inactive Catholic population, combined with a low amount of media attention, contributed to the easy passage of the laws. However, the promotion of abortion reform in the South came at a time when forced sterilization of women of color appeared epidemic in the region. As late as 1964, Mississippi legislators went so far as to propose a law requiring the forced sterilization of unwed mothers, a phenomenon noted and condemned by SNCC. African-American activists like Fanny Lou Hamer framed sterilization abuse as an expression of racial bias—and with some reason. In the Mississippi hospital that had forcibly sterilized Hamer, an estimated six out of ten women of color experienced the same trauma. If the South led the way in abortion reform, activists like Hamer found reason to worry.[87]

Moreover, in the late 1960s and 1970s, some population controllers, like Richard Bowers of ZPG and NARAL, justified coercive means of population control. This support for coercion seemed all the more troubling when the press reported on still more involuntary sterilizations performed in the South. In June 1973, in Montgomery, Alabama, two African-American girls, Minnie Lee Relf, aged twelve, and Mary Alice, aged fourteen, learned that they had been forcibly sterilized. Over a fifteen-month period, more than eighty other minors reported having suffered similar trauma. Adult women in North Carolina, South Carolina, Tennessee, Florida, and California—many of them non-white—came forward with stories of coerced sterilizations. If population controllers tolerated forced sterilization, rumors about coerced abortions seemed more credible.[88]

Population Controllers Distance Their Cause from Abortion Rights

White and non-white feminists recognized the costs of tying abortion to population control. If African-Americans viewed abortion reform as a tool to curb birth rates, feminists would struggle to win the trust of the civil rights movement. Moreover, women of color more often lacked access to reproductive health services—a problem only exacerbated by anxieties about race and population control.

The costs of tying legal abortion to lower birth rates increased in the later 1970s, when the very idea of population politics became more controversial. First, at the 1974 UN Conference on World Population in Bucharest, Hungary, leaders of developing countries accused the population-control movement of manipulating their citizens while ignoring the true cause of poverty in the developing world. News of compulsory sterilizations at home and in India convinced many that the population-control movement exploited the poor. These scandals made it seem too risky for population controllers to immerse themselves in the abortion battle of the mid- to late 1970s.[89]

After 1973 major organizations, including Hugh Moore's PCC and John D. Rockefeller III's Population Council, publicly endorsed legal abortion for the first time. Nonetheless, during the mid- to late 1970s, population organizations generally kept out of domestic abortion politics. In the mid-1970s, women like then-executive director of the PCC, Phyllis Piotrow, came to play a more pivotal role in the internal workings of the PCC. Piotrow, who had strong interests in international development and family planning, did not strongly identify with the women's movement or its demands for reproductive rights. By contrast, her protégée, Sharon Camp, had sought out an illegal abortion in Mexico during her senior year in college, nearly dying due to complications from the procedure. This experience crystallized Camp's interest in reproductive issues.[90]

When Camp began working for the PCC in the mid-1970s, she helped Piotrow to make women's-rights claims a more central part of demands for international family planning funding. For example, in 1977, when Jimmy Carter announced his opposition to Medicaid funding for abortion, Piotrow spoke out against the decision, describing abortion as a "human right."[91]

However, Piotrow and Camp agreed that the population-control movement could not afford to be on the front lines of the abortion wars. Instead, for the PCC, opposition to abortion became a convenient argument for family planning funding. In July 1976, the group released a report indicating that thirty to fifty-five million babies were aborted each year. Marilyn Brant Chandler, a member of the PCC Board of Directors, argued in the *New York Times*: "So let the issues in the United States be expanded family planning delivery systems and better and earlier family-life education in the schools and homes, not abortion."[92]

The Population Council also endorsed legal abortion after 1973. In the mid-1970s, Council leader John D. Rockefeller III also stepped up his funding of the abortion-rights cause, helping to finance the creation of a NARAL office in Washington, DC, the activities of the ACLU Reproductive Rights Project, and the establishment of the Religious Coalition for Abortion Rights.[93]

Nonetheless, as the American Life Lobby and other antiabortion groups mounted a fierce attack on family planning, the Council mostly kept out of the abortion conflict. Thus, when Christopher Tietze began a 1975 study on the rate of legal abortions and abortion-related deaths, the Council no longer sponsored his research, and he instead pursued funding from Planned Parenthood's Guttmacher Institute. Beginning in 1974, the Council worked primarily on research into or advocacy for access to oral contraceptives or other "alternatives" to abortion.[94]

Similarly, as population arguments stopped playing a central role in the abortion debate, ZPG focused less on the issue. For some time, ZPG members had disagreed about the relevance of abortion to their cause. After 1973, new concerns became more salient for ZPG, including recent waves of immigration from Mexico to California and other border states. In 1978, the *Chicago Tribune* reported that the ZPG's goals were "immigration reform, expansion of women's opportunities, continued emphasis on family planning, and perhaps an explicit national policy on population." Abortion did not make the list.[95]

For population-control organizations, the Supreme Court's decision represented something of a turning point. By legitimating abortion, the Court had strengthened the position of those in the movement who favored endorsing the procedure. Nonetheless, as the abortion conflict intensified, population controllers mostly stayed out of abortion politics, having their hands full with the growing controversy about sterilization abuse and coercive family planning in the Third World.

Feminists seeking to redefine the relationship between the abortion-rights and women's movements also responded to further changes to the landscape of civil-rights politics, as a powerful group of non-white feminists expanded their influence in the mid-1970s. These feminists of color helped to persuade colleagues in civil-rights organizations that abortion would advance both race and sex equality.

Some African-American and Chicana feminists viewed the mainstream women's movement with skepticism in the late 1960s and early 1970s. For many non-white feminists, the mainstream women's movement appeared too oblivious to the intersection of race, sex, and class discrimination, too indifferent to economic change, and too focused on changing the nuclear family at a time when many African-American families felt under attack. Fannie Lou Hamer voiced a widely shared skepticism about white feminists' willingness to understand the "special plight" that women of color had confronted for centuries. As Hamer said to white feminists at a 1971 speech at the NAACP Legal Defense Fund Institute, "[y]ou thought you *was* more because you was a white woman."[96]

At the same time, non-white feminists began to recognize that black-power organizations often replicated the gender hierarchies visible in the larger society. Black-power author Nathan Hare articulated the common view that "the black woman is, and can be, the black man's helper, an undying collaborator" who would bear and raise children.[97] Elaine Brown, a future chairwoman of the Black Panther Party, recalled that women shouldered a disproportionate share of kitchen work and had to wait for the men before they could eat.[98]

Experiences like Brown's convinced women within the civil-rights movement of the need to combat both race and sex discrimination, particularly when it came to access to reproductive health care. With the publication of works like Frances Beal's *Double Jeopardy: To Be Black and Female* (1969) and Florynce Kennedy's *Abortion Rap* (1971), African-American feminists condemned the population movement while insisting that women of color had a right to control their fertility. For example, Beal condemned population control as "the use of the black woman as a medical testing ground for the white middle class." At the same time, Beal presented "rigid abortion laws" as "another vicious means of subjugation and . . . outright murder" of poor women of color.[99] Before 1973, Beal formed a separate organization within SNCC that ultimately became the Third World Women's Alliance, a group focused on the rights and reproductive health of non-white women.[100]

After 1973, though, African-American feminists organized to an unprecedented extent. In 1973, following a meeting on "Black Women and Their Relationship to the Women's Movement," activists formed the National Black Feminist Organization (NBFO), members of which campaigned for legal abortion and a condemnation of sterilization abuse. In 1975 Barbara Smith formed the Combahee River Collective, a Boston-based organization that combined demands for legal abortion with criticism of sterilization abuse and calls for general improvements to the health care available to women of color. Organizations like Combahee and the NBFO convinced many of their male colleagues to reject the black-genocide narrative.[101]

Moreover, in the mid-1970s, feminists threw pro-lifers' accusations about racism back at them, charging the opposition with victimizing the poor. During the trial of Dr. Kenneth Edelin, the defendant presented himself as a champion of reproductive health for minority women often denied adequate care. Planned Parenthood and NARAL used the *Edelin* case to foreground the importance of legal abortion, the specter of racial bias in the pro-life movement, and the need for better health care access for poor women. Members of Combahee and the NBFO took a central part in protesting Edelin's conviction.[102]

In the mid-1970s, pro-life emphasis on funding bans also lent credibility to feminists' arguments that all women, and particularly minority women, needed abortion rights. A NOW lobbying campaign against the Hyde Amendment presented the law as "an effort that would, in effect, deny low-income women the right to abortion."[103] Organizations representing women of color and mainstream groups also mourned the death of Rosie Jimenez, a Chicana woman who died during an illegal abortion after Medicaid funding for the procedure ended. In 1977 Planned Parenthood and other mainstream groups held a joint rally to protest Jimenez's death and the Hyde Amendment. As Elisa Sanchez of the Mexican-American Women's National Association explained at the rally: "Though we may not make the choice of abortion for ourselves, surely we cannot argue that a woman must forfeit the right to that choice by circumstance of poverty."[104] With the success of the Hyde Amendment and the rise of Faye Wattleton to the Presidency of Planned Parenthood, the organization officially prioritized an effort "to restore to the poor access to safe, legal abortion."[105]

When abortion became less heavily associated with population control, feminists of color had an easier time bringing their male colleagues into the movement for reproductive rights. In 1975, the Black Panther Party, one of the organizations that had expressed the most concern about black genocide, endorsed abortion rights. The Panthers joined protests of Dr. Edelin's conviction. In 1977, in the wake of the passage of the Hyde Amendment, the Panthers went so far as to argue that "Black and poor women on welfare [would] suffer most" from the new restrictions.[106]

Feminists Use the *Roe* Decision to Remake the Identity of the Abortion-Rights Movement

While drawing on the changing politics of population control and civil rights, abortion-rights feminists also used the Supreme Court's decision to remake their movement's identity. At first, many movement members generally presented *Roe* as an opinion involving physicians' rights. Nonetheless, for a minority of feminists in the movement, *Roe* served as a signal of the Supreme Court's recognition that women had a right to control their own bodies. In reality, the Supreme Court had not framed abortion in the way feminists described, instead emphasizing physicians' interest in practicing medicine as they saw fit.

Nonetheless, in the mid-1970s, feminists reinterpreted *Roe* as a sign that the courts backed women's reproductive autonomy. Over time, feminists used this understanding of the Court's decision to create a different identity for the abortion-rights movement.

This use of *Roe* proved valuable to Planned Parenthood members ambivalent about the population-control movement or committed to the cause of the women's movement. Robin Elliott, then the director of information and education at Planned Parenthood, realized the risks involved in making population-control arguments. In October 1973 at a strategy meeting in Denver, Colorado, he encouraged the organization to redefine its cause.

In a confidential memorandum, Elliott suggested that antiabortion activists had successfully called into "question . . . Planned Parenthood's credibility in its reference to the population problem." Those present at the conference saw Planned Parenthood's support for population control as a liability, because pro-life organizers had successfully "sought to exploit to their own advantages the fears of minorities." Elliott suggested that his colleagues adopt a new strategy involving "the reaffirmation of the commitment to freedom of choice in parenthood."[107]

For several reasons, however, the organization did not stress women's-rights arguments until later in the decade. First, many members of the organization believed that the Court's decision had put an end to any meaningful debate about abortion. To the extent that the organization addressed abortion in 1974–1975, leaders tended to focus on convincing often-reluctant affiliates to offer the procedure. For the most part, the organization's new leader, Jack Hood Vaughn, a former head of the Peace Corps, and later, Ambassador to Colombia, focused on the backlash to family planning funding in the developing world.[108]

However, with the intensification of pro-life efforts in Congress, feminists in Planned Parenthood argued effectively that more needed to be done to preserve abortion rights. This shift began in 1975, at the start of a battle about the Hyde Amendment and the scope of funding restrictions on abortion. Abortion-rights lobbyists began emphasizing the harm that the Hyde Amendment and the larger antiabortion movement would do to poor and often non-white women. Given the charges of racism leveled against the population-control movement, arguments related to it seemed particularly inappropriate in debate about abortion funding. Even Vaughn described proposed abortion restrictions as a "travesty of equal rights" for women.[109]

Planned Parenthood sponsored a similar approach during Abortion Rights Strategy '77, a conference attended by a variety of abortion-rights groups. Those leading the meeting argued that the movement had made serious tactical mistakes since 1973, particularly in the context of the Hyde Amendment. In order to improve its chances of victory, Planned Parenthood first sought the support of civil-rights organizations charged with representing women of color and all those most immediately affected by the Hyde Amendment. As part of this effort, the organization also adopted a new statement on abortion, defending access to the procedure as a "fundamental, constitutional right belonging to all women in the United States."[110]

Faye Wattleton, the leader of an Ohio chapter of Planned Parenthood, also helped to remake Planned Parenthood's image. A charismatic speaker, Wattleton was also an African-American feminist. Her presence served to counter claims that Planned Parenthood prioritized population control over the rights of racial minorities. Her leadership reconfirmed Planned Parenthood's new commitment to the idea of women's rights.[111]

In defining the right to abortion, Wattleton explained in the winter of 1978 that "[w]hat's really important is that black women have equal access to determine when and how they will have children." By selecting Wattleton, Planned Parenthood identified abortion rights—and particularly those of women of color—as a priority. In defending abortion, the organization became more political, more feminist, and more focused on the issue of abortion.[112]

Similarly, younger, often more feminist members used the *Roe* decision to redefine NARAL. These activists included Sarah Weddington, the attorney who had argued *Roe* before the Supreme Court, and Karen Mulhauser, the woman who was hired to open a NARAL office in Washington, DC.

Weddington's own experiences informed the arguments about abortion rights that she presented before the Supreme Court. She had experienced sex discrimination before attending law school, while searching for work as a lawyer, and even at the Supreme Court building, which did not have a ladies' room in 1973. Weddington herself had chosen abortion when an unwanted pregnancy threatened a major disruption of her life and career, and she argued that such a choice was of constitutional significance.[113]

Like Weddington, Mulhauser had come to view sex equality and abortion rights as inextricably linked. She became aware of the issue as a young woman teaching science at a local high school. Time and again, female students asked Mulhauser about abortion, sharing stories about their own unwanted pregnancies. Convinced of the urgency of the issue, Mulhauser began working at a pregnancy-counseling service. With the financial assistance of donors like John D. Rockefeller III, NARAL's Washington, DC membership grew from 7,000 to 140,000 members during Mulhauser's tenure. Mulhauser and Weddington both viewed abortion as a women's-rights issue—unless women could decide for themselves when or whether to have a child, they could not avail themselves of other opportunities.[114]

In 1974, when pro-lifers managed to secure hearings on a fetal-protective amendment, the NARAL Executive Committee met to determine how best to defend legal abortion. Weddington used the meeting as a chance to promote women's-rights arguments for abortion. After speaking to Senator Birch Bayh (D-IN), a supporter of the Equal Rights Amendment, Weddington reported that she had persuaded him primarily by contending that "women cannot take advantage of opportunities guaranteed under the ERA if they cannot control their fertility."[115] In a series of debates about a fetal-rights amendment, Mulhauser similarly argued that "the right to decide whether or not to have children [was] central to the Equal Rights Amendment."[116]

The same year, as debate in Congress began to focus on the issue of abortion funding, Mulhauser, Weddington, and their allies exercised more control over their organization. In December 1975, Weddington became NARAL president. As she had done previously, she emphasized that abortion was a matter of women's rights to privacy and equality.[117]

Working together, Weddington and Mulhauser reinforced the view that abortion was a women's issue. The strategy remained in place after Weddington stepped down in 1977, replaced by former PCC lobbyist Robin Chandler Duke. As Duke's selection suggests, the transition from a population-control to a women's-rights frame was not seamless. Duke had been heavily involved in population-control advocacy. Nonetheless, after Duke took office, the organization continued prioritizing women's-rights claims.[118]

For example, in lobbying against stricter versions of the Hyde Amendment, Mulhauser and other NARAL members focused increasingly on the central importance of fertility control to women. In some instances, NARAL leaders referred directly to their personal experiences. Mulhauser, who had been raped at gunpoint, told her story in justifying abortion rights before Congress and in discussing Medicaid funding for abortion in cases of sexual assault. Similarly, during fundraising efforts, Carolyn Buhl, an Ohio activist who was to become a member of the NARAL Board in the 1970s, relied on her own abortion experience in defending and defining the *Roe* decision.[119]

Indeed, a new debate handbook issued by the organization denied any connection to population control: "Allegation: That abortion should not be used as a means of population control. [Response]: Agreed. The decision to have an abortion is and should be a private one, free from outside pressures or interferences. . . . The term 'population control' implies the use of coercive policies." The handbook denounced many of the consequence-based justifications that population controllers (and many in the abortion-rights movement) had once emphasized. "If we were pro-abortion, we would urge women to have abortions (to avoid out-of-wedlock births, to avoid having a defective baby . . . , to reduce welfare costs, to limit population growth, etc.)," the handbook stated. Instead of seeking to curb population growth, as the handbook explained, NARAL hoped to empower women.[120]

NOW members also made *Roe* into a symbol of judicial recognition of women's reproductive freedom. Using the 1973 decision in this way, NOW members restored the organization's earlier emphasis on sex equality. Karen DeCrow, who was to become the group's president in 1974, helped to oversee this transformation. When she won a contested presidential election, DeCrow made clear that a defense of abortion rights would be one of her priorities. She promoted a resolution labeling all antiabortion activists "determined opponents of women's rights."[121] By 1974, NOW lobbying materials called on local chapters to "defend a woman's right to make her own moral choice concerning her own body."[122] In April 1977, DeCrow continued to warn NOW members that they could not be "complacent about our right to choose."[123]

Generally, after DeCrow stepped down as president, NOW leaders still asserted that *Roe* guaranteed abortion rights for women. In the late 1970s, the organization passed a reproductive-rights resolution describing the importance of fertility control for women. In yearly lobbying against the Hyde Amendment, NOW invoked the equality interests of women and the poor. Working to preserve legal abortion, in turn, became a central part of fighting for self-determination for women. NOW showcased such arguments in its 1979 Call to Action for Reproductive Rights, an effort to shore up legal and popular support for abortion. The organization described abortion as a core aspect of women's liberation: "A woman's right to reproductive choice is the underpinning for the exercise of [all] her other rights."[124]

The Marginalization of Population Rhetoric

When Jesse Jackson began considering a run for the Presidency of the United States in August 1983, he no longer described abortion as part of a conspiracy to harm people of color. Instead, he viewed abortion rights as part of a broader progressive platform. Since Jackson sought the support of Democratic voters, he initially ran into trouble with feminists, many of whom remembered his alliance with the NRLC and his work on behalf of the Hyde Amendment. Just the same, in 1983 Jackson emphasized that notwithstanding any objections he might have to abortion, women had "the freedom to make that choice as a matter of theology and law."[125]

Although NOW ultimately endorsed Walter Mondale, the Democratic Party nominee, Jackson's Rainbow Coalition still reflected the success of feminist efforts to reframe reproductive freedom. As Jackson recognized, abortion-rights supporters no longer pointed to reduced welfare costs or birth rates. Instead, abortion rights were minority rights—the rights of all women to make important life decisions.[126]

Since the 1970s, *Roe* has drawn criticism from feminist scholars and activists. Describing abortion as freedom from state interference, the Supreme Court supposedly hamstrung the women's movement. In borrowing the Court's rhetoric, feminists emphasized reproductive autonomy at the expense of poor women's need for state assistance. Viewed in this way, the Supreme Court's decision aggravated tensions between feminists and people of color.

However, a study of abortion politics in the 1970s shows that we cannot so easily equate the movements for legal abortion and women's liberation. Before 1973, population-control arguments strongly appealed to some movement members. Some reformers expressed concern about the future of the environment and the need for sexual liberation. Others relied on population-control reasoning to gain a strategic advantage. In either case, in contesting the meaning of the abortion-rights cause, feminists seeking to connect abortion and sex equality often found themselves on the losing side.

Feminists used the *Roe* decision to influence the struggle unfolding within the abortion-rights movement. At first, movement leaders described the opinion as one involving rights for physicians and patients. Nonetheless, for feminists uncomfortable with population-control rhetoric, the Supreme Court seemed to have protected abortion rights from popular politics. When the movement believed that it could rely on courts, feminists could more effectively argue against an alliance with population controllers.

Later, when the antiabortion movement scored a string of victories in the courts and state legislatures, feminists had new leverage in internal debates. If the movement's old arguments had not worked, as feminists stressed, it was worth experimenting with new ones. In the mid-1970s, with the pro-life movement building momentum, feminists in leading organizations asserted themselves to an unprecedented extent, de-emphasizing population-control arguments, stressing women's interest in self-determination, and claiming positions of leadership for themselves.

Instead of highlighting concerns about illegitimacy, crime, welfare costs, or environmental damage, the movement positioned its cause as a fight for women's rights. Creating a new movement identity allowed feminists to deny pro-life allegations of racism more effectively. Moreover, as pro-lifers backed the Hyde Amendment, feminists could turn antiabortion allegations on their head, arguing that abortion rights, rather than pro-life activism, advanced the interests of poor, non-white women.

The Supreme Court did not constrain abortion-rights activists in the way we often think. Feminist activists made *Roe* a symbol of and argument for women's right to fertility control. The account of abortion rights given by NOW activists in the later 1970s reflected this change. Abortion was no longer justified by the consequences of its legalization. Instead, in *Roe*, the Court "said that reproductive rights . . . were civil rights guaranteed in the Constitution, . . . and were ultimately the rights of a woman."[127]

CHAPTER FOUR

The Rise of Choice: Single-Issue Politics and Privacy Arguments

AFTER THE MID-1970S, feminists enjoyed unprecedented influ-ence in the abortion-rights movement. The once-troubled relation-ship between abortion-rights activism and feminism had grown much closer, as prominent activists made *Roe* synonymous with autonomy for women. In what direction did the movement's new leaders take their cause after coming into power?

Karen DeCrow and Marilyn Katz experienced firsthand the intense battles of the late 1970s between activists seeking to chart a new course for the abortion-rights movement. Before 1973 while living in upstate New York, DeCrow had helped women seeking abortions from out of state. She picked them up at the airport, brought them into her home, and drove them to abortion clinics. After becoming NOW president, DeCrow oversaw the creation of several resolutions on abortion rights and led protests to build support for reproductive freedom.[1]

Katz, too, had a long history of involvement with the cause. After having an abortion, she made reproductive rights a central part of her work with feminist, antiwar, and civil-rights groups in Chicago and California. Later, Katz helped to found the Reproductive Rights Na-tional Network (R2N2), a group that fought for government-funded health care, child care, and education, for access to contraception and abortion, and against sterilization abuse. Katz, however, took issue with the way that DeCrow and the broader abortion-rights mainstream pursued their goals. She believed that organizations like NARAL and NOW had prioritized abortion at the expense of other reproductive-rights objectives. The mainstream approach, as Katz would still put it years later, was "silly and wrong."[2] As she explained: "You can't be a pole of attraction if you don't stand for something."[3]

In the early- to mid-1970s, feminists like Katz and DeCrow used *Roe* to renegotiate the relationship between the abortion-rights cause, the women's movement, and population control. But when feminists finally took positions of leadership, the vision of reproductive rights they advanced seems to many commentators to have fallen sadly short. This chapter explores the evolution of two crucial and widely criticized aspects of abortion-rights politics that emerged in the later 1970s: the privileging of arguments about choice and the focus on a single-issue agenda.

Commentators contend that *Roe* helped to narrow feminists' ambitions, standing in the way of efforts to create a broader reform platform or a more popularly resonant idea of reproductive rights. Scholars like Robin West and Rickie Solinger trace to the *Roe* decision the framing of abortion as a choice. The Supreme Court's decision encouraged those interested in developing a "respectable, non-confrontational movement" to adopt the justices' reasoning.[4] Framing abortion as a matter of choice, in turn, institutionalized long-standing race and class distinctions governing access to reproductive health care. In defending *Roe* at all costs, reproductive-rights activists also sacrificed a comprehensive reproductive-rights agenda.[5]

But as this chapter shows, a faction in the reproductive-rights movement did campaign for the kind of broad initiative that the Court's decision theoretically put out of reach. More surprisingly, in the late 1970s, feminist women's health activists used the idea of reproductive choice so often maligned by contemporary commentators in formulating revolutionary demands. Far from limiting the abortion-rights movement, the Court's rhetoric served as an important weapon for those seeking a radical reordering of reproductive-health law.[6]

Mainstream organizations like NARAL, NOW, and Planned Parenthood took a more cautious approach only after the pro-lifers scored a series of victories in the mid-1970s. In this period, abortion opponents built an impressive record in state legislatures, and some of the most painful restrictions—those on the public funding of abortion—succeeded in Congress and were upheld by the Supreme Court.[7]

Convinced that most Americans supported legal abortion, movement leaders blamed themselves for the defeats of mid-decade. While abortion-rights activists had invested too much in lobbying and litigation, pro-lifers had made a name for themselves in electoral politics. Abortion-rights leaders set out to surpass pro-lifers' record of success. If victory depended on the movement's ability to impact national elections, a single-issue agenda seemed more realistic, practical, and effective. Movement leaders also used choice arguments to court voters, since abstract concepts of privacy and autonomy enjoyed more support than did claims involving socioeconomic or sex equality.[8]

For a circle of feminists and women's health activists, by contrast, the defeats of mid-decade exposed mainstream movement strategies as overcautious and uninspiring. Organizations such as the Reproductive Rights National Network and the National Women's Health Network (NWHN) responded to the Supreme Court's decision by crafting a broader reform platform. These organizations argued that without protection from sterilization abuse and without access to adequate child care, health care, sex education, and contraception, women would not truly have reproductive freedom.[9]

By the early 1980s, political events forced many movement members to abandon demands for comprehensive reform. The 1980 election gave the White House and Senate to Republicans, many of whom favored abortion restrictions. Congress seriously considered a statute and a constitutional amendment that would either ban abortion outright or empower the states to do so. Defending abortion occupied all of the energies of a beleaguered abortion-rights movement.[10]

Furthermore, in a political landscape reshaped by neoliberalism and the New Right, abortion-rights leaders had reason to present themselves as the true defenders of individualism. In the late 1970s and early 1980s, leaders of both major political parties lauded market-based solutions, deregulation, and entitlement reform. Commentators across the ideological spectrum began agreeing that welfare represented a privilege rather than a right. To preserve tenuous gains, abortion-rights activists championed small government, setting aside their own demands for state support. Adopting a narrower focus made sense when broader reforms seemed politically out of reach.

A decade after the Supreme Court decision in *Roe*, various reproductive-rights groups coalesced around a single-issue approach that privileged abortion. This focus, however, did not follow inevitably from the *Roe* decision. Instead, the abortion-first agenda emerged in the shadow of a 1970s conservative ascendancy in American politics. As importantly, feminists made a deliberate decision to prioritize the abortion issue. Faced with an impossible choice between political relevance and ideological courage, supporters of abortion rights took the more pragmatic path.

The Abortion-Rights Movement Confronts Sterilization Abuse and Legal Setbacks

In the first half of the 1970s, feminists had worked successfully to reframe abortion as a matter of women's rights. Later in the decade, abortion-rights feminists again contested the meaning of their cause, this time disagreeing about how best to strike the proper balance between idealism and realism, between preserving legal abortion and pursuing the original principles movement members had espoused. The Supreme Court did not determine the course of this battle.

While some prominent activists had always described abortion as a matter of free choice, feminists and other abortion-rights supporters had experimented for some time with different ideas about the relationship between fertility control and equality for women. In the late 1960s, radical feminist groups like the Redstockings and New York Radical Women connected abortion to women's interests in both equal treatment and sexual freedom. Kate Millett, a member of both organizations and the author of the groundbreaking 1969 manifesto *Sexual Politics*, described the struggle to repeal abortion laws as an effort to "convert sexuality from pain and penalty to pleasure."[11] In cases like *Abramowitz v. Lefkowicz* and *Abele v. Markle*, Nancy Stearns and other feminist attorneys connected abortion to women's interest in equal citizenship. The idea of abortion as a freedom to make choices represented only one of many options available to feminists in the mid-1970s.[12]

The changing political environment of the 1970s helped make choice arguments more attractive. The Equal Rights Amendment (ERA) had seemed to be a certain success in the early 1970s, but as the decade wound to a close, feminists found the amendment in peril. In concert with Phyllis Schlafly, the New Right tied the ERA to both abortion and to the decline of the traditional family. Fearing for the future of the amendment, feminists steered clear of equality-based arguments.

Choice-based contentions also gained favor because of progress made by the pro-life movement. Starting in the mid-1970s, state and federal abortion funding became increasingly off-limits, a development upheld by the Supreme Court. Leaders of mainstream abortion-rights organizations generally blamed the failures of the mid-1970s on their movement's incompetence in electoral politics. These activists argued that the movement could succeed only if it beat pro-lifers at their own game: influencing elections and convincing prominent politicians of the movement's political strength. In the quest to build a "pro-choice majority," mainstream organizations downplayed claims about sex equality or socioeconomic justice for fear of alienating undecided voters.

The quest to rebuild the abortion-rights cause began in 1976, when Congress passed the Hyde Amendment. In 1977, with the reauthorization of the Hyde Amendment up for discussion, those on opposing sides fought bitterly about which narrow exceptions to funding bans would survive. Every year thereafter, abortion-rights activists found themselves in a standoff, endlessly debating whether any Medicaid funding could go to women seeking abortions in cases of rape or incest. The Hyde Amendment appeared to have become a permanent feature of the political terrain.[13]

Moreover, in 1977, in spite of a series of lower court decisions to the contrary, the Supreme Court upheld several state funding bans, dashing hopes that the courts would strike down the Hyde Amendment. In *Maher v. Roe*, the Court upheld a Connecticut law authorizing Medicaid funding only for first-trimester abortions that were deemed "medically necessary." In *Poelker v. Doe*, the Court similarly sustained a St. Louis policy preventing the performance of elective abortions in city-owned hospitals. In a final case, *Beal v. Doe*, the Court held that Title XIX of the federal Social Security Act did not require states participating in the Medicaid program to fund non-therapeutic abortions. The lower courts had often struck down funding- or facilities-based bans, and abortion-rights leaders had expected the Supreme Court to do the same.[14]

Abortion-rights activists viewed these developments as a disaster. Between 1977 and 1978, the number of Medicaid-eligible women unable to access abortion rose from 133,000 to 234,000. A study published in Planned Parenthood's *Family Planning Perspectives* concluded that roughly 23 percent of these women would have terminated a pregnancy if the law on Medicaid had been different. These numbers alarmed those committed to reproductive rights. In 1977, the ACLU stated: "[T]oday, the right to choose has been interfered with. It belongs only to those who can pay for it."[15] In 1978, NARAL identified as the primary new "area . . . of conflict" battles about "legislation to restore public funding—both state, federal, and local."[16] Individual abortion clinics, such as Reproductive Health Services, the St. Louis, Missouri, facility led by NARAL board member Judith Widdicombe, began working to mobilize opposition to the Hyde Amendment and the Supreme Court's funding decisions. Patients at the facility received a brochure requesting their support in unseating antiabortion legislators.[17]

At the same time, the sterilization-abuse scandal challenged the leaders of groups like NARAL and NOW to clarify what they meant by reproductive rights. While mainstream organizations considered a broader agenda, new groups mobilized, demanding a different definition of the right to choose. In California, Chicana feminists working in organizations like the Feminil Mexicana Nacional and the Chicana Service Action Center became involved in sterilization-abuse activism without explicitly addressing abortion rights. Other organizations like the National Black Feminist Organization (NBFO) tied sex discrimination and abortion rights to protection from sterilization abuse and bias based on race and class. In New York City, public-health activists, women of color, feminists, and city officials responded by forming the Committee to End Sterilization Abuse (CESA), a diverse feminist group that successfully championed a minimum age of consent, a thirty-day waiting period between the signing of an informed-consent form and the sterilization procedure, and stronger penalties for those who violated the law.[18]

While seeking to expose the ideology of population controllers, CESA members also pioneered new interpretations of choice and coercion. Whereas Planned Parenthood called for freedom from state interference, Karen Stamm of CESA argued that the State denied women a right to choose by failing to protect them against undue pressure. As she contended, coercion involved "being pressured [to choose sterilization] while you're in labor or about to have an abortion; it's being told that if you don't sign the consent form your welfare payments will be cut off; it's being told that there is a medical necessity for a hysterectomy when there is not; it's being told that sterilization is not permanent; it's not being offered other methods of contraception." As activists like Stamm maintained, reproductive choice prohibited some forms of state involvement and required others.[19]

Members of the mainstream abortion-rights movement had to determine whether this understanding of choice should command support, particularly in the context of sterilization abuse. At first, NOW leaders pushed not only abortion access but also rights to sterilization (and protections from forced sterilization), contraception, and child care. Over time, however, NOW strategists chose to treat abortion as a stand-alone issue, related primarily to individual freedom.

NOW leaders hoped that separating abortion from the ERA would prevent the controversy surrounding abortion from damaging the amendment's chances. In turn, NOW activists prioritized the abortion issue over other matters of reproductive health, seeking to consolidate an obviously fragile victory in the courts and in the political arena. NOW leaders feared that the campaign for sterilization protections would lend legitimacy to pro-life arguments about manipulative, dishonest, and coercive abortion providers. If the issue of sterilization abuse took center stage, voters might give credence to pro-life allegations about the misbehavior of abortion providers.

Abortion Restrictions and the Struggle for the ERA Increase the Appeal of Choice

By the time NOW leaders turned decisively away from population-control arguments in the mid-1970s, the ERA had run into major new obstacles. To the surprise of many observers, New York and New Jersey voters rejected state versions of the amendment in 1975. Moreover, after 1973, few additional states ratified the amendment, and campaigns to rescind votes in ratified states were underway.[20]

Phyllis Schlafly's STOP ERA had mobilized a committed group of antifeminists convinced that the amendment would destroy the family, force women out of the home, and make abortion a permanent fact of American life. Partnering with the New Right, Schlafly worked to befriend state legislators and to raise funds for politicians who voted "no" on the amendment. Rhetorically, antifeminists focused on the dire consequences supposedly connected to the ERA. In particular, ERA opponents contended that the amendment would stick the American people with the bill for "abortion on demand, financed by the government and made socially acceptable any time, any place." From the standpoint of NOW leaders, the New Right appeared to be using the abortion controversy to sink the ERA.[21]

NOW leaders recognized the momentum that Schlafly and her allies had built, particularly among homemakers. By waging war against the amendment, antifeminists claimed to protect housewives' rights to stay at home, gain child custody after divorce, collect alimony, and avoid the draft. Prominent NOW member Toni Carabillo stressed that feminists would lose the ERA struggle unless they could show that Schlafly "deserved neither credibility nor trust" when she claimed to be "homemakers' champion and defender."[22]

While showcasing the advantages of a sex-equality amendment for women in traditional roles, Carabillo and her colleagues also worked to play down issues, like abortion, that might frighten off homemakers. At a 1977 strategy meeting, NOW leaders contended that ERA opponents were "pursuing a deliberate strategy to link ERA, gay rights, and reproductive choice and will use any or all of this, as the situation dictates, to organize a power base."[23] To defuse this threat, NOW members separated the ERA from rallies and arguments for abortion rights. If the ERA stood for sex equality, abortion rights would have to mean something else entirely.[24]

Efforts to distance the ERA from the abortion issue spread across NOW campaigns. While battling a fetal-protective amendment, NOW lobbyists encouraged state activists to deemphasize sex-equality claims, stressing instead the difficult legal and practical questions that would follow ratification of a fetal-protective amendment: would fetuses count as citizens, for example, and would women choosing abortion be prosecuted for murder?[25]

In battling restrictions on abortion funding, NOW largely stayed away from sex-equality arguments. Lobbyists Jan Liebman and Ann Scott advised their colleagues to foreground the costs of denying women Medicaid funding for abortions: a funding ban would "hit poor women first and hardest." However, Liebman and Scott primarily highlighted the "probability that such a [funding] prohibition is unconstitutional." The strategy memorandum quoted a lower court opinion holding that states funding childbirth could not refuse to pay for abortion services, since, under *Roe*, "the selection of the method of treatment [of pregnancy] is an inviolable fundamental right."[26]

Just the same, NOW's adoption of a single-issue, choice-based strategy was not inevitable, even given the ERA politics of the late 1970s. The sterilization-abuse scandal of the mid-1970s prompted new dialogue within the organization about the meaning of reproductive freedom, particularly after the 1977 election of Eleanor Smeal as president. Smeal had worked with the Pittsburgh-area women's movement formerly led by Wilma Scott Heide, and she had distinguished herself as a master strategist in national NOW politics. Born to a Catholic family in Ohio, Smeal had become politically active in protesting in favor of the integration of her alma mater, Duke University. She joined NOW in 1970, and early in that decade she engineered the election of Karen DeCrow, moving the center of the organization's operations from Chicago back to the East Coast.[27]

When Smeal became NOW president in 1977, she presented herself as the symbol of a kinder, gentler feminism. She emphasized her healthy marriage and her role as a homemaker, and she expressed solidarity with other Catholic women. Under her leadership, NOW initially forged a reproductive-rights agenda that reached beyond abortion. For example, in a 1977 resolution on reproductive rights, NOW demanded the "passage of sweeping federal legislation guaranteeing access of all to sex education, contraception, voluntary sterilization, abortion, and prenatal and childbirth care."[28]

The resolution represented the first step in a vigorous debate about how to respond both to the progress made by the pro-life movement and to the sterilization-abuse controversy. In 1978, the diverse members of the NOW Reproductive Rights Committee took up this challenge. Committee members included veteran reproductive-rights activist Jean Marshall Clark and abortion provider Charlotte Taft. Other committee members, like Pennsylvania advocate Gloria Sackman-Reed, had focused on the creation of feminist political action committees or the campaign for the ERA. Beginning in April, the committee reconsidered the scope of NOW's reproductive-rights platform—particularly on issues beyond abortion. Citing a conflict between different state chapters, NOW leader Arlie Scott set a date for discussion of "arguments on Sterilization Regulations."[29]

Ultimately, preoccupied by the risk to legal abortion, NOW leaders struggled to create a comprehensive reproductive-rights initiative. First, in the fall of 1978, the national organization staked out its opposition to the waiting period and other informed-consent protections endorsed by CESA. Informed-consent regulations seemed dangerous to feminists fending off accusations that abortion exploited women. Conceding the need for protective legislation in the sterilization context seemed likely to strengthen the hand of pro-lifers making similar demands. While condemning sterilization abuse, the NOW resolution described all informed consent laws as "paternalistic and a denial of women's right to reproductive choice."[30]

For many white feminists in organizations like NOW, framing sterilization as a matter of reproductive choice made ideological sense. In the 1970s voluntary sterilization had gained popularity, particularly for white married couples. Nonetheless, physicians often rejected younger, middle-class white women seeking sterilization, especially when they had no children. Some NOW members could understand the experience of feminists like Sandra Moseley, a divorced mother of one and the founder of a pro-sterilization organization, Foresight. While using birth control, Moseley accidentally became pregnant. After finally managing to find a physician who would perform an abortion, Moseley had to "threaten . . . to become a Lesbian" before "the doctor agreed to do a tubal ligation at the same time."[31] At some feminist rallies in the 1970s, protestors like Moseley called for "free sterilization on demand."[32] For many white feminists, sterilization appeared to be an issue of access and free choice rather than one of coercion.[33]

Just the same, NOW's understanding of reproductive rights provoked internal dissent. For example, at the October 1978 NOW National Issues Conference, Elisa Sanchez, a representative of LaRaza, one of the nation's largest Hispanic civil-rights organizations, contended that NOW had not "consider[ed] the poor and the minority women . . . [who] might well require a 30 day waiting period."[34]

By April 1979, members of the Reproductive Rights Committee also disagreed about whether to emphasize arguments about choice. At an April 28–29 session, some members asserted that NOW "should encourage women to discuss their experiences [with abortion] and to share them with others." Others suggested that equality-based arguments for abortion could be made more indirectly, by attacking the opposition or by describing the history of the family planning movement and Margaret "Sanger's battle for reproductive choice." Regardless of how NOW members framed reproductive freedom, the group found itself constantly drawn back to the abortion fight. Although nominally focused on all reproductive-rights issues, the Reproductive Rights Task Force focused on how to address "frustration . . . with the Religious Right" and on how to "give [NOW members] information on abortion."[35]

Given the growing stigma surrounding abortion, a single-issue focus offered obvious tactical advantages. In the latter half of the 1970s, the press suggested that the connection between abortion and the ERA had helped to doom ratification efforts in Missouri, Florida, and Illinois. Abortion seemed to attract controversy and alienate the homemakers ERA proponents desperately wanted to court.[36]

At the same time, by framing abortion (and sterilization) as a matter of autonomy, NOW could describe pro-lifers as anti-choice—opponents not only of a controversial abortion procedure but also of any freedom in reproductive decision-making. By downplaying the abortion procedure, feminists hoped to score political points. Furthermore, in the 1970s, major donors like the Ford Foundation provided little direct funding for work on abortion rights. To build support among potential donors and voters, NOW had reason to emphasize more abstract concerns about freedom and choice. By 1979, Smeal portrayed her cause as a defense of birth control as much as of abortion. "Is this an attack on abortion, or is this an attack on contraception itself?" Smeal asked in criticizing the pro-life movement. "The issue of abortion must not be used to eliminate other avenues of reproductive choice."[37] If abortion was controversial, freedom of choice seemed likely to enjoy universal support. By describing the issue in these terms, NOW could enlist supporters who viewed abortion with ambivalence.[38]

NARAL's New Focus on Electoral Politics Centers on the Idea of Choice

For NARAL, a single-issue, choice-based strategy also seemed necessary. In fighting the Hyde Amendment in Congress, NARAL had prioritized lobbying, working in particular to help state affiliates to establish a presence in Congress and state legislatures. After the Hyde Amendment passed, NARAL leaders concluded that the organization had done too little to determine who won important elections. As NARAL explained in a 1978 press release: "The right to choose abortion is under serious attack with recent Congressional and state actions limiting public funding for legal abortion care."[39] Citing a wave of recent antiabortion legislation, Sarah Weddington of NARAL explained: "The only way to fight this threat is politically."[40]

In 1979, for example, NARAL's four-day national conference focused heavily on how to succeed in electoral politics. The message created for the new electoral efforts made no mention of the abortion procedure, sex equality, or welfare rights. Instead, bumper stickers and advertisements highlighted the idea of choice and the popularity of legal abortion. One campaign button, which read "I am pro-choice—and I vote," captured this message.[41] Karen Mulhauser elaborated on these arguments in a major NARAL fundraising campaign: "Why, you ask, are [abortion opponents] succeeding despite the ruling of the U.S. Supreme Court? . . . The answer is simple: they have frightened and intimidated our political leaders. . . . The battle for liberty is won or lost at the polls."[42]

Mulhauser also made apparent the kinds of choice-based claims NARAL would stress in appealing to voters. She described the struggle as a "battle between conservative and liberal ideologies," "a test of whether our society will protect the rights of the individual to lead his or her life, free of the dictates and dogma of others."[43]

In 1980, the organization confirmed this change in strategy. Announcing an initiative called Impact '80, NARAL members contended that politicians should support legal abortion because "choice" enjoyed substantial popular support. By extension, NARAL framed abortion in a way calculated to maximize public approval. As the *Chicago Tribune* reported in 1980, NARAL had "adopted a less offensive connection to abortion; it now calls itself pro-choice, recognizing that many persons generally opposed to abortion believe it is not a government's prerogative to forbid it."[44]

NARAL's choice-based arguments spread throughout the abortion-rights movement. In 1979, Planned Parenthood and NOW launched a campaign to celebrate the legacy of family planning pioneer Margaret Sanger. In its own fundraising campaign, Planned Parenthood described opponents of abortion as those "who want to impose their moral dogma on everybody."[45] "In the face of [the] outright attack on the most personal of human rights, Planned Parenthood must use its strength to preserve the ideals that Margaret Sanger so courageously represented," the letter asserted. "We must defend the right to choose."[46] Nationally, as early as 1978, state abortion-rights organizations held abortion rallies entitled "Freedom Is the Right to Choose" or "Freedom to Choose Is the American Way."[47] In October 1979, the national movement organized a major protest event, Abortion Rights Action Week, around the idea of choice. As one brochure on the event explained, the issue was "the political reality of the abortion issue—we are the majority, we are pro-choice, and WE VOTE!"[48]

The focus on free choice also dictated the attitudes of Planned Parenthood members on the sterilization protections advanced by CESA. Consider the telling example of the position taken by Planned Parenthood of New York on the issue. Some leaders of the organization understood that the danger of coerced sterilization was all too real for many poor women. Just the same, members of the group opposed informed-consent protections. This position stemmed from members' opposition to any "regulation in [the] area of human reproduction—encroaching on a basic human right." Adopting reasoning similar to NOW's sterilization resolution, Planned Parenthood of New York decided to oppose protective regulations because they "limit[ed] free choice."[49]

If the Constitution protected (and the American people demanded) freedom of choice, NARAL, Planned Parenthood, and NOW leaders presented sterilization rights, like abortion rights, as freedoms from government interference. Even when siding with CESA on the issue of sterilization abuse, leaders of mainstream organizations described themselves as champions of choice. By 1978, when Planned Parenthood President Faye Wattleton endorsed the thirty-day waiting period, the ideas of freedom and state non-interference still set the terms of discussion. "People have a right to decide to be sterilized," Wattleton told the *New York Times* in 1978, "and with abortion restrictions, more and more women are going to want sterilization."[50]

In the context of either sterilization or abortion, arguments about choice helped abortion-rights activists confront what appeared to be growing discomfort with fetal killing. As NARAL had concluded, the pro-life movement had successfully stigmatized the procedure itself. Since the early 1970s, antiabortion literature had portrayed abortion in graphic and emotional terms. In his touring presentation, Dr. John Willke described an abortion as follows: "The baby breathes and swallows it [saline solution], is poisoned, struggles, and sometimes convulses. It takes over an hour to kill the baby."[51] Missouri Citizens for Life, a major antiabortion organization, circulated a pamphlet with the following language: "The womb is opened. The baby's skull is crushed and its body dismembered. The baby is removed with forceps."[52]

Such arguments made abortion appear violent and disturbing. By contrast, in emphasizing an abstract constitutional right to choice, NARAL and its allies appealed to undecided voters. Many Americans opposed abortion, but no reasonable citizen, it seemed, would stand against freedom.

In focusing on the idea of choice, however, NARAL, NOW, and Planned Parenthood tended almost automatically to oppose protections against sterilization abuse that required state interference. The leaders of mainstream abortion-rights organizations worried in particular that state intervention in the sterilization issue would set a dangerous precedent for abortion regulation. If the government could restrict or ban one reproductive procedure, then why not another?

The setbacks of the 1970s convinced mainstream abortion-rights groups of the need for a change in strategy. Movement members attributed antiabortion successes, especially the Hyde Amendment, to abortion opponents' sophisticated electoral strategies. Fighting back meant outmaneuvering pro-lifers in state and national elections. In appearance and reality, NARAL worked to create a "pro-choice majority." This effort required activists to present their cause in the most broadly appealing terms. If an individual would not vote to preserve *Roe v. Wade*, she might vote for choice.

Movement Dissenters Forge a Multi-Issue Agenda

For a group of dissenting feminists, women of color, and women's health activists, the Hyde Amendment and the sterilization-abuse scandal also marked turning points in the struggle for reproductive rights. However, these activists drew a different lesson from the events of mid-decade, concluding that mainstream groups had wrongly disconnected abortion from other reproductive rights. In order to have a political impact, these activists believed that the abortion-rights movement could not be afraid to speak out for its basic principles.

Surprisingly, these advocates formulated radical demands for change by using the rhetoric of choice tied to the Supreme Court's decision. If a woman truly enjoyed reproductive autonomy, as activists suggested, she would have to have the resources to raise a child. True choice would thus require protections from sterilization abuse and the means to prevent or end a pregnancy. At the same time, real choice would require the State to guarantee women's access to child care, health care, education, and freedom from sex discrimination.

Recognizing that reproductive law and politics had systematically undervalued the interests of poor and non-white women, women's health activists drew on the more robust vision of reproductive choice offered by feminists of color. As Frances Beal explained in 1970: "The lack of the availability of safe birth control methods, the forced sterilization practices, and the inability to obtain legal abortions are all symptoms of a sick society that jeopardizes the health of black women."[53] In the mid-1970s, organizations led by women of color defined reproductive freedom broadly, linking the prevention of sterilization abuse and access to health care, child care, abortion, and contraception.[54]

Abortion-rights dissenters also drew inspiration from their own experiences. When Karen Stamm had an abortion, she learned that some physicians would grant poor women's request for the procedure only if they agreed to sterilization. Stamm's experience inspired her to join the Women's National Abortion Action Campaign (WONAAC). However, she soon came to resent what she saw as the organization's fixation on winning new members. Rather than standing up for its core values, as Stamm believed, WONAAC watered down its message to attract recruits. Later in the decade, convinced that leading groups had neglected sterilization abuse, Stamm joined CESA. When she became more engaged in abortion politics, she still defined herself as a critic of the mainstream movement. As she explained in 1981: "[W]e must be aware that the [abortion] laws have not been changed for [women's] benefit, but so that the government can have control over the population."[55]

Alice Wolfson shared a similar view of reproductive-health activism. She attended her first feminist consciousness-raising session in 1967. Within two years, she became a full-time activist, co-founding a feminist group called D.C. Women's Liberation. Wolfson belonged to the welfare-rights movement and to WITCH (Women's International Conspiracy from Hell), a radical feminist group. Although involved with a variety of issues, Wolfson prioritized women's health. In her view, the government's indifference to women's physical and mental well-being revealed deeper problems surrounding sex, equality, and power. This attitude motivated her to co-found the National Women's Health Network (NWHN). As she would still put it years later, she believed that "freedom of choice meant freedom to have a child if you wanted to."[56] She lobbied for publicly funded day care and against sterilization abuse at the same time that she fought to "bring abortion out of the closet."[57]

Activists like Wolfson and Stamm formed an emerging feminist women's health movement in the late 1970s. Abortion bans convinced some feminists of the need for a new approach to medical care. Even the reforms passed in most states in the 1960s and early 1970s often required women to clear a number of embarrassing hurdles before getting an abortion and denied access to some women altogether. Feminists stepped up to offer abortion services that were more private, discreet, and easy to access than those offered by hospitals or other providers, even after 1973.[58]

Like Mickey Stern in Ohio and Charlotte Taft in Texas, many feminist abortion providers developed a scathing critique of the medical establishment. In 1970, in *Our Bodies, Ourselves*, the Boston Women's
Health Collective detailed a vision of self-help for women. Some activists like Carol Downer, a member of the NOW Abortion Committee, also shared new ideas about health care delivery. Downer helped
to popularize the idea of women-centered care, embarking in 1971
with her colleague Lorraine Rothman on a national tour in which she
demonstrated cervical self-exams and menstrual extraction, a technique whereby women could terminate early pregnancies.[59]

Other feminists exposed the mistreatment some women suffered in
seeking medical care. In 1968, sales of the birth-control pill reached
the $150 million mark. One year later, in *The Doctor's Case against
the Pill*, columnist Barbara Seaman showcased the dangerous side effects of the popular contraceptive method. In 1971, studies revealed
that diethylstilbestrol (DES), a popular drug thought to reduce the
risk of miscarriage, dramatically increased the risk that women exposed to the drug in utero would develop vaginal tumors later in
life. These scandals magnified worries that medical professionals did
not tell women about all the consequences of different courses of
treatment.[60]

By the later 1970s, the disparate individuals and groups identifying
with the feminist women's health movement channeled their concerns
into a campaign for legal reforms. Founded in 1975, the National
Women's Health Network united well-known critics of the medical
establishment like Barbara Seaman with members of organizations
such as the DES Action Project in Louisiana, the Elizabeth Blackwell
Center for Women in Philadelphia, and the Federation of Feminist
Women's Health Centers.[61]

Initially, NWHN focused on previously-neglected health issues.
Organization leaders prioritized the regulation of intrauterine devices
(IUDs) and compensation for low-income women injured by DES.
Group members sought to fill a gap left by groups dedicated to preserving abortion rights. At the same time, informing women about
sterilization, DES, the birth control pill, or the IUD allowed feminist
women's health activists to add depth to popular discussion of reproductive rights. Earlier in the 1970s, leading abortion-rights groups
had demanded freedom for doctors to practice medicine as they saw
fit. By contrast, women's health activists argued that deregulation

could harm women, particularly when a physician failed to inform her patients of any risk they faced.

The Hyde Amendment put the abortion issue at the heart of NWHN's agenda. Because the organization addressed the intersection of race, class, and health care, the Hyde Amendment became a prime target for NHWN reformers. In 1977 the organization began a campaign to fund free abortions and joined groups like NOW and NARAL in coordinated protests against bans on the public funding of abortion.[62]

Deepening involvement in abortion politics required NWHN to differentiate itself from other organizations contesting the abortion wars. In a 1978 position paper, NWHN chastised NARAL and Planned Parenthood for treating abortion as a stand-alone issue. By contrast, NWHN members believed that abortion rights lost meaning if they were not made part of a comprehensive reproductive-rights platform. The organization argued that the "right to abortion [was] inextricably intertwined with a number of issues," including "sterilization abuse" and "child care services and pregnancy disability rights."[63]

NWHN did not reject the idea that abortion represented a right for women to choose. Instead, the organization's position paper invested the idea of choice with new meaning. The position paper suggested that decisional autonomy meant nothing to poor women who could not afford to raise children. "It is every woman's right to choose whether, when, and under what circumstances to bear children," the paper explained. "This choice will only be truly available to women when . . . there exists universal access to contraceptive information, . . . assured pregnancy disability rights for working women, universal access to decent infant healthcare, and high quality day care at low cost."[64]

An ally of NWHN, Abortion Rights Mobilization (ARM) organized in 1976 to offer an alternative to the approach used by the mainstream movement. Founded by former NARAL leader Larry Lader, ARM promised a more radical defense of legal abortion. Uniting movement veterans, attorneys, legal academics, and feminists, ARM worked heavily on the issue of abortion funding and launched a battery of lawsuits against public hospitals. In 1978 ARM considered going to court to challenge the tax-exempt status of the Catholic Church. Leaders of the group argued that the Catholic hierarchy "used tax-exempt money . . . for lobbying beyond legal limits"—an argument the group would make after filing suit in 1980.[65] Attorneys and law professors like Cyril Means Jr. of New York Law School endorsed ARM's mission. The group's message also attracted feminists like Barbara Seaman and Marion Banzhaf of NWHN, who believed in ARM's demand for a "revival of a feminist grass roots fight for abortion rights for all women"[66]

In the winter of 1979, tensions between NWHN and ARM and the mainstream movement escalated when Eleanor Smeal invited pro-lifers to a common-ground summit. She explained to the media: "We feel abortion must be one of the choices, but reasonable people must have a common goal for reducing the need for abortion."[67]

The NOW summit enjoyed the support of NARAL and Planned Parenthood, but NWHN and ARM members objected to Smeal's rhetoric and underlying objective. Summarizing these concerns, JoAnne Fischer, the NWHN Chair, argued that Smeal's approach did not "strongly affirm our commitment to abortion." NOW and NARAL representatives offered several responses to Fischer's objections—the summit would "expose the Right to Life's hypocrisy," "divide the ranks of Right to Life," and "assure support and passage for 'family planning.'"[68]

After the gathering, NWHN and ARM members largely rejected the pragmatic rationales offered by NOW and NARAL. As an NWHN press release explained, women's health activists insisted that the abortion issue could not be analyzed in isolation. Furthermore, as the press release explained: "[t]o say that abortion is 'an act of desperation' . . . is to negate the experiences of the millions of women in this country who choose abortion for themselves."[69]

The February meeting allowed NWHN to redefine reproductive choice. The organization concluded that it required state support for women who wanted to have a child. At the same time, feminist activists and the State would make choice hollow if they did not stop expressing so much disapproval of abortion. Presenting the procedure as a decision of last resort made some strategic sense, since the pro-life movement had exposed the deep ambivalence with which many Americans viewed the procedure. For NWHN and its allies, however, stigmatizing abortion undermined reproductive choice. If the public viewed abortion as an immoral decision, women would not feel free to choose it.

For NOW, the common-ground meeting with abortion opponents proved to be a disappointment. Representatives of most major antiabortion organizations, including the National Right to Life

Committee, refused to attend. Just the same, after the meeting, NOW still emphasized choice. While stating that "child care, job dislocation, [and] even the added burden of food and shelter are all economic implications of a woman's reproductive rights," the organization's major new rhetorical initiative, "Call to Action for Reproductive Rights," stressed that "[t]he Constitution is intended to protect individuals from the government."[70] In August 1980 when the Supreme Court rejected a constitutional challenge to bans on federal abortion funding, NOW President Eleanor Smeal again asserted that the Court had given "the government the right to decide if and when people will have or not have children."[71] Facing further setbacks on the abortion issue, the organization, as NOW Legal Defense and Education Fund Director Phyllis Segal explained, had to shift its "focus . . . back to Congress and to state legislatures," pursuing realistic goals and relying on popularly resonant rhetoric. When legal abortion seemed at risk, NOW leaders had little leverage to demand broader reproductive rights. And with public support for legal abortion in question, organizations like NOW and NARAL gravitated toward the choice claims that had long enjoyed public support.[72]

Within several years, however, even movement dissenters began to take a more single-issue approach. Mainstream groups had adopted tactics of this kind in response to a series of antiabortion victories in the mid-1970s. In the early 1980s, reproductive-rights dissenters found themselves facing equally difficult tradeoffs. With the landslide election of Ronald Reagan, the New Right and the Religious Right claimed powerful allies in both Congress and the White House. The ascendancy of the Right posed an imminent threat to legal abortion. Congress seriously considered both a statute and a constitutional amendment that would vitiate abortion rights.

Reagan and his supporters became powerful proselytizers for neoliberalism. In the 1930s and 1940s, theorists from Friedrich Hayek to Milton Friedman articulated a policy vision of individual liberty, deregulation, limited government, and the superiority of free markets. In the following decades, neoliberal academics at the Universities of Virginia and Chicago achieved scholarly success, lending new credibility to such ideas. By the mid-1970s, Democratic President Jimmy Carter began experimenting with neoliberal macroeconomic policies, deregulating the transportation and banking industries.[73]

During the 1980 election, Ronald Reagan made neoliberalism into a seductive electoral message. Drawing on policies developed by

Paul Weyrich's Heritage Foundation, Reagan promised market-based policy solutions, lower taxes, and trimmer government. Groups like NWHN had described state support as a woman's right. Increasingly, politicians in both parties instead presented welfare services as a source of dangerous dependency. Reagan's rhetoric of equal opportunity, individual achievement, and American greatness resonated with voters, who unseated some of the most prominent Senate liberals in the 1980 election. With grassroots conservatism on the rise, many Americans appeared to have rejected the liberal vision of social justice and welfare rights embraced by many in NWHN.[74]

The early 1980s forced abortion-rights feminists to weigh political survival against deeply-held beliefs. The Supreme Court did not create the narrow, freedom-based identity that activists ultimately chose. Instead, feminist dissenters had to compromise their basic commitments to succeed in a dramatically different political climate.

Movement Dissenters Narrow Their Agenda in Response to the Rise of the Right

In the late 1970s, another wing of the feminist women's health movement took on mainstream abortion-rights organizations. The Reproductive Rights National Network (R2N2) brought together a coalition of reproductive-rights organizations, feminist women's health providers, and labor and socialist groups. Like Karen Stamm, some founding members of R2N2 had first become active in the fight against sterilization abuse. Like Meredith Tax, other founders had ties to socialist feminist groups or welfare-rights organizations. R2N2 leaders set out to forge partnerships with labor organizations, minority-rights movements, and feminists. The group hoped to find a balance between "ultra-left isolationism and impotence" and the fate of being "eaten up by the large national [abortion-rights] groups."[75] By uniting a variety of feminist, socialist, and other dissenting groups, R2N2 blended practicality with radical philosophy, developing a principled and realistic politics of reproductive freedom. In accomplishing this mission, the organization took up the banner of choice. Significantly, however, R2N2 used that idea to make transformative demands on the larger society.[76]

The story of R2N2 began in 1977, when activists formed a forerunner of the organization, the Committee for Abortion Rights and Against Sterilization Abuse (CARASA), to tie existing sterilization-abuse activism to concerns about the public funding of abortion. In the late 1970s, CARASA operated primarily in New York and New Jersey, although the group partnered with organizations across the nation. CARASA set forth a much broader agenda than the one advanced by the mainstream movement. In 1979, the organization published *Women under Attack: Abortion, Sterilization, and Reproductive Freedom*, insisting on both a multi-issue approach to reproductive rights and on an understanding of choice that made room for the needs of poor women. As a CARASA draft outline on abortion explained, women needed not only the right to choose but also certain "[p]reconditions of free choice," including "birth control methods/info[rmation]," "child care facilities," "decent income," and "decent healthcare."[77]

In 1978, when R2N2 began organizing, over fifty member groups, including CARASA, identified problems with the approach of leading organizations. Founding members complained primarily about the degree to which the mainstream movement had ignored other reproductive-health issues in their quest to save legal abortion. R2N2 later described the reasons for its founding as follows: "We have purposefully chosen not to become a single issue organization because we feel the issues of access to childcare, jobs, and health care are inseparable parts of a woman's right to reproductive choice."[78]

Rather than rejecting choice as a framework, R2N2 gave the idea a new spin. In a draft of the organization's later-adopted Principles of Unity, CARASA maintained: "Reproductive freedom requires abortion rights, guarantees against sterilization abuse, [and ensures access to] safe, well-designed birth control, . . . good and accessible health care, . . . equal wages for women, . . . welfare rights, [and] reliable, skilled child care."[79] Abortion played only one part in a much more nuanced understanding of choice. As R2N2's position paper on abortion later explained, reproductive rights necessarily tied into a variety of social and economic issues affecting women. Instead of rejecting the language of reproductive freedom, R2N2 emphasized "the question of the social context in which 'individual choices' are made."[80]

R2N2 pursued its mission at a time of great political change. The 1980 election season witnessed the election of a president and congressional majority opposed to abortion. Pro-life leaders tried immediately to capitalize on this opportunity. In January 1981, Senator Jesse Helms (R-NC) proposed the human life bill, which would have directly contradicted the *Roe* decision and asserted that the fetus was a person from the moment of conception. Within months, Senator Orrin Hatch (R-UT) offered a states'-rights amendment as an alternative. The amendment asserted that the Constitution did not recognize a right to abortion and gave the abortion issue back to Congress and the states.[81]

These new measures seemed to stand a greater chance of success than had earlier constitutional proposals. The pro-life movement had more support in the Congress and the White House. Since it did not require a super-majority vote in the states, a statute such as the one Helms proposed would be far easier to pass than a constitutional personhood amendment. Even a federalism amendment, which would allow states to permit abortion, seemed more likely to succeed than did earlier proposals effectively banning the procedure across the nation.[82]

Reagan's triumph also heralded the success of neoliberalism as a popular political philosophy. Neoliberalism began with the scholarly output of a pioneering group of economists and academics, but by the early 1980s it had become a "conflicted political movement."[83] Before Reagan arrived in office, some key Democratic politicians had already proven receptive to neoliberal policies, particularly the deregulation of important industries. The welfare state also came under fire, characterized by Democratic leader Jimmy Carter as being too large and too great a threat to individual liberty. Like his opponent, Ronald Reagan, Carter promised to increase "self-sufficiency through work rather than welfare."[84]

"Reaganomics" translated these ideas into an overarching economic philosophy. His first August in office, Reagan signed into law what were then the largest tax cuts in American history, and he did so with strong support from Democrats in Congress. When it came to welfare, Reagan worked with the New Right to create a new narrative. In a 1981 speech, Reagan related the story of a victim of the welfare state—a young woman "who had become so dependent on the welfare check that she even turned down offers of marriage."[85] Reagan's story echoed statements made by the New Right connecting the welfare state and the decline of the traditional family. A healthy dose of economic self-sufficiency, Reagan suggested, would save the family and revive an ailing economy. Government, not social injustice, was the problem. In a famous speech, Reagan suggested that the government close shop for a time so that legislators could go fishing. "It would be fun," he said, "to see how long it would take the rest of the country to miss them."[86]

Reagan's war on the welfare state stopped short of delivering the results desired by the New Right. Just the same, his 1981 Omnibus Budget Reconciliation Act (OBRA) dramatically changed eligibility and benefit limits for the Aid to Families with Dependent Children program, taking 400,000 Americans off the welfare rolls and cutting benefits for an additional 300,000 recipients. More importantly, "ideas previously seen as distinctly conservative had become mainstream."[87] Reagan's Democratic opponents conceded the value of work and the merits of individualism. Increasingly, the public appeared to agree. For several years, the Gallup poll had asked whether "big government" or "big business" posed the greatest threat to the nation's future. Beginning in 1978, the number of Americans primarily concerned about big government started to climb, increasing approximately 10 percent over the decade to come. Politicians contested which policies best ensured equality of opportunity rather than questioning whether equal outcomes represented a desirable policy goal. The new political climate made little room for activists who viewed certain forms of welfare as a woman's right.[88]

In 1981, with Reagan's welfare reforms under consideration and pro-life bills gaining attention in Congress, R2N2 members met to set forth an abortion agenda. The dialogue within the organization exposed the stakes of abortion-rights decision-making in the early 1980s. On the one hand, activists did not want to bury their vision of social change in a more politically pragmatic platform. On the other hand, bold demands for reproductive freedom seemed counterproductive when Congress seemed ready to gut abortion rights.

R2N2 members clearly agreed on matters of principle. A draft of the R2N2 Abortion Task Force Paper first suggested that leading groups had too often relied on the law, rather than on grassroots support, in creating social change. The draft argued that *Roe* was "a fragile victory," since it "came almost prematurely, before a widespread, grass roots reproductive rights movement really took hold."[89] The draft also took aim at the choice-based rhetoric and single-issue approach adopted by mainstream groups. As the position paper explained: "What makes us . . . different may be our stand on sterilization abuse and the broad social/economic/political context in which we view our abortion work."[90]

While agreeing on matters of belief, R2N2 members hotly debated how best to respond to pro-life attacks. Midwestern affiliates, like the Chicago-based Women Organized for Reproductive Choice (WORC) argued: "We've learned that we can't win abortion without being part of a larger movement, that reproductive rights issues lose their credibility unless they are connected with a deeper socialist-feminist program."[91] Midwest R2N2 asked the national organization to consider whether "a focus on the Human Life Amendment removes us from working on issues of access, racism, and discrimination."[92]

By contrast, New York members leading CARASA believed that, at least temporarily, the abortion wars should take priority. These feminists agreed that "race, economic, class, and sexual orientation particularly [affected] women's right and access to reproductive freedom."[93] Nonetheless, CARASA urged other R2N2 members to postpone other struggles until abortion rights stood on firmer ground. "The actual physical threat . . . to all women cannot be stressed enough," CARASA argued.[94] A Minneapolis-based group agreed: "We think it is very important to focus on abortion at this time."[95] Certainly, as CARASA explained, R2N2 could "expose the New Right's broader program for women," drawing attention to the relationship between abortion, social justice, and sex equality. For the time being, however, activists could not afford a more comprehensive reproductive-rights agenda.[96]

In spite of the opposition of member groups in Connecticut and the Midwest, R2N2 ultimately adopted something similar to the CARASA approach. The position paper explained that R2N2 had "selected abortion rights as [its] focus for this period because of the immediacy of the attack from the New Right." In light of this threat, a majority of R2N2 leaders concluded that "the defense of abortion rights [was] the most urgent task facing the women's movement." As the position paper reasoned: "without the legal right to abortion, we have nothing to build upon."[97]

By 1981, different abortion-rights groups reached an uneasy consensus, prioritizing abortion rights. In the process, mainstream groups downplayed some reproductive-rights demands and used arguments calculated to appeal to the largest possible audience. Even organizations like R2N2 privileged the abortion issue. Although the abortion-rights movement remained internally divided, different member organizations generally treated the fight against abortion as a proxy for attacks on legal contraception, the ERA, and women's wish to play nontraditional roles.

The difficult choices facing R2N2 and CARASA became evident in both organizations' new rhetorical strategies. In the late 1970s, these groups assigned equal importance to the issues of child care, health care, contraception, and sterilization abuse. By contrast, in 1981, R2N2 primarily mentioned other reproductive-health issues in attacking pro-lifers. Instead of calling for government support of other reproductive options, R2N2 argued that pro-lifers "really want[ed] to punish women for being sexual."[98] CARASA agreed that activists should "consistently and aggressively work to show that our enemies are not so concerned with 'fetal personhood' as they are with furthering the oppression of women."[99] As R2N2 put it: "Opposition to abortion is an integral part of its misguided attempts to keep women in the home and in traditional nuclear family roles."[100]

Settling for Choice

In the first half of the 1970s, feminists gained the upper hand in battles to determine the identity of the abortion-rights movement. These activists rejected an alliance with population controllers and committed themselves to a rights-based vision of legal abortion. In the second half of the decade, with feminists in power, movement members still disagreed strongly about what it meant to defend reproductive freedom. Should the movement prioritize legal abortion, or should the movement pay equal attention to contraception, sterilization, child care, health care, and other related reproductive-rights issues? How should advocates describe their cause to the public?

These questions gained importance as the abortion-rights movement suffered setbacks in the mid-1970s. The passage of the Hyde Amendment, the retreat of the Supreme Court from its protection of abortion rights, reversals of fortune in the ERA campaign, and the emergence of effective antiabortion political action committees seemed to signal that the abortion-rights movement had made costly mistakes. In the area of reproductive rights, NOW responded by focusing more exclusively on the abortion battle. At the same time, NOW became more committed to privacy-based arguments, downplaying demands for government support. For its part, NARAL responded by increasing its investment in electoral politics. In appealing to voters, the organization pushed choice claims likely to appeal to those uncomfortable with the idea of abortion. In the process, NARAL de-emphasized supposedly controversial claims about sex equality and the needs of poor women.

A coalition of women's health advocates, women of color, and dissenting feminists viewed the defeats of the mid-1970s in a very different way. These activists attributed the failures of mid-decade to the mainstream movement's decision to neglect other reproductive-health issues. Organizations like NWHN, CARASA, and R2N2 argued that reproductive freedom required government support of contraception, child care, and health care. Only when women could afford to raise children without sacrificing other opportunities could they claim to have a true right to choose.

These different understandings of the reproductive-rights cause created conflict in the decade after the *Roe* decision. Mainstream groups came under attack for being too conciliatory and too willing to settle for legal abortion and nothing more. These fights spilled over into policy debates about sterilization abuse, abortion, and contraception.

Ultimately, by the end of the decade, abortion-rights groups generally adopted the single-focus approach of which feminist scholars have been so critical. Just the same, the Supreme Court did not create this movement consensus. The new threat to abortion evident after the 1980 election convinced even women's health activists of the urgency of defending the decision. Elements of an emerging neoliberal ideology spread to both political parties, and for many, welfare came to seem a threat rather than a right. At best, feminists could voice principled demands in criticizing what the opposition wanted to do. Any direct campaign for a broad reproductive-rights agenda seemed likely to end in failure.

By 1981, reproductive freedom had become a synonym for abortion, and choice had replaced previous arguments about sex discrimination or socioeconomic equality. The Supreme Court did not dictate the narrowing of abortion-rights demands. In the mid-1970s, mainstream groups endorsed a broader reproductive-rights agenda until the political costs of doing so became too high. Later in the decade, movement dissenters revamped the idea of choice associated with the *Roe* decision. The narrowing of movement ambitions did not come because of the Court's action in 1973. Instead, state funding bans, adverse Supreme Court decisions, the triumph of Republicans in the 1980 election, and the apparent popularity of limited-government ideology all pushed movement members to moderate their demands.

Years later, even R2N2 leader Marilyn Katz resigned herself to this outcome. Katz had long believed that the abortion-rights movement could not win supporters if it did not stand for something. Just the same, in the climate of the early 1980s, standing for something seemed a luxury. As Katz concluded later, asking for everything could easily have left the abortion-rights movement with nothing at all.[101]

PART III

The Movement-Countermovement Dynamic after *Roe*

CHAPTER FIVE

The Popular Reinterpretation of *Roe v. Wade*

THE CONVENTIONAL WISDOM holds that *Roe* not only re-
aligned the priorities of each movement but also fundamentally
changed the interactions between those on opposing sides. This chapter begins exploring how the Court's decision actually influenced
movement-countermovement dialogue. Drawing on the changing
interpretations of the *Roe* decision developed by competing activists, this chapter addresses a central question: did the Supreme Court
undermine popular experimentation with the scope, rationale, and
meaning of abortion rights? In the 1960s and early 1970s, opposing
activists participated in an innovative conversation about reproductive rights. Before the *Roe* decision, state legislatures could respond to
movement demands by devising a variety of solutions to the abortion
problem. By ending a process of state experimentation, the Supreme
Court allegedly short-circuited these conversations. It appears that
the Court's opinion alienated abortion opponents, suggesting that
their views on fetal life made no difference. At the same time, the
Court chilled popular discussion about what abortion ought to mean,
even among those who supported legal reform. In this way, the Court
theoretically cut short a promising public debate that might have produced an understanding of abortion rights that "commended itself to
the Court and the nation."[1]

However, over the course of the 1970s, contrary to the conventional account, activists and politicians on either side of the abortion debate continued battling to shape the justification for abortion rights.
After 1973, however, advocates channeled their views into discussion

about what *Roe v. Wade* actually said. Those on opposing sides of the abortion battle did not uniformly feel disenfranchised by the Court. Indeed, movement members worked actively to shape citizens' views of the Court and its reasoning.

Dr. Mildred F. Jefferson, then the president of the National Right to Life Committee (NRLC), sought to reap the benefits of reinterpreting the *Roe* decision. In September 1975, Jefferson sat for an interview with the *Los Angeles Times*. She had experience relating her personal journey: from her beginnings as a Texas minister's daughter, to her achievements as a general staff surgeon and assistant clinical professor at Boston University, and as the first African-American woman to graduate from Harvard Medical School. In her time as president of the NRLC, she had become something of a media fixture: major newspapers described her as attractive, impressive, and authoritative—"a small woman . . . with the figure and graceful movements of a ballerina."[2] In the middle of September 1975, however, Jefferson had come not to tell her own story but instead to promote a particular interpretation of *Roe v. Wade*.[3]

Her message was simple: in spite of what any abortion-rights organization might have suggested, *Roe* did nothing to help women. Women were "delu[ded] to feel the Supreme Court's decision [in *Roe* was] in their favor." The Court had not recognized abortion rights for women. "The final decision," she explained, was "the doctor's."[4]

Early in her term as president, Jefferson spread a related message. While condemning feminists who supported abortion, she appeared to symbolize the heights women could reach if they pursued an education or a career. Her motto, as she told the *New York Times*, was: "Decide what you wish to do most, then set out to do it."[5] In talking about the Supreme Court, Jefferson strove to convince women that *Roe* would only undermine their ability to pursue their dreams. She told women that *Roe v. Wade* promised women some measure of control over their lives. In reality, the Court had only reaffirmed physicians' control over women.[6]

Several years later, Jefferson gave another interview, this time to *Ebony Magazine*. She had just participated in a "pro-family" rally in Houston, Texas, designed to counter a feminist gathering held across town. In contrast to her earlier position, by 1978 Jefferson strongly opposed virtually every proposal endorsed by the feminists, from government-funded daycare to stronger protections against sex discrimination at work. Jefferson now agreed with feminists that *Roe v.*

Wade involved women's rights. Quite simply, she opposed *Roe* in the same way she opposed the women's movement. "We're at odds with everything they represent," she said of feminist activists. "There isn't anything they talk about that I can support in any way."[7]

As Jefferson's changing understandings of *Roe* suggest, activists seeking to persuade the public of what the Court had said in fact waged a larger war about the meaning of abortion rights. At times, opposing activists used *Roe* as a tool to recruit new members, raise money, and lay the groundwork for future legal changes. On other occasions, different interpretations of the Court's opinion reflected the changing ideology of movement members—the result of changing organizational leadership or larger cultural turns.

In the courts and in the political arena, advocacy groups offered their own ideas about what the *Roe* Court had said. This dialogue proved to be influential in political circles, ultimately producing the understanding of *Roe* that predominates today—the idea that the decision recognizes a woman's right to choose.

The shifts that produced this consensus came in two distinct phases. In the first period, roughly in the first half of the 1970s, organizations such as Planned Parenthood, NARAL, and NOW said little about the *Roe* decision or its interpretation. They argued that the Supreme Court had settled the abortion question and feared that further debate about *Roe* could only help the antiabortion movement. In the same period, pro-life organizations like the NRLC sought to build women's opposition to the Supreme Court's decision. As part of this effort, pro-lifers claimed that *Roe* addressed only physicians' rights and did nothing at all to help women. These arguments raised concerns for an abortion-rights movement anxious about losing female supporters, especially as pro-life women took a greater number of leadership positions in opposition organizations.

In the second half of the decade, organizations supportive of *Roe* responded by advancing a women's-rights interpretation of the decision. This understanding reflected the values of the feminists assuming leadership positions in the abortion-rights movement in the later 1970s. It also worked as an effective rebuttal to an evolving body of antiabortion, woman-protective arguments.

For their part, pro-lifers endorsed a similar interpretation of the *Roe* decision. As part of a long-standing effort to change their movement's image, pro-lifers worked to win over a larger number of non-Catholic recruits. After the rise of the New Right and Religious Right, some antiabortion leaders found a new way to broaden the movement's base. Paul Weyrich and his allies prioritized strength in numbers—the creation of an integrated coalition of single-issue groups. In crafting such an alliance, New Right leaders hoped to convince conservative Protestants and Catholics that they could work together. For this reason, New Right advocates offered a different interpretation of the *Roe* decision and of abortion rights, one that drew on some Americans' hostility to the women's movement. Promoting this interpretation helped pro-lifers earn new conservative Protestant supporters, all the while alienating others the movement had tried to attract.

The Supreme Court's decision did reorient discussion about abortion, focusing debate on the justices' reasoning. Nonetheless, activists deliberately reinterpreted *Roe*. Far from shutting down movement efforts to redefine abortion rights, the Court's decision became a vehicle for activists seeking to change the public's understanding of what the justices had said and whether reproductive freedom deserved support.

Reformers Frame Abortion Partly as a Medical Right

Immediately after the Supreme Court announced its decision in *Roe*, pro-life and abortion-rights activists gravitated toward a medical interpretation of the decision. For abortion-rights activists, arguing that *Roe* conferred rights on physicians and patients made abortion seem legitimate—a common-sense medical procedure overseen by responsible doctors. For pro-lifers, such an interpretation drove home the point that antiabortion activists looked out for women's best interests. Pro-lifers argued that the *Roe* decision made false promises to women while giving all real decision-making power to physicians. Interpreting the Court's decision in this way allowed pro-lifers to present themselves as the ones who would protect women and tell them the truth.

A medical understanding of reproductive rights had first emerged years earlier, when early reformers contested the best way to frame a right to abortion. Consider as an example two prominent movement members, Mickey Stern and Dr. Milan Vuitch. A native of Windsor, Ontario, Stern met her husband while both were involved in the civil-rights movement. As a young, married woman, Stern focused on homemaking. At the time, she recalls believing that men were smarter than women—that men at parties were more interesting than women. By 1972, Stern would be one of the leading figures in an underground abortion movement in Cleveland, a committed feminist, and in her words, an "expert on abortion."[8] She helped to found and operate a Preterm Clinic—an independent, nonprofit, feminist clinic—throughout the 1970s, seeking to make every aspect of the abortion experience responsive to women's needs and preferences.[9]

Stern's transformation came largely because of her involvement in the women's movement. Her introduction to feminism, through a local consciousness-raising group, made her question all of her previous assumptions. Wanting to do something concrete for women, she placed an ad in a local publication asking anyone interested in abortion to contact her. When she found herself flooded with calls, she and other members of a local feminist group began an abortion referral service. In Stern's view, everything about her job and about abortion rights had to do with women: in her words, "women's rights and choices."[10]

Dr. Milan Vuitch, a physician in Washington, DC known for openly defying bans on abortion, viewed rights to the procedure in a different way. A Serbian immigrant, Vuitch had survived imprisonment by the Nazis. After marrying an American woman, he moved to the United States and soon found himself facing a request for a then-illegal abortion. Vuitch granted that request and many more: he became one of the first physicians to denounce abortion bans publicly. Arrested sixteen times, Vuitch became the named defendant in a major abortion case before the Supreme Court. Vuitch did not see his crusade as one for sex equality. Instead, he described his work as an effort to get "rid of medical absurdities."[11] As he explained to a leading NARAL member: "If you think that abortion is a medical service, then you can't ignore it."[12]

These different ways of viewing the issue divided the abortion-rights movement in the years before 1973. The interpretation of reproductive rights adopted by the *Roe* Court and later reworked by opposing movement members—one centered on the physician—emerged partly from conflict within the abortion-rights movement. How much authority should physicians have over a woman seeking abortion, and why should the public back liberalized laws? In contesting these questions, many activists presented the abortion decision as a right belonging jointly to doctors and patients. This interpretation would influence the debate well into the mid-1970s.[13]

Given the roots of the struggle for abortion reform, a physician's-rights approach had obvious appeal for some movement leaders. The early movement to legalize abortion gathered momentum partly because of demands made by doctors anxious about ambiguous criminal laws. Moreover, framing abortion as a physician's right made sense to early reformers seeking to reassure legislators anxious about radical social change. Writing in the *New York Times*, for example, Larry Lader stressed that liberalizing abortion laws would free doctors from the specter of legal liability, allowing providers to deliver better care." However, beginning in the late 1960s, as women and physicians expressed frustration with reform laws, some feminists attacked a physician's rights approach as sexist—a distraction from the true reasons for the abortion struggle.[14]

For example, within NARAL, the question of how to define the organization's cause exposed fault lines based on gender, ideology, and strategy. Generally, before the *Roe* decision, members of organizations like NARAL disagreed about the extent to which the movement should emphasize women's rights. To some extent before the mid-1970s, mainstream groups took for granted that women would support access to the procedure, since they were the ones most immediately impacted by dangerous illegal abortion procedures. As importantly, the leaders of groups like NARAL believed that medical arguments would effectively achieve the organization's goals, presenting legal abortion as a relatively modest form of social change. By contrast, connecting abortion to sex equality might make the chances of legalization more remote.

In 1969 in NARAL's first press release, Representative Shirley Chisholm (D-NY), the organization's honorary president, a feminist, and a civil-rights activist, suggested that women would not exercise abortion rights without supervision. She clarified that "abortion must be a medical decision between a woman and her physician."[15] Larry Lader helped to head later efforts to tie abortion to public health. As part of this effort, the group sent out a statement that sympathetic doctors could issue, emphasizing the physician's interest in practicing medicine as he saw fit.[16]

The organization's emphasis on medical arguments stirred controversy in 1971, when NARAL challenged the constitutionality of Michigan's abortion ban. Several physicians, including NARAL leader Edward Keemer, had agreed to serve as petitioners in the suit. Prominent NARAL feminists, including Betty Friedan and Carol Greitzer, opposed the organization's decision to highlight physicians' rights in litigating the case. Emphasizing doctors' prerogatives reinforced a paternalism that Friedan and Greitzer found deeply disturbing. Ultimately, both women publicly criticized NARAL's neglect of women's rights in the Michigan case. By contrast, Lader and his colleague, Joseph Nellis, hoped to appeal to the broadest possible audience. The press described Lader's position as follows: "courts would more easily strike down state anti-abortion laws if the test case were presented in terms of interference [with] medicine than if it were done on the basis that many women's rights groups have advocated—namely, the right of a woman to control her own body."[17]

Similar strategic concerns animated the executive committee's decision to distance itself from a reproductive-rights protest led by feminists in the Women's National Abortion Action Campaign (WONAAC). As the group reported on December 10, 1971, "strategic reasons" informed the organization's "refusal . . . to participate in their demonstration and press conference."[18]

In the years before 1973, NARAL continued to emphasize the kind of medical rhetoric used by Lader and Nellis. The group hosted workshops entitled "Abortion as a National Public Health Issue," designed to create "official recognition of abortion as an urgent public health issue and legitimate public health concern."[19] NARAL also developed a standard presentation on legalization that made no mention of women's rights. The speaker began by showing "a picture presenting the negative effects of illegal abortion—the death of woman, infanticide, [and] defective babies." The presentation clearly identified one of the primary rationales for legalizing abortion: "The final section of this presentation would . . . highlight the public health benefits of legal abortion."[20]

In 1973, the Supreme Court appeared to have vindicated Lader's strategy. Justice Harry Blackmun's opinion presented abortion rights in primarily medical terms. *Doe v. Bolton* and *Roe v. Wade* emphasized "the right of the physician to administer medical treatment according to his professional judgment up to the point where important state interests provide compelling justifications for intervention." In closing, the majority opinion stressed: "the abortion decision in all its aspects is inherently, and primarily, a medical decision, and basic responsibility for it must rest with the physician."[21] As Blackmun wrote to Justice Lewis F. Powell Jr. in December 1972, the opinion all but said "what essentially is the obvious—namely, that the state is free to leave the decision to the attending physician."[22]

Pro-Lifers Connect the *Roe* Decision to Physicians' Rights

Press coverage of the Supreme Court opinion made clear what some pro-lifers had known already: the antiabortion movement needed to change its image. As early as December 1972 at an NRLC strategy meeting, Dr. John Willke called attention to "the continuance of 'Catholic' labeling of Right to Life groups by [the] opposition."[23] In June 1973 at its national conference in Detroit, the NRLC voted to formally separate itself from the Catholic Church and from the National Conference of Catholic Bishops.[24]

But how should the group describe the Court's decision, both to existing and potential supporters? Those present at the group's 1973 national conference targeted the "dehumanization . . . of American medicine."[25] The conferees would fight fire with fire: if *Roe* relied on scientific fact, so would the opinion's opponents. Nick Thimmesch, a correspondent sympathetic to the antiabortion movement, summarized the organization's proposal as follows: "the test for constitutional protection [should] be biological rather than political, sociological, or whatever."[26] Less than a year later, Mildred Jefferson, then an unofficial spokeswoman for the group, took a similar argument to the media. In criticizing the Court's decision in *Roe*, she relied primarily on the traditional medical "requirement that the physician not do harm to any patient."[27]

Pro-life attraction to a medical interpretation of *Roe* stemmed partly from deeply-held beliefs about the science of fetal life. Since the late 1960s, pro-lifers had deployed fetological studies, slideshows, and medical articles to establish the personhood of the fetus. Many pro-lifers believed that science could "demonstrate factually that abortion destroys an individuated and unique human life."[28] For this reason, the 1972 NRLC National Conference featured two films depicting "actual abortions," designed to energize existing movement members and recruit new ones. With the evolution of fetology as a specialty, as pro-lifers believed, the medical profession seemed convinced that the unborn child was a patient deserving the best possible care. As antiabortion activist Robert Byrn explained in the mid-1960s: "the ethics of the medical profession require a physician, who attends a pregnancy, to care for the lives of two human beings—the woman and the unborn child."[29]

If medicine treated the unborn child as a patient, pro-lifers believed fetal personhood to be self-evident. Unless the Court ignored the evidence scientists had presented, "the unborn child [would] qualify as a person within the purview" of the Fourteenth Amendment.[30] In turn, if the courts recognized fetal personhood, unborn children could claim the same constitutional rights as anyone else. As prominent pro-life academic David Louisell reasoned: "The progress of the law in the recognition of the fetus as a human person for all purposes has been strong and steady and roughly proportional to the growth of knowledge of biology and embryology."[31]

When the Supreme Court enlisted medical reasoning to reject fetal personhood, abortion opponents were shocked. Pro-lifers believed that the Supreme Court had consciously disregarded the truth about the unborn. In July 1973, NRLC members passed a resolution condemning the American Medical Association and the Court for ignoring the fact that "the primary task of the medical profession is to preserve human life."[32]

From a strategic standpoint, a medical interpretation could also reassure women that abortion opponents took their rights seriously. In the mid-1970s, the pro-life movement had to fight several different battles to establish that it was pro-woman. In 1973 when the Court issued its decision, gender divisions fractured national antiabortion organizations. In many states in the late 1960s and early 1970s, pro-life women in grassroots groups operated informally. Homemakers worked with their friends and neighbors, balancing strategy sessions and child care. As the national movement began formalizing a chain of command, organization leaders sometimes discounted the strategies most familiar to grassroots women activists.[33]

In 1974 many of the most influential female pro-life activists, including Marjory Mecklenburg, exited the NRLC, reinforcing the impression that the organization, and perhaps the entire national movement, belonged to pro-life men. Mecklenburg and her allies had many reasons for leaving the NRLC, including tactical disagreements with Edward Golden, then the NRLC president. In spite of the complexity of the conflict leading to Mecklenburg's exit, the Catholic press, which covered the departure the most closely, presented the divisions between different NRLC factions as a gender war. In turn, Ray White, the new executive director of the organization, publicly stated that the remaining leaders of the NRLC were "relieved, if not happy, to see the ladies go."[34]

Describing *Roe* as a decision recognizing rights for physicians factored into a larger effort to increase women's support for the pro-life movement. If the Court had offered hollow hope to women, pro-lifers could effectively claim to have women's best interests at heart. Pro-lifers asserted that the *Roe* decision made false promises to American women, offering a freedom that legal abortion could never deliver. As pro-lifers suggested, the Supreme Court stood with the medical establishment against women's best interests.

When congressional hearings on a fetal-protective amendment began in 1974, some pro-life witnesses began stressing that the Supreme Court had mostly created rights for doctors. Senator Jesse Helms (R-NC) argued that, contrary to what *Roe* stated, "an unborn baby is not a private affair between the mother and the abortionist."[35] Mildred Jefferson offered a similar interpretation of *Roe*, contending: "The highest Court of our land undermined respect for the medical profession by granting the doctor a nearly unlimited license to kill the unborn child."[36]

In 1975 with the election of Mildred Jefferson to the presidency of the NRLC, the organization redoubled its efforts to recruit women. As a physician, Jefferson held sincere concerns about what the *Roe* decision meant for the medical profession. In Jefferson's view, the Court had given doctors untrammeled power over women and unborn children while chipping away at the ethical rules that had always governed medical practice. In speeches, she described her work as a profoundly personal quest to remind doctors of "their obligations to protect and cure rather than to kill."[37] At the same time, Jefferson and her new executive director, Judie Brown, felt that the organization had not done enough to reach women.[38]

Working together, Jefferson and Brown spread the argument that *Roe* put women in the position of making decisions based on a false sense of autonomy. As Brown would put it years later, the abortion right did not provide any freedom for women but rather represented a contract between the woman and the abortionist. As early as the winter of 1975, Jefferson warned career women that *Roe* left them out in the cold. In her view, pro-lifers, not the Court or the abortion-rights movement, had women's best interests in mind.[39]

The Abortion-Rights Movement Turns to a Medical Interpretation of the *Roe* Decision

Before 1975, abortion-rights organizations largely agreed that the *Roe* decision recognized rights for physicians and patients. Activists who had joined the early movement for reform saw real value in freedom for physicians. Some of these activists, like Dr. Vuitch, provided abortions and knew firsthand the importance of physicians' freedom to deliver medical care as they saw fit. Moreover, when the Supreme Court seemed firmly behind abortion rights, NARAL members and other prominent activists focused on expanding access to abortion in public hospitals, private clinics, and family planning centers. Presenting *Roe* as a decision involving physicians' rights might help convince reluctant doctors to provide abortion services. Other activists, like Shirley Chisholm, did not view physicians' rights as conflicting with those of women. Some advocates believed that broader rights for physicians would improve medical care for women and save the lives that could be lost during botched, illegal abortions. Providing rights for physicians would, in the words of a NOW fundraising letter, ensure that women could "terminate a pregnancy without danger or humiliation." At the same time, the Supreme Court decision appeared to have confirmed the tactical value of medical arguments. Rearguing the rationale for abortion rights, it seemed, would do more harm than good.[40]

NARAL leaders hardly saw the Supreme Court's decision as the endpoint of the abortion wars. Indeed, in February 1973 the NARAL Executive Committee agreed that the abortion "fight [would] continue for years."[41] In particular, the executive committee expressed concern about the campaign to pass a fetal-protective constitutional amendment. In response, in early 1973 the organization worked to put together materials intended to "awaken a public that thinks that the battle has been won."[42]

At the same time, NARAL leaders remained convinced of the value of medical arguments. Later in February 1973, Lee Gidding, then the executive director of NARAL, suggested an offensive that would demonstrate that "[t]he Supreme Court clearly defines abortion as a medical concern, not a statutory one." Gidding proposed a number of steps that would build on *Roe*: efforts to push hospitals to perform abortions, the creation of a free referral service, and an initiative to "galvanize allies in the medical community" to draw up "regulations medically necessary for second-trimester abortions." Gidding justified the group's emphasis on medical rhetoric as follows: "Only the interest of official Roman Catholicism will be served by keeping the abortion debate going. Unquestionably, they will try to use us, and the vehicle of public debate, to keep their views before the public. I do not believe we should cooperate. The court has spoken, and the case is closed."[43]

Following the first round of testimony on a proposed fetal-protective amendment that spring, the NARAL Executive Committee agreed on the importance of a medical interpretation of *Roe*. After the July 1974 meeting, the NARAL Executive Committee concluded: "The importance of [medical] words was stressed. After 24 weeks, it is not an abortion but a premature delivery; before 12 weeks, it is not an embryo but a fetus. We must stress statistics showing that the majority of abortions are before 12 weeks. We agreed that to emphasize a 'woman's right to choose abortion' is sometimes not good strategy." Instead, as the executive committee suggested, NARAL leaders elected to follow *Roe* in "stress[ing] the legal aspects and public health benefits of legal abortion."[44]

NARAL emphasized these claims in part to establish its place among "respectable national organizations." In 1974 a coalition of abortion-rights groups adopted a similar goal. For example, members of NOW and NARAL attended a lobbying workshop hosted by the Women's Equity Action League that did not center on women's-rights claims. As NARAL reported, activists emphasized the importance of "evidence [that] points to myriad problems connected with implementing a law banning abortion."[45]

Similarly, when NOW mobilized to battle a proposed fetal-life amendment, its leaders carefully avoided any challenge to the medical interpretation of *Roe*. In 1974 Jan Liebman, a leading NOW lobbyist, circulated a strategy paper to state, regional, and local NOW affiliates. As Liebman explained in a confidential memorandum, "[b]ecause feminist arguments against a [fetal-protective amendment] are often ineffective, it is important that we learn to use a broad range of reasons for opposition." Rather than presenting *Roe* as a decision about women's rights, Liebman urged NOW members to showcase the unintended consequences of a fetal-protective amendment, such as contentions that "technology could make the abortion issue obsolete" or arguments that changing the Constitution would "open . . . the door to busing and school prayer amendments."[46]

Those on both sides of the abortion issue had a variety of reasons for identifying *Roe* with physicians' rights. For pro-lifers, such an interpretation gave voice to activists' disappointment in the medical establishment. Before 1973, pro-lifers felt that scientific progress would halt the momentum of abortion rights, putting fetal humanity beyond dispute. However, many physicians had called for the reform of abortion bans, and the Supreme Court had responded to doctors' advocacy. By tying *Roe* to physicians' rights, abortion opponents expressed anger about the perceived decline of medical ethics.

At the same time, medical interpretations helped pro-lifers reassure female recruits. Facing the argument that the antiabortion movement represented nothing more than a front for the Catholic Church, pro-lifers wanted to attract a larger number of Protestants and other non-Catholics to their cause. Pro-lifers also had to answer charges that their movement imposed the will of a small group of Catholic males on all American women. Even within the movement, activists had to heal an apparent rift that formed after the departure of prominent women from the NRLC. By presenting *Roe* as a pro-doctor decision, pro-lifers could identify themselves as women's real defenders.

Abortion-rights activists had similarly complex reasons for framing *Roe* as a medical-rights opinion. In spite of feminist criticism, some activists saw real value in abortion rights for physicians. Such a right would protect women's health, ensure abortion access, and protect courageous providers from liability. Strategically, a medical-rights interpretation built on the momentum provided by the Supreme Court. In making arguments about physicians' and patients' rights, the abortion-rights movement had achieved a string of victories. In the view of some leaders, activists stood to gain nothing from further debate about *Roe*'s rationale.

Activists Begin Emphasizing a Women's-Rights Interpretation of the *Roe* Decision

In the mid-1970s, organizations like NARAL, Planned Parenthood, and NOW dramatically reversed course, insisting that *Roe* stood for women's interests in decisional freedom and bodily integrity. With the rise of more women to visible positions in the pro-life hierarchy and with the movement's recent emphasis on woman-protective arguments, there was more reason than ever to stress the connection between *Roe* and rights for women.

Before 1973, abortion-rights leaders often took for granted that women would support liberalized laws. A 1972 NARAL strategy paper predicted that a majority of American women could be counted on to endorse the cause. At an October meeting of the NARAL Board of Directors, those present voted for a measure stating that it would "initiate a nationwide campaign to counter the Right-to-Life [movement . . .] by mobilizing women (who hold 53% of the vote)."[47]

If their movement could count on women's support, some abortion-rights activists saw no urgent reason to publicize a connection between *Roe* and women's rights. In 1974, NOW's Abortion Action Program described the opposition as the "fringe political right"—the same antifeminists opposed to the ERA. By extension, lobbyists assumed that most women favored legalized abortion.[48]

Abortion-rights leaders understood that women stood to lose the most if the government outlawed abortion. Particularly after feminists came into power in abortion-rights organizations, movement leaders often believed that they spoke for American women. At least in Congress, the most visible abortion opponents, such as Representative Henry Hyde (R-IL) and Senator Helms, were conservative, white, and male. Why would women not wish to take back control over their reproductive lives?[49]

In the first half of the 1970s, several political developments challenged the assumption that an obvious majority of women favored legal abortion. First, in that period, a variety of antiabortion activists disseminated new "pro-woman/antiabortion" arguments.

Dr. Eugene Diamond of Americans United for Life (AUL) argued that abortion threatened women's health. A devout Catholic, Diamond worked as a professor of pediatrics at Loyola University Strich School of Medicine in Chicago, and he served as guardian ad litem for the unborn in several cases brought by the group's legal defense fund. A father of ten, he considered himself a deeply religious and traditional family man. He disapproved of the women's movement and the ERA, believing that both were pro-abortion.[50]

Pat Goltz, a co-founder of Feminists for Life, defined herself quite differently. As a schoolchild she badly wanted to study chemistry, but since she was a girl, her mother urged her to take home economics instead. In 1969 she read Betty Friedan's *The Feminine Mystique*. She identified with those frustrated that gender could stand in the way of pursuing a chosen path in life. She had no question that she was a feminist. However, she had long found abortion to be morally inexcusable, and she was shocked when she learned that NOW had previously endorsed legalization. Having always considered herself pro-life, Goltz joined a NOW chapter in Columbus, Ohio, and began working to persuade members that abortion did not benefit women.

When this organization expelled her, Goltz worked harder than ever on the growth of Feminists for Life, a group she ran with Catherine Callaghan, a linguistics professor at Ohio State University.[51]

Feminists for Life expanded rapidly, recruiting members in forty states between 1972 and 1974. The group promoted not just bans on abortion but also efforts to allow married women to get credit in their own names. Feminists for Life urged members to boycott companies, like AT&T or General Mills, accused of discrimination against women. Members of the group also participated in the campaign for the Equal Rights Amendment, viewing constitutional protections against sex discrimination as indispensable. While Diamond condemned the women's movement and the sexual revolution, Goltz strongly favored greater social and legal equality for women.[52]

Nonetheless, in the early- to mid-1970s, both Goltz and Diamond worked to inform the public of the dangers they believed women faced in choosing abortion. In speaking to the *Chicago Tribune*, Diamond and his wife, a fellow antiabortion activist, presented women who chose abortion as victims, manipulated by scheming providers. In January 1974 Dr. Diamond asserted that physicians did not inform women that their fertility was "going to be compromised." As he explained: "[T]he principle difference between childbirth and even early abortion is that abortion is an invasive procedure."[53]

Goltz drew public attention to a second set of pro-woman/antiabortion arguments. She first echoed claims like those made by Dr. Gloria Volini Heffernan, a pro-lifer from Illinois who contended that abortion facilitated the sexual exploitation of women. Feminists for Life also spread claims that legal abortion would result in the disproportionate killing of female fetuses. Goltz called abortion "an insidious form of enslavement to the Playboy's 'right to [have sex' that] has no place in the women's movement."[54] The availability of legal abortion allowed men who used women sexually to avoid facing the consequences of their actions.[55]

By the mid-1970s, pro-lifers from across the ideological spectrum publicized arguments that abortion harmed women. Such contentions became a part of the argumentative agenda of major antiabortion organizations such as the NRLC. These claims appeared prominently in the amicus curiae briefs submitted by a variety of antiabortion groups in *Roe v. Wade*. Between 1968 and 1975, pregnancy crisis counselors told women about the dangers abortion supposedly posed. Similar reasoning figured centrally in the 1973 edition of the already

well-known *Handbook on Abortion* written by Dr. John and Barbara Willke. Between 1970 and 1974, related arguments also played
a major role in the advocacy of organizations as diverse as the United
States Coalition for Life, a group opposed to contraception as well as
abortion, and Women for the Unborn, the organization that would
later promote the first single-issue, antiabortion candidate for President of the United States.[56]

As pro-woman/antiabortion arguments became a more prominent
part of public discussion, organizations like NOW and NARAL responded by asserting that *Roe* advanced women's rights. When pro-
lifers focused primarily on the personhood of the fetus, abortion-
rights activists could easily portray the opposition as indifferent to
women's best interests. In the mid-1970s, however, leading pro-life
organizations developed an early form of what Reva Siegel calls
"woman-protective" arguments—claims that abortion threatened
women's physical and psychological well-being. By 1975 activists
on both sides presented themselves as women's true defenders, and
abortion-rights leaders had to stop the momentum built by the new
woman-protective claims.

Moreover, in the mid-1970s, as women took leadership positions in
major pro-life organizations, abortion-rights activists had additional
competition for female recruits. In the early 1970s, the press at times
suggested that antiabortion leaders were male and Catholic. By 1975,
however, women had taken the helm of least three major antiabortion
organizations representing a wide range of perspectives.

Marjory Mecklenburg, who favored sex education and family planning, remained a high- profile figure after leaving the NRLC. As a
confidential NOW strategy paper put it in 1978, Mecklenburg founded American Citizens Concerned for Life to offer a place to women
with "pro-birth control, pro-sex education," antiabortion positions.[57]
A more conservative group of women could identify with Mildred Jefferson. The NRLC and Jefferson appealed to women who wanted to
work within a more hierarchical and formal organization; as the *New
York Times* reported in 1977, physicians and attorneys dominated the
organization and "were disproportionately represented in the organization's leadership."[58]

Nellie Gray, the founder and leader of March for Life, appealed
to homemakers interested in a more grassroots and absolutist form
of antiabortion activism. Gray urged direct action and praised the
ingenuity of grassroots efforts. Under her leadership, March for Life

began attracting supporters who opposed the use of any "abortifa-cient," even when there was a significant risk that a woman would die.[59]

Women with varying political identities and tactical preferences could identify with these new female leaders. Moreover, the ascendancy of activists like Gray and Mecklenburg seemed to signal that the pro-life movement took women's views seriously. The visibility of these leaders lent credence to pro-life claims that their movement neither ignored nor marginalized women. As women became a more visible part of the antiabortion movement, opposing organizations had new impetus to present *Roe* as advancing women's interests and rights.

As importantly, the feminists assuming new leadership positions in the abortion-rights movement saw profound value in a women's-rights interpretation of the *Roe* decision. As the 1970s progressed, abortion-rights feminists like Sarah Weddington, Eleanor Smeal, and Faye Wattleton exercised greater influence over movement rhetoric and priorities. For these activists, abortion rights—and the *Roe* decision—mattered because of the freedom fertility control conferred on American women. Whether or not the Court prioritized the doctor's role, the *Roe* decision made a difference because it expanded women's access to abortion. For this reason, abortion-rights organizations played up the rights *Roe* had assigned to women alone. Under Smeal, NOW characterized abortion funding bans as denying "women the right to abortion upheld by the 1973 U.S. Supreme Court decision." In 1980 Wattleton maintained that, in *Roe*, the "Supreme Court ruled that the Constitution protected a woman's right to abortion." These feminists valued the Supreme Court's decision primarily because of the liberty it created for women. By tying *Roe* to women's rights, feminist leaders gave voice to their own beliefs about the value of the abortion battle.[60]

By the mid-1970s, partly because of the strategic choices made by the opposition, NARAL, Planned Parenthood, and NOW took action. Advocates in these organizations offered different interpretations of *Roe* as a way of building support for their cause and did so in Congress. The first wave of such interpretations came in 1975, when NARAL member Betty Friedan and Audrey Rowe Colom of the National Women's Political Caucus (NWPC) testified against one of the proposed human life amendments. Women's-rights interpretations of *Roe* served a dual purpose. First, in opposing a fetal-protective amendment, feminists could use such an interpretation to insist that the rights of the woman, not the unborn child, mattered most. More importantly, in confronting new woman-protective arguments, abortion-rights activists could present themselves as the real champions of sex equality. If the *Roe* decision recognized a right to abortion that advanced women's interests in liberty and equal citizenship, defending women's rights required the protection of the Supreme Court's opinion.

In testifying against a fetal personhood amendment, Betty Friedan explained that *Roe* did not ignore the personhood of the fetus but demanded recognition of "the personhood of woman." In 1975, Friedan explained: "[T]he Supreme Court . . . said that the right of [a] woman to control her own body and to choose privacy in the matter of bearing children was far more fundamental than many of the rights recognized in the Bill of Rights."[61] During the hearings on the amendment, Colom took a similar position. As the head of the NWPC, she represented a different understanding of feminism and a very different organization, one founded to help women achieve elected or appointed positions. In talking about abortion, Colom brought to bear her personal experience as a woman of color, a Republican feminist, a former welfare recipient, and a welfare rights activist. Nonetheless, during the same hearings, Colom made Friedan's point even clearer, asserting: "the *Roe* and *Doe* decisions" recognized that "[t]he right to control one's family size [and] the right to safe legal abortion" were "central to [women's] essential being and growth."[62]

In the mid-1970s, a woman's-rights interpretation spread. At a 1975 meeting of the NARAL Executive Committee, organization leaders reported that influential members of Congress responded when the group connected abortion and the ERA. In the late 1970s, an updated version of NARAL's "Debating the Opposition" featured a larger number of women's-rights arguments about *Roe* and did so more prominently. The central claim in the updated manual read as follows: "What we favor is not abortion but a woman's right to choose."[63]

NOW followed a similar course in the mid-1970s, emphasizing a women's-rights interpretation of *Roe*. In a January 1976 public service announcement, NOW members explained that the *Roe* decision had been made "on behalf of all women in this country," giving them "the right to choose and to privacy."[64] By 1978, the NOW standard "Chronology of Major Events Affecting Women's Right to Choose" described *Roe* as a decision in which the Court "declare[d] women ha[d] a right to an abortion based on the constitutional rights to equal protection and privacy."[65]

Planned Parenthood also began presenting *Roe* as a decision involving women's liberation. In May 1975 the organization approved a policy declaring that, under *Roe,* "[p]arenthood [had] cease[d] to be the primary . . . means to self-fulfillment for women, and [had become] a matter of genuine choice, one among many."[66] In January 1976 the organization adopted a measure stating: "growing opposition to the Supreme Court Decision on Abortion" threatened women's "freedom of choice."[67] In June the board adopted a plan of action on abortion that described *Roe* as a women's-rights decision. By the fall of 1977, the board began circulating a copy of the National Plan of Action generated at the National Women's Conference for International Women's Year, describing *Roe* as a decision "which guarantee[s] reproductive freedom to women."[68]

Pro-Lifers Seeking New Allies Connect the *Roe* Decision to Women's Rights

In the later 1970s, pro-life organizations similarly equated the *Roe* decision with women's rights. Reinterpreting the *Roe* decision advanced the interests of pro-lifers seeking a new identity for their movement. In working to convince the public and the media that they represented more than just Catholic America, antiabortion activists pursued supporters with a wide variety of political commitments. By not formally opposing contraception, pro-lifers hoped to increase support for their cause among left-leaning believers and nonbelievers. Conversely, by courting fundamentalist and evangelical ministers, pro-lifers tried to recruit more right-wing Protestants, many of whom might be expected to oppose abortion. Prior to the late 1970s, many of these efforts fell short.

With the emergence of the New Right and Religious Right, antiabortion leaders identified a new strategy for pursuing non-Catholic supporters. In spite of the religious differences and clashing policy preferences of various single-issue right-wing groups, Paul Weyrich and his allies made headway in building a powerful socially conservative coalition. At the same time, new theological understandings of abortion reached evangelical Protestants previously unmoved by the abortion battle. In creating a new coalition, New Right leaders worked to convince conservative Protestants of the importance of the abortion issue. In service of this goal, social conservatives formulated a new understanding of the *Roe* decision and of abortion rights, one that reflected the deep harm supposedly done by feminism to the American social fabric.

By advancing such an interpretation, activists advanced two long-standing antiabortion goals: increasing the religious diversity of the pro-life movement and maximizing overall social support for abortion bans. Just the same, this understanding of *Roe* proved to be a double-edged sword for a movement intent on becoming larger and more diverse. On the one hand, infusing interpretations of *Roe* with hostility to the women's movement promised to scare off the left-leaning Americans that leading antiabortion organizations had long tried not to offend. On the other hand, identifying antiabortion sentiment with antifeminist politics promised to increase the membership of the pro-life movement dramatically. In choosing to woo conservative Protestants, pro-lifers helped to solidify a movement interpretation of the *Roe* decision rooted in women's rights.

The antiabortion movement had long struggled to win over nonbelievers, Protestants, and Jews. Within the NRLC, the Education Committee and Interfaith/Intergroup Committee set out to attract a broad array of members with divergent views. At first, the NRLC Education Committee largely stayed away from "biblical tracks" and "sectarian issues," fearing that in using either, the movement "might be hitting one or two religions and missing others—perhaps alienating others."[69] Pro-lifers wanted to reach left-leaning Protestants, Jews, and others generally supportive of contraception while also reaching out to religious conservatives. As Judith Fink explained on behalf of the Interfaith/Intergroup Committee, the NRLC primarily sought to "broaden the base of the movement and bring the pro-life message to many millions more people than are now being reached."[70] The NRLC worked to recruit evangelical Protestants, at least some of whom seemed likely allies of the antiabortion movement. The organization urged its members to do pro-life workshops at "seminaries and Bible colleges" and to establish a "cooperative relationship" with the "Evangelical Press Association."[71] At the same time, NRLC leaders wanted to develop a relationship with the left-leaning National Council of Churches. NRLC leaders also adopted what Fink called the organization's "no policy statement" on birth control—refusing to say anything about contraception one way or another—to attract the largest possible number of recruits.[72]

Well into the mid-1970s, however, pro-lifers struggled to overcome the view that the movement represented a single religion. Since movement leaders disagreed about both contraception and a variety of other social questions, the "no policy statement" approach spread across a range of issues. At the same time, abortion-rights activists described the opposition as a front for Roman Catholicism. In 1976, for example, the Religious Coalition for Abortion Rights, an interdemoninational abortion-rights group founded three years earlier, attacked pro-lifers for seeking "to impose their religious doctrines on . . . people of other faiths."[73] Afraid of offending potential constituents, the NRLC struggled to dispel the impression that it championed a purely Catholic cause.[74]

With pro-lifers so publicly associated with Catholicism, a wide variety of religious organizations kept their distance from the movement. The National Council of Churches, which had endorsed reform in the early 1970s, remained committed to the cause of abortion rights. Before the late 1970s, certain prominent evangelical organizations, like the Southern Baptist Conference (SBC), actually favored limited reform of abortion bans. While some evangelical Protestants kept out of politics altogether, other religious conservatives remained on the sidelines because of a general anxiety about the Catholic Church and the causes it embraced. For example, Foy Valentine, the head of the SBC's Christian Life Commission for much of the 1970s, viewed the crusade against abortion as a Catholic conspiracy.[75]

As importantly, for conservative Protestants concerned about the ERA or the broader agenda of the women's movement, abortion appeared to be an isolated issue. Abortion-rights activists often presented legal abortion as a matter of population control or public health, largely disconnected from the politics of sex equality. Moreover, NOW leaders and other feminists consistently distanced the amendment from abortion politics, fearing that pro-life advances would otherwise stand in the way of the progress of the ERA.[76]

At the same time, pro-lifers struggled to win over left-leaning Protestants concerned, as Judith Fink put it, that their movement "opposed . . . contraception."[77] Leading organizations' decision to remain largely on the sidelines of battles about the ERA and family planning funding did nothing to change the minds of Protestants, Jews, and other Americans convinced that they did not fit in what many viewed as a Catholic movement.[78]

The New Right Unites Single-Issue Groups around a New Understanding of Abortion

Pro-lifers were not alone in seeking to build a broader, more diverse movement. In the later 1970s, leaders of the emerging New Right and Religious Right also worked to create a new socially conservative base for the Republican Party. To smooth out the differences between potential Catholic and Protestant recruits, New Right leaders not only emphasized the rhetoric of judicial activism but also helped to create a different understanding of both the *Roe* decision and the right to abortion. Appealing to the existing anxieties of some conservative Protestants about the women's movement and changes to the American family, Weyrich and his colleagues tied the *Roe* decision to the vision of women's rights championed by second-wave feminists. In doing so, New Right leaders hoped to create an effective alliance between conservative Catholics and Protestants.

The connection between antifeminism and antiabortion sentiment made by New Right activists reflected both advocates' strategic priorities and shifting beliefs. Tactically, redefining the *Roe* decision helped the New Right present a united front to the American public and to the Republican Party. Just the same, a number of political shifts made the relationship between the women's movement and abortion reform seem something far more than a political ploy.

First, antifeminist organizations like the Happiness of Women (HOW) and Phyllis Schlafly's STOP ERA reacted to the changing priorities of NOW and other leading feminist organizations. Under Karen DeCrow, NOW had put greater emphasis on issues of sexual liberty, including lesbian rights and reproductive autonomy. In 1976, when the Democratic Party platform did not endorse gay or lesbian rights, DeCrow and other NOW members led a rally outside Madison Square Garden to protest it. Observing NOW's new agenda, Schlafly and leading New Right figures began to see lesbianism and abortion as related evils—part of an effort by feminists to change the basic meaning of sex and sexuality. In expanding abortion rights and protections for gays and lesbians, the ERA would make women less like women and men less like men. Under the ERA, as Schlafly argued, abortion would make women "equal to men in their ability not to become pregnant."[79]

The rise of Schlafly's anti-ERA movement represented an important political opportunity for New Right leaders interested in coalition-building. Weyrich and other New Right veterans saw the relationship between antifeminism and antiabortion belief as an opening for a broader, conservative interfaith alliance. Schlafly and her supporters discovered a shared value system that cut across religious lines. Although there were strategic and ideological disagreements within the antifeminist movement, Schlafly's STOP ERA suggested that opposition to both abortion and the women's movement united religiously diverse social conservatives and made them into a potentially potent political force.[80]

The 1976 election served as a reminder of the power of voters who shared Schlafly's views. In the fall of that year, President Jimmy Carter gave an interview with *Playboy* magazine, explaining that his religious beliefs prevented him from passing judgment on free lovers and hedonists. Shocked by Carter's statements, conservative Protestants from Jerry Falwell to Bob Jones III became involved in the presidential race, making it clear that Carter—a fellow evangelical Protestant—did not represent their views, especially on the issues of sex, abortion, the ERA, and the women's movement. The uproar about Carter's *Playboy* interview again demonstrated that opposition to abortion and the ERA brought together otherwise diverse religious conservatives. Similarly, presidential candidate Ellen McCormack's pro-life and anti-ERA strategy identified an influential group of swing voters.[81]

To organize a new socially conservative coalition, the New Right reframed abortion as a feminist plot to undermine the traditional family and presented the *Roe* decision as a weapon of godless feminists. In 1980 Senator Jesse Helms, a powerful ally of the New Right, also described abortion as one of several threats to the American family. "[T]he permissiveness, the pornography, drugs, abortion, living together [outside of wedlock], divorce," Helms recited. "Somewhere, you've got to put the flag down and draw the line and say 'Enough is enough.'"[82]

To some extent, New Right operatives could claim credit for increasing evangelical participation in the pro-life movement—a strategic coup for those seeking to build a socially conservative political alliance. However, the evangelical wing of the pro-life movement also took shape because of a changing understanding of abortion and its theological stakes. In 1978, Francis Schaeffer, an evangelical theologian, called believers to account for staying on the sidelines of the abortion wars. Until the late 1970s, Schaeffer had worked mostly outside the spotlight, founding L'Abri, a religious retreat, in Switzerland. In 1977, however, Schaeffer stepped onto a larger public stage when his son, Frank, made his father's book, *How Shall We Then Live? The Rise and Decline of Western Culture*, into a film. In speaking to the camera, the theologian made an emotional plea to his fellow believers, describing legal abortion as a signal of cultural decay. The charismatic Schaeffer argued that legal abortion signaled the breakdown of "the Christian consensus." He called the *Roe* decision a harbinger of future rights to "kill the old, the incurably ill, [and] the insane."[83]

Schaeffer's admonitions inspired a number of evangelical popularizers, including Jerry Falwell and Timothy LaHaye, to take up pro-life politics. *How Shall We Then Live?* strengthened the position of conservative evangelicals seeking to reverse the SBC's support for legal abortion. Significantly, however, both Religious Right and New Right leaders reformulated Schaeffer's concerns about abortion, describing the *Roe* decision as an offshoot of the women's liberation movement. As evangelical leaders redefined the abortion issue, more believers identified with the pro-life cause.[84]

In the late 1970s, Falwell's Moral Majority called supporters to action, describing the amendment as "a satanic attack upon the family and the Bible."[85] The ERA, as the Moral Majority asserted, defied "the Scriptural mandate that the husband is the head of the wife, even as Christ is the head of the Church."[86]

Inspired partly by Schaeffer, Falwell and other Religious Right leaders combined antifeminist and pro-life sentiment. While evangelicals had previously believed that the ERA battle had nothing to do with abortion, groups like the Moral Majority came to insist that the issues were one and the same. Under the ERA, the Moral Majority insisted that "abortion on demand would be finalized."[87] Falwell related "the human and civil rights of millions of unborn babies" to the belief that the "only acceptable family form begins with the marriage of a man to a woman."[88]

By presenting abortion as one of several feminist threats to the traditional family, New Right and Religious Right leaders energized evangelicals who had not responded to the fetal-rights claims highlighted by the pro-life movement for much of the 1960s and 1970s.

In becoming politically active, evangelicals reacted to perceived federal interference with the family—conditions put by the IRS on tax-exempt evangelical schools, recognition of rights for gays and lesbians, Supreme Court decisions on school prayer, and the push for the ERA. The New Right convinced conservative evangelicals that abortion was one of several related moral cancers: "abortion on demand . . . , pornography, homosexuality, and godless humanism."[89] Only when conservative evangelicals viewed abortion as a threat to the traditional family did they flock to the pro-life movement.[90]

Pro-Lifers Use a Reinterpretation of *Roe* to Court New Allies

Leaders of the NRLC and other mainstream antiabortion groups seized on new interpretations of the *Roe* decision as part of an ongoing effort to create a more religiously diverse pro-life movement. Connecting *Roe* to women's rights resonated with potential recruits in the Religious Right who worried that second-wave feminism could destroy the American family. At the same time, linking pro-life politics to antifeminism put off the moderate and progressive believers and non-believers that the mainstream antiabortion movement had also courted. The movement's new understanding of the *Roe* decision reflected a difficult and costly set of tactical tradeoffs—a choice dictated in part by a rapidly shifting political reality.[91]

In 1976 testimony before the House Judiciary Committee, for example, NRLC member Professor Joseph Witherspoon emphasized that the "Court in [*Roe v.*] *Wade* created a constitutional right in a pregnant woman to direct a physician to perform an abortion on her mere demand"—a right that undercut the "power of fathers to protect their unborn children."[92]

Later in 1976, when testifying before the House Judiciary Committee against appropriations for International Women's Year, Nellie Gray linked women's rights, International Women's Year, and *Roe* and *Doe*. In Gray's view, all three wrongly recognized and endorsed "a woman's right to control her reproduction or her right to kill her children."[93]

Legal briefs submitted by the movement similarly described abortion as a right belonging only to women. As late as 1976, Americans United for Life contended that *Roe* involved both "a woman's right to an abortion or a physician's right to practice medicine."[94] By contrast, in 1978 the organization made no mention of physicians' rights. Arguing in favor of a law requiring a minor to consult her parents before seeking an abortion, Americans United for Life emphasized that in *Roe* and its progeny, "the major reason for the abortion right is . . . to free the woman of the burdens of an unwanted child."[95] In *Williams v. Zbaraz*, one of a series of late-1970s cases on abortion funding, an amicus brief submitted by the National Right to Life Committee explained that in *Roe*, the "Court . . . extend[ed] a woman's right to decide whether or not she desires an abortion."[96]

By 1980, even as conflict within the NRLC reemerged, the new leadership of the group stressed similar arguments. In 1978, Jefferson failed to win reelection. Brown left the organization, and a new leader, Dr. Carolyn Gerster, took the helm. A physician from Scottsdale, Arizona, Gerster played an influential part in the Arizona pro-life movement in the early 1970s. She had a powerful personal narrative about her reasons for joining the movement: she had been traumatized by a late-term miscarriage and could not understand why anyone would choose to end a pregnancy.[97]

Like Jefferson and Brown before her, Gerster described *Roe v. Wade* as a decision involving women's rights and the women's movement. In 1980 she told the *New York Times* that *Roe* reflected a "certain Uncle Tomism" that was latent "in the women's movement, a desire to emulate men." She explained to the *New York Times* that neither *Roe* nor the women's movement could change the fact that biology "[was,] to a great extent[,] destiny." Gerster did not question that *Roe* had a women's-rights rationale. Instead, she argued that *Roe* and its rationale were misguided. As she stated, "[w]omen bear children. It may not be fair, but that's the way things are."[98]

By the late 1970s, both abortion-rights and pro-life activists concluded that the Supreme Court's decision involved a woman's right to choose. In social-movement struggle, *Roe* no longer described only the Supreme Court's decision. Instead, opposing activists used *Roe* as a weapon in the war to reshape public attitudes toward legal abortion. At times, movement members projected changing views about gender and abortion onto the Court's opinion.

Abortion-rights activists began describing *Roe* as a women's-rights decision after the opposition ate away at their assumed monopoly on female support. Presenting the decision as a vindication of women's reproductive freedom made sense to a movement trying to solidify the support of female voters. As importantly, as feminists gained influence over abortion-rights politics, a women's-rights interpretation of *Roe* reflected the values of new movement leaders.

For its part, the pro-life movement adopted a women's-rights interpretation of *Roe* in seeking to create an interfaith movement against abortion. With the mobilization of the New Right and Religious Right, however, the antiabortion movement identified a powerful new rhetorical tool. As part of an effort to unite activists with deeply different religious views and policy priorities, New Right leaders had redefined both abortion rights and the *Roe* decision, tapping into conservative Protestants' opposition to second-wave feminism. By borrowing this tactic, pro-lifers hoped finally to make their movement stronger and more diverse. At the same time, linking the *Roe* decision to antifeminism distanced the antiabortion movement from other potential recruits.

How to Think of Roe

Leading accounts suggest that the Supreme Court put an end to popular dialogue about the scope and rationale of abortion rights. The Supreme Court forced a single solution on the nation. Faced with the *Roe* decision, pro-life activists supposedly understood that their views of abortion rights no longer mattered. Scholars often contend that *Roe* undermined a previously promising process of innovation. Because the Court intervened prematurely, activists did not arrive at an interpretation of abortion rights that won widespread support.

However, the story of *Roe*'s reinterpretation makes clear that the Supreme Court hardly ended creative discussion about the meaning of abortion rights. Instead, opposing advocates channeled their beliefs and strategic priorities into discussion of what *Roe* truly said. At times, activists used *Roe* to win new supporters, raise money, and change citizens' minds about legal abortion. On other occasions, new interpretations of *Roe* mirrored the shifting ideological commitments held by opposing activists.

Immediately after 1973, the leaders of organizations like NARAL saw little reason to present abortion as anything but a right for physicians and patients. Arguments of this kind invoked the respectability of the medical profession and the authority of the Supreme Court.

While challenging the Supreme Court's reasoning appeared likely to provoke more debate, interpreting *Roe* as a medical decision allowed NARAL members to insist that meaningful disagreement about legal abortion had come to an end. Such an interpretation also reflected deeply-held convictions of activists who wanted to remove the stigma and danger surrounding abortion. Some reformers believed that treating abortion as both a standard medical procedure and a physician's right would allow the movement to make abortion safer, more accessible, and more socially legitimate.

Pro-life leaders interpreting the *Roe* decision in this way voiced genuine disappointment in both the medical profession and the Supreme Court. Focusing on physicians allowed pro-life activists to condemn what they saw as doctors' decision to forsake their duty to preserve life. Strategically, such an interpretation formed part of a larger effort to convince women that legal abortion promised a freedom that it could never deliver. By drawing attention to physicians' rights, pro-lifers argued that the Supreme Court's decision did nothing for women.

As antiabortion activists successfully bid for the loyalty of a larger group of female supporters, opposing groups began reinterpreting *Roe* as a decision involving women's rights to equality and liberty. Pro-lifers ultimately turned to such an interpretation in an effort to sway a larger group of supporters. Connecting the *Roe* decision to the movement for women's liberation appealed to an influential group of potential partners in the New Right and Religious Right. At the same time, such an interpretation alienated left-leaning Americans that the pro-life movement had tried to recruit.

Mildred Jefferson had her own reasons for redefining what the Supreme Court said. In July 1977, Jefferson issued a press release condemning a major feminist conference. She made sure that the press knew about all of her professional accomplishments, particularly her post at Boston University's School of Medicine. At the same time, she insisted that the abortion rights set forth by the Supreme Court made women "social terrorists."[99] She harshly criticized the women's movement that had unleashed *Roe* on society. "The abandonment of the nurturing and sustaining role of women," Jefferson argued, "is a threat to the future of all mankind."[100]

In remaking *Roe*, activists like Jefferson listened to and borrowed from their opponents. Together, the abortion-rights and pro-life movements created an interpretation of *Roe* that has had staying power.

Most observers have come to take for granted the interpretation of *Roe* that emerged from interest-group debate. Does *Roe* protect a woman's right to choose, instead of the right of a doctor, a patient, or some other actor? In current debate, the answer is simple, and it is an answer owed in large part to the work of abortion interest groups. Of course, *Roe* recognizes a woman's right to choose. It always has.

CHAPTER SIX

Compromise and Polarization

THE SUPREME COURT'S decision did not short-circuit social movement experimentation with the meaning of abortion rights. Indeed, in the later 1970s, opposing activists used different interpretations of *Roe* to advance competing ideas about the women's movement. By focusing on those who ultimately found themselves out of place in the abortion debate, this chapter explores a related and equally important historiographical question surrounding movement-countermovement interaction: did *Roe v. Wade* undermine promising compromises on other gender issues?

Scholars argue that the Supreme Court's decision polarized debate about the Equal Rights Amendment (ERA), sex-discrimination law, and family planning. By exposing fundamental differences in worldview about women's proper role in American society, *Roe* theoretically made compromise on any gender issue virtually impossible.[1]

However, by focusing on advocates eventually marginalized in either movement, we gain a significantly different understanding of post-1973 efforts to reach consensus. This chapter tells the story of an influential group of activists who, for the better part of a decade after the Supreme Court decision, strove to work with those on the other side of the abortion issue. While not seeking a shared solution on abortion, these activists fought to find common ground on legal issues from fetal research to pregnancy discrimination. Their experiences spotlight the diversity of members of both the antiabortion and abortion-rights movements in the decade after *Roe*. Some advocates on either side of the issue fit poorly within the "pro-choice" and "pro-life" categories now familiar to us. By the early 1980s, many of the activists studied in this chapter faced a Hobson's choice: giving up on abortion politics or fitting within a movement that no longer fully reflected their basic beliefs.

Studying the journey of those who struggled to keep a place in abortion politics also offers crucial insight into how the conflict became so polarized. Consider, for example, the stories of Warren Schaller, Mary Meehan, and Mary Ann Kuharski.

Having moved up quickly through the ranks of the Episcopal Church in Minneapolis/St. Paul, Schaller preached from a progressive point of view. He and his wife supported the ERA and had trouble understanding why anyone would oppose equality for women. They believed in rights to contraception as well, and expected that they would feel the same about abortion. After attending a lecture on the subject, however, Warren left opposed to the procedure. He became involved in Marjory Mecklenburg's Minnesota Citizens Concerned for Life (MCCL), as well as national groups such as the National Right to Life Committee (NRLC) and American Citizens Concerned for Life (ACCL). Schaller believed that refusing to seek common ground with supporters of abortion rights was the equivalent of "putting the shotgun in your mouth and pulling the trigger."[2]

Meehan first became active in the antiwar movement in the late 1960s. She grew up in a patriotic household; four of her uncles served in World War II, and two of her mother's first cousins—young brothers—died in that war. However, as Meehan moved through high school and learned more about the bombing of Hiroshima and American military intervention in Latin America, she found herself deeply troubled by the question of when—or if—war was just. When the United States escalated the war in Vietnam, Meehan stood up against it, mourning the lost lives of young soldiers and civilians. She also worked passionately for the 1968 presidential campaign of Democratic antiwar candidate Eugene McCarthy. Although she didn't follow the women's movement closely, Meehan in some ways considered herself a "born feminist." She felt that consciousness-raising was the most valuable part of the women's movement. Concerned about the limited career options available to women at the time, she wanted to stand up and cheer the first time she saw a woman who was driving a public bus in Washington, DC.[3]

After the decision of *Roe v. Wade*, Meehan identified abortion as a great American tragedy. She waited for her colleagues in the peace movement to take a stand for the unborn and did not understand when friends stayed silent. She began researching, writing, and protesting against abortion, identifying a relationship between abortion and eugenics that she believed explained efforts to legalize the procedure. Meehan's writing launched a lifelong quest to advance what she considered a consistent vision of the right to life—an effort to value all lives, whether in war or peace, whether poor or rich, whether born or unborn.[4]

A liberal Democrat like Meehan, Kuharski lived in a working-class, pro-union neighborhood in Minneapolis, and she had worked to help rebuild African-American neighborhoods devastated by the rioting that followed the death of Dr. Martin Luther King Jr. She eventually became a mother of thirteen, including several mixed-race children she adopted. In the 1970s Kuharski saw the fight against abortion as the quintessential liberal struggle. As she still recalls, the two most disheartening and memorable events of her life were the assassination of President John F. Kennedy and the announcement of *Roe v. Wade*. In the early- to mid- 1970s, she played a major part in Minnesota Democratic Party Politics, as well as in Feminists for Life and Minnesota Citizens Concerned for Life.[5]

In telling the stories of those, like Schaller, Kuharski, and Meehan, who found themselves estranged from either movement, the chapter exposes the complex origins of the clash of absolutes we know today. Non-judicial actors did as much as the Supreme Court to escalate the abortion conflict. In part, the leaders of the abortion-rights and antiabortion movements reacted to the reordering of American politics—particularly, the rise of the New Right and the Religious Right and the realignment of party politics.[6]

However, the leaders of the opposing movements did not simply react to the growing polarization of the abortion battle; they made conscious choices that contributed to it. The New Right and the Religious Right promised pro-lifers badly-needed funding and political influence. At the same time, as pro-lifers allied with antifeminists, abortion-rights leaders came to view compromise with the opposition as impossible. Finally, with the party politics of abortion still in flux, the leaders of each opposing movement began to view consensus-seeking as a liability. To pressure politicians effectively, both movements presented their supporters as absolutely unwilling to compromise. Seeking middle-ground solutions, it increasingly seemed, could spell defeat at the polls.

The Supreme Court's intervention did not sabotage all efforts to forge creative compromises on other issues involving women's rights. If anything, some influential activists believed that the Court's decision had made consensus-seeking more urgent. A variety of actors share the responsibility for the gradual polarization of gender politics in the late 1970s and early 1980s. For reasons beyond the *Roe* decision, solutions that had once appeared within reach began to seem politically impossible.

Influential Pro-Lifers Present Women's Rights as an Alternative to Abortion

What kind of compromise remained after the Supreme Court's decision in *Roe v. Wade*? Certainly, some pro-lifers supported exceptions to bans on abortion, and for strategic reasons, incrementalist activists focused on laws that would restrict access to abortion rather than outlawing it altogether. In the late 1970s, however, an influential group of abortion opponents argued that the *Roe* decision had made the effort to find common ground on other gender issues more important than an ever. According to a 1977 editorial in *Commonweal*, a progressive Catholic journal, the Supreme Court had "left open the possibility that moderate elements . . . might, through dialogue, evolve some kind of compromise social policy." The editorial suggested that activists for and against abortion rights could work together in demanding "grants for sex education, family planning, and family support," "an enormous public and private investment . . . in health care . . . , allowances for food, clothing, and education; a guaranteed job, . . . subsidized housing and more generous welfare payments."[7]

The *Commonweal* editorial reflected continued interest among some influential pro-lifers in working with the opposition to make abortion less necessary. Certainly, some conservatives, including those who would form the absolutist wing of the antiabortion movement, had little interest in any partnership with the opposition. With few exceptions, pro-lifers tolerated no exceptions to abortion bans. Indeed, the constitutional amendments favored by most movement members throughout the decade would have criminalized all abortions. Later, incrementalists pursued what some saw as middle-ground solutions but did so for purely tactical reasons. The quest for common ground on abortion itself seemed all but dead, either before or after 1973.[8]

However, if we focus on efforts to seek compromise on other gender issues—and on activists ultimately marginalized in either movement—a different picture emerges. Although sometimes in conflict with their colleagues, prominent pro-lifers fought to find agreement with the opposition on other gender issues. Unlike incrementalists, who agreed primarily on questions of strategy, those interested in compromise often shared a similar vision of the ideal relationship between law and reproductive health. While sometimes embracing incrementalist strategies in the abortion struggle, many activists in the latter group had a different focus—finding ways to make abortion less necessary and devising strategies to advance a particular idea of reproductive choice. Some pro-lifers worked side by side with feminists in the fight for the ERA. More importantly, abortion opponents fought for laws banning pregnancy discrimination, ensuring financial support for new mothers, and guaranteeing the right to child care. These activists remained steadfastly opposed to legal abortion. However, influential pro-lifers called for the government to guarantee a different kind of choice, ensuring that women could afford to have children without sacrificing their careers, educations, or economic security.

Pat Goltz's Feminists for Life believed that opposition to abortion formed an integral part of the fight for sex equality. While mainstream legal feminists saw fertility control as necessary for women seeking equal citizenship, Goltz and her allies regarded abortion as an obstacle to women's efforts to overcome sex discrimination in the home or the workplace. Juli Loesch (later, Juli Loesch Wiley), a member of Feminists for Life and the Pax Center, a liberal Catholic organization, argued that legal abortion offered a false solution to women's problems: "This is finally what it comes down to: women whose pregnancies are an emotional, social, or financial burden are thrown up against a rather heartless individualism. . . . We . . . deserve, and have a right to demand, that men accept their role in nurturing babies. *We insist that the men must change*—[that men] accept equal male-female cooperation, decision-making, and responsibility in the earliest, most demanding stages of their children's lives. What we need is not abortion. What we need is revolution."[9]

Loesch and other members of the organization argued that the State used legal abortion as an excuse for withholding support for women who decided to work while raising children. A resolution passed by national Feminists for Life in January 1978 similarly contended: "A responsible society must make room for woman-as-childbearer. . . . It is a degradation of woman's rights that she should feel compelled to destroy human life she carries to safeguard her basic, human, civil, and economic rights."[10]

Members of Feminists for Life saw the ERA as a critical part of the effort to make women equal citizens, to give them "equal rights," and to allow them "to protect and nourish the lives of their children."[11] Feminists for Life argued that women should not have to sacrifice other opportunities in order to fulfill their role as mothers. The ERA would help eliminate the discrimination that forced women into this false choice, making it easier for activists to create "those support services in the community without which a woman in a desperate situation really has no good choice."[12]

Partly because of the mobilization of antifeminists, the ERA campaign eventually ended in disappointment. In voting for the ERA, the 92nd Congress had introduced a seven-year time limit, but when the deadline passed, only thirty-five states had ratified the amendment. Even after a simple majority in Congress voted in August 1978 to extend the deadline, the amendment did not make progress. In June 1982, when the extension expired, ERA supporters remained three states short of the required thirty-eight.[13]

In spite of the setbacks faced by ERA proponents after 1973, support for women's rights in the antiabortion movement reached beyond Feminists for Life. Throughout the mid- to late 1970s, prominent pro-lifers articulated a new vision of reproductive choice, demanding new rights for mothers and redefining the law of sex discrimination. One of the greatest contributors to this strategy, Marjory Mecklenburg, played a crucial role in the early years of the NRLC. A former home economics teacher, she had defined herself as the supportive spouse of an influential physician and family planning activist. In the antiabortion movement, however, her husband, Fred, came to seem the helpmate of a more powerful partner. It was Marjory who held positions of leadership and popularized a surprising new vision of what it meant to oppose abortion. Pro-lifers nationwide selected Marjory as the first chairman of the NLRC, and her views influenced the organization's first statement of purpose. She helped to spearhead the campaign to separate the NLRC from the Catholic Church and ensured that the organization would select her friend and colleague Warren Schaller to serve as the organization's first executive director.[14]

During her time in the NRLC, Mecklenburg and her allies called on pro-lifers to condemn sterilization abuse and refrain from opposing contraception. Of course, Mecklenburg's views sparked debate within the NRLC, and her battles with Edward Golden, then-president of the NRLC, nearly crippled the organization. In spite of this conflict, Mecklenburg retained strong support. Before she left the organization in June 1973, NRLC members resoundingly reelected her to the NRLC Executive Committee. Partly because of her influence, the NRLC also adopted a major 1974 policy resolution, calling for the removal of the word "illegitimate" from birth certificates and insisting that the "marital status of the mother" should not "affect the privileges and responsibilities conferred by the United States government and the several states."[15]

Well into the 1970s, Mecklenburg's ideas appealed to a majority in the NRLC—and to a significant group of pro-lifers. Gradually, in the wake of the mobilization of the New Right and Religious Right, a variety of antiabortion activists voiced greater discomfort with the women's movement as a whole, but the connections between antifeminism and pro-life activism tell only part of the story. The NRLC's illegitimacy resolution sheds light on a broader effort to reconcile some form of reproductive freedom with opposition to abortion—to join protection for the fetus with rights for unwed mothers, working women, and the poor. Some within the antiabortion movement believed that penalizing unwed mothers might help deter women from engaging in premarital sex and might encourage what Mecklenburg called "responsible interpersonal relationships between men and women."[16] Nonetheless, Mecklenburg convinced many of her colleagues that punishing sexually active women mattered less than ensuring rights for both mothers and the unborn. Instead of ostracizing women who violated sexual conventions, as Mecklenburg had previously written, society could reduce the number of abortions and "rescue the girl . . . by showing her that we value her and have confidence in her."[17]

In the mid- to late 1970s, Mecklenburg's allies foregrounded the plight of unwed mothers and women who faced discrimination at work, believing that rights for all mothers, including those who gave birth outside of wedlock, would reduce the number of abortions performed. At the same time, by providing mothers with the resources to raise a child, the government would for the first time provide women with meaningful reproductive freedom. Focusing on rights for women allowed Mecklenburg and her allies to seek some form of consensus with those on the opposing side of the abortion issue. With the procedure legal and accessible, these pro-lifers believed that it was more important than ever to convince all Americans, even those who favored a right to choose, to give women better alternatives.

Pro-Lifers Demand Protections for Poor Women, New Mothers, and Pregnant Workers

In the later 1970s, Mecklenburg and her supporters translated her vision of rights and respect for mothers into legal reform. For the most part, she worked through an alternative antiabortion organization, American Citizens Concerned for Life (ACCL), the national equivalent to Mecklenburg's Minnesota group. To some contemporary scholars, the ACCL appears to be small and relatively unimportant: founded prior to *Roe* and no longer functioning by the mid-1980s.[18]

However, Mecklenburg and the ACCL helped to reshape the law on pregnancy discrimination. Her allies forged a new understanding of reproductive choice that resonated with prominent politicians in favor of abortion rights. As Warren Schaller, then an ACCL leader, explained, influential pro-lifers opposed abortion while insisting that "women should be able to control their own reproductive functions and [that] couples should be able to determine the size of their family."[19] Moreover, the ACCL sought, whenever possible, to identify reforms that those on both sides of the abortion issue could support, such as laws on public funding for child care and family planning. As one ACCL leader explained: "[I]f we persist in avoiding and rejecting the help of concerned citizens who may promote sex education or family planning programs or welfare programs to support the unwed, we deserve to be left frustrated and angry."[20]

Beginning in the mid-1970s, public panic about teenage pregnancy offered Mecklenburg and her supporters an opportunity to redefine reproductive choice. Like many of her colleagues, Mecklenburg supported a constitutional amendment outlawing all abortions except when the woman's life was at risk. Just the same, Mecklenburg and her allies championed an alternative understanding of choice— one that denounced abortion but recognized the importance of both combating sex discrimination and providing a social safety net for the poor. If women had a right to choose, as Mecklenburg argued, then the government had to ensure that all women, including juveniles, could afford to bear and raise children. Her allies lobbied for state and federal laws prohibiting discrimination on the basis of marital status or pregnancy, and she asked Congress to consider funding "well-run daycare facilit[ies]," sex education, and family planning initiatives. Her supporters also endorsed laws "designed to eliminate the social stigma which much of our society still places on single parenthood."[21]

Mecklenburg started to elaborate on this idea of choice in the push for the School Age Mother and Child Health Act of 1975, a comprehensive aid program for unwed mothers. The law would have authorized funding for pregnancy testing, health care for newborns and toddlers, family planning, day care, continuing education, and adoption assistance. Planned Parenthood endorsed the reform, as did the ACCL. In 1975, in testifying in favor of the bill, Mecklenburg explained what she meant by reproductive choice: "Surely advocacy of 'the right of a woman to choose' does include the right for her to choose to continue her pregnancy. . . . In the process, she should be able to maintain her own self-respect, dignity and physiological and psychological health."[22]

Mecklenburg saw a better social safety net as a guarantee that fewer women would choose abortion. By saving women from poverty, discrimination, and joblessness, Mecklenburg asserted that pro-lifers could save unborn lives. At the same time, Mecklenburg argued that without state support and respect for the caretaking work performed by women, freedom of choice would "be just an empty word."[23]

The School Age Mother and Child Act of 1975 did not pass, but the ACCL continued lobbying for state financial support for adolescent mothers. After the 1976 presidential election, Mecklenburg's supporters found themselves in an advantageous position. President Jimmy Carter came into office seeking out a moderate position in the abortion wars. Carter's interest in compromise made a good deal of sense under the circumstances. In 1976 the passage of the Hyde Amendment began a series of battles about the scope of abortion-funding restrictions, struggles so intense that Congress found itself repeatedly unable to pass major appropriations legislation. In such an environment, compromise in and of itself was appealing. At the same time, reports released by both Planned Parenthood's Guttmacher Institute and by university researchers highlighted a spike in the rate of pregnancy for unwed teenagers. The Carter Administration responded by creating the kind of abortion policy long promoted by the ACCL: Carter supported both Medicaid funding bans and greater funding for sex education and family planning, especially for juveniles.[24]

With the spotlight on adolescent pregnancy, Mecklenburg's allies continued to promote their vision of a right to choose. The ACCL partnered with Planned Parenthood in lobbying for the Adolescent Health, Services, and Pregnancy Prevention and Care Act, a 1978 law funding family planning, sex education, and child care for teenagers. For Mecklenburg and her allies, protecting teenage mothers would serve as the opening battle in a war for mothers' rights. Poor, unmarried adolescents had the fewest reproductive choices, sometimes sacrificing their health, freedom, education, and career prospects to raise children. If lawmakers truly respected motherhood, as Mecklenburg believed, the government would not demand so much from its youngest parents.[25]

In the later 1970s, reproductive rights activists in organizations like the Committee for Abortion Rights and Against Sterilization Abuse (CARASA) and the Reproductive Rights National Network (R2N2) began to develop a similarly broad understanding of the right to choose. Of course, feminists disagreed strongly with the ACCL on abortion and a variety of other issues. While leaders of CARASA and R2N2 emphasized the unique challenges faced by women of color, Mecklenburg's allies made little mention of racial differences in women's access to reproductive health care. Moreover, whereas leaders of CARASA and R2N2 demanded sexual freedom for women, Mecklenburg's followers presented non-marital sex as a problem (although not as a justification for punishing women).[26]

Just the same, some pro-life activists and feminists partly agreed about the meaning of a right to choose. Regardless of their disagreements about abortion, influential feminists and pro-lifers both reasoned that reproductive freedom would be a reality only when the government guaranteed that women could afford to bear and raise children.

While Mecklenburg and her allies built a transformative reform program around the rights of unwed mothers, her supporters made the greatest difference in the fight against pregnancy discrimination. For much of the 1970s, feminists made pregnancy disability reform part of a larger project to separate women's biological and social roles in parenting—an effort that included demands for a universal right to free, quality child care. Feminists began reconceptualizing pregnancy discrimination in 1970, when the Citizens Advisory Council on the Status of Women announced a new paradigm for pregnant workers. Rather than demanding a separate maternity leave program, the

Council urged employers to define pregnancy- and childbirth-related conditions as "temporary disabilities" covered by existing, sex-neutral workplace policies on health insurance and sick leave. As developed by feminists throughout the 1970s, the temporary-disability paradigm promised economic security for childbearing women. At the same time, as feminists envisioned it, the temporary-disability framework "challenged sex-role stereotypes by affirming individual opportunity, by distinguishing between women's biological and social roles in reproduction, and by seeking benefits for women workers within a universal framework."[27]

In the late 1970s, some prominent pro-lifers supported protections against pregnancy discrimination, albeit for different reasons. In 1976 Mecklenburg's allies first took notice when the Supreme Court concluded that pregnancy discrimination did not violate the federal Civil Rights Act of 1964. In a class action lawsuit against General Electric, a group of female employees challenged the company's disability policy, which afforded no medical leave for pregnancy or childbirth. Members of the class argued that pregnancy discrimination counted as sex discrimination and thus ran afoul of the Civil Rights Act of 1964. In *General Electric Company v. Gilbert*, the Supreme Court rejected this argument. Reasoning that not all women were pregnant, the justices differentiated sex and pregnancy discrimination. In doing so, the Court effectively barred any pregnancy-discrimination claim, since an earlier decision, *Geduldig v. Aiello*, had held that pregnancy discrimination did not constitute sex discrimination under the Equal Protection Clause of the Fourteenth Amendment.[28]

The ACCL's campaign to undo *Gilbert* reveals the complexity of the views held by its members on sex discrimination and reproductive choice. We can better understand these nuances by examining the relationship between the ACCL and feminist members of the Committee to End Discrimination against Pregnant Workers (CEDAPW), a coalition of labor, civil rights, and women's groups that included leading abortion-rights supporters like NOW and the American Civil Liberties Union (ACLU). Both the ACCL and CEDAPW endorsed federal protections against pregnancy discrimination, and both groups backed a version of such a law that did not exclude the cost of medical care after an abortion. Members of each organization, however, took dramatically different paths to arrive at this conclusion.[29]

Drawing on a 1977 *New York Times* editorial by Susan Deller Ross and Ruth Bader Ginsburg, CEDAPW presented the fact of pregnancy as a central excuse for the subordination of women. Ginsburg, then a professor at Columbia Law School and a co-founder of the ACLU Women's Rights Project, led litigation efforts establishing that the Equal Protection Clause of the Fourteenth Amendment prohibited some forms of sex discrimination. For her part, Deller Ross had worked as a staff attorney at the Equal Employment Opportunity Commission in 1972 when that body had interpreted Title VII of the Civil Rights Act of 1964 as prohibiting pregnancy discrimination. Ginsburg and Deller Ross both insisted that sex discrimination in the workplace often stemmed from the fact that women could become pregnant.[30]

When hearings began in Congress on the Pregnancy Discrimination Act of 1978 (PDA), a federal law designed to overturn *Gilbert*, Deller Ross and prominent feminist advocate Wendy Webster Williams again presented pregnancy discrimination as the root cause of the bias women faced at work. Williams insisted that "[t]he common thread of justification running through most policies that discriminated against women . . . rested ultimately on the capacity and fact of pregnancy."[31] In Deller Ross's view, Congress could not eradicate sex discrimination without attacking pregnancy-based bias, which served as "the central justification of and support for discrimination against women workers."[32]

Other feminists promoting the PDA forged what Deborah Dinner has called neomaternalist arguments—describing pregnancy, childbearing, and childrearing as a service to the community. Feminists like Sylvia Law, a law professor at New York University Law School, and Letty Cottin Pogrebin, a founding editor of *Ms.* magazine, argued that since society benefited from women's willingness to carry children, the government should bear some of the costs of reproduction. At a minimum, given the value of childbearing women to the larger society, the government had a duty to protect them from sex discrimination.[33]

Mecklenburg's supporters shared some feminists' view that society undervalued motherhood and forced women to bear more than their fair share of its costs. However, sex stereotypes surrounding pregnancy played almost no part in the April 1977 testimony offered by the ACCL General Counsel, Jacqueline Nolan-Haley, a former prosecutor who had defended the *Edelin* prosecution before Congress. Speaking on behalf of the ACCL, Nolan-Haley presented women's defenselessness as an indisputable fact. Williams emphasized the career setbacks faced by women who took maternity leave. Nolan-Haley instead stressed that pregnancy was involuntary, especially for women who opposed abortion. Williams and Nolan-Haley agreed, however, that *Gilbert* would force women to have abortions in order to save their jobs.[34]

Over the course of 1977, the ACCL came to share more of the concerns about reproductive choice voiced by Williams and other feminists. In March, ACCL leader Judith Fink stated: "We hope that the Supreme Court did not mean to say that a woman worker must choose between wages and her unborn baby's life—that she does not have a constitutional right to both. But it looks that way."[35] Nolan-Haley described reproductive liberty in similar terms, asserting: "When a woman is faced with losing her income . . . because of pregnancy, her decision to abort cannot be said to be the product of free choice."[36]

The events of 1977–1978 tested the ACCL's commitment to a principle of meaningful choice. In both the House and the Senate, members of Congress, including Senator Thomas Eagleton (D-MO) and Representative Edward Beard (D-RI), introduced amendments providing that the proposed PDA would not require employer coverage of anything related to abortion. ACCL leaders urged their supporters to endorse the law whether or not it prohibited funding for post-abortion care.[37]

Why did an organization opposed to legal abortion take this position? In her June 1977 testimony, Dr. Dorothy Czarnecki, a Pennsylvania obstetrician-gynecologist and a leading ACCL member, explained the reasoning behind the organization's decision. She expressed support for women who wished to work. According to Czarnecki, *Gilbert* would force women "into a backup method of destructive obstetrics, such as abortion."[38]

Pro-life members of Congress demanded that she explain why her organization would support the bill if it required employers to cover post-abortion treatment. She responded that the ACCL advocated for a certain form of reproductive choice. For activists like Czarnecki, reproductive freedom required the government to protect women from sex discrimination—to ensure that they did not have to make a false choice between work and family. As she explained, the PDA "would encourage a woman to keep a pregnancy or do what she wants. It gives women a choice."[39]

The PDA passed in 1978. The final bill did not require an employer to provide health-insurance benefits for abortion unless a woman's life would be at risk if she carried a pregnancy to term or if complications arose after an abortion. The struggle for the PDA exposed the differences between ACCL members and many feminists. Mecklenburg and the ACCL believed abortion to be wrong, and those who shared her perspective argued that fetuses enjoyed rights equal (and often superior) to those of women, a position that many feminists certainly denounced. Nonetheless, the ACCL identified areas of agreement with abortion-rights supporters. Like feminists who supported abortion rights, ACCL members campaigned for publicly funded family planning services. ACCL members also argued, as did some feminists who favored abortion rights, that the State should subsidize child care and contraception services and guarantee freedom from sex discrimination. Only under such circumstances would reproductive decisions be truly voluntary.

Significantly, the idea of reproductive choice outlined by the ACCL resonated with influential policymakers supportive of abortion rights. Indeed, there is evidence that Mecklenburg's perspective on the right to choose shaped the success of the PDA campaign. Key sponsors of the PDA echoed this idea of reproductive choice. Senator Eagleton, a committed pro-lifer, argued that sex discrimination could effectively coerce women into terminating a pregnancy: "[T]here are a number of reasons why a woman would want to have an abortion. One of the reasons is that she cannot afford the expenses attendant to a prolonged pregnancy and childbirth. . . . We are removing that [situation] where the price tag of a baby determines whether it is born or not."[40] Representative Ronald Sarasin (R-CT) similarly argued that women with real reproductive choice would be better able to participate in the economic and social life of the nation. The PDA gave a woman "the right to choose both [childrearing and career], to be financially and legally protected before, during, and after her pregnancy."[41]

Working in groups like the ACCL, some pro-lifers had principled and tactical reasons for endorsing certain rights for women. Laws like the PDA provided both symbolic and material support for mothers—something prized by Mecklenburg's followers. As importantly, ACCL leaders believed that the search for common ground lent respectability to what many saw as a fringe pro-life movement. Working with feminists to guarantee mothers' rights appeared both strategically necessary and morally correct. As the ACCL's fundraising materials asserted: "Respect for life can eventually be reinstated, but only if we persuade—not pressure; educate—not intimidate; gather—not divide."[42]

The Supreme Court did not undermine the work of activists attracted to groups like Feminists for Life or the ACCL. Instead, in adjusting to major political changes in the late 1970s and early 1980s, the mainstream pro-life movement drifted away from the principles these groups embraced. In 1980 both parties took stronger stands on the abortion issue. As Republicans proved to be receptive allies, leaders of the antiabortion movement pushed their colleagues to work with conservative candidates. At the same time, the New Right and Religious Right provided struggling pro-lifers with financial resources and political reinforcements. In return, the antiabortion movement put greater emphasis on the rhetoric and reforms favored by its new allies.

Mecklenburg found her agenda transformed by the political trends that reshaped antiabortion politics. In 1981 Ronald Reagan selected her to head the Office of Adolescent Pregnancy Programs. Mecklenburg's appointment nearly coincided with the release of a new report by the Guttmacher Institute, indicating the rate of adolescent pregnancy had remained roughly constant notwithstanding broader access to contraception. The Reagan Administration seized on the report as evidence of the need for a change in federal support for family planning. If contraception had not addressed the problem of adolescent pregnancy, as some argued, the only solution was abstinence. Mecklenburg adopted the Administration's position, explaining in a co-authored piece in 1983 that family planning efforts would then be "aimed at preventing adolescent sexual activity."[43]

Under Mecklenburg, the Reagan Administration would propose a "squeal rule," requiring any federally funded clinic to inform parents whenever a teenager requested birth control. When Congress passed the Adolescent Family Life Act of 1981 (AFLA), Mecklenburg headed efforts to advance an agenda that was both pro-abstinence and antiabortion. AFLA provided funding for a series of projects designed to reduce the rates of adolescent pregnancy. Mecklenburg reportedly led efforts to ensure that both reviewers of AFLA applications and grantees had an explicitly pro-life, religious, and anti-contraception stance. When Mecklenburg resigned in 1985, hounded by rumors about an affair with a co-worker and the misuse of travel funds, she seemed very different from the woman who had stood for the possibility of compromise in a post-*Roe* era. A former advocate for protections against sex discrimination and access to family planning had become the public face of the Reagan Administration's efforts to "promote self-discipline and other prudent approaches to the problem of adolescent premarital sexual relations."[44]

The Quest for Political Influence and Financial Security Pushes Pro-Lifers to the Right

Mecklenburg's position aside, the antiabortion movement as a whole had begun to change dramatically in the later 1970s. In 1975 the NRLC took a vote highlighting uncertainty about the ERA's impact "on the rights of unborn children." The resolution proposed that pro-lifers stand against the ERA until "such a time as this ambiguity is removed."[45] NRLC leaders resoundingly defeated the proposal by a vote of thirty-five to fifteen. In 1977 the organization again voted on a similar resolution, this time easily approving it.[46]

The NRLC's growing hostility to the ERA stemmed from larger changes to the identity of the pro-life movement. In the mid- to late 1970s, it took in new evangelical Protestant members and organizations, including national groups like the Christian Action Council or Christian Voice and smaller local groups like Christians for Life and the Christian Freedom Foundation. The new conservative Protestant antiabortion groups contributed to a change in the rhetoric of the pro-life movement as a whole. Significantly, however, activists already engaged in the abortion battle also began to view their cause in different terms.[47]

In part, a mix of political and legal developments surrounding abortion funding bans made Phyllis Schlafly's arguments about the ERA more compelling to pro-lifers in the later 1970s. In 1977, when the Supreme Court upheld state funding bans, abortion opponents celebrated, with some demanding greater resources for court-oriented strategies. Playing on pro-lifers' investment in the Hyde Amendment and similar state laws, Schlafly pointed to evidence that the federal ERA would undermine the antiabortion movement's hard-won gains. In Hawaii and Massachusetts, feminist attorneys had claimed that funding bans violated state ERAs. Schlafly suggested that, if the amendment passed, feminists could successfully make the same claim at the federal level, forcing the American taxpayer to foot the bill for women's abortions.[48]

Schlafly also transformed a conference celebrating International Women's Year (IWY) into a symbol of feminist hostility toward the pro-life movement. In early 1977, the National Commission on the Observance of International Women's Year sent out a letter outlining the core agenda that would be discussed at state conferences. Pro-life newsletters highlighted a statement on "Reproductive Freedom" that expressed support for abortion rights. Women opposed to abortion, like Mary Schmit of Minnesota Citizens Concerned for Life and Ann O'Donnell of Missouri Citizens for Life, organized to protest this position at various state conventions. In 1977 *The Phyllis Schlafly Report* told stories of rigged state elections and shortcuts taken to prevent antiabortion women from attending meetings. At least some of these rumors were false, as pro-life (and even antifeminist) delegations influenced state proceedings in Indiana, Montana, Missouri, Alabama, Hawaii, Ohio, and Mississippi. Just the same, Schlafly found a receptive audience when she urged pro-lifers to study the IWY proceedings, particularly given that women supportive of abortion rights constituted a majority at the national conference. What more evidence did abortion opponents need that the women's movement would never be pro-life?[49]

Schlafly's campaign had a striking effect on the antiabortion movement. Ray White, then-executive director of the NRLC, urged members to protest IWY funding. In 1977 Dr. John Willke issued a similar request. In spite of evidence that pro-life and antifeminist women had made a difference in several conventions, abortion opponents generally came to agree that "state conferences [were] being manipulated to promote causes espoused by militant feminists and that other women are not being allowed to participate."[50]

Schlafly's efforts formed part of a larger New Right campaign to recruit abortion opponents. Some pro-lifers like Randy Engel or Charles Rice naturally sympathized with the positions advanced by the New Right or the Religious Right. Other advocates, however, found new practical reasons for working with social conservatives.

In particular, a partnership with the New Right and the Religious Right promised pro-lifers a way out of crippling financial troubles and political isolation. Between 1975 and 1979, the evangelical Christian Action Council, a major new player on the pro-life scene, struggled to stay afloat. The Society for a Christian Commonwealth, a formerly influential antiabortion organization, ran out of money to publish its flagship magazine, *Triumph*. In 1976 the NRLC's third executive director, Judie Brown, began work as a volunteer because the organization could not afford to pay her. When Dr. Carolyn Gerster replaced Dr. Mildred Jefferson as president in 1978, some reports indicated that the organization was $25,000 in debt. By contrast, Christian Voice, an influential Religious Right organization, had raised as much as $3 million for the 1980 presidential campaign by the end of summer 1979. By 1981 the *Moral Majority Report* reached 840,000 homes, and the Moral Majority boasted a $6 million budget. Facing financial strain, pro-lifers had reason to partner with better-funded, politically powerful organizations in the Religious Right and New Right.[51]

As importantly, between 1977 and 1979 new absolutist pro-life groups, funded and supported by Richard Viguerie and Paul Weyrich, began to challenge the NRLC's dominance in the antiabortion movement. When hardliners took center stage in pro-life politics, mainstream groups like the NRLC moved to the right to outmaneuver their new competitors. After Judie Brown resigned from the NRLC, Viguerie recruited her to lead a new, more conservative antiabortion organization, christened the American Life League/American Life Lobby (ALL). In 1977 Brown's husband Paul had begun an antiabortion political action committee, Life Amendment PAC (LAPAC), with the support of Viguerie and Weyrich. In 1978 LAPAC quickly made a mark in national elections. Indeed, that July, Weyrich publicly made unfavorable comparisons between LAPAC and the NRLC, explaining "the [National] Right to Life Committee doesn't have the political sophistication it needs to accomplish its goal."[52]

The NRLC responded to the challenge to its dominance by drawing on the recruits and sources of financial support that LAPAC and the ALL had identified. The organization strengthened its ties to existing evangelical organizations and built relationships with groups that had formed more recently. In allying with the Religious Right, pro-life organizations adopted a more religious and antifeminist message. In June 1977, the NRLC had passed a resolution describing the organization as a religious one, asserting that the "Right to Life Movement is founded on the belief that God creates LIFE."[53] That year at the National March for Life, several of the most prominent speakers presented antiabortion activism as an act of faith. In 1978 the *National Right to Life News* began describing the ERA, lesbian rights, and other "women's rights" issues as "anti-life causes."[54]

The changing complexion of party politics further convinced pro-lifers to move to the right. In the early 1970s, powerful liberal members of Congress opposed abortion. These included Democrats such as Representative Dick Gephardt (D-MO), Senators Albert Gore (D-TN) and Joseph Biden (D-DE), and leading opponents of the Vietnam War like Senators Mark Hatfield (R-OR) and Thomas Eagleton (D-MO). Indeed, between 1973 and 1984, Democrats sponsored most of the antiabortion legislation considered in Congress. By contrast, well-known Republicans like Senator Jacob Javits (R-NY) and Governor Nelson Rockefeller (R-NY) counted among the abortion-rights movement's strongest allies. Throughout the 1970s, some influential Democrats like Eagleton and Representative James Oberstar (D-MN) still worked with abortion opponents.[55]

However, by 1976 the Republican and Democratic positions began to diverge more dramatically. That year, just as they had for several election cycles, Republican feminists organized to shape their party's platform. Activists like Audrey Rowe Colom and public figures like Betty Ford had made a place for feminists in the Republican Party. That August, however, Representative Philip Crane (R-IL) and Senator Jesse Helms (R-NC) drafted platform proposals on behalf of forty conservative activists intent on taking the party in a different direction. One of the proposed planks expressed support for those who pursued a fetal-protective amendment. The platform also condemned the *Roe* opinion as "an intrusion into the family structure."[56]

The Republican Women's Task Force, a feminist group, decided to deemphasize an attack on the abortion plank "for fear of confusing the issue with its priority concern, the Equal Rights Amendment."[57] On August 18, a belated effort by Republican feminists to change the platform position on abortion failed. By contrast, the Democratic platform more clearly avoided any endorsement of a fetal-protective amendment, at most acknowledging that many Americans had moral objections to abortion. As the women's movement built a tighter bond with the Democratic Party, its leaders began more often—and more vocally—expressing support for abortion rights.[58]

By 1980 the difference between the two parties had become pronounced. The Democratic platform, which generally reflected the positions of President Jimmy Carter, endorsed the Supreme Court's 1973 decision as "the law of the land" and opposed a constitutional amendment undoing it. By contrast, the Republican platform condemned the ERA, endorsed a fetal-protective amendment, and put the party on record as favoring bans on the public funding of abortion.[59]

As the official party positions diverged, fewer Democrats—especially those new to Congress—sided with the antiabortion movement.

In 1979 Carolyn Gerster of the NRLC complained publicly about the difficulty she had faced in recruiting Democrats to the antiabortion cause. Paul Brown of LAPAC agreed that "the Democratic Party doesn't provide a home for us."[60]

When Ronald Reagan won the 1980 election and Republicans, many of them social conservatives, took both houses of Congress in 1980, the stakes of an alliance with the Religious Right and the New Right had never seemed higher. In 1980 Sandra Faucher, the head of the NRLC PAC, reported that majorities in both houses of Congress opposed abortion. These legislators seemed ready to pass some kind of major antiabortion legislation, as well as a constitutional amendment outlawing abortion. Many pro-lifers, such as Judie Brown, Randy Engel, and Harold O. J. Brown, had always taken conservative positions on issues like contraception and feminism. For those with a different perspective, however, an alliance with social-conservative organizations provided irresistible tactical advantages.[61]

The Supreme Court's *Roe* decision did not make a pro-life alliance with social conservatives inevitable. Nor did the Court destroy abortion-rights interest in middle-ground solutions. For much of the 1970s, members of Congress and organizations supportive of abortion rights endorsed limited protections for fetuses. While respecting a woman's abortion rights, as some activists insisted, the State should guarantee fetuses' access to lifesaving treatment after the termination of a pregnancy. Some supporters of abortion rights also called for the appointment of a proxy decision-maker before fetal research could begin.

Gradually, supporting any fetal rights began to seem incompatible with backing legal abortion. As the pro-life movement scored a string of victories in state legislatures, supporters of reproductive freedom began to reject any law that could set a precedent for recognizing fetal personhood. Moreover, with the mobilization of the New Right and Religious Right, abortion-rights activists came to see fetal-protective laws as an offshoot of antifeminism. How could feminists compromise with an opposition so hopelessly opposed to sex equality?

Civil Libertarians Work to Reconcile Woman's Reproductive Liberty and Fetal Rights

In July 1973, several members of the National Institutes of Health (NIH) proposed restrictions on fetal research. An unpublished staff paper urged the recognition of "human rights" for the aborted fetus "whether the mother is concerned over its . . . fate or not."[62] The NIH report began an intense debate about medical ethics, fetal personhood, and human rights that reshaped the abortion politics of the later 1970s.[63]

In the second half of the decade, abortion-rights sympathizers debated whether any fetal rights, including the kind proposed by the NIH, deserved support. Surprisingly, the lawmaker leading the campaign to recognize limited fetal rights, Senator Edward Kennedy (D-MA), strongly supported legal abortion. Before *Roe*, Kennedy, a devout Catholic, had opposed the outright repeal of abortion laws. Later in the decade, however, Kennedy became a leading advocate for reproductive freedom. He played a key role in the defeat of the Bartlett Amendment, an early effort to ban Medicaid funding for abortion. Later, in fights over the Hyde Amendment, Kennedy maintained strong support for the abortion rights of poor women.[64]

Nonetheless, Kennedy, like other Americans on the pro-choice side, favored regulation of fetal research. The *New York Times* explored the complexity of the relationship between fetal research and abortion: "[D]oes anyone have the right to [do] research on [the fetus] without consent—and whose consent? The mother would ordinarily be the one to ask, but she has already asked for an abortion."[65] When Congress held hearings on the subject of fetal research, Kennedy asked "where, if at all, [the] issue overlap[ped] with the abortion issue."[66]

For Kennedy, fetal research raised questions not so much about abortion rights as about the risk that scientists would conduct unethical experiments on other human beings. He could easily call to mind several disturbing examples of the latter. In July 1972, the Associated Press ran a story revealing the details of the Tuskegee study, a project begun forty years before on the effects of untreated syphilis on African-American men. No one had informed the individuals involved in the study what it entailed; none, including 201 of whom had not been infected at the beginning of the study, had received proper treatment for the disease. The forced sterilizations of women of color across the South reinforced concern about disregard for the rights of patients. To observers like Kennedy, fetal research represented one example of the medical exploitation of people who could not defend themselves.[67]

But did fetal research really stand apart from the abortion battle? Beginning in the mid-1970s, commentators across the ideological spectrum identified differences between the issues of abortion and fetal research. At congressional hearings on fetal research chaired by

Kennedy, pro-life witness Andre Hellegers explained these distinctions as follows: "It is not sufficient to analyze the problem in light of the Supreme Court abortion decision. [A]n extrauterine fetus can no longer interfere with a woman's privacy. . . . In brief, there is no longer any possible conflict between the fetus and its mother."[68]

In the absence of a conflict with the woman's interest in bodily integrity, did the fetus have any rights, and how should researchers obtain informed consent? Dr. Richard Behrman, a champion of fetal research, argued that the only actors who could give proxy consent were "adequately informed . . . individuals whose interests are substantially overlapping or identical to those of the proposed subject."[69] Who could consent to research in the event of abortion? Hellegers and Behrman ruled out a woman who had terminated a pregnancy. For his part, Kennedy favored the creation of a permanent scientific commission that would regulate all human experimentation, including fetal research.[70]

The Kennedy hearings raised a number of difficult questions for the reproductive-freedom movement. Did abortion rights guarantee that a fetus would die? Did fetuses have rights after a provider completed an abortion? After choosing abortion, did women have any say over what subsequently happened to a fetus? Could supporters of abortion rights recognize any fetal protections without undermining women's reproductive freedom?

In the mid- to late 1970s, such questions proved difficult for a variety of abortion-rights organizations. In lobbying against an antiabortion constitutional amendment, NOW carefully avoided the issue of fetal research. An influential committee within the ACLU, a group on the front lines of the battle for reproductive freedom, went further, endorsing limited fetal rights.[71]

In part, the ACLU's interest in fetal rights reflected the organization's troubled history with the women's movement. In 1966, for example, the ACLU Board of Directors rejected a proposal to prohibit sex discrimination, arguing that the "liberation of the black male" must be given priority. Other board members believed that a fight against sex discrimination would only endanger existing civil-rights protections. ACLU leaders expressed similar reservations about abortion. In 1967, adopting a more moderate resolution, the board rejected the more absolute position advanced by feminist Dorothy Kenyon—that no legitimate interest justified state interference with women's right to control their own bodies.[72]

Women, and feminists in particular, did appear to exercise more influence over the organization in the 1970s. In December 1970, the board committed to increasing "significantly the representation of women in all policy-making bodies and committees."[73] In December 1972, Suzanne Post, Ruth Bader Ginsburg, and two members of NOW, Faith Seidenberg and Wilma Scott Heide, won approval and a $30,000 budget for a Women's Rights Project (WRP), and by 1974, the ACLU spun off a separate Reproductive Freedom Project. Nonetheless, as late as 1972, while women were the best represented on the organization's subject-matter committees, they held only 23 percent of those seats. Fewer women were represented on the group's national board, executive committee, or structural committees.[74]

In the later 1970s, the politics of fetal rights within the ACLU stemmed partly from the low priority some members assigned to women's liberation. Like Kennedy, however, most ACLU members remained steadfast in their support for women's right to abortion—and to the safest available procedure in each individual case. Nonetheless, members of the ACLU Privacy Committee believed that the Constitution could protect certain fetal rights without denying women reproductive autonomy. Particularly after the completion of an abortion, the fetus had the right to medical care and lifesaving support at the end of a procedure. As the committee reasoned, favoring reproductive autonomy did not require abortion-rights activists to disregard the value of fetal life.

The committee's discussion laid bare the social anxieties linking abortion, fetal research, fetology, and neonatology in the mid-1970s. Fetal research did not debut in 1973. Indeed, between 1964 and 1974, researchers conducted thousands of studies, many of them drawing on a massive increase in congressional funding. Well-known studies had played a part in the development of vaccines for polio and rubella. Just the same, the Supreme Court's abortion decision began a new chapter, bringing debate about fetal rights into the open, increasing the relative availability of non-viable, later-term fetuses, and thereby making possible new avenues of research.[75]

The debate about fetal research took place at a time when technological changes made it easier to imagine the fetus as a patient. Prior to the mid-1960s, premature infants, especially those younger than twenty-eight weeks, stood little chance of survival. After 1965, however, the emergence of respiratory-support mechanisms increased the life expectancy of infants under thirty-two weeks. With warming beds and ventilators, infants could survive as long as they received around-the-clock care. This led to the creation of the first neonatal intensive-care units.[76]

These technological developments changed the age of fetal viability, as well as popular perceptions of it. If the age of viability moved to twenty-four or even twenty-one weeks, the survival of younger and smaller infants seemed possible in the near term. Technological advances also influenced how medical professionals, politicians, and patients defined fetal life. CT scans, ultrasounds, and fetal heartbeat monitors made it easier to visualize and identify with fetuses. Moreover, as the age of viability changed, "signs of life," like fetal heartbeat or respiration, became more meaningful, bringing to mind what ethicist Daniel Callahan called "the growing power of medicine to push back the time of viability of an infant earlier and earlier."[77]

In the midst of a broader cultural conversation about fetal viability and fetal research, the ACLU Privacy Committee met to consider whether fetuses had any rights. The unresolved question through much of the committee's June 1975 meeting involved the impact of the *Roe* decision on this discussion. Had the Supreme Court given a woman the right to "reliev[e herself] of the pregnancy," or did abortion rights necessarily require "killing the fetus?" Unable to reach consensus, the committee scheduled another meeting on the meaning of fetal rights.[78]

In the period, conventional definitions of abortion presented the procedure as both the termination of the fetus's life and its removal from the woman's body. Just the same, in the mid- to late 1970s, the spread of prostaglandin abortions increased the possibility that a fetus would show signs of life after completion of the procedure. Very few women had abortions after the twenty-seventh week of pregnancy, and fetal survival seemed impossible following first-trimester procedures. For the committee and other commentators, the issue was whether relatively common second-trimester abortions would produce a live birth.[79]

Before the mid-1970s, when saline abortion remained the most common second-trimester technique, studies put the rate of live births at no higher than .17 per 100 procedures. However, because providers believed saline abortions posed risks for patients with a variety of health conditions, prostaglandin abortions grew in popularity by mid-decade. The procedure required providers to inject the hormone prostaglandin into the amniotic sac, thereby inducing premature labor. Because prostaglandin abortions did not destroy fetal tissue, they more often led to live births. Indeed, some studies of prostaglandin abortion completed in the 1970s and early 1980s reported a live birth rate as high as between two and eight percent. Nonetheless, pinning down an accurate figure, or assessing its meaning, remained difficult. Disagreement about the definition of a live birth, coupled with reluctance to report such incidents, made reliable statistics on the subject hard to find.[80]

For some committee members, however, the possibility of a live birth post-abortion, together with the changing definition of viability, created an opening for efforts to protect fetal rights. In October 1976, the committee again plunged into debate about the scope and meaning of fetal rights—and reproductive autonomy. Member Peter Birnbaum asserted that the Fourteenth Amendment imposed "an affirmative obligation to protect life." Member Alvin Schorr, a social worker and child welfare expert, replied that "the right to abort is the right to kill," which was the "full implication . . . of the Supreme Court's definition of abortion." Others insisted that "the medical profession [should] make decisions" about the breadth of abortion rights. The meeting ended with the committee deeply divided.[81]

Between October and November, the committee arrived at a compromise, seeking to balance fetal rights and women's right to choose abortion. The committee acknowledged that recognizing any fetal rights could impact a woman's decision-making, even if she still had the power to terminate a pregnancy. Just the same, the committee concluded that society should assume responsibility for any child born alive after the completion of the procedure. Moreover, the committee argued that a woman's right not to know the fate of an unborn child should give way to the First Amendment rights of those seeking to inform her and to the fetal interests in survival.[82]

What happened if a child lived through an abortion? What obligations, if any, did the government, the physician, and the woman have at that point? Again, the committee concluded that the fetus had rights that did not conflict with women's reproductive freedom. Without undermining a woman's abortion rights, the government could ensure that a child received lifesaving care at the end of an abortion. As importantly, the committee concluded that if policymakers had a genuine interest in protecting fetal life, the government "should assume financial responsibility for the child," at least insofar as the costs of medical care were concerned.[83]

As the federal government considered how best to regulate fetal research, policymakers similarly sought to balance reproductive freedom and fetal rights. After Congress chartered a group to study the question—the National Commission for the Protection of Human Subjects of Biomedical and Behavioral Research—the Department of Health, Education, and Welfare approved regulations requiring the preclearance of any research that harmed a fetus. As the National Institutes of Health explained in 1976: "Essentially, the Commission would permit research on a dead fetus, fetal tissues and other fetal material, and, with respect to non-therapeutic research, [would] ensure that the research design not affect the advisability, timing, or method of abortion."[84] The Commission allowed abortion-related research only in the first twenty weeks of pregnancy and only when a study did not reduce the probability of fetal survival. Like the ACLU Privacy Committee, the Commission envisioned fetal protections that did not interfere with women's abortion rights.[85]

In spite of the Supreme Court's decision, some proponents of reproductive freedom worked to reconcile the rights of women and unborn children. The ACLU Privacy Committee reached the kind of compromise that *Roe* was supposed to have rendered all but impossible. This solution went considerably further than the trimester framework set out by the Court. Under *Roe*, the states could regulate abortion in the interests of the fetus only after viability. Whereas *Roe* discussed what the states could do, the Privacy Committee had voted that the government and physicians owed unborn children certain rights.[86]

The committee's efforts reflected ambivalence within the abortion-rights movement about the treatment of fetal life. In the mid- to late 1970s, some doctors, activists, and feminists in favor of legal abortion viewed fetal research—and other questions of fetal rights—as legally and morally distinct from the abortion issue. These activists did not question the paramount value assigned to women's interests in bodily integrity and decisional freedom. Nonetheless, abortion-rights activists could imagine fetal rights to dignity, life, and ethical treatment deserving of support.

Well into the 1980s, many of these fetal-protective proposals remained scientifically or financially impracticable. By 1980, dilation and evacuation (D&E) abortions, which required the dilation of the cervix and the evacuation of the fetus, had become the most common second-trimester method, since women reported D&E to be faster, more comfortable, and less traumatic than prostaglandin procedures, which required long and painful deliveries. Significantly for the committee's proposals, D&E abortions virtually precluded a live birth. Even providers performing prostaglandin abortions began using saline to reduce the chances that an aborted child would show signs of life. However defined, live births became exceedingly rare by the early 1980s. Moreover, given the extremely high cost of neonatal intensive care, neither states nor biological parents often could have paid for the kind of care that might have been helpful in preserving the lives of fetuses after an abortion.[87]

By the early 1980s, however, movement leaders generally lost interest in the very idea of fetal rights. For proponents of legal abortion, the alliance between the pro-life movement, the New Right, and the Religious Right seemed to expose the antifeminist biases of pro-lifers. Strategically, movement leaders also stood to gain a great deal by presenting the opposition as anti-woman rather than pro-life. Over the course of the 1970s, abortion opponents had monopolized discussion of what the procedure actually involved. Slide shows, placards, and billboards humanized the fetus and stigmatized abortion. Abortion-rights activists could gain an advantage by demonstrating that the opposition took no genuine interest in the unborn.

Moreover, as both political parties staked out their positions on abortion in the early 1980s, the idea of compromise came to appear risky. To maintain influence over the Democratic Party, abortion-rights activists had to convince politicians of the costs of siding with the opposition. In the new world of abortion politics, both sides began to see consensus-seeking as a strategic handicap.

Political Party Realignment Undercuts Interest in Balancing the Rights of Women and Fetuses

By the late 1970s, Juli Loesch Wiley, a member of Feminists for Life, found it virtually impossible to build partnerships of any kind with anyone supporting abortion rights. Loesch approached fellow anti-nuclear activists and often found herself rebuffed. Pro-choice feminists proved to be equally hostile.[88]

Loesch's frustrations testify to the polarization of abortion-rights politics in the late 1970s. Feminists in groups from NOW to R2N2 saw the new pro-life partnership with the Religious Right and the New Right as evidence of rampant sexism within the antiabortion movement. In part, abortion-rights leaders responded to some pro-lifers' public criticism of the women's movement. In 1977 Phyllis Schlafly's Pro-Family Rally featured antifeminist speeches by abortion opponents like Dr. Mildred F. Jefferson and Nellie Gray. Between 1977 and 1980, Paul Weyrich and Richard Viguerie, who proved to be brilliant organizers, emphasized antifeminist rhetoric, as did antiabortion groups aligned with them, like the Ad Hoc Committee in Defense of Life. For example, a 1977 version of the Ad Hoc Committee in Defense of Life's *Lifeletter* described "women's lib groups" as "always-abrasive and often-shrewish."[89]

Furthermore, by questioning pro-lifers' sincerity, movement leaders could more effectively address public ambivalence about the abortion procedure. Over the course of the 1970s, the antiabortion movement had become increasingly adept at using fetal ultrasound images and pictures in support of their claims. Questioning the motives of the opposition offered pro-choice leaders a way to effectively counter fetal-protective arguments. By focusing on the supposed sexism of the opposition, abortion-rights activists avoided hard questions about fetal rights, instead presenting interest in the unborn as a political trick.

Between 1978 and 1980, NOW, NARAL, and Planned Parenthood presented pro-life positions as a smokescreen for extremist, anti-woman views. In a June 1978 *New York Times* editorial, Larry Lader focused on the pro-life movement's alliance with the New Right and the Religious Right, maintaining that "[o]pposition to abortion has now become the spearhead of political fanaticism."[90] In 1979 members of the NOW Reproductive Rights Task Force similarly asserted: "Right wing involvement in the abortion controversy must be brought to the public's attention. We are the ones who care about life."[91] In 1980, Planned Parenthood President Faye Wattleton described abortion opponents as "an increasingly vocal and at times violent minority which seeks to deny all of us our fundamental rights."[92] A 1979 NOW campaign echoed claims that the antiabortion movement focused on "biblical tyranny and paternal condescension." "Their goal," the campaign explained, "is the suppression of women."[93]

The emergence of abortion as a national political issue further discouraged activists interested in building a cross-movement consensus. Movement leaders like Karen Mulhauser believed that the future of the abortion issue lay in electoral politics. To preserve reproductive rights, activists like Mulhauser sought to mobilize the largest possible number of new voters. To do so, the leaders of organizations like NARAL and Planned Parenthood presented their opponents as anti-contraception, anti-equality, anti-woman, and anti-sex. By suggesting that pro-lifers condemned women who refused traditional roles, the abortion-rights movement hoped to reach more Americans who were ambivalent about the procedure.[94]

Furthermore, in the early 1980s, abortion-rights leaders had to convince members of the Democratic Party of the importance of the movement's support. Officially, beginning in 1976, leaders of the Democratic Party had started to side with the abortion-rights movement. Just the same, feminists had reason to worry about the fragility of this alliance. Indeed, into the early 1980s, many Americans with pro-life views continued voting for the Democratic Party in major national elections. Beginning in the late 1970s and early 1980s, feminist organizations like NOW responded by organizing more effective campaigns to influence the Democratic national convention. Groups like NARAL and Planned Parenthood began channeling most of their campaign contributions to Democratic candidates. Nonetheless, with both parties' positions in flux, abortion-rights leaders wanted Democratic leaders to believe that switching sides would be costly.[95]

In this political climate, efforts to seek common ground seemed to send the wrong message to wavering politicians. In 1980, Karen Mulhauser explained that "some politicians have been persuaded by anti-abortionists that they are strong enough to make a difference in their campaigns."[96] In crafting its own electoral initiatives, NARAL members wanted to demonstrate that they would prioritize the abortion issue and brook no compromise on reproductive rights. As Jean Weinberg, an architect of the NARAL strategy, explained, "[W]e realize that a majority that doesn't vote is a powerless majority."[97]

In particular, leaders like Mulhauser and Weinberg felt they had to match the intensity of pro-life voters. In the 1978 and 1980 elections, pro-lifers highlighted the commitment, rather than mere numbers, of antiabortion voters. The 1978 election season witnessed the defeat of incumbent (and abortion-rights supporter) Senator Dick Clark (D-IA), a turn of events that the *New York Times* described as evidence that "a small but undeniably fervent group, . . . the antiabortionists, can upset a highly favored candidate."[98] By 1980 newly active evangelical voters added not only "new numbers to the political Right but also served as a kind of cement holding together the single issue groups in the name of family."[99]

Political commentators suggested that abortion opponents had neither a united front nor the support of a majority of voters. While disputing this claim, pro-lifers sometimes drew attention to the zealousness of their supporters—supposed single-issue voters who could determine the outcome of a race. In June 1981, Sandra Faucher, the activist who oversaw the NRLC's political action committee, focused on the strength of voter preferences. When pro-lifers successfully backed Senator Chuck Grassley (R-IA) against then-incumbent John Culver (D-IA), Faucher emphasized that 10 percent of voters had chosen Grassley for his pro-life position, whereas only 5 percent selected Culver because of his stand on abortion rights.[100]

To create an effective majority, organizations like NARAL and NOW urged abortion-rights voters to display the same unwillingness to give in. In a fundraising letter, Karen Mulhauser warned: "Up until now, those of us who believe in individual liberty . . . have not taken a strong enough stand to effectively impress upon our legislators that they can disregard the fanatics with impunity."[101] NOW President Eleanor Smeal similarly suggested that abortion-rights activists would not give an inch to an opposition "who wanted to return women and the nation to the last century."[102] Abortion-rights organizations presented their supporters as a rational majority unwilling to strike bargains with "the fanatics" of whom Mulhauser spoke. Between 1975 and 1980, partly for this reason, a number of feminist organizations including NOW all but expelled members who opposed abortion, and at its formative meeting, CARASA leaders voted to exclude pro-lifers. Partly to maintain the allegiance of the Democratic Party, movement members demonized pro-lifers and concluded that compromise on abortion was impossible. As NARAL activist Nanette Falkenberg would later explain: "We had to be able to prove that the abortion-rights position was good politics."[103]

The Supreme Court did not bear the primary responsibility for the polarization of abortion-rights politics. Tensions between the abortion-rights and pro-life movements increased well before 1973. Divisive rights-based arguments played a prominent part in state battles to reform abortion laws. Political party realignment, which impacted the abortion debate after 1973, began before the *Roe* decision.

Moreover, well into the late 1970s, compromise remained attractive to some abortion-rights activists. When movement members more uniformly rejected any middle-ground solution, they responded to the new antifeminist rhetoric of the opposition. They also questioned pro-lifers' motives to secure a tactical advantage, particularly as the antiabortion movement successfully stigmatized the abortion procedure. Finally, because the support of the Democratic Party seemed tenuous, abortion-rights leaders had to convince politicians of the intensity and inflexibility of voters' support for reproductive freedom. If feminists gave away too much on any issue regarding fetal life, politicians might feel free to betray them.

Compromise in a Brave New World

Over the course of the 1970s, abortion politics changed dramatically. The *Roe* decision not only revolutionized access to legal abortion but also opened new avenues for fetal research. Confronted with these developments, influential activists worked harder than ever to find common ground. Some pro-lifers argued that women turned to abortion only because of discrimination on the basis of sex, class, and marital status. While endorsing outright bans on the procedure, these advocates campaigned successfully for their own idea of reproductive choice—one that required state protection against pregnancy discrimination and some of the burdens of poverty. Members of the abortion-rights movement remained open to the idea that some fetal rights could be compatible with women's reproductive freedom, particularly in the context of fetal research.

A new political reality helped to marginalize those interested in such shared solutions. With the mobilization of the New Right and Religious Right in the late 1970s, pro-lifers pursuing political influence or shoring up financial resources could do so by allying with social conservatives. The rise of Ronald Reagan helped convince pro-lifers that only the Republican Party would promote a fetal-protective amendment to the Constitution—the pro-life movement's central goal since the *Roe* decision. Political-party realignment also chilled efforts by pro-choice activists to recognize a limited form of fetal rights. With the support of the Democratic Party still in some doubt, the leaders of organizations like NARAL had everything to gain by refusing compromise of any kind.

Faced with these profound changes to the political environment, a number of activists fought to keep a place in abortion politics. In the late 1970s, Mary Meehan found her way to a small group, Pro-Lifers for Survival, an organization founded by Juli Loesch Wiley and designed to facilitate dialogue and action among left-leaning people who shared opposition to war and abortion, as well as, in many cases, to euthanasia and the death penalty. Although Meehan says that there was some "genuine dialogue" on the abortion issue on the left, she recalls that at some point in the early 1980s "the debate kind of closed down."[104]

A major anti-nuclear coalition refused to accept Pro-Lifers for Survival as a member, and mainstream pro-life groups stayed away from the positions embraced by Meehan and Loesch, increasingly aligning with the Right and the Republican Party. Meehan found herself very uncomfortable with pro-life groups that embraced the Right and felt alienated from the Democratic Party. Meehan recalls that Pro-Lifers for Survival had "the great virtue of giving a lot of lonely folks the realization that they were not alone."[105]

By the early 1980s, Warren Schaller, a former spokesman for pro-life moderation, no longer belonged to any antiabortion organization. Mary Ann Kuharski, a powerbroker in both pro-life and Democratic Party circles, lost her standing in Democratic politics. Like Schaller, Meehan, and Kuharski, an influential and sizable group of activists found themselves lost in a new world in which neither movement fully reflected their fundamental beliefs.[106]

The years to come presented these advocates with a series of painful choices. As did Warren Schaller, activists could give up, leaving abortion politics to someone else. Others, like Kuharski, tried to adapt to the new political reality, reconsidering formerly progressive positions. With little support or public attention, embattled activists like Meehan and Loesch continued to seek out consensus. Similarly, for abortion-rights supporters, the kind of interest in fetal protections expressed by Ted Kennedy or the ACLU Privacy Committee came to seem a contradiction of the movement's guiding principles. To fit within the abortion-rights or pro-life movements of the early 1980s, many activists sacrificed what had been defining beliefs.[107]

Only later did the narrow definitions of pro-life or pro-choice come to seem inevitable to absolutists like Phyllis Schlafly. Years later, Schlafly would recall the late 1970s and early 1980s as the beginning of beautiful friendships between social conservatives and anti-abortion activists, and between Catholics and evangelical Christians. She fondly remembers speaking with Jerry Falwell about abortion: Falwell stated that he did not favor the ordination of women, but if he had to choose only one woman to preach, it would be Schlafly herself.[108]

Today, efforts to seek shared solutions appear to be an interesting but largely irrelevant footnote to the broader culture wars. Few remember the many activists who believed that *Roe v. Wade* made compromise on the abortion issue more crucial. In contemporary battles, Dr. John and Barbara Willke's book, *Why Can't We Love Them Both?* serves as a blueprint for abortion opponents seeking to win the support of undecided women. In the decade after *Roe*, those words would have meant something quite different. Honoring the rights of both women and fetuses seemed possible, politically realistic, and morally necessary.[109]

Conclusion

During a summer 2012 interview, Todd Akin, a Republican Senate candidate from Missouri, answered a reporter's question about whether abortion should be legal in cases of sexual assault. In cases of "legitimate rape," Akin explained, women's bodies would naturally reject a pregnancy. Quite simply, women victimized by sexual assault would never need an abortion. "If it's a legitimate rape," Akin stated, "the female body has ways to try to shut the whole thing down."[1]

Akin's comments once again put abortion at the center of American political debate. For Democratic commentators, Akin's remarks revealed the gender bias underlying pro-life activism. At the same time, Akin's statements prompted a debate within both the Republican Party and the antiabortion movement. Pragmatists generally agreed that Akin should bow out, as Reince Priebus, the chairman of the Republican National Committee explained, in favor of "someone . . . [who would have] a better chance of winning."[2] Absolutists, Akin among them, insisted that only his wording was regrettable. State pro-life leaders in Missouri agreed with Akin that "if God has chosen to bless [a rape victim] with a life, you don't kill it."[3] Abortion should be illegal in cases of rape as a matter of principle. Akin had taken a courageous and ethical position.[4]

As the Akin debate suggests, the battles of the 1970s and early 1980s still affect American abortion politics. The decade after *Roe* gave rise to a women's-rights interpretation of the decision still prominent in political circles. Dominant features of contemporary debate—the influence of choice-based arguments for abortion, the divide between absolutists and incrementalists, pro-lifers' use of arguments against judicial activism, and the alliance between abortion opponents and social conservatives—appeared in the decade after the decision.

Recently, the history of social-movement reactions to the *Roe* decision itself has also become an important subject of political discussion. Did the Court's rhetoric only paper over an unholy alliance between population-control activists and supporters of abortion rights? This question has become central to pro-life allegations about the racism of abortion providers and opposition activists. Citing the history of the abortion-rights movement's "racist roots," pro-lifers call for the defunding of Planned Parenthood. These activists insist that if their colleagues "counter the racism inherent in the abortion business, more African-American babies will be saved."[5]

As the battle for marriage equality for gays and lesbians builds momentum, commentators across the ideological spectrum have also looked to responses to *Roe*. Proponents of marriage equality have waged a successful fight in the state and federal courts. In the Supreme Court, in *United States v. Windsor*, the marriage-equality movement effectively challenged the constitutionality of part of the federal Defense of Marriage Act (DOMA), a law denying federal benefits to married same-sex couples. With the justices weighing in on DOMA, commentators predicted that the Supreme Court would soon resolve the issue at the national level, deciding once and for all whether the federal Constitution entitled same-sex couples to marry. However, in October 2014, the Court declined to hear an appeal from five states seeking to preserve existing bans, leaving in place decisions holding some laws unconstitutional and leaving other prohibitions in limbo.[6]

To be sure, the Court's decision defied many predictions, but did the justices make the best choice? Would a broad, national ruling create the kind of reaction we associate with the *Roe* decision? Or, as some commentators suggest, might there be something different about the abortion issue, about gender questions, or even about the *Roe* decision that explains the dramatic change produced by the 1973 opinion? In battles about marriage equality, the aftermath of *Roe* remains a touchstone for those debating when and whether litigation works—and when the Court can create social change. As Robert P. George argues, *Roe* supposedly "inflamed the culture war that has divided our nation" by "short-circuiting the democratic process."[7]

But how, in fact, did movements react to *Roe*? The materials assembled here make clear that this is not the right way to ask the question.

By paying attention so exclusively to the Supreme Court, we have lost a much richer story about the evolution of abortion politics. Rather than remaining preoccupied by the Court's actions, competing social movements had to navigate the realignment of both major political parties, the mobilization of the Religious Right and the New Right, the changing politics of population control and civil rights, and the popularization of neoliberalism. Activists also made choices that intensified abortion conflict. Opposing movement members sometimes made these decisions to obtain a tactical advantage. On other occasions, advocates pursued a polarizing course of action as the result of shifting ideological commitments.

Certainly, the Supreme Court's decision marked a turning point. The opinion undid the statutes applied by the vast majority of American states. The Court also impacted the strategies pursued by both abortion-rights and pro-life activists. Before 1973, most pro-lifers assumed that the law and the Constitution already protected fetal rights. After 1973, the struggle for a fetal-protective amendment brought together previously fragmented state groups. By making such an amendment the priority of the movement, the *Roe* decision encouraged pro-lifers to vote for whichever party stood for constitutional change. In demanding an amendment, national organizations became larger and more focused on their constitutional goals. As importantly, faced with the Court's decision, some movement members invested much more in the possibility of common ground on other gender issues.

For abortion-rights activists, the Supreme Court decision guaranteed a result the movement would not likely have obtained by working through ordinary politics, at least in the near term. Since the justices had legitimated legal abortion, a variety of reproductive-rights activists borrowed from and often transformed the rhetoric of the Court's decision. Moreover, by making the procedure legal and more widely available, the Supreme Court gave the movement a precious victory that its members sacrificed a good deal to preserve.

Just the same, the *Roe* decision hardly determined the course of abortion politics. Indeed, when scholars and social-movement members speak of the far-reaching impact of *Roe*, they only sometimes refer to the decision itself, often using it instead as a symbol for a range of deeply held political values and important social shifts. For some, *Roe* stands for certain aspects of Harry Blackmun's majority opinion, such as a medical justification for abortion rights or the trimester system that the Court used to analyze abortion cases. *Roe* can mean simply legal abortion or the importance of fertility control for women. Critics use *Roe* to discuss the influence of judicial review on American politics.

We have attributed so much about contemporary abortion politics to *Roe* partly because we have not adequately separated the Supreme Court's decision from everything that followed. We think we need to study the impact of the Supreme Court decision, but we would learn more from asking how we arrived at the present moment in the abortion wars.[8]

Abortion Politics after 1983

A good deal happened after the period studied in this book, and we should not equate the world examined in this volume with the abortion wars of later decades. The history of that period reaches beyond the bounds of this work. Just the same, if we briefly consider the developments of later decades, we see first that political and social changes still contribute to the polarization of abortion conflict. As importantly, surveying the abortion battle of later decades shows that crucial aspects of the struggle have held constant since 1983. The decade after the *Roe* decision set the stage for much of what defines contemporary abortion politics.

As had been the case in the 1970s and early 1980s, post-1983 abortion conflict continued to intensify for reasons beyond the intervention of the Supreme Court. Beginning in the mid-1980s, a spike in anti-clinic violence further poisoned the relationship between the abortion-rights and pro-life movements. Between 1980 and 1993, clinics reported a total of 153 bombings or acts of arson. While condemned by many pro-lifers, death threats, chemical attacks, and break-ins persuaded abortion-rights activists and providers alike that the opposition was violent and irrational. Beginning in 1993 with the killing of Pensacola provider Dr. David Gunn, clinic staff came under fire. At the time of this writing, ten others have died or received gun-shot wounds as the result of clinic violence.[9]

Together with clinic violence, the rising use of direct-action tactics increased hostilities. In the late 1980s a group of pro-lifers forged a new "rescue movement," focused on "sidewalk counseling" and massive protests that blocked clinics. Over the course of the late 1980s and early 1990s, clinics experienced 525 blockades, and law enforcement officials arrested over 31,000 pro-life protestors. With a militant wing of the pro-life movement making its mark, fewer physicians were willing to perform the procedure, leaving the task increasingly to independent clinics. At the same time, however, abortion providers more often immersed themselves in activism, joining established abortion-rights organizations or founding their own.[10]

Tensions in the abortion wars also continued to rise as the result of American party politics. In particular, since 1983 both the abortion-rights and pro-life movements have helped to politicize the judicial nomination process, dedicating tremendous amounts of time, research, and energy to the selection of ideal candidates. Beginning with Justice Sandra Day O'Connor's 1983 dissent in *City of Akron v. Akron Reproductive Health Services (Akron I)*, activists on either side of the abortion question invested more in the vetting of judicial nominees. In 1981 pro-lifers dug up O'Connor's Arizona voting record and concluded that she would be a solid supporter of abortion rights. By 1983, however, O'Connor had penned a dissent criticizing the trimester framework set forth in the *Roe* decision. In the aftermath of *Akron I*, the possibility that sympathetic presidents could reshape the Supreme Court seemed more real than ever before. The explosive (and ultimately failed) nomination of Robert Bork in 1987 only heightened activists' interest in the composition of the Court. The process of selecting Supreme Court justices has also changed substantially, as potential nominees confront many questions about abortion and often feel safer answering almost none of them. With newfound focus on the nomination process, both movements made the abortion issue a more hotly contested feature of presidential politics.[11]

Moreover, much as the evolution of fetology and fetal research raised the stakes of the abortion battles of the 1970s, an ever-changing medical context still marks conflict about abortion. The age of viability remains in flux. In recent decades, assisted reproductive technologies have flourished. Whereas individuals could easily access only artificial insemination in the 1970s, the following decades witnessed dramatic progress, with the spread of various forms of in vitro fertilization, gestational surrogacy, and prenatal genetic diagnosis. Legally, politically, and ethically, assisted reproductive technologies bear an ambiguous relationship to abortion rights. Should the courts analyze access to reproductive technologies using the existing constitutional framework? Politically, would the abortion-rights movement benefit or lose out if assisted reproductive technologies remain a stand-alone issue? As these technologies become more sophisticated and widely used, both the pro-life and abortion-rights movements will have to clarify what their causes mean.[12]

After 1983, the Supreme Court certainly continued to insert itself into the abortion wars, retreating from the protections announced in *Roe* and creating new uncertainty about the state of the law. Over the course of the 1980s, Republican nominees to the Supreme Court expressed increasing skepticism about the trimester framework set out in the *Roe* decision. By 1992 Court watchers concluded that the justices might be ready to overrule the 1973 opinion. Instead, the justices steered a middle course. In *Planned Parenthood of Southeastern Pennsylvania v. Casey*, a majority preserved what it called the essential holding of *Roe*. To an unprecedented extent, *Casey* linked abortion rights to women's interest in equal citizenship. The majority described the abortion decision as "too intimate and personal for the State to insist . . . upon its own vision of the woman's role." *Casey* insisted that a woman's destiny should mainly reflect "her own conception of her spiritual imperatives and her place in society."[13]

However, *Casey* also dramatically revised the constitutional test governing abortion law. Jettisoning the trimester framework set out in 1973, the Court suggested that abortion restrictions should survive unless they had the purpose or effect of creating a substantial obstacle for women seeking abortions. Apparently, very few laws would create such a burden. *Casey* struck down only one part of the challenged Pennsylvania law, a provision requiring married women to notify their husbands before obtaining an abortion. Lower courts charged with interpreting *Casey* have created significant leeway for states restricting abortion. Some legal commentators conclude that, under *Casey*, only the woman's decision to seek an abortion receives protection, even if access to the procedure remains out of reach.[14]

At the time of this writing, the Court has cast further doubt on the fate of abortion rights. In 2007 a divided court upheld the federal Partial Birth Abortion Act, a law prohibiting a particular late term abortion procedure, intact dilation and extraction (D&X). D&X required a provider to remove an intact fetus rather than extracting pieces of the unborn child. In *Gonzales v. Carhart*, Justice Anthony Kennedy, a member of the *Casey* majority, reasoned that the statute served a valuable purpose for women who might later regret their abortions. Kennedy assumed that women did not fully understand what abortion entailed, and providers often failed to tell their patients what they needed to know. "While we find no reliable data to mea-sure the phenomenon," Kennedy wrote, "it seems unexceptionable to conclude some women come to regret their choice to abort the infant life they once created and sustained. . . . Severe depression and loss of esteem can follow."[15]

By creating so much uncertainty, *Casey* and *Carhart* have height-ened tensions in the abortion wars. The Court has connected abortion to women's interest in equal citizenship. At the same time, as Jus-tice Ruth Bader Ginsburg asserted in a forceful dissenting opinion in *Carhart*, the justices endorsed what amounted to a stereotype about the bonds women experienced with unborn children and the regret suffered after an abortion. Those on either side cannot easily predict how far the current Court will go in remaking abortion rights. The re-strictions upheld by the *Casey* Court have already become a template for legislators seeking to regulate the procedure. Pro-lifers have tried to push beyond the boundaries set by *Casey*, promoting new laws defunding abortion-rights organizations or banning abortion when providers could detect a fetal heartbeat or when a fetus could theo-retically experience pain.[16]

Nonetheless, to explain the trajectory of the post-1983 abortion battle, we need to look far beyond any doctrinal changes in the Court. The polarization of contemporary debate makes sense only if we un-derstand the rise and fall of the rescue movement, the increasing po-litical mobilization of abortion providers, the dissemination of new reproductive technologies, and the ongoing entanglement of abortion and party politics. If we focus too much on the judiciary, we lose sight of much of what continues to make abortion politics so bitter and so complex.

Abortion politics have changed a great deal since 1983. Just the same, the 1970s and early 1980s teach us about how many of the defining features of the contemporary abortion wars came about. The Supreme Court did not provoke pro-lifers into opposing judicial ac-tivism in 1973. Indeed, abortion opponents wished that the courts would recognize a far-reaching right not spelled out in the text of Constitution. When the pro-life movement adopted a new position on judicial overreaching, movement leaders did so partly to benefit from political changes of the period, particularly the rise to power of Ronald Reagan, the New Right, and the Religious Right.

The split between incrementalists and absolutists that appeared in the late 1970s and early 1980s also continues to plague the pro-life movement. The Supreme Court's decision did not reveal this schism. Instead, over the course of the 1970s, pro-life pragmatists more often gained the upper hand in internal debates about both ideology and strategy. Since 1983, critical pro-life disagreements continue to turn on the desirability of incrementalism.[17]

The decade after *Roe* also helped to redefine the contemporary movement for reproductive freedom. A previously strong alliance between the movements for population control and abortion rights gradually lost influence, as feminists gained positions of leadership. By mid-decade, feminists had played up women's-rights arguments for abortion.

In this period, the campaign for a broad reproductive-rights agenda gave way to the single-issue, choice-oriented strategy now familiar to us. Abortion-rights supporters gravitated to this strategy as a way of creating a presence in electoral politics. At the same time, major political changes narrowed the options available to supporters of reproductive freedom. In the aftermath of the 1980 election, the pro-life movement seemed poised to gut legal access to abortion. Ronald Reagan had popularized a neoliberal vision that undercut support for welfare rights. Interest in single-issue, choice-based tactics came partly as a result of the difficult decisions confronting the reproductive-rights movement in the early 1980s. Forced to choose between political pragmatism and ideological consistency, leaders of the abortion-rights movement increasingly charted a more realistic and cautious course.

Moreover, the decade after the Supreme Court's decision witnessed the appearance of several defining features of the dynamic between the abortion-rights and the pro-life movements. In the period, compromise became more difficult, even on other gender issues. To uncover the cause of the polarization of abortion conflict, however, we have to look not only to the Court but also to the mobilization of the New Right and the Religious Right, the financial and political vulnerabilities of the pro-life movement, the reconfiguration of party politics, the arc of the ERA battle, and the tactical needs of abortion-rights leaders. Activists had pursued shared solutions on pregnancy disability, public financial support for mothers, post-abortion fetal rights, fetal research, and even the meaning of reproductive choice. Confronted with a radically different political world, both movements reached decisions that made common ground much harder to find. What was more, some activists had to sacrifice a great deal to fit within the emerging pro-choice and pro-life categories that came to define movement identity.

Finally, understanding the decade after 1973 provides crucial insight into the evolution of the popular meaning of the *Roe* decision. Rather than openly debating the rationale for abortion rights, opposing activists redirected discussion to what the *Roe* decision meant. At times, this dialogue advanced the tactical objectives of activists seeking to raise money, attract new supporters, or redefine public perception of the Supreme Court decision. On other occasions, reinterpreting *Roe* allowed activists to express changing beliefs.

The question, then, is not just how movements reacted to *Roe* but also how and why abortion politics and the dominant interpretation of the holding of the case changed so substantially. Significantly, several influential debates turn at least partly on questions about *Roe*'s historical impact. What difference should it make if we better understand the world activists fashioned in the wake of the Supreme Court decision?

The Relationship between the *Roe* Decision and Popular Opposition to Judicial Activism

Legal scholar William Eskridge and Justice Antonin Scalia, among others, argue that *Roe* precipitated a crisis of legitimacy for the Supreme Court. To some abortion opponents, the decision more closely resembled legislation than it did a conventional judicial decision, and the Court endorsed an abortion right that the public did not fully support. For this reason, abortion opponents saw *Roe* as antidemocratic and unfair. Challenges to the Court's authority came as the price of the justices' decision to proceed before public support for legal abortion had solidified. As Scalia contends, "The Court would profit . . . from giving less attention to the *fact* of [the challenge to judicial legitimacy], and more attention to the *cause* of it[:] . . . a new mode of constitutional adjudication that relies [neither] upon text [nor] traditional practice to determine the law."[18]

As we have seen, however, the antiabortion movement did not focus on challenges to the Court's legitimacy (or on arguments about it) for some time. In the aftermath of the decision, pro-lifers opposed efforts to return the abortion issue to the democratic process. Movement leaders believed that the right to life was rooted in substantive due process, the Thirteenth and Fourteenth Amendments, the Declaration of Independence, and human rights precedents—a right that should not be left to the mercy of popular majorities.

Abortion opponents fought against states-rights amendments that would overrule *Roe* and return the abortion question to the people. Rather than focusing on judicial activism, pro-lifers instead prioritized arguments about the medical evidence for fetal personhood, the importance of protecting the weak against discrimination, or the constitutional foundation of a right to life. It was not until the early 1980s that the evils of judicial overreaching gained prominence. Just the same, when abortion opponents put greater emphasis on the evils of judicial overreaching, incrementalists did so partly for pragmatic reasons: strengthening alliances with the Religious Right and the New Right and influencing the Reagan White House and the Republican Party. Gradually, some activists also began to view the courts in a different way. Perceiving the *Roe* decision as a betrayal of the courts' duty to protect vulnerable minorities, some pro-lifers began to use the rhetoric of judicial activism to voice sincere disappointment in the judiciary.

Studying the origins of popular perceptions of judicial legitimacy will be a complicated but rewarding endeavor. Even in the context of abortion, scholars should examine the legal, political, and cultural factors that contribute to the continuing prominence of arguments about judicial activism within the antiabortion movement. Commentators appear to have overstated the importance of the *Roe* decision in making judicial legitimacy an important issue for abortion opponents. For this reason, concerns about the effects of opinions like *Roe* on the Court's authority may be exaggerated. It is possible, however, that *Roe* did damage to the Court's credibility, albeit not in the ways we have often believed. In either case, we have a good deal to learn about the politics of judicial activism, both in the context of abortion and beyond. This book lays the foundation for studies of this kind.

Reaction to the *Roe* Decision as a Case Study in Backlash

The history of reactions to *Roe* plays a part in scholarly debates about the ability of the courts to create social change. One vein of scholarship focuses on the relationship between the courts and popular opinion. Michael Klarman and Jeffrey Rosen agree that the Supreme Court is "never truly at the vanguard of a social reform movement."[19] As Rosen suggests, the courts tend to act more in conformity with public attitudes than do their elected counterparts in other branches of government. A second line of argument addresses the effects of decisions that run ahead of public views. In Klarman's account, *Roe* serves as an example of the repercussions of judicial decisions that outpace popular opinion. He suggests that the 1973 decision gave hardliners new momentum and generated "an enormous political backlash that undermined the cause of abortion reform in the long term."[20] Scholars measuring backlash to a decision tend to look partly to the empowerment of extremists. As Rosen suggests, these strongly adverse responses help to explain the courts' tendency to adhere closely to public opinion. Gerald Rosenberg similarly asserts that litigation rarely produces meaningful social change, since the courts can achieve little without the support of the public and the elected branches of government.[21]

The evolution of pro-life incrementalism makes clear how difficult it is to evaluate the extent of backlash to the *Roe* decision. Starting in the mid-1970s, incrementalists gradually increased their influence over the antiabortion movement. To a greater extent than earlier in the decade, abortion opponents did build alliances with the New Right and adopt socially conservative arguments similar to those made by their new allies. While some of them held traditionalist views, however, incrementalists pursued an alliance with social conservatives largely because of the political advantages such a coalition promised.

The same pragmatism helped to explain the willingness of incrementalists to prioritize compromise laws that restricted abortion without banning it. Some incrementalists believed that these restrictions struck the right balance between protecting unborn life and allowing access to abortion. Many more believed instead that compromise legislation was the most effective tool available in limiting the impact of the opinion and in undermining the foundation of the decision.

The aftermath of the *Roe* decision reveals the difficulties inherent in assessing a movement's response. Did the decision undermine possible compromises and empower extremists? Much depends on which compromises we dignify and which activists we qualify as extremists. Was Marjory Mecklenburg an extremist? She favored a constitutional amendment that banned abortion unless the procedure was needed to save a woman's life. She also favored funding for contraception and sex education, and she sometimes sympathized with the women's movement.

Do we consider James Bopp Jr. an extremist? Primarily for strategic reasons, Bopp came to oppose an immediate push for a constitutional amendment banning all abortions, instead favoring incremental restrictions on the procedure. However, Bopp did not favor compromise for its own sake, viewing incremental restrictions as the best way to attack *Roe*. Characterizing these activists as either extremists or moderates does not do justice to the complexity of their motivations, decisions, and values.

In describing backlash to the decision, we should continue to ask whether courts can deliver profound social change, and we should examine how the rhetoric and holding of opinions such as *Roe* make a difference to social movements like the one against abortion. To the extent that the history here offers an example, however, we should pay as much attention to the internal battles that shape movement politics. The incrementalist ascendancy came partly as the result of a series of struggles within the antiabortion movement about the meaning and desirability of compromise in the short term. As the history of abortion politics in the 1970s and early 1980s suggests, our emphasis on backlash has obscured much of what shaped the pro-life movement in the years after 1973.

Roe and the Relationship between the Movements for Legal Abortion and Women's Rights

Feminist scholars have described the troubling legacy of *Roe* for members of the women's movement. Catharine MacKinnon and Martha Minow, among others, suggest that the decision laid the foundation for later rulings on abortion funding. By highlighting individualism, choice, and freedom, *Roe* did not encourage feminists to prioritize the interests of poor or non-white women.[22]

The history of abortion politics in the decade after *Roe* shows that we have taken for granted the close relationship between the women's movement and the abortion-rights cause. Both immediately before and after 1973, movement activists hotly contested what that relationship ought to be. Pragmatists stressed consequence-based claims—including those related to population control—believed more likely to advance the abortion-rights cause. Others favored legalizing abortion primarily as a means to eliminate botched illegal abortions. Feminists struggled to convince their colleagues to prioritize claims concerning women's rights.

In the mid-1970s, feminists changed the identity of the movement by leveraging changes to the politics of population control and civil rights. Beginning in the mid-1970s scandal followed the population-control movement, deepening concerns about racism. Within the civil-rights movement of the 1960s, a longstanding tradition based on nationalism, separatism, and cultural pride attracted new attention, as the leaders of high-profile organizations like the Student Non-Violent Coordinating Committee and the Congress for Racial Equality called for "black power." Women of color formed feminist organizations of their own, convincing male colleagues that reproductive rights deserved support. Within the abortion-rights movement, feminists pointed to these shifts as evidence that population-control arguments did more harm than good.

As importantly, feminists reinterpreted the Supreme Court's decision for strategic reasons, making *Roe* a symbol of a woman's right to control her own body. Abortion-rights activists relied on the authority of the Court and the efficacy of pro-life challenges to demand a new rhetorical strategy. By the mid-1970s, feminists had helped to rework both the racial politics of abortion and the relationship between the abortion-rights and women's movements.

Unearthing the contested relationship between feminism and legal abortion gives us reason to reexamine the identity of the abortion-rights movement. Certainly, the needs, work, and dreams of women have fueled demands for legal abortion. Just the same, there is nothing inevitable about the close ties between the movements for abortion rights and sex equality in America. Recognizing this contingency will allow us to map out later battles about whether, why, and how abortion rights relate to the movement for women's liberation.

Roe, Single-Issue Politics, and Choice Arguments

Much as the *Roe* decision did not subvert the relationship between the women's movement and people of color, the Supreme Court's intervention did not inexorably lead to the dominance of either a single-issue approach or the choice-based contentions now associated with the debate. In response to the *Roe* decision, activists in organizations like the Committee for Abortion Rights and Against Sterilization Abuse (CARASA), the Reproductive Rights National Network (R2N2), and the National Women's Health Network (NWHN) set forth a broader agenda, arguing that reproductive freedom did not mean anything unless the government supported women's decisions to use contraception, raise children, work, or receive adequate health care. These activists transformed the Supreme Court's idea of reproductive choice, asserting that women enjoyed true freedom only when they had the resources to select among various alternatives.

Moreover, in putting greater emphasis on choice-based arguments in the later 1970s, mainstream organizations like NARAL or NOW responded not to the Supreme Court but rather to the political setbacks of the mid-1970s. Ultimately, in the early 1980s when abortion-rights activists settled on the idea of a right to choose, they did so partly in response to the election of Ronald Reagan, the success of small-government rhetoric, the victories of the antiabortion movement, and the imminent threat to legal abortion.

By linking the influence of choice-based rhetoric or a single-issue agenda so exclusively to *Roe*, we have ignored important questions about the persistence of arguments based on autonomy and privacy. Choice-based claims gained influence partly because of the political exigencies of the 1970s and early 1980s. Scholars should offer a fuller account of why similar arguments have had such staying power in the past several decades.

Roe certainly framed abortion as a privacy-based right, offering support for activists who prioritized the abortion decision itself rather than the preservation of funding for those who could not afford an abortion. Nonetheless, the emphasis put on arguments about a right to choose—and the creation of a single-issue agenda—arose for reasons beyond the decision. In the late 1970s, mainstream organizations responded to the emergence of abortion as a major issue in electoral politics, to a series of unfavorable abortion funding cases, to the need to appeal to a broader segment of the voting public, and to the imminent threat to legal abortion posed by the human life bill and the human life amendment in the early 1980s.

As was the case in the decade after *Roe*, we should not explain the continuing influence of choice-based rhetoric and law-reform strategies solely by looking at the Supreme Court's actions in 1973. In later decades, what political events, tactical contests, and changing beliefs contributed to the continuing relevance of this strategy? Has the choice framework varied in influence, or have supporters of legal abortion challenged, reshaped, and revived it? What can abortion-rights activists do, if anything, to move away from this approach? Like single-issue politics, the idea of a right to choose has a long and complicated history. *Roe* is certainly a part of this story, but there is likely a good deal more of it that remains to be told.

Roe and Popular Interpretation of Abortion Rights

Roe has become synonymous with a woman's right to choose abortion, but it was not always that way. Commentators often conclude that the opinion undermined a productive popular dialogue about what abortion rights ought to mean. Before 1973, while states reached a variety of solutions to the abortion problem, pro-lifers felt that policymakers took their views seriously. Those pushing for the liberalization of abortion laws had the freedom to experiment with new ideas about the scope and justification for abortion rights. *Roe* supposedly put an end to these innovative exchanges. "*Roe* essentially declared a winner in one of the most difficult and divisive public law debates of American history," explains William Eskridge. The Court supposedly sent a powerful message: "Don't bother going to state legislatures to reverse the decision. Don't bother trying to persuade your neighbors."[23]

Contrary to what many scholars and advocates claim, however, opposing social movements continued to debate the meaning, scope, and justification for abortion rights after 1973, this time reformulating their views as claims about what the *Roe* Court had said. In popular politics, the women's-rights understanding of *Roe* now central to abortion debate emerged as the result of dialogue and competition between those on opposing sides, as activists vied to win supporters, raise money, and build public sympathy.

Changing popular interpretations of *Roe* shed light on other lost ideas about what the *Roe* Court meant and what difference its decision could have made to sexual politics. In the 1970s, for example, civil libertarians, sex workers, feminists, and members of the gay-liberation movement cast *Roe* as a decision about sexual freedom. In the mid-1970s, the ACLU formed the Sexual Privacy Project to build on this understanding of *Roe*. Marilyn Haft, the attorney leading the Project, brought cases on behalf of gay men, prostitutes, women in non-marital heterosexual relationships, and men convicted of fornication. The Project worked with COYOTE (Call Off Your Old Tired Ethics), a sex workers' union, and the National Gay Task Force (later to become the National Gay and Lesbian Task Force) in fighting for a right to sexual privacy. Outside the courts, COYOTE held an annual "hooker's ball" attended by sex workers, feminists, and celebrities. Street theater, marches, and protest rallies dramatized claims that all Americans had a right to control their own bodies. *Roe* played an important part in these claims. Sexual dissenters framed *Roe* as a decision about adults' sexual liberty—a case about adults' sexual liberty.[24]

Beginning in the late 1970s, abortion providers also began to forge their own interpretations of the abortion right in *Roe*. Feminist women's health activists like Charlotte Taft began to identify what they believed to be a gap between abortion-rights rhetoric and the experience of women who had abortions. Some providers wanted to confront more directly the difficult questions abortion raised. Did abortion involve killing? When, if at all, did women regret abortion? Why did women elect abortion at all? Some providers redefined *Roe* as a decision about the evils of state intervention rather than as an opinion identifying abortion as a fundamental right. Providers insisted that rights-based rhetoric failed to capture the nuances of real women's experiences. Criticism of rights arguments began to appear in the late 1970s, as providers organized the National Abortion Federation (NAF). By the 1990s when the National Coalition of Abortion Providers (NCAP), an alternative group, formed, similar contentions gained momentum.[25]

Future studies can reveal a good deal about our own understanding of and commitment to *Roe* by examining the history of these popular interpretations. Why did different groups draw on *Roe* in pursuing a particular program of social change? Why did these popular interpretations fail to capture the public imagination? At present, have other groups created their own, dramatically different understandings of *Roe*? Current views of the decision, as we have seen, depend partly on the contingencies of the 1970s and early 1980s. Once we realize this, other lost interpretations may come into view.

Roe and Compromise on Other Gender Issues

The Todd Akin controversy revived discussion about whether the antiabortion movement has waged "a war on women." This debate raises questions about when and why the antiabortion movement became committed to traditionalist positions on gender issues. Current scholarship indicates that traditionalist worldviews define antiabortion activism. Kristin Luker's seminal study shows that *Roe* prompted a younger, more socially conservative group of women to mobilize.

In the aftermath of the decision, the abortion debate became "so passionate and hard-fought" because it turned into a "referendum on the place and meaning of motherhood."[26]

Based on her own study of North Dakota activists, Faye Ginsburg also asserts that opposing activists disagree about the proper place for women in society. Ginsburg argues that, for abortion opponents, legalizing the procedure "represents an active denial of two essential conditions of female gender identity: pregnancy and the obligations of nurturance that should follow."[27] According to Ginsburg, the abortion battle involves "an intense, almost populist struggle for contending interpretations of gender, sexuality, and reproduction."[28]

Ginsburg and Luker also offer valuable diagnoses of the future of abortion conflict. Ginsburg believes that activists with such differing views of gender will rarely find common ground. "As the abortion debate has come increasingly to stand for opposing views of gender," she concludes, "the possibility of mutual recognition seems to decrease."[29] Luker agrees that, because of divisions about gender issues, "the abortion debate will not become noted for civility, calm, or reasoned discourse."[30]

Similar arguments shape legal and historical scholarship. For example, Reva Siegel has argued that nineteenth-century and contemporary abortion restrictions reflect a desire to keep women in traditional roles. "Restrictions on abortion," she explains, "reflect the kind of bias that is at the root of the most invidious forms of stereotyping: a failure to consider, in a society always at risk of forgetting, that women are persons, too."[31] In his work on possible common ground in the abortion debate, Laurence Tribe also suggests that abortion regulations reflect hostility to women who seek out sexual pleasure without wishing to parent.[32]

The materials assembled here do not challenge the conclusions drawn by Luker, Ginsburg, Siegel, and Tribe but rather better place those conclusions in historical context. Although some dissenting groups remain, traditionalist rhetoric, positions, and beliefs often characterize the work of contemporary abortion opponents, even in incrementalist organizations like the NRLC. Just the same, the alliance between the New Right and the antiabortion movement did not fall into place immediately after or because of the *Roe* decision. Indeed, throughout much of the 1970s and early 1980s, gender issues divided the antiabortion movement.[33]

Organizations like Feminists for Life or American Citizens Concerned for Life sided with the women's movement in battles about the Equal Rights Amendment, federally funded family planning or child care, and sex discrimination laws. Leaders sympathetic to these positions played a prominent role in larger antiabortion organizations like the NRLC. Advocates such as Pat Goltz and Marjory Mecklenburg had complex views about sex equality and mothering. Some saw nurturance and parenting as the fate of all women. At the same time, members of these organizations endorsed efforts to eliminate sex discrimination in the workplace, to keep unwed mothers in school, to improve contraceptive access, to encourage men to take greater responsibility for child care, and to allow women to parent without sacrificing their career aspirations or financial independence. These activists challenged some aspects of traditional gender roles while reaffirming others.

Some abortion-rights supporters wanted to recognize protections for fetuses that would not directly interfere with women's access to abortion. For many of these activists, the *Roe* decision offered an additional reason to find consensus.

The Supreme Court alone did not guarantee that these activists would lose influence. The realignment of political party position, the mobilization of the New Right and the Religious Right, abortion-rights activists' need to respond to the stigmatizing of the abortion procedure, and pro-lifers' financial struggles all affected the abortion battle. The alliance between the political Right and the antiabortion movement was not inevitable. Instead, that coalition formed as the result of still-understudied changes to the American political landscape.

The history explored in this volume makes clear that we cannot blame the contemporary gender wars so heavily on the Supreme Court. In the 1970s and early 1980s, a variety of politicians, strategists, attorneys, and grassroots activists contested the relationship between sex-equality politics and abortion. To the extent that reproductive politics turn on activists' beliefs about motherhood or gender roles, views about sex equality within either movement have varied a good deal.

Recovering the lost history of those who sought middle-ground positions on gender issues opens up promising avenues of future study. First, the partnership between social conservatives and abortion opponents has been so prominent in recent years that we may sometimes neglect current divisions within each movement. We ought to study whether those on opposing sides have, in fact, come to hold more uniform views on gender issues. If not, the participants in the abortion wars might still forge promising alliances on issues from equal pay for women to welfare reform. If compromise remains impossible, we have important questions to answer about how and why leaders of opposing movements struggle to find any shared solutions on issues like contraception or sex-discrimination law. Furthermore, we have seen that the polarization on gender issues that defines contemporary abortion debate resulted partly because of political events that took place in the 1970s and early 1980s. If conflict continues to escalate, we have more reason than ever to identify the more recent political, cultural, and social trends that continue to affect abortion politics.

Current scholarship points to the importance of gender issues in setting the terms of the abortion battle. Nonetheless, in the decade after 1973, the relationship between the antiabortion movement and antifeminism (or between the abortion-rights movement and feminism) was in almost constant flux. We should not be surprised if the gender dimensions of the abortion battle that today seem to be a permanent feature of the American political landscape once again change dramatically.

Roe as a Touchstone for Debate about the Best Method of Constitutional Interpretation

Roe's critics, Justice Antonin Scalia among them, suggest that public opposition to the decision would have been less intense had the Court focused on the intentions of the framers and the text and history of the Constitution. Influential supporters of legal abortion generally favor a reframing of the abortion right. Proponents of equality-based rationales also rely on reactions to Roe in arguing for an alternative constitutional rationale for abortion rights. According to Justice Ruth Bader Ginsburg, "[t]he Roe decision might have been less of a storm center had it . . . homed in more precisely on the women's equality dimension of the issue."[34] In Laurence Tribe's view, the Court's privacy approach required the justices to "needlessly insult . . . and alienate . . . those for whom the view that the fetus is a person represents a fundamental article of faith," and the backlash produced by

Roe intensified accordingly.[35] Ginsburg and Tribe suggest that if *Roe* had relied on the Equal Protection Clause, the abortion conflict might have been less anguished.[36]

For some commentators, reactions to *Roe* illustrate the negative consequences of certain forms of constitutional interpretation. Cass Sunstein uses *Roe* to highlight the problems with decisions that have unnecessarily broad holdings or philosophical rationales. One of Sunstein's preferred methods, minimalism, prizes modest, under-theorized decisions tailored to the facts in an individual case. By contrast, in using a "many minds" approach to the Constitution, a court consults a variety of interpretations of the Constitution, and if a majority adheres to one in particular, the court should assign more weight to this view. Sunstein suggests that "[i]ntense public opposition is a clue that [an] interpretation of the Constitution is incorrect."[37] For this reason, Sunstein explains, the Court should learn from "the experience of *Roe*."[38] In Sunstein's view, *Roe* "raised serious and enduring issues about judicial legitimacy."[39]

William Eskridge and John Ferejohn agree that *Roe* was a "mistake" because it "announce[d] a Constitutional right prematurely."[40] Eskridge and Ferejohn defend a method of constitutional change whereby Americans create statutory and administrative rights that fill gaps in our constitutional fabric. This method of change creates a strong foundation for government structures and constitutional values by facilitating public deliberation, encouraging interbranch cooperation, and building consensus. By contrast, when, as in *Roe*, the Court mandates sweeping social changes, its decisions can be counterproductive, especially when the Court acts in conflict with popular opinion. For pro-lifers, Eskridge and Ferejohn write, *Roe* "marginalized the interests of the fetus . . . without a solid theory."[41]

Similarly, Richard Posner uses *Roe* to showcase the shortcomings of decision-making that ignores the practical impact a judicial opinion would have. Posner contrasts *Roe* with pragmatism, an empirical, forward-looking mode of decision-making. Given that abortion law was undeveloped in the 1970s, a pragmatist would have decided *Roe* on narrow grounds, citing prudence and the need for experimentation before the Court imposed a single, national solution. Posner suggests that because the *Roe* Court did not fully consider the consequences of its decision, it straight-jacketed state legislatures, incited the antiabortion movement, and undermined the Court's legitimacy.[42]

Generally, as the materials assembled here suggest, scholars analyzing the consequences of *Roe* sometimes miss other political and social events in shaping movement politics. Too often, commentators also describe movement members as bound by forces beyond their control. At least in the period studied here, a variety of grassroots activists freely and knowingly made choices that raised the stakes of the abortion wars. Focusing so narrowly on the influence of the Supreme Court has partly blinded commentators to the wide array of factors that helped to create the current struggle about abortion.[43]

The challenges inherent in evaluating the consequences of *Roe* may well apply whenever scholars address the effects of different methods of constitutional interpretation. This body of research is important, and it will benefit considerably from a detailed historical examination of the aftermath of other high-salience cases like *Roe*. Future studies of this kind should pay as much attention to changing movement strategy discussions and political circumstances as to the details of an opinion. If we have a better historical foundation for studying the consequences of various interpretive methods, different conclusions may well emerge. Given the wide variety of factors shaping movement politics in the 1970s and the early 1980s, we may have overstated the negative consequences of *Roe*'s interpretive approach or others like it.

Roe at Forty and Beyond

The abortion debate following *Roe* has already lasted for almost half a century. The Supreme Court has played a crucial role in the politics of abortion, but public debate about the procedure has been infinitely complex. In a single decade after *Roe*, the popular interpretation of the decision changed. Through a series of internal battles, the leadership, identity, and arguments that defined the opposing sides shifted.

Roe itself has altered the constitutional landscape. The decision helped to launch an important discussion about the justification for judicial review and the best method of constitutional interpretation. For many, *Roe* is a symbol: of freedom or indifference to the weak, of equality for women or the devaluation of life.

However important that single decision has been, the abortion wars themselves are more complicated than anything that could be explained by one Supreme Court decision. We cannot easily generalize about the activists involved in the discussion. They were homemakers who became full-time breadwinners and activists, demographers, feminists, traditionalists, physicians, lawyers, and religious leaders. The story of the decade after *Roe* is their story. That struggle has been both deeply personal and politically influential, and it has continued in the decades that followed. Better understanding the abortion debate will require us to do justice to these activists—to their contradictions, commitments, savvy, strategies, and beliefs. This book begins that project.

Notes

Preface

1. For Barron's personal story: Thea Rossi Barron, interview with Mary Ziegler, April 23, 2012. For further discussion of Barron's career in the movement, see "National Right to Life, Political Right Interlink," *National Catholic Reporter* 15 (November 10, 1978): 1; Thea Rossi Barron, "Hyde Amendment Big Victory; Fight Goes On," *National Right to Life News*, January 1977, JRS, 1977 National Right to Life News Box.
2. Barron, interview.
3. Ibid. For archival evidence of the common ground summit, see "Implementation of Consensus Working Paper" (April 19, 1979), 1, NOW, Box 96, Folder 21; American Citizens Concerned for Life, "Statement for February 15, 1979 National Dialogue on Abortion" (February 14, 1979), NOW, Box 96, Folder 21.
4. Frances Kissling, interview with Mary Ziegler, January 9, 2012. For further discussion of Kissling's life and influence, see Gene Burns, "Abandoning Suspicion: The Catholic Left and Sexuality," in *What's Left? Liberal American Catholics*, ed. Mary Jo Weaver (Bloomington: Indiana University Press, 1999), 67–74.
5. Kissling, interview. For more on the Jimenez story, see Jennifer Dunning, "Books: *Rosie*, a Death after an Illegal Abortion," *New York Times*, October 12, 1979, C27; Karen DeWitt, "Abortion Foes March in Capitol on Anniversary of Legalization," *New York Times*, January 23, 1979, C10.
6. See generally Laurence H. Tribe, *Abortion: The Clash of Absolutes* (New York: W. W. Norton, 1992).
7. In abortion scholarship, terminology has become ideologically charged. Hereafter, this book follows contemporary activists in using the terms

"pro-choice" and "pro-life" to refer to the competing movements studied here. At other times, the book refers to these movements as "abortion-rights" or "antiabortion." By using these terms, I do not mean to signal the rightness of either side's position. Nor do I mean to suggest that these terms accurately capture the identity of either movement in the period studied here. Generally, I use each movement's chosen labeling as part of a broader effort to describe, rather than judge, the positions opposing activists took in response to *Roe*. A rich legal, philosophical, political, and theological literature argues the rights and wrongs of abortion. Just the same, this scholarship often provides a distorting lens through which to view post-1973 history. By asking how activists understand and describe themselves, this project offers a deeper understanding of what happened after the *Roe* decision.

8. For an understanding of legal feminists and their aims, see Serena Mayeri, "Constitutional Choices: Legal Feminism and the Historical Dynamics of Change," *California Law Review* 92 (2004): 758; see also Deborah Dinner, "The Costs of Reproduction: History and the Legal Construction of Sex Equality," *Harvard Civil Rights-Civil Liberties Review* 46 (2011): 419n17.

9. For discussion of the impact of rising violence against abortion clinics and providers, see Faye D. Ginsburg, "Rescuing the Nation: Operation Rescue and the Rise of Anti-Abortion Militance," in *Abortion Wars: A Half-Century of Struggle, 1950–2000*, ed. Rickie Solinger (Berkeley: University of California Press, 1998), 227–251; James Risen and Judy L. Thomas, *Wrath of Angels: The American Abortion War* (New York: Basic Books, 1998), 74–76, 339–371; Suzanne Staggenborg, *The Pro-Choice Movement: Organization and Activism in the Abortion Conflict* (New York: Oxford University Press, 1991), 130–132; Donald T. Critchlow, *Intended Consequences: Birth Control, Abortion, and the Federal Government in Modern America* (New York: Oxford University Press, 1999), 215–222. For recent Supreme Court decisions remaking abortion law, see *Planned Parenthood of Southeastern Pennsylvania v. Casey*, 505 U.S. 833 (1992); *Gonzales v. Carhart*, 550 U.S. 124 (2007).

10. On the advantages and risks inherent in snowball sampling, see Alan Bryman, *Social Research Methods*, 4th ed. (New York: Oxford University Press, 2012), 63, 424–425; Patrick Biernacki and J. K. Waters, "Targeted Sampling: Options for the Study of Hidden Populations," *Social Problems* 36 (1989): 416–430; Patrick Biernacki and Dan Waldorf, "Snowball Sampling: Problems and Techniques of Chain Referral Sampling," *Sociological Methods & Research* 10 (1981): 141–163.

11. On volunteer bias, see Robert Rosenthal and Ralph Rosnow, "The Volunteer Subject," in *Artifacts in Behavioral Research: Robert Rosenthal and Ralph L. Rosnow's Classic Books* (New York: Oxford University Press, 2009), 48–93. On challenges related to social network size and isolated individuals, see J. Faugier and M. Sargeant, "Sampling Hard to Reach Populations," *Journal of Advanced Nursing* 26 (1997): 790–797; Douglas

A. Heckathorn, "Development of a Theory of Collective Action: From the Emergence of Norms to AIDS Prevention and the Analysis of Social Structure," in *New Directions in Contemporary Sociological Theory*, eds. Joseph Berger and Morris Zelditch Jr. (Lanham, MD: Rowman and Littlefield, 2002), 79–106; Douglas A. Heckathorn, "Respondent-Driven Sampling: A New Approach to the Study of Hidden Populations," *Social Problems* 44 (1997): 174–199.

12. On methods used to reduce bias in snowball sampling, see Faugier and Sargeant, "Sampling," 790–797; Piergiorgio Corbetta, *Social Research: Theory, Method, and Techniques* (London: Sage, 2003), 229; V. M. Hendricks and P. Blanken, "Snowball Sampling: Methodological Analysis," in *Snowball Sampling: A Pilot Study on Cocaine Use*, eds. V. M. Hendricks, P. Blanken, and N. Adriaans (Rotterdam: IVO, 1992), 83–100. On sampling strategy and oral history, see Patricia Leavy, *Oral History: Understanding Qualitative Research* (New York: Oxford University Press, 2011), 34–35, 75–76, 84–90, 135–136; Lynn Abrams, *Oral History Theory* (New York: Routledge, 2010), 6–8, 95–103.

13. For discussion of the study of oral memory and public memory, see Graham Smith, "Toward a Public Oral History," in *The Oxford Handbook of Oral History*, ed. Donald A. Ritchie (New York: Oxford University Press, 2011), 437–443; see also generally Paul Thompson, *Voice of the Past: Oral History*, 3rd ed. (New York: Oxford University Press, 2000).

Introduction

1. See Leigh Ann Wheeler, *Against Obscenity: Reform and the Politics of Womanhood in America, 1873–1935* (Baltimore: Johns Hopkins University Press, 2004), 9–12; Nicola Kay Beisel, *Imperiled Innocents: Family Reproduction in Victorian America* (Princeton: Princeton University Press, 1997), 3–25.

2. On the creation of new antiabortion laws in the period, see Michael Grossberg, *Governing the Hearth: Law and the Family in Nineteenth-Century America* (Chapel Hill: University of North Carolina Press, 1985), 171–193; Lawrence M. Friedman, *Crime and Punishment in American History* (New York: Basic Books, 1993), 229–230, 400. On the AMA and the antiabortion movement, see James C. Mohr, *Abortion in America: The Origins and Evolution of National Policy* (New York: Oxford University Press, 1978), 147–200; see also Leslie J. Reagan, *When Abortion Was a Crime: Women, Medicine, and Law in the United States, 1867–1973* (Berkeley: University of California Press, 1997), 53–80.

3. Margaret Sanger, *The Pivot of Civilization* (New York: Brentano's, 1922), 259.

4. On Sanger's influence and view of women's rights, see Ellen Chesler, *Woman of Valor: Margaret Sanger and the Birth Control Movement in America*

(New York: Simon and Schuster, 2007), 60–61, 66–67; David M. Kennedy, *Birth Control in America: The Career of Margaret Sanger* (New Haven, CT: Yale University Press, 1970), 60, 134. In the early twentieth century, supporters of birth control and "voluntary motherhood" explicitly positioned contraception within feminist discourse. See Harriet Sigerman, "Laborers for Liberty: 1865–1890," in *No Small Courage: A History of Women in the United States*, ed. Nancy F. Cott (New York: Oxford University Press, 2000), 347; Linda Gordon, *The Moral Property of Women: A History of Birth Control Politics in America* (Champaign: University of Illinois Press, 2002), 55–72.

5. Francis Galton, *Inquiries into the Human Faculty and Its Development* (London: Macmillan, 1883), 25.

6. On the history of the eugenic legal reform movement, see generally Daniel J. Kevles, *In the Name of Eugenics: Genetics and the Uses of Human Heredity* (Berkeley: University of California Press, 1985); Wendy Kline, *Building a Better Race: Gender, Sexuality, and Eugenics From the Turn of the Century to the Baby Boom* (Berkeley: University of California Press, 2001); Stefan Kühl, *The Nazi Connection: Eugenics, American Racism, and German National Socialism* (New York: Oxford University Press, 1994). On eugenic-marriage laws and their shortcomings, see Kevles, *In the Name of Eugenics*, 99–100, 120, 277; Paul A. Lombardo, *Three Generations, No Imbeciles: Eugenics, the Supreme Court, and* Buck v. Bell (Baltimore: Johns Hopkins University Press, 2008), 44–46. On the success of compulsory sterilization laws, see Mark Largent, *Breeding Contempt: The History of Coerced Sterilization in the United States* (Piscataway, NJ: Rutgers University Press, 2008), 65–66, 127–128. For the Supreme Court decision upholding a model compulsory sterilization law: *Buck v. Bell*, 274 U.S. 200 (1927).

7. On the relationship between eugenics and Progressivism, see Michael Willrich, "The Two Percent Solution: Eugenic Jurisprudence and the Socialization of American Law, 1900–1930," *Law and History Review* 16 (1998): 63–111. On anxieties about masculinity and self-employment, see Gail Bederman, *Manliness and Civilization: A Cultural History of Gender and Race in the United States, 1880–1917* (Chicago: University of Chicago Press, 1995), 11–13. On women's increasing workforce participation, see Alice Kessler-Harris, *Out to Work: A History of Wage-Earning Women in the United States* (New York: Oxford University Press, 2003), 3–5, 23, 91–128, 142, 277, 300–304. On the rate of elite women's college attendance, see Diana B. Turk, *Bound by a Mighty Vow: Sisterhood and Women's Fraternities, 1870–1920* (New York: New York University Press, 2004), 15.

8. On postwar, reform eugenics, see Kevles, *In the Name of Eugenics*, 171–192; Christine Rosen, *Preaching Eugenics: Religious Leaders and the American Eugenics Movement* (New York: Oxford University Press, 2004), 165–180. On the Nazi sterilization regime, see Lombardo, *Three*

Generations, 193–210, 236–239; Kuhl, *The Nazi Connection*, 23–25, 62–63; Rebecca M. Kluchin, *Fit to Be Tied: Sterilization and Reproductive Rights in America, 1950–1980* (Piscataway, NJ: Rutgers University Press, 2009), 16.

9. Chapter 3 discusses these connections in greater depth. For a sample of historical scholarship on the population-control movement, see Donald T. Critchlow, *Intended Consequences: Birth Control, Abortion, and the Federal Government in Modern America* (New York: Oxford University Press, 1999); Simone M. Caron, *Who Chooses? American Reproductive History since 1850* (Gainesville: University Press of Florida, 2008), 150–151, 153–155, 160–163; Matthew Connelly, *Fatal Misconception: The Struggle to Control World Population* (Cambridge, MA: Harvard University Press, 2008).

10. See Hugh Moore, "Voluntary Sterilization: Is It an Answer to the Population Bomb?" (December 1959), 14, HMP, Box 20, Folder 5. For more on Moore's career in the movement, see Critchlow, *Intended Consequences*, 4–5, 29–33, 147, 150–152, 229; Ian Dowbiggin, *A Merciful End: The Euthanasia Movement in Modern America* (New York: Oxford University Press, 2003), 125–132, 144–145. On the early days of the Population Council, see "Documentation of the Conference on Population Problems" (June 22, 1952), JDR, Series 2, Box 45; Thomas Parran to John D. Rockefeller (October 28, 1952), JDR, Series 2, Box 45.

11. "Catholics in Poll Back Birth Curbs," *New York Times*, September 1, 1968, 46. For further discussion of the changing attitudes of the Catholic laity toward contraception, see Leslie Woodcock Tentler, *Catholics and Contraception: An American History* (Ithaca, NY: Cornell University Press, 2004), 1–14; Jay P. Dolan, *In Search of an American Catholicism: A History of Religion and Culture in Tension* (New York: Oxford University Press, 2002), 163–164, 250–255. On the changing stance of Protestant denominations toward contraception: Linda Greenhouse and Reva B. Siegel, eds., *Before* Roe v. Wade: *Voices That Shaped the Abortion Debate before the Supreme Court's Ruling*, 2nd ed. (New Haven, CT: Yale Law Library, 2012), 73–75.

12. For discussion of the increasing use of birth control, see Jane E. Brody, "The Pill: Revolution in Birth Control," *New York Times*, May 31, 1966, 1. On rates of premarital sex, see "Vanishing Virginity," *New York Times*, May 14, 1972, E2. On feminist engagement with the issue of reproductive freedom in the early 1970s, see Greenhouse and Siegel, *Before* Roe v. Wade, 276–293, 328–337; Christine Stansell, *The Feminist Promise: 1792 to the Present* (New York: Random House, 2010), 303, 326–328, 342–343; Leslie J. Reagan, *When Abortion Was a Crime: Women, Medicine, and Law in the United States, 1867–1973* (Berkeley: University of California Press, 1997), 224–252.

13. See "Looking into The ZPGeneration," *Time Magazine*, February 28, 1977, 71. For further discussion of ZPG's activities in the period, see Critchlow,

Intended Consequences, 156–158, 185, 191; Connelly, *Fatal Misconception,* 248–269; Suzanne Staggenborg, *The Pro-Choice Movement: Organization and Activism in the Abortion Conflict* (New York: Oxford University Press, 1991), 9, 18–19, 84–90, 162–164, 182–197. Chapter 3 offers further discussion of the organization's involvement in the abortion wars.

14. On physicians' reasons for pursuing reform in the period, see Jennifer Nelson, *Women of Color and the Reproductive Rights Movement* (New York: New York University Press, 2003), 8–14; Reagan, *When Abortion Was a Crime,* 138–142, 223–260. On the ALI and early reform efforts, see Staggenborg, *The Pro-Choice Movement,* 14, 31–34; Faye D. Ginsburg, *Contested Lives: The Abortion Debate in an American Community* (Berkeley: University of California Press, 1998), 35–37; Reagan, *When Abortion Was a Crime,* 221–239. On the changing indications for abortion, see Kristin Luker, *Abortion and the Politics of Motherhood* (Berkeley: University of California Press, 1984), 51–61, 73–90.

15. For contemporary coverage of Finkbine's struggles, see "Mrs. Finkbine Undergoes Abortion in Sweden," *New York Times,* August 19, 1962, 69; "Mother Loses Round in Legal Battle for Abortion," *New York Times,* July 31, 1962, 9; "Mother, Rebuffed in Arizona, May Seek Abortion Elsewhere," *New York Times,* August 1, 1962, 19. For discussion of the influence of Finkbine's story, see Sara Dubow, *Ourselves Unborn: A History of the Fetus in Modern America* (New York: Oxford University Press, 2010), 64–65; Leslie J. Reagan, *Dangerous Pregnancies: Mothers, Disabilities, and Abortion in Modern America* (Berkeley: University of California Press, 2010), 55–59, 85–91.

16. On the influence of the German measles on the abortion wars, see Reagan, *Dangerous Pregnancies,* 144–152, 166–179; Laurence H. Tribe, *Abortion and the Clash of Absolutes* (New York: W. W. Norton, 1992), 37–42; Luker, *Abortion,* 80–90.

17. Lawrence Lader, "The Scandal of Abortion Laws," *New York Times,* April 25, 1965, SM32.

18. Keith Monroe, "How California's Abortion Law Isn't Working," *New York Times,* December 29, 1968, SM10. For more on the lack of access to abortion under reform laws, see Martin Tolchin, "Doctors Divided on Issue," *New York Times,* February 27, 1967, 1; Robert D. McFadden, "Flaws in Abortion Reform in an 8-State Study," *New York Times,* April 13, 1970, 1. On doctors' anxieties about the reform laws, see "Abortion Experts, Saying Women Should Decide, Ask End to Curbs," *New York Times,* November 24, 1968, 77.

19. Betty Friedan, "Abortion: A Woman's Civil Right: Keynote Speech before the First National Conference for the Repeal of Abortion Laws" (February 14, 1969), 2, BFP, Box 121, Folder 1467. On the feminist activists joining the repeal movement, see Reagan, *When Abortion Was a Crime,* 190, 223–234; Nelson, *Women of Color,* 45–55; Greenhouse and Siegel, *Before Roe v. Wade,* 256–268.

20. Chapters 1 and 2 further discuss the history of the pro-life movement. On state adoption of repeal laws, see Jerry M. Flint, "Abortion Backers Hopeful of Gains," *New York Times*, October 9, 1972, 9; "Bill to Legalize Abortion Clears Hawaii Legislature," *New York Times*, February 25, 1970, 1.

21. On the effort to repeal New York's liberalized law, see William E. Farrell, "Governor Vetoes Abortion Repeal As Not Justified," *New York Times*, May 14, 1972, 1; William E. Farrell, "Assembly Votes to Repeal Liberalized Abortion Law," *New York Times*, May 10, 1972, 1; Alfonso A. Narvaez, "Abortion Repeal Passed by Senate, Sent to Governor," *New York Times*, May 11, 1972, 1. On the Michigan referendum, see Staggenborg, *The Pro-Choice Movement*, 35–38, 48; Critchlow, *Intended Consequences*, 556–557, 577–579; David J. Garrow, *Liberty and Sexuality: The Right to Privacy and the Making of* Roe v. Wade (Berkeley: University of California Press, 1998), 562–567, 577.

22. See Linda Greenhouse and Reva B. Siegel, "Before (and after) *Roe v. Wade*: New Questions on Backlash," *Yale Law Journal* 120 (2011): 2052–2071. For discussion of abortion as a wedge issue in the early 1970s, see Rick Perlstein, *Nixonland: The Rise of a President and the Fracturing of America* (New York: Simon and Schuster, 2008), 528, 745; Robert Mason, *Richard Nixon and the Quest for a New Majority* (Chapel Hill: University of North Carolina Press, 2004), 153; Critchlow, *Intended Consequences*, 148–149, 169–175.

23. *Griswold v. Connecticut*, 381 U.S. 479, 485–486 (1965).

24. *United States v. Vuitch*, 402 U.S. 62, 67–68 (1971).

25. Ibid., 71–73.

26. *Abele v. Markle*, 342 F.Supp. 800, 802 (D.Conn.1972).

27. *Cheaney v. State*, 285 N.E.2d 265, 267–270 (Ind. 1972); *People v. Nixon*, 201 N.W.2d 635, 635–643 (Mich. App. 1972).

28. *Eisenstadt v. Baird*, 405 U.S. 438, 453–454 (1972).

29. George Gallup, "Abortion Seen up to Woman, Doctor," *Washington Post* (August 25, 1972), A2, HBP, Box 151, Folder 4.

30. On the medicalized frame advanced in *Roe*, see Burns, *The Moral Veto*, 222–227; Greenhouse and Siegel, *Before* Roe v. Wade, 255–256; Garrow, *Liberty and Sexuality*, 595.

31. On the Texas law, see *Roe v. Wade*, 410 U.S. 113, 117–119 (1973). On the Georgia law, see *Doe v. Bolton*, 410 U.S. 179, 202–205 (1973). For press speculation about the outcome of the decisions, see Glen Elsasser, "Supreme Court Compromise Expected on Abortion Issue," *Chicago Tribune*, October 12, 1972, B5; Glen Elsasser, "Capitol Views: Supreme Court Secrecy Broken," *Chicago Tribune*, August 31, 1972, 16.

32. See *Roe v. Wade*, 148. Linda Greenhouse traces Blackmun's interest in a medical framing of abortion partly to his time at the Mayo Clinic. See Linda Greenhouse, *Becoming Justice Blackmun: Harry Blackmun's Supreme Court Journey* (New York: Henry Holt, 2005), 72, 90, 99. For *Roe's* survey of medical history, see *Roe v. Wade*, 139–148.

33. *Roe v. Wade*, 153, 164.
34. Ibid., 156–160.
35. See ibid., 164.
36. The *Roe* decision did spark debate in the legal academy about the best method of constitutional interpretation and the justification for judicial review. For a sample of the academic responses to the decision, see John Hart Ely, "The Wages of Crying Wolf: A Comment on *Roe v. Wade*," *Yale Law Journal* 82 (1973): 920–949; Thomas Gray, "Do We Have an Unwritten Constitution?" *Stanford Law Review* 27 (1975): 703–718; Philip Heymann and Douglas Barzelay, "The Forest and the Trees," *Boston University Law Review* 53 (1973): 765–784. For more on the scholarly discussion *Roe* inspired, see Stephen M. Griffin, *American Constitutionalism: From Theory to Politics* (Princeton: Princeton University Press, 1996), 141–142; Jack M. Balkin, "*Roe v. Wade*: An Engine of Controversy," in *What* Roe v. Wade *Should Have Said: The Nation's Top Legal Experts Rewrite America's Most Controversial Decision*, ed. Jack M. Balkin (New York: New York University Press, 2005), 3 ("Attacking and defending the reasoning and principles of *Roe v. Wade* has been a central preoccupation of constitutional theorists ever since it was decided").
37. See Laura Kalman, *Right Star Rising: A New Politics, 1974–1980* (New York: W. W. Norton, 2010), 22–28. For more on the New Right, see Rebecca Klatch, *A Generation Divided: The New Left, the New Right, and the 1960s* (Berkeley: University of California Press, 1999), 85–89, 223–239; Daniel K. Williams, *God's Own Party: The Making of the Religious Right*, 2nd ed. (New York: Oxford University Press, 2012), 167–178; Donald T. Critchlow, *The Conservative Ascendancy: How the GOP Right Made Political History* (Cambridge, MA: Harvard University Press, 2007), 128–136; Clyde Wilcox and Carin Robinson, *Onward Christian Soldiers? The Religious Right in American Politics*, 4th ed. (Boulder, CO: Westview, 2011); Darren Dochuk, *From Bible Belt to Sun Belt: Plain-Folk Religion, Grassroots Politics, and the Rise of Evangelical Conservatism* (New York: W. W. Norton, 2011).
38. On the Conservative Caucus, see Critchlow, *The Conservative Ascendancy*, 129–130; Chip Berlet, "The New Political Right in the United States: Reaction, Rollback, and Resentment," in *Confronting the New Conservatism: The Rise of the Right in America*, ed. Michael J. Thompson (New York: New York University Press, 2007), 83–85; Donald T. Critchlow, *Phyllis Schlafly and Grassroots Conservatism: A Woman's Crusade* (Princeton: Princeton University Press, 2005), 252, 263. On NCPAC, see Kalman, *Right Star*, 145; Jerome L. Himmelstein, *To the Right: The Transformation of American Conservatism* (Berkeley: University of California Press, 1990), 81–84; Williams, *God's Own Party*, 169. On Weyrich's background, see Andrew Rich, *Think Tanks, Public Policy, and the Politics of Expertise* (New York: Cambridge University Press, 2004), 53–54; Williams, *God's Own Party*, 167–171. On the CSFC, see Himmelstein, *To*

the Right, 81, 86; Gillian Peele and Joel D. Aberbach, "Introduction: The Ending of the Conservative Era?" in Crisis of Conservatism? The Republican Party, the Conservative Movement, and American Politics after Bush, eds. Joel D. Aberbach and Gillian Peele (New York: Oxford University Press, 2011), 28. On Viguerie's fundraising acumen, see Sara Diamond, Spiritual Warfare: The Politics of the Christian Right (Montreal: Black Rose Books, 1990), 58. For more on Viguerie's background, see Critchlow, The Conservative Ascendancy, 97, 128–130; Himmelstein, To the Right, 80–82.

39. See Williams, God's Own Party, 167–171; Patricia Miller, Good Catholics: The Battle over Abortion in the Catholic Church (Berkeley: University of California Press, 2014), 85–86; Michele McKeegan, Abortion Politics: Mutiny in the Ranks of the Right (New York: Free Press, 1992), 21–25.

40. "Year of the Evangelicals," Newsweek, October 25, 1976, 68–75. On changing patterns of evangelical turnout, see Jeff Manza and Clem Brooks, Social Cleavages and Political Change: Voter Alignments and U.S. Party Coalitions (New York: Oxford University Press, 1999), 97; Jon A. Shields, The Democratic Virtues of the Christian Right (Princeton: Princeton University Press, 2009), 120; Corwin Smidt, "Evangelical Voting Patterns: 1978–1988," in No Longer Exiles, ed. Michael Cromartie (Washington, DC: Ethics and Public Policy Center, 1993), 85–117. On the diversity of the evangelical community and the history and origins of the Christian Right, see Williams, God's Own Party, 1–11. On the hardening of conservative Protestants' opposition to abortion, see Steven P. Miller, The Age of Evangelicalism: America's Born-Again Years (New York: Oxford University Press, 2014), 53–55.

41. On Christian Voice, see Joel Kotkin, "Ready on the Right: Christian Soldiers Are on the March," Washington Post, August 25, 1979, A10; Williams, God's Own Party, 153–170; Dochuk, From Bible Belt, 384–388. On the Moral Majority's activities in the period, see Dr. Jerry Falwell, "What Is the Moral Majority?" Moral Majority Capitol Report (August 1979), 1, MMP, Series 1, Box 1, Folder 1; The Moral Majority, ERA Brochure (n.d., ca. 1979), 3, JFP, Series 3, Box 1, Folder 2; Brochure, "What Is the Moral Majority?" (n.d., ca. 1979), MMP, Series 1, Box 1, Folder 1. On the Religious Roundtable, see Critchlow, The Conservative Ascendancy, 130, 175–176; Elizabeth Anne Oldmixon, Uncompromising Positions: God, Sex, and the U.S. House of Representatives (Washington, DC: Georgetown University Press, 2005), 94–96; Dochuk, From Bible Belt, 384–385.

42. "Resolution on Abortion and Sanctity of Human Life" (June 1974), accessed April 9, 2014, http://www.sbc.net/resolutions/search/results. asp?query=abortion. For the 1971 resolution, see Southern Baptist Convention, "Resolution on Abortion" (June 1971), accessed April 10, 2014, http://www.sbc.net/resolutions/search/results.asp?query=abortion. On evangelical opposition to Roe before 1973, see Williams, God's Own

Party, 114, 155–156, 172; Susan Friend Harding, *The Book of Jerry Falwell: Fundamentalist Language and Politics* (Princeton: Princeton University Press, 2000), 190.

43. For the decision in *Engel*, the Court's seminal school prayer decision, see *Engel v. Vitale*, 370 U.S. 421 (1962). Chapter 1 studies Weyrich's use of *Roe* in greater depth.

44. For the text of the amendment, see Gayle Graham Yates, *What Women Want: The Ideas of the Movement* (Cambridge, MA: Harvard University Press, 1975), 52.

45. For discussion of the amendment's history and fate, see generally Donald G. Mathews and Jane Sherron De Hart, *Sex, Gender, and the Politics of ERA: A State and a Nation* (New York: Oxford University Press, 1990); Jane J. Mansbridge, *Why We Lost the ERA* (Chicago: University of Chicago Press, 1986); Mary Frances Berry, *Why ERA Failed: Politics, Women's Rights, and the Amending Process of the Constitution* (Bloomington: University of Indiana Press, 1986).

46. Phyllis Schlafly, "What's Wrong with Equal Rights for Women?" *The Phyllis Schlafly Report*, February 1972, vol. 5, no. 7, sec. 2, PSR. On the backgrounds of ERA opponents, see Val Burris, "Who Opposed the ERA? An Analysis of the Social Bases of Antifeminism," *Social Science Quarterly* 64 (June 1983): 305–317; Kent L. Tedin et al., "Social Background and Political Differences Between Pro- and Anti-ERA Activists," *American Politics Quarterly* 5 (July 1977): 395–404; David W. Brady and Kent L. Tedin, "Ladies in Pink: Religion and Political Ideology in the Anti-ERA Movement," *Social Science Quarterly* 56 (March 1976): 564–575.

47. For examples of Schlafly's efforts to persuade pro-lifers that the ERA would strengthen abortion rights, see Phyllis Schlafly, "ERA Means Abortion and Population Shrinkage," *The Phyllis Schlafly Report*, December 1974, vol. 8, no. 5, sec. 2, PSR; Phyllis Schlafly, "What Really Happened in Houston," *The Phyllis Schlafly Report*, December 1977, vol. 11, no. 5, sec. 2, PSR. On the conversion of evangelicals to the pro-life cause, see Williams, *God's Own Party*, 105, 114–115, 157, 241, 250; Miller, *The Age of Evangelicalism*, 53–55; James Risen and Judy L. Thomas, *Wrath of Angels: The American Abortion War* (New York: Basic Books, 1998), 119–121, 128.

48. Chapter 6 explores the strategic advantages, for pro-lifers, of an alliance with the New Right and Religious Right.

49. On Gerald Ford and the official Republican position on abortion in 1976, see Williams, *God's Own Party*, 168–173; Tribe, *The Clash of Absolutes*, 149; Critchlow, *Intended Consequences*, 201–204. On Carter's position, see J. Brooks Flippen, *Jimmy Carter, The Politics of Family, and the Rise of the Religious Right* (Athens: University of Georgia Press, 2011), 64–69; Tribe, *The Clash of Absolutes*, 149; David Karol, *Party Position Change in American Politics: Coalition Management* (New York: Cambridge University Press, 2009), 65–66.

50. On the 1980 Democratic Party platform, see David Rosenbaum, "Platform Drafters Back Carter Stands," *New York Times*, June 25, 1980, A1. Chapter 3 discusses the reframing of abortion as a woman's right and its consequences for the Democratic Party.

51. Chapter 3 examines the post-*Roe* disengagement of population-control organizations from abortion politics.

52. On the influence of feminists of color on the civil-rights movement, see Kimberly Springer, "Black Feminists Respond to Black Power Masculinism," in *The Black Power Movement: Rethinking the Civil Rights-Black Power Era*, ed. Peniel E. Joseph (New York: Routledge, 2006), 105–119; Sherie M. Randolph, "'Women's Liberation or . . . Black Liberation, You're Fighting the Same Enemies': Floryence Kennedy, Black Power, and Feminism," in *Want to Start a Revolution? Radical Women in the Black Freedom Struggle*, eds. Dayo F. Gore, Jeanne Theoharris, and Komozi Woodard (New York: New York University Press, 2009), 223–248; Nelson, *Women of Color*, 53–64. On the history of black power ideology earlier in the politics of civil rights, see Clayborne Carson, *In Struggle: SNCC and the Black Awakening of the 1960s*, 2nd ed. (Cambridge, MA: Harvard University Press, 1995), 1–9; Christopher B. Strain, *Pure Fire: Self-Defense as Activism in the Civil Rights Era* (Athens: University of Georgia, 2005), 1–8; Lance Hill, *The Deacons for Defense: Armed Resistance and the Civil Rights Movement* (Chapel Hill: University of North Carolina Press, 2004), 1–10; William L. Van Deburg, *New Day in Babylon: The Black Power Movement and American Culture, 1965–1975*, 2nd ed. (Chicago: University of Chicago Press, 1993), 1–11, 29–62; Cedric Johnson, *Revolutionaries to Race Leaders: Black Power and the Making of African American Politics* (Minneapolis: University of Minnesota Press, 2007), xix–xxxvi; Waldo E. Martin, *No Coward Soldiers: Black Cultural Politics in Postwar America* (Cambridge, MA: Harvard University Press, 2005), 1–10.

53. On shifting attitudes on gender roles and the women's movement, see Susan Welch, "Support Among Women for the Issues of the Women's Movement," *The Sociological Quarterly* 16 (Spring 1975): 216–227; Karen Oppenheim Mason, John L. Czaja, and Sara Arber, "Change in U.S. Women's Sex Role Attitudes, 1964 to 1974," *American Sociological Review* 41 (1976): 573–596. On legal reforms sought by feminists in the period, see Estelle B. Freedman, *No Turning Back: The History of Feminism and the Future of Women* (New York: Ballantine, 2002), 215–223; Sara M. Evans, *Tidal Wave: How Women Changed America at Century's End* (New York: Simon and Schuster, 2003), 107–122; Susan M. Hartmann, *The Other Feminists: Activists in the Liberal Establishment* (New Haven, CT: Yale University Press, 1998); Serena Mayeri, *Reasoning from Race: Feminism, Law, and the Civil Rights Revolution* (Cambridge, MA: Harvard University Press, 2011).

54. On Reagan's commitment to shrinking government, see Bernard Weinraub, "Democrats Say Reagan Program Would Hit Pensions of 1.2

Million," *New York Times*, June 25, 1981, B14; "The Truly Needy," *New York Times*, February 20, 1981, A26. For an example of Democrats' use of small-government language in the period, see Joyce Purnick, "Moynihan Hails a Carter Pledge on Welfare Cost," *New York Times*, October 22, 1980, B1. On stagflation and Reagan's explanation of it, see Chris J. Dolan, John Frendreis, and Raymond Tatalovich, *The Presidency and Economic Policy* (Lanham, MD: Rowman and Littlefield, 2008), 183. Chapter 4 discusses the popularization of neoliberalism and its impact on abortion politics. On perceptions of the economy under Carter, see W. Carl Biven, *Jimmy Carter's Economy: Policy in an Age of Limits* (Chapel Hill: University of North Carolina Press, 2002), 191–197; Kathleen Hall Jamieson, *Packaging the Presidency: A History and Criticism of Presidential Campaign Advertising*, 2nd ed. (New York: Oxford University Press, 1996), 366–369, 424–426.

55. See Mayeri, *Reasoning from Race*, 34, 36, 191–198, 217, 213, 226; Serena Mayeri, "A New E.R.A. or a New Era? Amendment Advocacy and the Reconstitution of Feminism," *University of Pennsylvania Law Review* 103 (2009): 1233, 1243–1244; Reva B. Siegel, "Sex Equality Arguments for Reproductive Rights: Their Critical Basis and Evolving Constitutional Protection," *Emory Law Journal* 56 (2007): 828–829.

56. Luker, *Abortion*, 145.

57. Ibid., 214.

58. Ginsburg, *Contested Lives*, 15.

59. Ibid., 43, 220.

60. Staggenborg, *The Pro-Choice Movement*, 66; see also Carol J. C. Maxwell, *Pro-Life Activists in America: Meaning, Motivation, and Direct Action* (New York: Oxford University Press, 2002), 37.

61. Ziad W. Munson, *The Making of Pro-Life Activists: How Social Movement Mobilization Works* (Chicago: University of Chicago Press, 2008), 84.

62. Ibid., 85.

63. *Planned Parenthood of Southeastern Pennsylvania v. Casey*, 505 U.S. 833, 997, 1001 (1992) (plurality decision) (Scalia, J., dissenting).

64. Ruth Bader Ginsburg, "Some Thoughts on Autonomy and Equality in Relation to *Roe v. Wade*," *North Carolina Law Review* 63 (1985): 384; see also Ruth Bader Ginsburg, "Speaking in a Judicial Voice," *New York University Law Review* 67 (1992): 1199–1200.

65. Jonathon Bullington, "Ginsburg: *Roe v. Wade* Not Ideal," *Chicago Tribune*, May 12, 2013, 6.

66. Cass R. Sunstein, *One Case at a Time: Judicial Minimalism on the Supreme Court*, 2nd ed. (Cambridge, MA: Harvard University Press, 2001), 37, 114.

67. Ibid., 114; see also Cass R. Sunstein, "Civil Rights Legislation in the 1990s: Three Civil Rights Fallacies," *California Law Review* 79 (1991): 766–767;

Cass R. Sunstein, "If People Would Be Outraged by Their Rulings, Should Judges Care?" *Stanford Law Review* 60 (2007): 183.

68. William N. Eskridge Jr. and John A. Ferejohn, *A Republic of Statutes: The New American Constitution* (New Haven, CT: Yale University Press, 2010), 378; see also William N. Eskridge Jr., "Channeling: Identity-Based Social Movements and Public Law," *University of Pennsylvania Law Review* 150 (2001): 455; William N. Eskridge Jr., "Pluralism and Distrust: How Courts Can Support Democracy by Lowering the Stakes of Politics," *Yale Law Journal* 114 (2005): 1312.

69. Richard A. Posner, *Law, Pragmatism, and Democracy* (Cambridge, MA: Harvard University Press, 2003), 46; see also Richard A. Posner, *Overcoming Law* (Cambridge, MA: Harvard University Press, 1995), 4–13, 29–33; Richard A. Posner, *The Problematics of Moral and Legal Theory* (Cambridge, MA: Harvard University Press, 1999), 240–243, 261–265.

70. Posner, *The Problematics of Moral and Legal Theory*, 254.

71. Posner, *Law, Pragmatism, and Democracy*, 125.

72. See Robert Post & Reva B. Siegel, "*Roe* Rage: Democratic Constitutionalism and Backlash," *Harvard Civil Rights-Civil Liberties Law Review* 42 (2007): 374–433.

73. See Jeffrey Rosen, *The Most Democratic Branch: How the Courts Serve America* (New York: Oxford University Press, 2006), 91–102. For more on Rosen's view, see Jeffrey Rosen, "The Supreme Court: Judicial Temperament and the Democratic Ideal," *Washburn Law Journal* 47 (2007): 8. For Rosenberg's view, see Gerald N. Rosenberg, *The Hollow Hope: Can Courts Bring about Social Change?* 2nd ed. (Chicago: University of Chicago Press, 2008), 173–178, 199; Gerald N. Rosenberg, "Courting Disaster: Looking for Change in All the Wrong Places," *Drake Law Review* 54 (2006): 810–812; Gerald N. Rosenberg, "The Implementation of Constitutional Rights: Insights from Law and Economics," *University of Chicago Law Review* (1997): 1218–1223. For more on Klarman's view, see Michael J. Klarman, *From Jim Crow to Civil Rights: The Supreme Court and the Struggle for Racial Equality* (New York: Oxford University Press, 2004), 465; Michael J. Klarman, *From the Closet to the Altar: Courts, Backlash, and the Struggle for Same-Sex Marriage* (New York: Oxford University Press, 2013), x.

74. Klarman, *From Jim Crow to Civil Rights*, 465.

75. Rosenberg, *The Hollow Hope*, 423; see also Staggenborg, *The Pro-Choice Movement*, 66; Balkin, "*Roe v. Wade*," 12.

76. Leigh Ann Wheeler, *How Sex Became a Civil Liberty* (New York: Oxford University Press, 2013), lx.

77. Critchlow, *Intended Consequences*, 7.

78. Dubow, *Ourselves Unborn*, 64; see also Williams, *God's Own Party*, 117; Paul Boyer, "The Evangelical Resurgence in 1970s American Protestantism," in *Rightward Bound: Making America Conservative in the 1970s*,

eds. Bruce J. Shulman and Julian E. Zelizer (Cambridge, MA: Harvard University Press, 2008), 36–37.

79. See Nelson, *Women of Color*, 7. For a sample of the legal scholarship, see Robin West, "From Choice to Reproductive Justice: De-Constitutionalizing Abortion Rights," *Yale Law Journal* 118 (2009): 1411; Joan Williams, "Gender Wars: Selfless Women in the Republic of Choice," *New York University Law Review* 66 (1991): 1561; Catharine MacKinnon, "Reflections on Sex Equality under Law," *Yale Law Journal* 100 (1991): 1281, 1318.

Chapter 1. Judicial Activism and the Pro-Life Movement

1. Pat Goltz, interview with Mary Ziegler, March 15, 2011; Kenneth Vanderhoef, interview with Mary Ziegler, August 7, 2011; Juan Ryan, interview with Mary Ziegler, August 6, 2011. A number of sociological studies address the motives and identities of pro-life activists, and some historians have discussed the movement's evolution. See Andrew H. Merton, *Enemies of Choice: The Right to Life Movement and Its Threat to Abortion* (Boston: Beacon Press, 1981); Connie Paige, *The Right to Lifers: Who They Are, How They Operate, Where They Get Their Money* (New York: Summit, 1983); Keith Cassidy, "The Right to Life Movement: Sources, Development, and Strategies," in *The Politics of Abortion and Birth Control in Historical Perspective*, ed. Donald T. Critchlow (University Park: Penn State Press, 1996), 128–151; Dallas A. Blanchard, *The Anti-Abortion Movement and The Rise of the Religious Right: From Polite to Fiery Protest* (New York: Twayne Publishers, 1994); Marian Faux, *Crusaders: Voices from the Abortion Front* (New York: Birch Lane Press, 1990); Kerry N. Jacoby, *Souls, Bodies, Spirits: The Drive to Abolish Abortion Since 1973* (Westport, CT: Praeger, 1998); James Risen and Judy L. Thomas, *Wrath of Angels: The American Abortion War* (New York: Basic Books, 1998); Ziad W. Munson, *The Making of Pro-Life Activists: How Social Movement Mobilization Works* (Chicago: University of Chicago Press, 2008); Cynthia Gorney, *Articles of Faith: A Frontline History of the Abortion Wars* (New York: Simon and Schuster, 2000).

For more on the reaction of abortion opponents to *Roe*, see Faye D. Ginsburg, *Contested Lives: The Abortion Debate in an American Community* (Berkeley: University of California Press, 1998), 72–73; Elizabeth Mensch and Alan Freeman, *The Politics of Virtue: Is Abortion Debatable?* 2nd ed. (Durham, NC: Duke University Press, 1995), 107–109; Kristin Luker, *Abortion and the Politics of Motherhood* (Berkeley: University of California Press, 1984), 137. Interestingly, a number of antiabortion activists remember being relatively unsurprised by the outcome of *Roe*. Randy Engel, interview with Mary Ziegler, February 5, 2010; Ryan, Interview;

Charles Rice, interview with Mary Ziegler, August 11, 2011; John Gorby, interview with Mary Ziegler, August 22, 2011.

2. For Willke's personal story: Dr. John Willke, interview with Mary Ziegler, December 19, 2010. For more on Willke: Deal Wyatt Hudson, *Onward, Christian Soldiers: The Growing Political Power of Catholics and Evangelicals in the United States* (New York: Simon and Schuster, 2008), 138–140; Linda Greenhouse and Reva B. Siegel, eds., Roe v. Wade: *Voices That Shaped the Abortion Debate Before the Supreme Court's Ruling*, 2nd ed. (New Haven, CT: Yale Law Library, 2012), 99–100; Carol A. Stabile, "The Traffic in Fetuses," in *Fetal Subjects, Feminist Positions*, eds. Lynn Marie Morgan and Meredith W. Michaels (Philadelphia: University of Pennsylvania Press, 1999), 145.

3. Steven Smith, "The Pursuit of Pragmatism," *Yale Law Journal* 100 (1990): 447.

4. For further discussion of this view: Cass R. Sunstein, *One Case at a Time: Judicial Minimalism on the Supreme Court*, 2nd ed. (Cambridge, MA: Harvard University Press, 2001), 37, 114; William N. Eskridge Jr. and John A. Ferejohn, *A Republic of Statutes: The New American Constitution* (New Haven, CT: Yale University Press, 2010), 242; Richard A. Posner, *Law, Pragmatism, and Democracy* (Cambridge, MA: Harvard University Press, 2003), 80, 82–85,126, 270. For arguments of this kind outside the legal academy, see Thomas M. Keck, "The Neoconservative Assault on the Courts: How Worried Should We Be?" in *Confronting the New Conservatism: The Rise of the Right in America*, ed. Michael J. Thompson (New York: New York University Press, 2007), 165 ("Since *Roe v. Wade* [1973], the primary conservative position on abortion rights has been that the courts should defer to state and federal legislative institutions"); Nancy MacLean, "Guardians of Privilege," in *Debating the Conservative Movement: 1945 to Present*, eds. Donald T. Critchlow and Nancy MacLean (Lanham, MD: Rowman and Littlefield, 2009), 156 (arguing that *Roe* upset many religious conservatives because it "seemed to give the imprimatur of federal authority to a practice they saw as sinful"); Paul Boyer, "The Evangelical Resurgence in 1970s American Protestantism," in *Rightward Bound: Making America Conservative in the 1970s*, eds. Bruce J. Shulman and Julian E. Zelizer (Cambridge, MA: Harvard University Press, 2008), 36–37.

5. For a sample of the relatively rare arguments against judicial activism offered by pro-lifers in the mid-1970s, see Celebrate Life Committee and Women for the Unborn, Booklet (November 1973), 33–36, ACCL, Box 4, Folder on Miscellaneous Reference Materials; National Right to Life Committee Legal Advisory Board, "Analysis of Decisions" (January 27, 1973), ACCL, Box 4, 1973 NRLC Board and Executive Committee Folder 6. The definition of judicial activism is famously hard to pin down. As Kermit Roosevelt writes, "we each have our own definition of judicial activism." Kermit Roosevelt, *The Myth of Judicial Activism: Making Sense of*

Supreme Court Decisions (New Haven, CT: Yale University Press, 2006), 2 (internal citation and quotation omitted).

6. Charles Rice, "Memorandum to the National Right to Life Committee" (July 28, 1975), CRP. On early state organizations, see Donald T. Critchlow, *Intended Consequences: Birth Control, Abortion, and the Federal Government in Modern America* (New York: Oxford University Press, 1999), 137; Cassidy, "The Right to Life Movement," 139–141; Munson, *The Making of Pro-Life Activists*, 82–86. For personal recollections of the early years of these organizations: Pam Manning, interview with Mary Ziegler, August 19, 2011; Jan Boyle, interview with Mary Ziegler, August 18, 2011; Mary Ann Kuharski, interview with Mary Ziegler, February 5, 2011; Elenor Schoen, e-mail interview with Mary Ziegler, September 10, 2011; Honor Leitzen, e-mail interview with Mary Ziegler, August 25, 2011; Suzanne Harmon, interview with Mary Ziegler, September 5, 2011; Jane Gilroy, interview with Mary Ziegler, August 22, 2011; Margie Montgomery, interview with Mary Ziegler, August 11, 2011; Sandra Faucher, interview with Mary Ziegler, February 4, 2012; Philip Moran, interview with Mary Ziegler, February 1, 2012; Mary Beliveau, interview with Mary Ziegler, February 7, 2012; Willke, interview. For more on those who shared Rice's perspective in the period, see Charles Rice, *The Vanishing Right to Live: An Appeal for a Renewed Reverence for Life* (New York: Doubleday, 1969), 120–130; Rice, "Memorandum to the National Right to Life Committee"; Society for a Christian Commonwealth, "The Movement to Make America Christian" (1970–1971), WC, Society for a Christian Commonwealth Folder. For the personal stories of activists holding these views: Rice, interview; Moran, interview; Engel, interview; Judie Brown, interview with Mary Ziegler, August 9, 2011; Dr. Eugene Diamond, interview with Mary Ziegler, February 6, 2011; Joseph Scheidler, interview with Mary Ziegler, August 20, 2011.

7. Chapter 2 discusses the influence and emergence of these pragmatists. For further discussion of the ideological diversity of the movement, see Cassidy, "The Right to Life Movement," 138; Munson, *The Making of Pro-Life Activists*, 192. For more on those favoring a broader social safety net or other goals associated with the political left, see William Hunt and Joseph Lampe, "Strategy Considerations for ACCL Involvement in Abortion and Related Issues" (n.d., ca. 1977), ACCL, Box 17, 1977 Strategy File; George Huntston Williams, "The Sacred Condominium," in *The Morality of Abortion*, ed. John T. Noonan (Cambridge, MA: Harvard University Press, 1970), 171; David Louisell and John T. Noonan, "Constitutional Balance," in *The Morality of Abortion*, ed. John T. Noonan (Cambridge, MA: Harvard University Press, 1970), 220, 230–236; "The New Abortion Debate: Decision on Medicaid Funding," *Commonweal*, July 22, 1977, 451–452; American Citizens Concerned for Life, "Philosophy and Objectives" (n.d., ca. 1978), ACCL, Box 18, ACCL Philosophy and Objectives Folder; Mary Meehan, "Abortion and 'The Consistency Thing,'" *Human*

Life Review 7 (1981): 60–68; Feminists for Life, "Feminists for Life State-ment on the Occasion of the Fifth Anniversary of the Supreme Court Deci-sion on Abortion" (January 22, 1978), LEP, Box 1, Folder 1. For the recol-lections of activists who identified in the period with the Democratic Party or the political left: Joseph Lampe, interview with Mary Ziegler, February 9, 2011; Kuharski, interview; Faucher, interview; Goltz, interview; Mary Meehan, interview with Mary Ziegler, March 20, 2012; Juli Loesch Wiley, e-mail interview with Mary Ziegler, April 1, 2012; Thea Rossi Barron, interview with Mary Ziegler, April 23, 2012; Warren Schaller, interview with Mary Ziegler, February 11, 2011.

8. On criticism of the Court's sex-discrimination jurisprudence, see Ser-ena Mayeri, *Reasoning from Race: Feminism, Law, and the Civil Rights Revolution* (Cambridge, MA: Harvard University Press, 2011), 75–80. For discussion of scholarly criticism of *Griswold*, see David J. Garrow, *Liberty and Sexuality: The Right of Privacy and the Making of* Roe v. Wade (Berkeley: University of California Press, 1998), 263–268. For the decisions in *Griswold*, *Reed*, and *Frontiero*, see *Griswold v. Connecticut*, 381 U.S. 479 (1965); *Reed v. Reed*, 404 U.S. 71 (1971); *Frontiero v. Rich-ardson*, 411 U.S. 677 (1973) (plurality decision). On the history of pro-tests against school prayer, see Daniel K. Williams, *God's Own Party: The Making of the Christian Right*, 2nd ed. (New York: Oxford University Press, 2012), 62–67; Barry Friedman, *The Will of the People: How Public Opinion Has Influenced the Supreme Court and Shaped the Meaning of the Constitution* (New York: Farrar, Straus, and Giroux, 2009), 261–267. On protests against busing, see Ronald P. Formisano, *Boston against Bus-ing: Race, Class, and Ethnicity in the 1960s and 1970s*, 2nd ed. (Chapel Hill: University of North Carolina Press, 2012); Jonathan Rieder, *Canar-sie: The Jews and Italians of Brooklyn against Liberalism* (Cambridge, MA: Harvard University Press, 1985), 2–3, 207–232.

9. For pro-life accounts of the role the courts should play in recognizing a right to life, see Patrick Conley and Robert J. McKenna, "The Supreme Court on Abortion—A Dissenting Opinion," *Catholic Lawyer* 19 (1973): 25–27; Robert M. Destro, "Abortion and the Constitution: The Need for a Life-Protective Amendment," *California Law Review* 63 (1975): 1327; Joseph P. Witherspoon, "The New Pro-Life Legislation: Patterns and Rec-ommendations," *St. Mary's Law Journal* 7 (1976): 640–641.

10. For examples of arguments of this kind made in the 1970s, see Nation-al Right to Life Committee, Resolution on Human Life Constitutional Amendment (June, 30 1973), ACCL, Box 4, 1973 National Right to Life Convention Folder; "News from Senator Mark Hatfield" (June 9, 1973), 5–8, ACCL, Box 4, 1973 National Right to Life Convention Folder; The National Right to Life Committee, "Give the Unborn Their First Civil Right: Life" (1975), ACCL, Box 10, 1975 NRLC Folder 2; "A Further Statement from the March to Life" (January 22, 1976), ACCL, Box 10, 1976 NRLC Folder 1 ("[D]isparagement of the value and dignity of a

human being is destructive evil to our society, which by our Declaration of Independence embraces certain inalienable rights for all people"); Robert M. Byrn, "An American Tragedy: The Supreme Court on Abortion," *Fordham Law Review* 41 (1973): 848–849 (locating a fundamental right to live in the Fourteenth Amendment and the Declaration of Independence); Hunt and Lampe, "Strategy Considerations," 1.

11. Brief of Amicus Curiae for the United States Catholic Conference, 16–17, *Planned Parenthood of Central Missouri v. Danforth*, 428 U.S. 52 (1976) (Nos. 74–1151, 74–1419).

12. Chapter 2 will discuss the evolution and reception of incrementalism in the late 1970s and early 1980s. I follow antiabortion activists in their use of the term incrementalism and do not adopt the definitions advanced by sociologists. For an overview of the latter category of definitions, see Scott H. Ainsworth and Thad A. Hall, *Abortion Politics in Congress: Strategic Incrementalism and Policy Change* (New York: Cambridge University Press, 2011), 24–36.

13. On Reagan's use of arguments against judicial activism on the campaign trail and in office, see Stuart Taylor Jr., "Politics of the Bench: Carter and Reagan Seek Gains from Prospective Judiciary Appointments," *New York Times*, October 28, 1980, A27; Fred Barbash and Mary Thompson, "Smith Outlines Strategy to Curb Court Activism," *Washington Post*, November 30, 1981, A1; Michael Uhlmann to Edwin Meese, Memorandum (July 6, 1981), EMP, OA 2408, Folder on Appointments—Supreme Court—O'Connor.

14. On strategies to increase the movement's influence on the nomination process, see Joseph M. Scheidler, "Editorial," *Illinois Right to Life Committee Newsletter*, November/December 1977, 2, PLN, Carton 1, Illinois Right to Life Committee Newsletter Folder; Ellen McCormack, "Can Right to Life Do Anything about the Power of the Courts?" *The Ellen McCormack Report*, January 1978, 1, 6, WC, Ellen McCormack Report Folder; "Federal Judgeships Denied to Pro-Lifers, Says Horan," *National Right to Life News*, February 1979, 17, JRS, 1979 National Right to Life News Box. On the perceived benefits of arguments for states' rights or against judicial activism, see "Anti-Abortion Group Backs Hatch Proposal," *New York Times*, December 13, 1981, 39; Kenneth Briggs, "Bishops Debate Strategy on Abortion Battle," *New York Times*, November 17, 1981, A20.

15. On Weyrich's efforts to mobilize hostility to the judiciary, see Hudson, *Onward, Christian Soldiers*, 13–14, 70; David M. Ricci, *The Transformation of American Politics: The New Washington and The Rise of Think Tanks* (New Haven, CT: Yale University Press, 1993), 158.

16. On antiabortion professionals, see Luker, *Abortion*, 131–145. On the importance of relational ties in antiabortion recruitment, see Munson, *The Making of Pro-Life Activists*, 52. On Mecklenburg's mobilization: Dr. Fred E. Mecklenburg, "Minnesota Should Seek Sexual Responsibility, Not 'Easier' Abortion" (n.d., ca. 1972), ACCL, Box 20, ACCL Speakers

Folder; "Biographical Sketch: Dr. Frederick E. Mecklenburg, M.D." (n.d., ca. 1979), ACCL, Box 20, ACCL Speakers Folder. On Jefferson's mobilization: Anthony J. Lauinger, "Focus: Mildred F. Jefferson, M.D.," *National Right to Life News*, January 1977, 5, JRS, 1977 National Right to Life News Box; Dennis Hevesi, "Mildred Jefferson, 84, Anti-Abortion Activist, Is Dead," *New York Times*, October 18, 2010, accessed April 7, 2014, http://www.nytimes.com/2010/10/19/us/19jefferson.html?_r=0; "Mildred Jefferson, Anti-Abortion Activist, Dies at 84," *Los Angeles Times*, October 16, 2010, accessed April 7, 2014, http://latimesblogs.latimes.com/afterword/2010/10/mildred-jefferson-anti-abortion-activist-dies-at-84.html. For recollections of the Horans' mobilization: Gorby, interview; Patrick Trueman, interview with Mary Ziegler, September 13, 2011. For an example of antiabortion physicians' recollections of their reasons for joining the movement: Diamond, interview. For an example of the stories of mobilized law professors: Rice, interview.

17. On the professional identity of pro-life attorneys, see Ann Southworth, *Lawyers of the Right: Professionalizing the Conservative Coalition* (Chicago: University of Chicago Press, 2008), 5, 71, 84, 116. For the personal stories of pro-life attorneys: Vanderhoef, interview; Ryan, interview; Rice, interview; Gorby, interview; Trueman, interview.

18. For Engel's recollections: Engel, interview. For a sample of Engel's writings from the period, see Randy Engel, *A Pro-Life Report on Population Growth and the American Future*, 2nd ed. (Pittsburgh: Pennsylvanians for Human Life, 1972). On the influence of the Catholic Church in shaping early antiabortion organizations, see Munson, *The Making of Pro-Life Activists*, 82; Michael W. Cuneo, "Life Battles: The Rise of Catholic Militancy within the American Pro-Life Movement," in *Bearing Right: Conservative Catholics in America*, eds. Mary Jo Weaver and R. Scott Appleby (Bloomington: University of Indiana Press, 1995), 270–275; Critchlow, *Intended Consequences*, 137. On Vanderhoef's decision to become involved in the movement: Vanderhoef, interview.

19. Fred C. Shapiro, "Right to Life Has Message for New York State Legislators," *New York Times*, August 20, 1972, SM10. On Golden's influence and background, see Critchlow, 137; Eyal Press, *Absolute Convictions: My Father, a City, and the Conflict that Divided America* (New York: Henry Holt, 2007), 68; Gorney, *Articles of Faith*, 119.

20. On Mecklenburg, see Garrow, *Liberty and Sexuality*, 579; Critchlow, *Intended Consequences*, 138. On Minnesota Citizens Concerned for Life, see Cassidy, "The Right to Life Movement," 139, 157; Munson, *The Making of Pro-Life Activists*, 82–87.

21. Articles of Incorporation of Minnesota Citizens Concerned for Life, Inc., 302 (1968), NDR, Box 4, Folder 30.

22. Society for a Christian Commonwealth, "The Movement to Make America Christian." On the Human Life Center, see Critchlow, *Intended Consequences*, 137. On the SCC: see Carol Mason, *Killing for Life: The*

Apocalyptic Narrative of Pro-Life Politics (Ithaca, NY: Cornell University Press, 2002), 68, 140–141.

23. On the early days of the NRLC, see Risen and Thomas, *Wrath of Angels*, 19–39; Cassidy, "The Right to Life Movement," 140–141; Cuneo, "Life Battles," 273–274. For a sample of the NRLC's activities in the period, see National Meeting: Right to Life Movement Agenda (July 31–August 3, 1970), ACCL, Box 4, 1970 National Right to Life Folder; National Right to Life Committee Board of Directors Meeting Minutes (December 9, 1972), 3, ACCL, Box 4, 1970 National Right to Life Folder.

24. Americans United for Life, Fundraising Letter (September 20, 1972), 2, AUL, Executive File Box, Folder 91. For further examples of the AUL's activities in the period, see Fundraising Letter (April 17, 1974), AUL, Executive File Box, Folder 91; Fundraising Letter (September 1, 1972), AUL, Executive File Box, Folder 91; Dr. Joseph Stanton to AUL Officers et al. (December 14, 1972), GHW, Box 4, Folder 4. The AUL also helped to produce an influential book on abortion. See Dennis Horan and Thomas Hilgers, eds., *Abortion and Social Justice* (New York: Sheed and Ward, 1972).

25. As Chapter 2 studies at length, pragmatists holding such views came to exercise greater influence over the mainstream movement in the late 1970s and early 1980s.

26. Rice, *The Vanishing Right*, 125; see also Charles Rice, "The Population Commission Report: New Mandate for the Pro-Life Movement," *Triumph*, May 1972, 11–15.

27. Rice, *The Vanishing Right*, 125.

28. On Rhys Williams, see F. Forrester Church and Timothy George, eds., *Continuity and Discontinuity in Church History: Essays Presented to George Huntston Williams* (Leiden, Netherlands: E. J. Brill, 1979), 9. For George Huntston Williams' critique of McCarthyism, see George Huntston Williams, *The Reluctance to Inform* (Princeton: Theology Today, 1957).

29. See Williams, *The Sacred Condominium*, 171. For an example of Williams' earlier antiabortion writings, see George Huntston Williams, "Religious Residues and Presuppositions in the Abortion Debate," *Theological Studies* 30 (1970): xxiv.

30. See John Archibald to George Huntston Williams (February 4, 1972), CRP; Julie Grimstad, "'Profound Obligation, Highest Privilege': Dr. Joseph R. Stanton and the Prolife Movement" (unpublished manuscript, February 20, 1991), 131–138, CRP; Letter from Charles E. Rice, Professor of Law, Notre Dame Law School, to George Huntston Williams, Professor, Harvard Divinity School (February 10, 1972), CRP.

31. See Americans United for Life, Meeting Minutes (March 10–11, 1972), 4, 6–7, AUL, Executive File Box, Folder 91.

32. Ibid., 4.

33. Ibid., 6.

34. Charles Rice to L. Brent Bozell (March 15, 1972), CRP.

35. On Byrn's background, see "'Friend of Fetus' Battling New York's Abortion Law," *Eugene Register-Guard*, December 21, 1971, 3C. For discussion of the "contraceptive mentality" thesis adopted by some pro-life opponents of contraception, see Mason, *Killing for Life*, 142, 226; Michael W. Cuneo, *The Smoke of Satan: Conservative and Traditionalist Dissent in Contemporary American Catholicism* (New York: Oxford University Press, 1999), 61–69; Cuneo, "Life Battles," 278–279. For discussion of the abortifacient argument, see Cuneo, "Life Battles," 279. On the lawsuit and Byrn's background: see Robert Tomasson, "A Lawyer Challenges the Abortion Law," *New York Times*, December 4, 1971, 29; "Order Is Sought in Abortion Suit: Judge Is Asked to Put Curb on Practice During Trial," *New York Times*, December 10, 1971, 32; Judy Klemesrud, "He's the Legal Guardian for the Fetuses About to Be Aborted," *New York Times*, December 17, 1972, 48.

36. Minnesota Citizens Concerned for Life, "A Sample Presentation on Abortion," (n. d., ca. 1970), NDR, Box 8, Folder 13.

37. For example, Jane Gilroy, a member of the New York pro-life organization Women for the Unborn, recalls that her organization allowed its members to hold a variety of views on artificial contraception. Although Gilroy and leading members opposed artificial birth control, avoiding any official position on the issue allowed Women for the Unborn to attract a broader membership and to focus on abortion itself. For Gilroy's account of Women for the Unborn and of her involvement in Ellen McCormack's presidential campaign, see Jane Gilroy, *A Shared Vision: The 1976 Ellen McCormack Presidential Campaign* (Parker, CO: Outskirts Press, 2010). For personal recollections of other activists in organizations that avoided the issue of birth control: Pam Manning, interview; Geline Williams, interview with Mary Ziegler, February 8, 2012; Beliveau, interview.

38. Montgomery, interview.

39. See Bill of Rights Committee Hearing, Minnesota State Legislature, June 21, 1972, 3 (Statement of Darla St. Martin). Mecklenburg served as an ad hoc chairperson of Women for Universal Human Rights, urging members of the Minnesota Women's Political Caucus to focus on initiatives to help unwed mothers. See Resolution Prepared and Distributed by Women for Universal Human Rights (n.d., ca. 1971), NDR, Box 8, Folder 16. Chapter 6 offers more on the organizations promoting this view.

40. See Americans United for Life, "Statement of Purpose" (n.d., ca. 1973), AUL, Executive File Box, Folder 91; Pennsylvanians for Life, National Right to Life Committee Statement of Purpose (n.d., ca. 1972), ACCL, Box 4, 1973 National Right to Life Convention Folder.

41. See Brief as Amicus Curiae for Americans United for Life, 8–10, *Roe v. Wade*, 410 U.S. 113 (1973) (Nos. 70–18, 70–40). For related arguments made before 1973, see Martin McKernan, NRLC Legal Counsel, "Legal Report: Court Cases" (July 1970), 3–4, ACCL, Box 4, 1970 National Right to Life Meeting Folder; Robert M. Byrn, "The Abortion Question:

A Nonsectarian Perspective," *Catholic Lawyer* 11 (1965): 317, 322; David W. Louisell, "Abortion, The Practice of Medicine and the Due Process of Law," *UCLA Law Review* 16 (1968–1969): 234, 235–244; A. James Quinn and James A. Griffin, "The Rights of the Unborn," *Jurist* 31 (1971): 578–580.

42. Robert M. Byrn, "Abortion on Demand: Whose Morality?" *Notre Dame Lawyer* 46 (1970): 19.

43. See, e.g., Brief as Amici Curiae for Certain Physicians, Professors, and Fellows of the American College of Obstetrics et al., 61–62, *Roe v. Wade*, 410 U.S. 113 (1973) (Nos. 70–18, 70–40); Brief as Amicus Curiae for Robert Sassone, 6, *Roe v. Wade*, 410 U.S. 113 (1973) (Nos. 70–18, 70–40); McKernan, "Legal Report," 4 ("That most fundamental of rights—not to be deprived of this right to life without Due Process of Law—cannot be ignored"). For a recollection of pre-*Roe* support for a fetal life amendment, see *Congressional Record—Senate: Proceedings and Debates of the 107th Congress 2nd Session*, vol. 144, pt. 1 (1998), 11264 (Statement of Senator John Ashcroft).

44. Conley and McKenna, "The Supreme Court on Abortion," 25 (internal quotations omitted); see also Destro, "Abortion and the Constitution," 1327; Witherspoon, "The New Pro-Life Legislation," 644, 649, 670.

45. See Luker, *Abortion*, 137. On the Ad Hoc Committee in Defense of Life, see Ad Hoc Committee in Defense of Life, Fundraising Letter (October 21, 1982), WC, Ad Hoc Committee in Defense of Life Folder (narrating the founding of the organization); J. Brooks Flippen, *Jimmy Carter, the Politics of Family, and the Rise of the Religious Right* (Athens: University of Georgia Press, 2011), 199. On the CUL, see Cuneo, *Smoke of Satan*, 64. For a sample of the CUL's materials, see "Mother Theresa Blesses CUL Supporters," *Catholics United for Life Newsletter*, October 1981, WC, Catholics United for Life Folder.

46. See Munson, *The Making of Pro-Life Activists*, 83–94. For Neary's story: Denise Neary, interview with Mary Ziegler, February 18, 2012. On Biviano's story: Garnett Biviano, interview with Mary Ziegler, February 23, 2012. For further recollections of movement homemakers: Pam Manning, interview; Gilroy, interview; Engel, interview.

47. Brief as Amicus Curiae for Eugene Diamond and Americans United for Life, 17–18, 35–43. For related arguments, see Byrn, "An American Tragedy," 848–849; The National Right to Life Committee, "Give the Unborn Their First Civil Right: Life," 1; "A Further Statement from the March to Life," 1. For more on natural law theory, see Robert P. George, *In Defense of Natural Law* (New York: Oxford University Press, 2001); Robert P. George, "Natural Law and Human Nature," in *Natural Law Theory: Contemporary Essays*, ed. Robert P. George (New York: Oxford University Press, 1992). The theories endorsed by abortion opponents immediately after *Roe* bear some resemblance to what Ken Kersch and others have called declarationism—a belief that the Constitution should be

interpreted and understood in light of the principles set forth at the start of the Declaration of Independence. See Ken Kersch, "Beyond Originalism: Conservative Declarationism and Constitutional Redemption," *Maryland Law Review* 71 (2011): 229–282.

48. Brief as Amicus Curiae for the United States Catholic Conference, 16–17.

49. Testimony before the House Subcommittee on Civil and Constitutional Rights of the House Judiciary Committee, 94th Congress, 2nd Session (1976), 26 (Statement of Professor Joseph Witherspoon). For Destro's argument, see Destro, "Abortion and the Constitution," 1327.

50. See NRLC Ad Hoc Strategy Meeting Minutes (February 11, 1973), ACCL, Box 4, 1973 National Right to Life Committee Folder 1.

51. Ibid., 5, 7.

52. Celebrate Life Committee and Women for the Unborn, Booklet, 33.

53. National Right to Life Committee Resolution #4 (July 10, 1973), ACCL, Box 4, 1973 NRLC Folder 3.

54. National Committee for a Human Life Amendment, "Human Life Amendment: Major Texts, 1973–2003," 1–2, accessed February 14, 2014, http://www.nchla.org/datasource/idocuments/HLAmajortexts.pdf. For analysis of the Hogan Amendment, see Harriet F. Pilpel, "The Fetus as Person: Possible Legal Consequences of the Hogan-Helms Amendment," *Family Planning Perspectives* 6 (1974): 6–7; James Bopp Jr., *Restoring the Right to Life: The Human Life Amendment* (Provo, UT: Brigham Young University Press, 1984), 44.

55. Proposed Constitutional Amendments on Abortion, Part 1: Testimony before the House Judiciary Subcommittee on Civil and Constitutional Rights, 94th Congress, 2nd Session (1976), 366–367 (Statement of Representative G. William Whitehurst). Whitehurst first introduced his amendment in 1974. See Malcolm Potts, Peter Diggory, and John Peel, *Abortion* (Cambridge, UK: Cambridge University Press, 1977), 367.

56. Abortion Part 1: Testimony on S. 119 and S. 130 before the Subcommittee on Constitutional Amendments of the Senate Judiciary Committee, 93rd Congress, 2nd Session (1974), 354 (Statement of Paul Ramsey). For a sample of Ramsey's pre-*Roe* writings on abortion, see Paul Ramsey, "Abortion: A Theologian's View," *Journal of Operating Nurses* (November 1970): 55–62; Paul Ramsey, "Feticide/Infanticide upon Request," *Religion in Life* 9 (Fall 1970): 170–186; Paul Ramsey, "Reference Points in Deciding About Abortion," in *The Morality of Abortion*, ed. John T. Noonan (Cambridge, MA: Harvard University Press, 1970), 40–100.

57. Proposed Constitutional Amendments on Abortion, Part 1: Testimony before the House Judiciary Subcommittee on Civil and Constitutional Rights, 94th Congress, 2nd Session (1976), 164–166 (Statement of David Louisell). For more on Louisell's background, see C. B. Mueller, "David Louisell: In Memoriam," *California Law Review* 66 (1978): 921–922.

58. On the priority put on a fetal-rights amendment: see Cassidy, "The Right to Life Movement," 146. For further discussion of the preference for a

personhood amendment, see Dennis J. Horan to NRLC Board of Directors et al. (January 19, 1974), 1–5 ACCL, Box 8, 1974 Board and Executive Committee Folder 3 (reporting that after consulting with seventeen attorneys and law professors, the NRLC Legal Advisory Committee drafted a model amendment recognizing the personhood of the fetus and forbidding the depriving the fetus of life without due process); Joseph Witherspoon to NRLC Executive Committee (August 14, 1973), ACCL, Box 4, 1973 NRLC Folder 4; Nellie Gray, Memorandum: A Mandatory Human Life Amendment, ACCL, Box 4, 1973 NRLC Folder 5; Resolution #4, 1. For activists' recollections about the preference for a personhood amendment: Engel, interview; Pam Manning, interview; Kuharski, interview; Schoen, e-mail interview; Leitzen, e-mail interview; Gilroy, interview; James Bopp Jr., interview with Mary Ziegler, February 22, 2012; Judie Brown, interview; Paul Brown, interview with Mary Ziegler, August 12, 2011; Scheidler, interview; Williams, interview; Faucher, interview. On Witherspoon's background, see "In Memoriam, Joseph Parker Witherspoon," accessed March 30, 2014, http://www.utexas.edu/faculty/council/1998–1999/memorials/Witherspoon/witherspoon.html. For a sample of Witherspoon's writings on abortion, see Joseph Witherspoon, "Representative Government, the Federal Judicial and Administrative Bureaucracy, and the Right to Life," *Texas Tech Law Review* 6 (1975): 363–384; Joseph Witherspoon, "Impact of the Abortion Decisions upon the Father's Role," *Jurist* 35 (1975): 41–47; Witherspoon, "The New Pro-Life Legislation," 637. On Horan's life: "Dennis M. Horan, 56, A Lawyer and Author," *New York Times*, May 3, 1988, accessed February 4, 2011, http://www.nytimes.com/1988/05/03/obituaries/dennis-m-horan-56-a-lawyer-and-author.html. Horan was also involved in several important post-*Roe* cases. See *Hodgson v. Anderson*, 378 F. Supp. 1008 (D. Minn., 1974); *Wynn v. Scott*, 449 F. Supp. 1302 (N.D. Ill. 1978). For individuals' recollections of Horan: Gorby, interview; Trueman, interview. For Vanderhoef's personal journey: Vanderhoef, interview. For others' recollections of his work: Schoen, e-mail interview; Leitzen, e-mail interview. On Nellie Gray, see Dave Jolivet, "At 84, Pro-Life Leader Nellie Gray Marches On," *Catholic News Service*, January 22, 2010, accessed April 8, 2014, http://www.americancatholic.org/news/report.aspx?id=2135; Denise Grady, "Nellie Gray, Abortion Foe and Leader of Annual March, Dies at 88," *New York Times*, August 15, 2012, accessed April 13, 2014, http://www.nytimes.com/2012/08/16/us/nellie-gray-anti-abortion-activist-dies-at-88.html?_r=0.

59. Abortion Part 4: Testimony on S. 119 and S. 130 before the Senate Judiciary Subcommittee on Constitutional Amendments, 94th Congress, 1st Session (1974), 107–108 (Statement of Professor Robert Byrn); Robert Byrn to Edward Golden, Re: Right to Life Amendment to the United States Constitution (February 16, 1973), 1–2, ACCL, Box 4, 1973 NRLC Folder 2. For a similar argument, see National Right to Life Committee, Press

Release (March 6, 1974), 1–9, ACCL, Box 8, 1974 Board and Executive Committee Folder 5.

60. Statement of Professor Robert Byrn, 107.

61. NRLC Memorandum "Progress" (September 21, 1973), ACCL, Box 6, 1973 Constitutional Amendment Folder.

62. Resolution #4, 1.

63. For discussion of Mecklenburg's role in the hiring of Schaller, see National Right to Life Committee Board of Directors Meeting Minutes (December 9, 1972), 2, ACCL, Box 4, 1972 NRLC Folder; Michael Taylor to the National Right to Life Committee Board of Directors (October 24, 1973), 1–3, ACCL, Box 5, 1973 NRLC Board and Executive Committee Folder 6.

64. On the conflict between the Mecklenburg and Golden factions, see Judith Fink to Edward Golden et al., "Re: Policy Statement of the NRLC Concerning 'Birth Control'" (May 15, 1973), ACCL, Box 4, 1973 NRLC Folder 3 (complaining about the organization's refusal to take a position on birth control); National Right to Life Committee Board of Directors Meeting Minutes (December 8, 1973), 1–8, ACCL, Box 5, 1973 NRLC Board and Executive Committee Folder 7 (discussing the replacement of Schaller and the organization's internal disagreements); William P. Maloney, "The Owl in the Saguaro: Report to Officers and Board of Directors of the Right to Life Committee of New Mexico" (January 23 1974), 1–4, ACCL, Box 8, 1974 NRLC Board and Executive Committee Folder 1 (same). For a sample of Schaller's comments to the press, see Clipping, "Former 'Pro-Abortion' Pastor New 'Right to Life' Executive," *St. Paul Pioneer Press*, August 1, 1973, ACCL, Box 4, 1973 Folder 5; Clipping, Clifford Simak, "Pro-Life Leader Fears Extension of Euthanasia," *Minneapolis Star Tribune*, August 3, 1973, ACCL, Box 4, 1973 NRLC Folder 5.

65. Warren Schaller to NRLC Board of Directors (February 25, 1974), ACCL, Box 8, 1974 NRLC Board and Executive Committee Folder 4.

66. Abortion Part 3: Testimony on S. 119 and S. 130 before the Senate Subcommittee on Constitutional Amendments of the Senate Judiciary Committee, 93rd Congress, 2nd Session (1974), 12 (Statement of Dr. Mildred Jefferson). For Holbrook and Bleich's testimony, see Abortion Part 1: Testimony on S. 119 and S. 130 before the Senate Subcommittee on Constitutional Amendments of the Senate Judiciary Committee, 93rd Congress, 2nd Session (1974), 287–288 (Statement of Rabbi David Bleich); ibid., 329–358 (Statement of Pastor Robert Holbrook).

67. Abortion Part 3: Testimony on S. 119 and S. 130 before the Senate Subcommittee on Constitutional Amendments of the Senate Judiciary Committee, 93rd Congress, 2nd Session (1974), 448–449 (Statement of Representative Lawrence Hogan).

68. Abortion Part 1: Testimony on S. 119 and S. 130 before the Senate Subcommittee on Constitutional Amendments of the Senate Judiciary Committee, 93rd Congress, 2nd Session (1974), 35 (Statement of Senator James Buckley). For an extensive story on Buckley's personality and politics, see

Richard Reeves, "Isn't It Time That We Had a Senator?" *New York Magazine*, February 25, 1974, 38.

69. Abortion Part 2: Testimony on S. 119 and S. 130 before the Senate Subcommittee on Constitutional Amendments of the Senate Judiciary Committee, 93rd Congress, 2nd Session (1974), 463 (Statement of Dr. William Colliton Jr.).

70. Ibid., 474–475 (Statement of Dr. William Godfrey); ibid., 487 (Statement of Dr. Thomas Hilgers).

71. See Constitutional Amendments on Abortion, Part II: Testimony before the House Subcommittee on Civil and Constitutional Rights of the House Judiciary Committee, 94th Congress, 2nd Session (1976), 408 (Statement of Dr. John and Barbara Willke); see also Statement of Dr. William Colliton Jr., 452; Statement of Representative Lawrence Hogan, 453. For the *Dred Scott* decision, see *Dred Scott v. Sandford*, 60 U.S. 393 (1857).

72. See Americans United for Life, "Statement of Purpose;" Christian Action Council, "Con-Con," *Action Line*, December 1978, 1, WC; Ad Hoc Committee in Defense of Life, Fundraising Letter (May 17, 1973), 1, WC, Ad Hoc Committee in Defense of Life Folder; "From the Office of Senator Mark O. Hatfield," 5; Resolution #4, 1; Hunt and Lampe, "Strategy Considerations," 1–7. For Cuneo's argument, see Cuneo, "Life Battles," 273–280.

73. See Ray White to Warren Schaller (June 2, 1974), ACCL, Box 8, 1974 NRLC Folder 4 (terminating Schaller's employment); Randy Engel to National Right to Life Committee Board of Directors et al. (March 30, 1974), ACCL, Box 8, 1974 NRLC Board and Executive Committee Folder 6 (complaining about the influence of the Mecklenburg faction on the NRLC). On Mecklenburg's falling out with the NRLC, see Marjory Mecklenburg to the NRLC Board of Directors, "Point of Personal Privilege" (October 8, 1974), ACCL, Box 8, 1974 NRLC Board and Executive Committee Folder 12.

74. On the early days of March for Life, see Nellie Gray to the National Right to Life Committee Board of Directors (December 8, 1973), ACCL, Box 4, 1973 NRLC Board and Executive Committee Folder 6; Nellie Gray to the National Right to Life Committee Board of Directors (February 10, 1974), ACCL, Box 8, 1974 NRLC Board and Executive Committee Folder 3.

75. On the alliance between Golden and Vanderhoef, see Kenneth Vanderhoef to NRLC Executive Committee (August 8, 1973), 1–2, ACCL, Box 4, 1973 NRLC Board and Executive Committee Folder 5 (Vanderhoef's taking Golden's side on the issue of Warren Schaller's leadership and salary); NRLC Executive Committee Meeting Minutes (January 17, 1974), 6–12, ACCL Box 8, 1974 NRLC Board and Executive Committee Folder 2 (detailing Vanderhoef's role in supporting Golden's leadership).

76. On Jefferson's life, see Hevesi, "Mildred Jefferson"; Lauinger, "Focus: Mildred F. Jefferson, M.D.," 5. For activists' recollections of Jefferson: Moran, interview; Judie Brown, interview; Barron, interview.

77. Jefferson gave a number of press interviews in the period. See Kathleen Hendrix, "Impassioned Argument for Right to Life," *Los Angeles Times*, September 26, 1975, F1; "A Fighter for Right to Life," *Ebony Magazine*, April 1978, 78–88; Judy Klemesrud, "Abortion in the Campaign: Methodist Surgeon Leading the Opposition," *New York Magazine*, March 1, 1976, 44.

78. See Robert Reinhold, "Boston v. The Doctors: Strange Case," *New York Times*, April 21, 1974, 223; see also Sara Dubow, *Ourselves Unborn: A History of the Fetus in Modern America* (New York: Oxford University Press, 2010), 90–101. For Edelin's recollections of the case, see also generally Kenneth Edelin, *Broken Justice: A True Story of Race, Sex, and Revenge in a Boston Courtroom* (Martha's Vineyard, MA: Pondview Press, 2007). For a sample of news coverage of the *Edelin* case, see Lawrence K. Altman, "Doctor Guilty of Death of Fetus in Abortion," *New York Times*, February 16, 1975, 1; Monroe Anderson, "Pro-Life Groups Here Laud Edelin Decision," *Chicago Tribune*, February 16, 1975, 3.

79. *Roe v. Wade*, 165.

80. See Frank Susman to Robert Sunnen (February 3, 1975), 1–4, ACLU, Series 4, Box 1355, *Edelin v. Massachusetts* File (reporting on the events unfolding in the *Edelin* trial). For a sample of the prosecutions of nonphysician abortion providers, see *Commonwealth v. Page*, 303 A.2d 215, 216–218 (Pa. 1973); *Wright v. State*, 351 So. 2d 708, 709–711 (Fla. 1977); *State v. Norflett*, 337 A.2d 609, 611–620 (N.J. 1975); *State v. Haren*, 307 A.2d 644, 646–647 (N.J. Super. 1973).

81. Affidavit of the Commonwealth Opposing the Defendant's Motion for a Dismissal of the Indictment (n.d., ca. 1974), 48–49, ACLU, Box 1355, *Edelin v. Massachusetts* File. On Jefferson's testimony at the *Edelin* trial, see Frank Susman to Robert Sunnen (February 3, 1975), 1–3.

82. See Anderson, "Pro-Life Groups," 3. On the controversy surrounding Edelin's conviction, see Altman, "Doctor Guilty in Death of a Fetus," 1; John Kifner, "Abortion Foe Cites Role," *New York Times*, February 17, 1975, 41. Ultimately, the Massachusetts Supreme Judicial Court reversed Edelin's conviction, holding that there was insufficient evidence to support a manslaughter conviction and that the trial court's instructions varied impermissibly from the charges in the indictment. *Com. v. Edelin*, 359 N.E.2d 4 (Mass. 1976).

83. Mary R. Hunt to NRLC Board Members Who Attended October Meeting (March 25, 1975), 1, ACCL, Box 10, 1975 NRLC Board and Executive Committee Folder 2.

84. For example, Dr. Mildred F. Jefferson, a key witness in the *Edelin* trial, denied that the NRLC wanted much to do with the prosecution of Dr. Edelin. See Dr. Mildred F. Jefferson, "Lifelines," *National Right To Life News*, February 1977, 11, JRS, 1977 National Right to Life News Box.

85. Gorby, interview. Chapter 2 further examines the litigation strategies developed by incrementalists.

86. *Lorillard Tobacco Co. v. Reilly*, 553 U.S. 535, 541 (2001).

87. For examples of these cases, see *Roe v. Norton*, 522 F.2d 928 (2d Cir. 1975) (holding that a funding ban was constitutional and did not conflict with federal Medicaid law); *Roe v. Ferguson*, 515 F.2d 279 (6th Cir. 1975) (upholding such a law against a supremacy-clause challenge); *Doe v. Beal*, 523 F.2d 611 (3d Cir. 1975) (en banc) (holding that Pennsylvania regulations were unconstitutional and conflicted with federal Medicaid law); *Doe v. Westby*, 402 F. Supp. 140 (D.S.D. 1975) (holding that a policy issued by State Social Services Department impermissibly conflicted with federal Medicaid law).

88. Roncallo's amendment failed in the House in 1974. See "House Rejects Plan to Prohibit Federal Funds in Abortion Work," *New York Times*, June 29, 1974, 24. The Bartlett Amendment failed in 1975. See Marjorie Hunter, "Senate Upholds U.S. Abortion Funds," *New York Times*, April 11, 1975, 28. For an example of Hyde's larger-than-life reputation, see Arthur Siddons, "'Evil' Hyde: Nice Enough to Be a Jekyll," *Chicago Tribune*, June 19, 1977, 16.

89. Henry Hyde, "The Heart of the Matter," *The Human Life Review* 3 (June 1977): 90–96.

90. *Congressional Record—House: Proceedings and Debates of the 95th Congress 1st Session*, vol. 123, pt. 16 (1977), 19698–19715 (Statement of Henry Hyde). For individuals' recollections of Hyde's emphasis on the constitutionality of his proposal: Gorby, interview; Bopp, interview; Trueman, interview.

91. Herbert Wechsler, "Toward Neutral Principles of Constitutional Law," *Harvard Law Review* 73 (1959): 19.

92. For discussion of massive resistance and attacks on judicial overreaching, see Michael J. Klarman, *From Jim Crow to Civil Rights: The Supreme Court and the Struggle for Racial Equality* (New York: Oxford University Press, 2004), 403–407; Reva B. Siegel, "'Equality Talk': Antisubordination and Anticlassification Values in Constitutional Struggles over *Brown*," *Harvard Law Review* 117 (2004): 1485–1501. For the Court's decision in *Brown*, see *Brown v. Board of Education*, 347 U.S. 483 (1954). For discussion of scholarly responses to Wechsler, see Siegel, "'Equality Talk,'" 1491–1497.

93. For the decision in *Engel*, see *Engel v. Vitale*, 370 U.S. 421 (1962). On protests against *Engel* and the school prayer decisions, see Friedman, *The Will of the People*, 261–267; Williams, *God's Own Party*, 62–67. On the movement to impeach Earl Warren, see Christine L. Compston, *Earl Warren: Justice for All* (New York: Oxford University Press, 2001), 130; G. Edward White, *Earl Warren: A Public Life* (New York: Oxford University Press, 1982), 247–248.

94. On the anti-busing movement, see generally Formisano, *Boston against Busing*; Rieder, *Canarsie*, 207–232. For Bork and Berger's criticisms of the Court's Fourteenth Amendment jurisprudence in the 1960s and 1970s, see

Robert Bork, "Neutral Principles and Some First Amendment Problems," *Indiana Law Journal* 47 (1971): 4–11; Raoul Berger, *Government by Judiciary: The Transformation of the Fourteenth Amendment* (Cambridge, MA: Harvard University Press, 1977), 7, 35. For a summary of scholarly criticisms of *Roe* in the 1970s, see Garrow, *Liberty and Sexuality*, 608–614. For Ely's argument, see John Hart Ely, "The Wages of Crying Wolf: A Comment on *Roe v. Wade*," *Yale Law Journal* 18 (1973): 920–949.

95. For internal discussion of the preference for the National Right to Life Amendment, see Ray White to NRLC Board of Directors and Others (June 30, 1975), ACCL, Box 10, 1975 NRLC Board of Directors Folder 4; Ray White to NRLC Board of Directors and Others (July 31, 1975), ACCL, Box 10, 1975 NRLC Board of Directors Folder 4; On efforts to introduce a human life amendment after 1975, see National Committee for a Human Life Amendment, 1–3.

96. Robert M. Byrn, "Which Way for Judicial Imperialism?" *The Human Life Review* 3 (Winter 1977): 20.

97. Dr. Joseph Stanton to George Huntston Williams (December 10, 1979), JRS, Dr. Joseph Stanton Papers. For Brown's article, see Harold O. J. Brown, "What Makes the Law the Law," *The Human Life Review* 5 (Winter 1979): 68–79.

98. For a summary of the fate of various fetal-life amendment proposals, see National Committee for a Human Life Amendment, 1–2.

99. On Meskill's nomination, see "Meskill Facing More Opposition," *New York Times*, September 15, 1974, 22. For further discussion of Meskill's views on abortion, see Jonathan Kandell, "Tough Abortion Law in Connecticut Is Attributed to Meskill and Catholics," *New York Times*, May 25, 1972, 38. On Carter's supposed effort to block pro-life nominees and Horan's letter on the subject, see "Federal Judgeships Denied to Pro-Lifers, Says Horan," 16.

100. McCormack, "Can Right to Life Do Anything about the Power of the Courts?" 1, 6.

101. Scheidler, "Editorial," 2.

102. McCormack, "Can Right to Life Do Anything about the Power of the Courts?" 5.

103. On the New Right's efforts to unite disparate conservative groups, see Paul Weyrich, "Comments," in *No Longer Exiles: The Religious New Right in American Politics*, ed. Michael Cromartie (Washington, DC: Ethics and Public Policy Center, 1993), 25–26; Williams, *God's Own Party*, 167–169; James Harold Farney, *Social Conservatives and Party Politics in Canada and the United States* (Toronto: University of Toronto Press, 2012), 42, 47; Laura Kalman, *Right Star Rising: A New Politics, 1974–1980* (New York: W. W. Norton, 2010), 27.

104. Leslie Bennetts, "Conservatives Join on Social Concerns," *New York Times*, July 30, 1980, A1.

105. Chapter 6 will further discuss these developments.

106. Taylor, "Politics of the Bench," A27. For an excellent analysis of Nixon's "strict constructionism," see Keith Whittington, "William Rehnquist: Nixon's Strict Constructionist, Reagan's Chief Justice" in *Rehnquist Justice: Understanding the Court Dynamic*, ed. Earl Malz (Lawrence: University of Kansas Press, 2003), 8–11.

107. Taylor, "Politics of the Bench," A27.

108. Christian Action Council, Fundraising Letter (February 4, 1980), 2, WC, Action Line Folder.

109. Ad Hoc Committee in Defense of Life, Fundraising Letter (October 21, 1980), WC, Ad Hoc Committee in Defense of Life Folder.

110. On antiabortion reactions to the O'Connor nomination, see Merilee Melvin, Memorandum to Ed Thomas (July 8, 1981), EMP, OA 2408, Appointments—Supreme Court—O'Connor. For further discussion of this subject, see Memorandum from Max Friedersdorf to Jim Baker, Edwin Meese, Michael Deaver et al. (July 6, 1981), EMP, OA 2408, Appointments—Supreme Court—O'Connor. On O'Connor's positions on abortion and the ERA, see Samuel Walker, *Presidents and Civil Liberties from Wilson to Obama: A Story of Poor Custodians* (New York: Cambridge University Press, 2012), 385.

111. Hedrick Smith, "Reagan's Court Choice: A Deft Maneuver," *New York Times*, July 9, 1981, A17. For more on the indifference of the Reagan Administration to pro-life protests of the O'Connor nomination, see Patrick Buchanan, "Reagan Letter Fuel for 'Pro-Lifers,'" *Chicago Tribune*, August 15, 1981, 7.

112. See Uhlmann to Meese, 1–2.

113. Confirmation of Sandra Day O'Connor to the Supreme Court: Testimony before the Senate Judiciary Committee, 97th Congress, 2nd Session, 334 (1981) (Statement of Dr. John Willke).

114. Sandra Salmans, "Abortion Opponents See Reagan as 'Clear-Cut' Choice in Campaign," *New York Times*, June 10, 1984, 30.

Chapter 2. The Incrementalist Ascendancy

1. Chapter 1 further studies Willke's strategic use of arguments against judicial activism.

2. Judie Brown, interview with Mary Ziegler, August 9, 2011. For a sample of Brown's autobiographical writings, see Judie Brown, *It Is I Who Have Chosen You: An Autobiography of Judie Brown* (Stafford, VA: American Life League, 1997); Judie Brown, *Not My Will but Thine: An Autobiography* (Stafford, VA: American Life League, 2002). For news coverage of Brown's activities in the period, see Laurie Johnston, "Abortion Foes Gain Support as They Intensify Campaign," *New York Times*, October 23, 1977, 1; Royce Rensberger, "March of Dimes Group Declares Genetic Aid

Program Will Go On," *New York Times*, March 15, 1978, A20; "Conservative Group to Monitor TV," *New York Times*, February 3, 1981, C8.

3. James Bopp Jr., interview with Mary Ziegler, February 22, 2012. For a sample of Bopp's writings on abortion, see James Bopp Jr., *Restoring the Right to Life: The Human Life Amendment* (Provo, UT: Brigham Young University Press, 1984); James Bopp Jr. and Richard Coleson, "The Right to Abortion: Anomalous, Absolute, and Ripe for Reversal," *Brigham Young University Journal of Public Law* 3 (1989): 181–209; James Bopp Jr., "An Examination of Proposals for a Human Life Amendment," *Capital University Law Review* 15 (1986): 417–474.

4. For discussion of these state campaigns, see "Ruling on Akron Abortion Ordinance Called Victory," *National Right to Life News*, September/October 1979, 1, 3, JRS, 1979 National Right to Life News Box; James Bopp Jr., "Akron Analysis," *National Right to Life News*, September/October 1979, 3, JRS, 1979 National Right to Life News Box; James Bopp Jr., "Akron Type Laws Buoyed by Court Decisions," *National Right to Life News*, November 1979, 20, JRS, 1979 National Right to Life News Box; Suzanne Glasow, "Sweeping Pro-Life Bills Stalled Until December," *National Right to Life News*, December 7, 1981, 1, JRS, 1981 National Right to Life News Box; "Louisiana's Stringent New Abortion Law Deemed 'Standard Bearer,'" *New York Times*, August 1, 1978, B6; Reginald Stuart, "Akron Divided By Heated Abortion Debate," *New York Times*, February 1, 1978, A10; Joseph Sullivan, "Bill on Detailing Risk in Abortion Passed in Jersey," *New York Times*, November 14, 1979, B2; Martin Waldron, "New Abortion-Law Proposal Sets Stage for Confrontation," *New York Times*, January 21, 1979, NJ1; Helen Epstein, "Abortion: An Issue That Won't Go Away," *New York Times Magazine*, March 30, 1980, SM111.

5. Bopp, "Akron Analysis," 3.

6. This view became the plainest during the battle for the Hatch Amendment. See Steven Roberts, "Catholic Bishops for Amendment Allowing States to Ban Abortion," *New York Times*, November 6, 1981, A1; Kenneth A. Briggs, "The Bishops Take a Risk: New Peace Position Sure to Ignite Dissent," *New York Times*, November 23, 1981, B10; "Anti-Abortion Group Backs Hatch Proposal," *New York Times*, December 13, 1981, 39. For pro-life individuals' recollections and views of incrementalism: Pam Manning, interview with Mary Ziegler, August 19, 2011; Margie Montgomery, interview with Mary Ziegler, August 11, 2011; Sandra Faucher, interview with Mary Ziegler, February 4, 2012; Philip Moran, interview with Mary Ziegler, February 1, 2012; Mary Beliveau, interview with Mary Ziegler, February 7, 2012; Bopp, interview; Jack Gorby, interview with Mary Ziegler, August 22, 2011; Patrick Trueman, interview with Mary Ziegler, September 13, 2011; Denise Neary, interview with Mary Ziegler, February 18, 2012; Geline Williams, interview with Mary Ziegler, February 8, 2012; Dr. John Willke, interview with Mary Ziegler, December 19, 2010.

7. "President's Column: Personhood, Please," *A.L.L. About Issues*, January 1982, 1, WC, A.L.L. About Issues Folder.

8. For articulations of the absolutist vision, see "President's Column: Beware of False Friends," *A.L.L. About Issues*, September 1981, WC, A.L.L. About Issues Folder; Judie Brown, "Down the Hatch: The Hatch Federalism Amendment Will Not Save Babies," *A.L.L. About Issues*, January 1982, 3, WC, A.L.L. About Issues Folder; Paul Brown, "The Hatch-Catholic Bishops' Amendment—A Recipe for Disaster," *A.L.L. About Issues*, January 1982, 2, WC, A.L.L. About Issues Folder; James Schall, SJ, "Political Wrong Turn Disheartens Pro-Lifers," *A.L.L. About Issues*, April 1982, 3, WC, A.L.L. About Issues Folder.

9. Brown, "Down the Hatch," 3.

10. This chapter later discusses the explosion of tensions between absolutists and incrementalists during the battle for the Hatch Amendment.

11. Elizabeth Mensch and Alan Freeman, *The Politics of Virtue: Is Abortion Debatable?* 2nd ed. (Durham, NC: Duke University Press, 1995), 127, 135 (describing how *Roe* pushed abortion supporters toward "the utterly secularized claims of the pro-choice extreme" and encouraged abortion opponents to become "ever more resolutely absolutist in theologically defending the pro-life position"). For Klarman's argument linking extremism after *Roe* and *Brown v. Board of Education*, see Michael J. Klarman, *From Jim Crow to Civil Rights: The Supreme Court and the Struggle for Racial Equality* (New York: Oxford University Press, 2004), 464–465. Political scientists have offered a number of definitions of extremism, based, among other things, on the rigidity of a group's positions, its fixation on particular issues or positions, and its recourse to violent or disruptive tactics. See Guido Ortona, "De Bello Omnium, Contra Omnes," in *Political Extremism and Rationality*, eds. Albert Breton, Gianluigi Galeotti, Pierre Salmon, and Ronald Wintrobe (New York: Cambridge University Press, 2002), 217–218; Manus I. Midlarsky, *Origins of Political Extremism: Mass Violence in the Twentieth Century and Beyond* (New York: Cambridge University Press, 2011), 7; Nancy L. Rosenblum, *On the Side of the Angels: An Appreciation of Parties and Partisanship* (Princeton: Princeton University Press, 2010), 17, 389. This chapter does not aim to contribute to scholarly understandings of extremism. Instead, by recovering part of the lost history of the pro-life movement, the chapter complicates leading understandings of the kind of pro-life leader who came to power after 1973 and the reasons those leaders came to exercise influence.

12. Jeffrey Rosen, *The Most Democratic Branch: How the Courts Serve America* (New York: Oxford University Press, 2006), 91 (arguing that *Roe* "continues to inflame and distort our judicial confirmation process, giving social conservatives and liberal extremists an exaggerated sense of their own political power").

13. Ziad W. Munson, *The Making of Pro-Life Activists: How Social Movement Mobilization Works* (Chicago: University of Chicago Press, 2008),

85; see also Sara Dubow, *Ourselves Unborn: A History of the Fetus in Modern America* (New York: Oxford University Press, 2010), 185.

14. Rosen, *The Most Democratic Branch*, 91.

15. Cass R. Sunstein, *Radicals in Robes: Why Extreme Right Wing Courts Are Wrong for America* (New York: Basic Books, 2005), 151.

16. Kristin Luker, *Abortion and the Politics of Motherhood* (Berkeley: University of California Press, 1984), 205. Some scholars, from Carol Maxwell to Michael Cuneo, also identify as extremists members of a smaller wing of the pro-life movement committed to direct-action tactics and a broader social conservative agenda. See Carol J. C. Maxwell, *Pro-Life Activists in America: Meaning, Motivation, and Direct Action* (New York: Oxford University Press, 2002), 70–82; Michael W. Cuneo, *The Smoke of Satan: Conservative and Traditionalist Dissent in Contemporary American Catholicism* (New York: Oxford University Press, 1999), 61–68. While Cuneo and Maxwell detail events that fall outside the scope of this book, this chapter draws on the understanding of pro-life absolutism these scholars develop—particularly, hardliners' interest in a broad agenda and new tactics.

17. For examples of scholars' portrayal of the conservatism or extremism of abortion opponents in the wake of *Roe*, see William N. Eskridge Jr. and John A. Ferejohn, *A Republic of Statutes: The New American Constitution* (New Haven, CT: Yale University Press, 2010), 242; Cass R. Sunstein, "Civil Rights Legislation in the 1990s: Three Civil Rights Fallacies," *California Law Review* 79 (1991): 766–767; Luker, *Abortion*, 193–208.

18. See Dennis Horan to NRLC Policy Committee (September 5, 1973), 1–3, ACCL, Box 8, 1973 NRLC Folder 4 (telling colleagues that an amendment would "solve only some, but not all, of our problems" and would require "further state legislation in order to plug the loopholes").

19. For examples of briefs signed by Dolores Horan, see Brief and Appendices of Dr. Bart Heffernan, Amicus Curiae in Support of Appellant, *United States v. Vuitch*, 402 U.S. 62 (No. 84); Brief as Amicus Curiae of Certain Physicians, Professors, and Fellows of the American College of Obstetrics and Gynecology, 3, *Roe v. Wade*, 410 U.S. 113 (1973) (Nos. 70–18, 70–40); Motion and Brief as Amicus Curiae for Dr. Eugene Diamond and Americans United for Life, 17, *Planned Parenthood of Central Missouri v. Danforth*, 428 U.S. 52 (1976) (Nos. 74–1151, 74–1419); Motion and Brief Amicus Curiae for Americans United for Life, Inc., *Poelker v. Doe*, 432 U.S. 519 (1977) (No. 75–442); Brief of Amicus Curiae of Americans United for Life, *H. L. v. Matheson*, 450 U.S. 398 (1981) (No. 79–5903); Brief of Amicus Curiae for the American Pro-Life Association of Obstetricians and Gynecologists et al., *Webster v. Reproductive Health Services*, 492 U.S. 490 (1989) (No. 88–605). For individual recollections about the Horans' partnership: Gorby, interview; Trueman, interview.

20. On the early activities of the Illinois Right to Life Committee, see "Abortion Talk to Be Given at Loyola U," *Chicago Tribune*, September 23, 1970,

5; "Abortion Foes Begin to Fight," *Chicago Defender*, February 13, 1971, 21; Stanley Ziemba, "400 at Workshop Hear Abortion Branded as Legalized Murder," *Chicago Tribune*, February 22, 1971, A17; "State Right to Life Group Offers Film," *Chicago Tribune*, March 21, 1971, S4; "Doctor Will Give Antiabortion Talk," *Chicago Tribune*, October 8, 1972, S5. For individual activists' experience of the early days of the IRLC: Dr. Eugene Diamond, interview with Mary Ziegler, February 6, 2011; Joseph Scheidler, interview with Mary Ziegler, August 20, 2011.

21. Dennis Horan to NRLC Policy Committee (September 5, 1973), 2. For individuals' recollections of Horan's changing priorities: Trueman, interview; Gorby, interview.

22. For Gorby's story: Gorby, interview; John Gorby, "Letter to Jack" (2010), on file with the author. For a sample of Gorby's scholarship, see John Gorby and Dennis Horan, "The Legal Case for the Unborn," in *Abortion and Social Justice*, eds. Thomas Hilgers and Dennis Horan (New York: Sheed and Ward, 1972): 105–141; John Gorby and Dennis Horan, "Abortion and the Supreme Court: Death Becomes a Way of Life," in *Abortion and Social Justice*, eds. Thomas Hilgers and Dennis Horan (New York: Sheed and Ward, 1972), 301–328; John Gorby, "The 'Right' to an Abortion and the Scope of Fourteenth Amendment 'Personhood,' and the Supreme Court's Birth Requirements," *Southern Illinois University Law Review* 4 (1979): 1–36; Dennis Horan and John Gorby, "Abortion and Human Rights," *Human Life Review* 2 (1976): 21–33.

23. For discussion of Trueman's work on abortion, see Lee Strobel, "Abortion Ruling a Plum for Lawyers, Nightmare for Clinics," *Chicago Tribune*, July 6, 1980, 6; Robert Enstad, "Void Parental Abortion Okay," *Chicago Tribune*, November 17, 1979, 1. For an example of Trueman's work during his time at the AUL, see Patrick Trueman to AUL Board of Directors (July 10, 1977), GHW, Box 5, Folder 7.

24. For discussion of Rosenblum's background and work on abortion, see Nick Thimmesch, "Right to Life Fights for Human Values," *Chicago Tribune*, June 17, 1973, A6; Marcia Chambers, "Advocates for a Right to Life," *New York Times*, December 16, 1984, SM94; "Victor Rosenblum, 1925–2006," *Chicago Tribune*, March 15, 2006, accessed February 22, 2012, http://articles.chicagotribune.com/2006–03–15/news/0603150265_ 1_anti-abortion-mr-rosenblum-law-schools.

25. On the founding of the AUL LDF, see David Mall to AUL Board of Directors, "First Quarterly Report" (February 28, 1975), GHW, Box 5, Folder 6. On the Moore case, see Letter to AUL Members (1978), AUL, Executive File Box, Folder 92; Strobel, "Abortion Ruling," 6. For individual activists' recollections of the Moore case: Gorby, interview; Trueman, interview.

26. See *Planned Parenthood of Central Missouri v. Danforth*, 428 U.S. 52, 59–84 (1976).

27. See Brief as Amicus Curiae for Dr. Eugene Diamond and Americans United for Life, 17, 88–89–105 (explaining that "*Roe v. Wade* teaches that the right to practice medicine, just as any other right, is a limited one at best").

28. *Planned Parenthood of Central Missouri v. Danforth*, 76–77.

29. See ibid. (emphasizing that the State "may not impose a blanket provision" or create a "veto power exercisable for any reason whatsoever or for no reason at all"). For activists' recollections on the subject: Gorby, interview; Trueman, interview.

30. Patrick Trueman to the AUL Board of Directors, Report on the AUL Legal Defense Fund (July 10, 1977), 5, GHW, Box 5, Folder 7. On the elevation of Trueman to the position of AUL Executive Director, see AUL Board of Directors Meeting Minutes (October 29, 1977), 4–6, GHW, Box 5, Folder 7.

31. Trueman to AUL Board of Directors, Report on the AUL Legal Defense Fund, 1. For further discussion of the AUL's strategies and criteria for case collection, see also Chambers, "Advocates for a Right to Life," SM94; E. R. Shipp, "Foes of Abortion Examine Strategies of NAACP," *New York Times*, April 2, 1984, A15.

32. For a discussion of the lead-up to *Poelker, Maher,* and *Beal*, see Joyce Maynard, "Health Aides and Abortion Groups Assail Proposed Medicaid Control," *New York Times*, September 18, 1976, 9; Max H. Siegel, "U.S. Courts Bar Curb on Funding Some Abortions: Restraints Are Imposed on Medicaid Statute," *New York Times*, October 2, 1976, 1; "Curb on Medicaid Funds for Abortion Defended," *New York Times,* February 15, 1977, 49.

33. Motion and Brief as Amicus Curiae for Americans United for Life, *Poelker v. Doe*, 7, 15.

34. Ibid., 13.

35. See *Doe v. Wohlgemuth*, 376 F.2d 173, 178–184 (W.D. Pa. 1978) (holding that a state funding ban was not contradicted by the federal Social Security Act and thus was constitutional); *Doe v. Westby*, 402 F. Supp. 140, 143–144 (D.S.D. 1975) (invalidating such a law on supremacy-clause grounds); *Roe v. Casey*, 464 F. Supp. 487, 499–500 (E.D. Pa. 1978) (striking down such a statute on supremacy-clause grounds); *Roe v. Norton*, 522 F.2d 928, 937–938 (2d Cir. 1975) (holding that a funding ban did not violate the Social Security Act but leaving open the constitutionality of the law under the Equal Protection Clause).

36. See *Doe v. Rose*, 49 F.2d 1112, 1115–1117 (10th Cir. 1974); *Wulff v. Singleton*, 508 F.2d 1211, 1215–1216 (8th Cir. 1974), aff'd on different grounds sub nom. *Singleton v. Wulff*, 428 U.S. 106 (1976); *Doe v. Wohlgemuth*, 190–191, aff'd on other grounds sub nom., *Doe v. Beal*, 523 F.2d 611 (3rd Cir. 1975) (en banc); *Klein v. Nassau County Medical Center*, 374 F. Supp. 496 (E.D. N.Y. 1972) rem. in light of *Wade* and *Bolton*, 412 U.S. 924 (1973); dec. on rem. 409 F. Supp. 733, 733–734 (E.D. N.Y. 1976); *Doe v. Rampton*, 366 F. Supp. 189, 193 (D. Utah 1973).

37. *Maher v. Roe*, 432 U.S. 464, 474, 481–490 (1977). For the decisions in *Poelker* and *Beal*, see *Poelker v. Doe*, 432 U.S. 519, 521–522 (1977); *Beal v. Doe*, 432 U.S. 438, 445–448 (1977).

38. Dr. Joseph Stanton to AUL Board of Directors (August 1977), 1, GHW, Box 5, Folder 7 (calling victories in *Poelker*, *Maher*, and *Beal* evidence that AUL-led litigation was "the most important aspect of the pro-life movement at this time"). For more on movement perceptions of *Maher*, *Poelker*, and *Beal*, see Liz Jeffries, "Court Rules Funding Not Required," *National Right to Life News*, August 1977, 1, 3, JRS, 1977 Right to Life News Box (calling the state funding cases "historic"); Mildred Jefferson, "Lifelines," *National Right to Life News*, August 1977, 9, JRS, 1977 National Right to Life News Box (urging "[e]veryone who speaks in the right to life movement or who participates in the educational effort in any way" to read *Maher*, *Beal*, and *Poelker*).

39. See Arlene Doyle, "Do You Need Permission to Save an Unborn Baby? A Pro-Life Study of Struggles within the Right to Life Movement and a Comparison of Two Kinds of Organization, Directorship vs. Coalition" (June 1977), 17, 19–20, The United States Coalition for Life Archive, accessed April 2, 2014, http://uscl.info/edoc/doc.php?doc_id=88&action=inline.

40. AUL Board of Directors Meeting Minutes (October 29, 1977), 5, 8.

41. Gorby, interview. For further discussion of the importance of *Maher* and other early incrementalist cases to the movement, see NRLC Informational Letter (March 1978), 1, JRS, Dr. Joseph Stanton Papers (emphasizing that, because of *Maher* and its companion cases, there were "35 states which provide no funding for abortions and [similar] legislation is now pending in many more").

42. On Bopp's personal experience and recollections of incrementalism: Bopp, interview.

43. Bopp, "Akron Analysis," 3. For further examples of the incrementalist approach: "Active Court Cases," *Lex Vitae*, February 22, 1978, 1, WC, Lex Vitae Folder (detailing AUL's involvement in cases on abortion funding and parental consultation); "AUL Perspective," *Lex Vitae*, February 1, 1979, 5–6, WC, Lex Vitae Folder (using an adverse decision on a Pennsylvania law as guidance for legislators drafting new incremental restrictions); "Louisiana's Stringent New Abortion Law Deemed 'Standard Bearer,'" B6 (describing incrementalists' campaign to introduce model legislation in Louisiana); Stuart, "Akron Divided," A10 (detailing pro-lifers' campaign to introduce a model law likely to be upheld in the courts); Sullivan, "Bill on Detailing Abortion Risk," B2 (reporting on an incrementalist law debated in New Jersey).

44. Williams, interview. For further discussion of Williams' involvement in the movement, see James Risen and Judy L. Thomas, *Wrath of Angels: The American Abortion War* (New York: Basic Books, 1998), 19. Williams would go on to become the second woman to serve as the mayor of Richmond, Virginia. See The Virginia Society for Human Life, "Honoring

Geline B. Williams," accessed May 1, 2014, http://www.vshl.org/honoring-mrs-geline-b-williams-vshl-director-to-nrlc.html.

45. For Faucher's individual experience: Faucher, interview. On Faucher's involvement with the movement, see "Right to Life Committee Plans Drive for Anti-Abortion Amendment," *New York Times*, June 30, 1980, A17; William Saletan, *Bearing Right: How Conservatives Won the Abortion Wars* (Berkeley: University of California Press, 2004), 113.

46. Faucher, interview.

47. NRLC Information Letter (March 1978), 2.

48. For examples of the incrementalist perspective, see Ray White to NRLC Board of Directors, "Regarding the Bartlett Amendment" (September 1974), ACCL, Box 8, 1974 NRLC Board and Executive Committee Folder 14 (calling abortion funding bans "one of the biggest fights we will ever have"); "Our Legislative Counsel Speaks," *Footnotes*, July 15, 1977, ACCL, Box 10, 1976 NRLC Folder 2 (explaining the importance of strict language in the Hyde Amendment to the movement); "Iowa Passes New Bill on Born Alive Baby," *National Right to Life News*, 7, July 1976, JRS, 1976 National Right to Life News Box (stressing the importance of state legislation requiring physicians to care for children surviving abortion); "Abortionists Attack Live Baby Care Law," *National Right to Life News*, July 1976, 7, JRS, 1976 National Right to Life News Box (same); Thea Rossi Barron, "Hyde Amendment Big Victory; Fight Goes On," *National Right to Life News*, January 1977, 1, JRS, 1977 National Right to Life News Box (calling a strong version of Hyde "no small victory in pro-life circles").

49. The qualifications for "pro-life" candidates set by the movement in the period will be discussed later in this chapter.

50. Dr. John Willke to Dr. Joseph Stanton (April 20, 1977), JRS, Dr. Joseph Stanton Papers.

51. Pro-lifers often emphasized the political power their movement supposedly enjoyed. See Dolores Barclay and Victoria Graham, "Abortion: It Ends Political Lives, Too," *Chicago Tribune*, February 15, 1976, 1; John Herbers, "Anti-Abortionists' Impact Felt In Elections across the Nation," *New York Times*, June 20, 1978, A1. Mildred Jefferson of the NRLC went so far as claiming that pro-lifers made up "the biggest movement in America." William Robbins, "Abortion Foes Look to Ultimate Victory," *New York Times*, June 19, 1977, 24. For an individual recollection of the importance of political influence to the NRLC and efforts to emphasize its size: Judie Brown, interview.

52. The chapter later discusses the importance, from the movement's standpoint, of "swing" votes in Congress and state legislatures.

53. On the diversity of the antiabortion movement, see Keith Cassidy, "The Right to Life Movement: Sources, Development, and Strategies," in *The Politics of Abortion and Birth Control in Historical Perspective*, ed. Donald T. Critchlow (University Park: Penn State Press, 1996), 138; Munson,

The Making of Pro-Life Activists, 192. On the antiabortion movement's
wish to appear non-partisan, see Robert Mason, *Richard Nixon and the
Quest for a New Majority* (Chapel Hill: University of North Carolina
Press, 2004), 230; Daniel K. Williams, *God's Own Party: The Making of
the Christian Right*, 2nd ed. (New York: Oxford University Press, 2012),
130–132.

54. "Right to Life Television Commercials: Proposal for Right to Life People
and Groups" (October 1974), JRS, Ellen McCormack Papers. For more
on Keating's campaign, see Barbara Keating, "Right to Life Television
Commercials" (n.d., ca. 1973), JRS, Ellen McCormack Papers.

55. "Proposal for Right to Life People: A Right to Life Candidate in the 1976
Presidential Primaries" (Fall 1976), JRS, Ellen McCormack Papers.

56. Fran Watson, "Response to President Ford's Statement on Abortion" (February 5, 1976), JRS, Ellen McCormack Papers.

57. See "Wanted: Your Support for a Right to Life Presidential Candidate"
(October 1976), 1, JRS, Ellen McCormack Papers.

58. Fundraising Letter, "Ellen McCormack for President" (March 8, 1976), 2,
JRS, Ellen McCormack Papers (arguing that "an important swing Right to
Life vote is to be found . . . throughout the country").

59. Nominating Speech for Ellen McCormack (n.d., ca. July 1976), JRS, Ellen
McCormack Papers. For analysis of the evolution of the Democratic plat-
form, see "Ellen McCormack to Address Nation on Jimmy Carter" (June
26, 1976), JRS, Ellen McCormack Papers; "Memorandum: Democratic
Platform Statement on Abortion" (June 31, 1976), JRS, Ellen McCormack
Papers.

60. On Sean Morton Downey Jr., see "Dear Reader," *LAPAC Reports*, June
15, 1979, WC, LAPAC Reports Folder (on Downey's idea of running for
president); "Abortion Foe Will Seek Presidential Nomination," *New York
Times*, June 8, 1979, A21 (same). For more on his antiabortion advocacy,
see John Herbers, "Convention Speech Stirs Foes of Abortion," *New York
Times*, June 24, 1979, 16; Randall Rothenberg, "Morton Downey, Jr. Is
Taking His Abrasive Style Nationwide," *New York Times*, May 16, 1988,
C16. On Downey's entry into pro-life politics, see "Downey Has Several
Careers," *Milwaukee Sentinel*, January 31, 1979, 6, 8.

61. Paul Brown, interview with Mary Ziegler, August 12, 2011.

62. On Paul Brown's career in the movement: Paul A. Brown, "Ronald Reagan, George Bush, and the Republican Platform," *LAPAC Reports*, Summer 1980, WC, LAPAC Reports Folder; Leslie Bennetts, "Anti-Abortion
Group Asks Defeat of Javits and Five Others at Polls," *New York Times*,
January 19, 1980, 11; Leslie Bennetts, "Abortion Foes Gird for Iowa Cau-
cuses," *New York Times*, January 13, 1980, 22.

63. On Sassone's career in the movement, see Marjory Mecklenburg to Robert Sassone (November 8, 1973), ACCL, Box 4, 1973 NRLC Board and
Executive Committee Folder 6; Robert Sassone, "The Meaning of Person
in the Fourteenth Amendment," *A.L.L. About Issues*, August 1981, 12,

WC, A.L.L. About Issues Folder; Nathaniel Sheppard, "Group Fighting Abortion Planning to Step Up Its Drive," *New York Times*, July 3, 1978, 9. For Sassone's personal story, see "Sassone—A Democrat Who Can Win It All," *34th Congressional District News*, June 1974, 1, WC, Ellen Mc-Cormack Papers.

64. Paul Brown, interview.

65. On LAPAC's strategy in the primaries, see Sheppard, "Group Fighting Abortion," 20; Bennetts, "Antiabortion Group Asks Defeat of Javits and Five Others," 11. On LAPAC's campaign against McGovern, see Lee Epstein and Joseph F. Kobylka, *The Supreme Court and Legal Change: Abortion and the Death Penalty* (Chapel Hill: University of North Carolina Press, 1992), 204, 209; Sara Diamond, *Roads to Dominion: Right-Wing Movements and Political Power in the United States* (New York: Guilford Press, 1995), 170; Leslie Bennetts, "Conservatives and Antiabortion Groups Press Attack Against Abortion," *New York Times*, June 2, 1980, B11. For recollections of the tactics used to unseat McGovern: Paul Brown, interview.

66. For discussion of LAPAC's 1978 victories, see Richard Viguerie, *The New Right: We're Ready to Lead* (Falls Church, VA: Viguerie and Co., 1981), 102 (claiming that LAPAC played a "decisive role" in the defeat of several members of Congress who favored abortion); Diamond, *Roads to Dominion*, 170.

67. On NRLC debt at the time of Jefferson's exit, see Connie Paige, *The Right to Lifers: Who They Are, How They Operate, Where They Get Their Money* (New York: Summit, 1983), 87. For discussion of the conflict between Jefferson and the AUL (as well as Jefferson and other Massachusetts activists), see Dr. Mildred Jefferson to Dr. Joseph Stanton (September 20, 1978), JRS, Dr. Joseph Stanton Papers (accusing Stanton of considering state pro-life organizations his "private domain"); Dr. Joseph Stanton to Harold O. J. Brown (October 2, 1979), JRS, Dr. Joseph Stanton Papers (claiming that Jefferson had "caused certain problems" for Massachusetts pro-life organizations); Dr. Joseph Stanton to Ann O'Donnell et al. (December 14, 1979), JRS, Dr. Joseph Stanton Papers (reporting on newspaper article detailing Jefferson's disagreement with other NRLC members and contending that Massachusetts Citizens for Life was "one of the jewels in NRLC's crown . . . not because of, but in spite of Jeffersonian manipulations"). For activists' recollections of this conflict: Moran, interview; Judie Brown, interview.

68. Scott Sherry, "Political Action Committee Formed," *National Right to Life News*, September/October 1979, 4, JRS, 1979 National Right to Life News Box (emphasizing that candidates supported by pro-life PACs were winners in general elections); see also Joann Rubeck, "Political Action Committees Wave of Future," *National Right to Life News*, July 1979, 7, JRS, 1979 National Right to Life News Box ("As the pro-life movement continues to flex its 'political muscle,' groups are being formed to insure

the tone and strength of this political arm"). For individuals' memories of the strategy pursued by the National Right to Life PAC in the period: Faucher, interview; Bopp, interview; Willke, interview.

69. Rubeck, "Political Action Committees the Wave of the Future," 7. On antiabortion frustrations with the official indifference of the Democratic Party, see Herbers, "Convention Speech Stirs Foes of Abortion," 16; John Herbers, "Sweeping Right to Life Goals Set as Movement Gains New Power," *New York Times*, November 27, 1978, A1; cf. Ad Hoc Committee in Defense of Life, "'Continuing Resolution' Extends Hyde Fight," *Lifeletter* #15, October 18, 1977, 4, WC, Lifeletter Folder (complaining that the "liberal media" tended incorrectly to "link the anti-abortion movement with what is being called the 'New Right'").

70. On the Senate vote, see "Senate Votes to Empower State to Approve Funds for Abortion," *New York Times*, September 30, 1980, A16. On the House vote, see Martin Tolchin, "Abortion Agreement Breaks Deadlock on Spending Bill," *New York Times*, October 1, 1980, A16. On similar votes taken in 1978, see B. Drummond Ayres Jr., "House Votes to Curb Funds for Abortion," *New York Times*, June 14, 1978, NJ23. For Faucher's claim, see "Right to Life Committee Plans Drive for Anti-Abortion Amendment," *New York Times*, June 30, 1980, A17.

71. Dr. John Willke to Dr. Joseph Stanton (April 20, 1977), 1.

72. Dr. Joseph Stanton to Nellie Gray (January 30, 1978), 2, JRS, Dr. Joseph Stanton Papers.

73. On the passage of the Akron ordinance, see William Hershey, "Council Passes Abortion Control Bill; Opponents Vow Challenge in Court," *Akron Beacon Journal*, February 28, 1978, A1.

74. On the use of the Akron anti-abortion statute as a model, see Nick Thimmesch, "Akron Abortion Proposal Could Fuel the National Debate," *Chicago Tribune*, January 25, 1978, B2; Reginald Stuart, "Akron Divided by Heated Abortion Debate," *New York Times*, February 1, 1978, A10 (explaining that what happened in Akron "could influence what will happen in other cities across the nation"); Nadine Brozan, "Abortion Rights In Peril, Say Advocates at Conference," *New York Times*, July 20, 1979, A14 (calling the Akron ordinance one of the issues with "the most serious consequences" in the abortion wars).

75. "Louisiana's Stringent New Abortion Law Deemed 'Standard Bearer,'" B6. On the effort to spread Akron-style laws to other cities, see "Goose-Stepping on Abortion . . . and Some Tripping Attempts," *Off Our Backs*, March 1978, 13.

76. See Bopp, "Akron Type Laws Buoyed by Court Decision," 20.

77. Thimmesch, "Akron Abortion Proposal," B2. In many states, Akron-style statutes became a prime concern for abortion-rights activists. See, for example, "SCR 4015. Testimony of North Dakota NOW before the House Special Services Committee," (March 9, 1979), JBP, Box 1, Folder 19; Testimony against H.B. 1581 Presented Jointly for North Dakota

Council for Legal, Safe Abortion and North Dakota NOW, JBP, Box 1, Folder 19.

78. "Ruling on Akron Abortion Ordinance Called Victory," 3.

79. "President's Column: Beware of False Friends," 1.

80. Schall, "Political Wrong Turn Disheartens Pro-Lifers," 3.

81. For articulations of this approach, see Dr. John Willke to Dr. Joseph Stanton (April 20, 1977), 1; Bopp, "Akron Type Laws Buoyed by Court Decision," 20; Thimmesch, "Akron Abortion Proposal," B2. For activists' recollections of incrementalist goals: Manning, interview; Montgomery, interview; Faucher, interview; Bopp, interview; Willke, interview.

82. "Personhood, Please," 1.

83. Christian Action Council, "Quiz," *Action Line*, March 31, 1981, 3, WC, Action Line Folder.

84. Ibid.

85. "A Positive Step," *A.L.L. About News*, September 1981, 3, WC, A.L.L. About News Folder.

86. On the constitutional-convention strategy, see Laurence H. Tribe, *Abortion: The Clash of Absolutes* (New York: W. W. Norton, 1992), 150–151. For movement discussion of the strategy from the period, see Ad Hoc Committee in Defense of Life, "The Action on Con-Con Suddenly Shifted to Washington," *Lifeletter No. 9*, July 6, 1977, 6, WC, Lifeletter Folder. The NRLC, by contrast, continued to focus on efforts to get Congress to endorse the human life amendment rather than campaigning first in the states for a constitutional convention. See Robbins, "Abortion Foes Look to Ultimate Victory," 24.

87. Doyle, "Do You Need Permission to Save an Unborn Baby?" 4.

88. See ibid.; see also Tribe, *The Clash of Absolutes*, 150–151.

89. Robbins, "Abortion Foes Look to Ultimate Victory," 24. For further discussion of the con-con campaign, see "Pro-Abortion Groups Rallying," *New York Times*, June 8, 1975, 83 (on the campaign in New Jersey); "Massachusetts Is 9th State to Seek a Convention on Issue of Abortion," *New York Times*, June 9, 1977, 88 (on the Massachusetts campaign); Harriet Pilpel, "Constitution Changing," *New York Times*, January 20, 1979, 21 (criticizing the con-con concept).

90. See Doyle, "Do You Need Permission to Save an Unborn Baby?" 21.

91. On the founding of the American Life League, see Carol Mason, *Killing for Life: The Apocalyptic Narrative of Pro-Life Politics* (Ithaca, NY: Cornell University Press, 2002), 15; "The New Right: A Special Report," *Conservative Digest*, June 1979, 10, 16; Brown, *It Is I Who Have Chosen You*, 72–75.

92. For Judie Brown's recollections on the subject: Judie Brown, interview. On the early activities of the ALL, see Michael W. Cuneo, "Life Battles: The Rise of Catholic Militancy within the American Pro-Life Movement," in *Bearing Right: Conservative Catholics in America*, eds. Mary Jo Weaver and R. Scott Appleby (Bloomington: University of Indiana Press, 1995),

270–275; Cuneo, *Smoke of Satan*, 62–63, 65. For examples of the early goals and values set forth by the ALL, see "President's Column: Guts," *A.L.L. About Issues*, February 1981, 1, WC, A.L.L. About Issues Folder; "President's Column: Pro-Life or Right to Life . . . Big Wheel or Square?" *A.L.L. About Issues*, June 1981, WC, A.L.L. About Issues Folder; "President's Column: Facing the Battle," *A.L.L. About Issues*, August 1, 1981, 1, WC, A.L.L. About Issues Folder. For individuals' recollections of the early years of the ALL: Judie Brown, interview; Paul Brown, interview.

93. Sister Paula Vandegaer, S. S. S., "Problem Pregnancy? Get an Abortion!" *A.L.L. About Issues*, July 1981, 3, WC, A.L.L. About Issues Folder.

94. "Teenagers, 'Responsible Sex Education,' and Contraceptives," *A.L.L. About Issues*, April 1981, 8, WC, A.L.L. About Issues Folder. On the growth of the ALL, see "Your Prayers and Dollars at Work," *A.L.L. About Issues*, September 1981, 4, WC, A.L.L. About Issues Folder; "Growth Brings Change to A.L.L." (April 1982), 1, WC, A.L.L. About Issues Folder.

95. On Scheidler's career in the movement, see Risen and Thomas, *Wrath of Angels*, 101–119; Lee Strobel, "Right to Life Groups Muster Their Forces," *Chicago Tribune*, June 20, 1974, N14; Brenda Stone, "After Two Years, An Ominous Future for Legal Abortion," *Chicago Tribune*, January 22, 1975, B1–B2; Mitchell Locin, "Bill to Ban Tax-Paid Abortion Is Vetoed," *Chicago Tribune*, September 14, 1977, 3; Patrick Buchanan, "Fighting Planned Parenthood," *Chicago Tribune*, November 7, 1978, B4; "8 Abortion Foes Arrested at Clinic," *Chicago Tribune*, September 9, 1979, 10.

96. Scheidler, interview. On Scheidler's techniques, see generally Joseph M. Scheidler, *Closed: 99 Ways to Stop Abortion* (Westchester, IL: Crossway Books, 1985).

97. For Cuneo's argument, see Cuneo, "Life Battles," 280–285. Faye Ginsburg, by contrast, dates the emergence of absolutism to 1983, when the Supreme Court rejected a major challenge to *Roe* and when another human life amendment failed by an eighteen vote margin in the Senate. Ginsburg, *Contested Lives*, 49–52. Ginsburg's view has merit, but it fails to account for the rise of absolutist organizations in the late 1970s.

98. Joseph M. Scheidler, "Editorial," *Illinois Right to Life Committee Newsletter* (November/December 1977), 2, PLN, Carton 1, Illinois Right to Life Committee Newsletter Folder. For expressions of frustration and desperation on the part of some abortion opponents, see Christian Action Council, "The Need for Con Con Is Pressing," *Action Line*, December 1978, WC, Action Line Folder; Ad Hoc Committee in Defense of Life, Fundraising Letter (n.d., ca. 1976), WC, Ad Hoc Committee in Defense of Life Folder (arguing that unless the pro-life movement made progress on abortion, the issue would "rip apart the very fabric of our society"); Robert Greene to NRLC Board of Directors Re: Evaluation and Critique of Past Efforts with Recommendations (May 23, 1975), 13, ACCL, Box

10, 1975 NRLC Board and Executive Committee Folder 4 ("We have arrived at a point where a different strategy is needed if we are to continue to support only a mandatory human life amendment").

99. Moral Majority, "Fighting for a Moral America in this Decade of Destiny" (1980), MMP, Record Group 1, Subgroup 1, Series 1.

100. "NRLC Says We Will Support a Candidate Who Is Pro-Life and Pro-Gay," *LAPAC Reports*, Summer 1980, WC, LAPAC Reports Folder.

101. For articulations of the views shared by members of the New Right and absolutist abortion opponents, see Brochure, "What Is the Moral Majority?" (n.d., ca. 1980), 1, MMP, Record Group 1, Subgroup 1, Series 1 (outlining the ways in which the organization was "pro-traditional family"); see also Dr. Jerry Falwell, "Why the Moral Majority?" *Moral Majority Capitol Report* (August 1979), MMP, Record Group 1, Subgroup 1, Series 1; "Guts," 1. The two groups sometimes held joint conferences. See Leslie Bennetts, "Abortion Foes, At Conference, Plan Strategy of Political Activism," *New York Times*, January 21, 1980, A18 (detailing a conference involving New Right leader Paul Weyrich and abortion opponents like Joseph Scheidler).

102. Scheidler, interview; Judie Brown, interview.

103. See Bennetts, "Abortion Foes," A18.

104. Ad Hoc Committee in Defense of Life, Fundraising Letter (October 21, 1980), 2, WC, Ad Hoc Committee in Defense of Life Folder.

105. "Pro-Life or Right to Life . . . Big Wheel or Square?" 1.

106. "Informed Consent, Abortion Restrictions Upheld," *AUL Newsletter*, December 1979, 3, WC, AUL Newsletter Folder.

107. "AUL Perspective," 6.

108. "Passage of Human Life Amendment Within Reach," *The Moral Majority Report*, December 15, 1980, MMH, Box 9, Folder 73. On Scheidler's comments on incremental restrictions, see Bennetts, "Abortion Foes," A18 (Scheidler encouraging pro-lifers to push for restrictive legislation).

109. Dave Gaetano, "Pro-Life Gains: President, 10 Senators and More," *National Right to Life News*, November 10, 1980, 1, JRS, 1980 National Right to Life News Box; "NRL PAC Proclaims Victories," *National Right to Life News*, November 10, 1980, 12, JRS, 1980 National Right to Life News Box (Dr. John Willke of NRLC explaining that the 1980 election was "a major step forward for the Right to Life Movement").

110. Jack Willke, "From the President's Desk: We Did It," *National Right to Life News*, November 10, 1980, 7, JRS, 1980 National Right to Life News Box.

111. Chapter 1 addresses Reagan's judicial-nomination strategy. This chapter later discusses the antiabortion movement's increasing interest in federal-court nominations.

112. On the effort to draft a unity amendment in the period, see "Report of NRLC Human Life Amendment Committee," *National Right to Life News*, January 27, 1981, 5, JRS, 1981 National Right to Life News Box;

"NRLC Board Reaches Historic Consensus on HLA Wording," *National Right to Life News*, October 18, 1981, 1, JRS, 1981 National Right to Life News Box. While movement attorneys had reached consensus on the broad outlines of a fetal-protective amendment, the details of such a proposal divided pro-life activists inside and outside the NRLC until members of the organization agreed on the "unity amendment" set forth in 1981.

113. On the promotion and nature of the human life bill, see Joan Beck, "The Pro-Life Groups Turn to Congress on Abortion," *Chicago Tribune*, January 30, 1981, B2; Jon Margolis, "The Abortion Struggle on Capitol Hill," *Chicago Tribune*, March 2, 1981, A2; "Senate OKs New Limit on Abortion," *Chicago Tribune*, May 22, 1981, 1–2.

114. On the human life bill, see Tribe, *The Clash of Absolutes*, 162; Suzanne Staggenborg, *The Pro-Choice Movement: Organization and Activism in the Abortion Conflict* (New York: Oxford University Press, 1991), 83; Edward Keynes and Randall K. Miller, *The Courts v. Congress: Prayer, Busing, and Abortion* (Durham, NC: Duke University Press, 1989), 296. For East's view, see The Human Life Bill: Testimony on S. 158, A Bill to Provide that Human Life Shall Be Deemed to Exist from Conception, Before the Senate Judiciary Subcommittee on Separation of Powers, 97th Congress, 1st Session (1981), 2 (Statement of Senator John East).

115. On the view that the human life bill was not constitutional, see The Human Life Bill: Testimony on S. 158, A Bill to Provide that Human Life Shall Be Deemed to Exist from Conception: Testimony Before the Senate Judiciary Subcommittee on Separation of Powers, 97th Congress, 1st Session (1981), 242–256 (Statement of Prof. Laurence Tribe); The Human Life Bill: Testimony on S. 158, A Bill to Provide that Human Life Shall Be Deemed to Exist from Conception, Before the Senate Judiciary Subcommittee on Separation of Powers, 97th Congress, 1st Session (1981) 515–519 (Statement of Prof. Norman Dorsen).

116. The Human Life Bill: Testimony on S. 158, A Bill to Provide that Human Life Shall Be Deemed to Exist from Conception, Before the Senate Judiciary Subcommittee on Separation of Powers, 97th Congress, 1st Session (1981), 309 (Statement of Prof. Robert Bork).

117. The Supreme Court would later adopt this view of Congress's power under Section Five. See *City of Boerne v. Flores*, 521 U.S. 507 (1997).

118. For Rice's view about the human life bill, see Charles Rice to Judie Brown (June 1, 1981), CRP. For Willke's support of the bill, see The Human Life Bill: Testimony on S. 158, A Bill to Provide that Human Life Shall Be Deemed to Exist from Conception, Before the Senate Judiciary Subcommittee on Separation of Powers, 97th Congress, 1st Session (1981) 1065–1080 (Statement of Dr. John Willke) (endorsing the human life bill and explaining that even a fetal-protective amendment would not affect any form of birth control, absent further legislation, unless there was "positive proof of pregnancy"). For further favorable testimony from NRLC members, see The Human Life Bill: Testimony on S. 158, A Bill to Provide

that Human Life Shall Be Deemed to Exist from Conception, Before the Senate Judiciary Subcommittee on Separation of Powers, 97th Congress, 1st Session (1981), 962–974 (Statement of Dr. Carolyn Gerster). By contrast, Wilfred Caron, a ranking legal advisor to the United States Catholic Conference, argued that the Supreme Court would likely strike down the human life bill. See Bernard Weinraub, "Issue and Debate: Determining When Life Begins and Abortion Stops," *New York Times*, April 23, 1981, B9.

119. David O'Steen, Confidential Memorandum, "The Case for a New Pro-Life Strategy—Two Amendments" (1981), CRP. For further discussion of O'Steen's role in the movement in the decade after the *Roe* decision, see Christopher Lydon, "Humphrey Leads in Minnesota, as Former Foes Rally to Him," *New York Times*, February 26, 1976, 20; Leslie Bennetts, "Antiabortion Forces in Disarray Less Than a Year After Victories in Elections," *New York Times*, September 22, 1981, B5.

120. See O'Steen, Confidential Memorandum, 1–15.

121. See Bennetts, "Antiabortion Forces," B5.

122. Charles Rice to Judie Brown (June 1, 1981), 1, CRP.

123. Ibid.

124. Bennetts, "Anti-Abortion Forces," B5.

125. Williams, interview. For further discussion of NRLC support of the Hatch Amendment, see Dave Andrusko, "Hatch Could Pass This Session, Willke Says," *National Right to Life News*, December 21, 1981, 1, JRS, 1981 National Right to Life News Box; John Willke, "From the President's Desk: The NRLC Board—A Hatch Endorsement," *National Right to Life News*, December 21, 1981, 3, JRS, 1981 National Right to Life News Box.

126. "Beware of False Friends," 1.

127. Ibid.; see also Judie Brown, "Down the Hatch: The Hatch Federalism Amendment Will Not Save Babies," 3; Paul Brown, "The Hatch-Catholic Bishops' Amendment—A Recipe for Disaster," 2.

128. Christian Action Council, *Action Line*, March 22, 1982, 4, WC, Action Line Folder. For further discussion of the antiabortion opposition to Hatch, see Cuneo, *Smoke of Satan*, 66–67.

129. Roberts, "Catholic Bishops for Amendment Allowing States to Ban Abortion," A1; see also Briggs, "The Bishops Take a Risk," B10.

130. "Anti-Abortion Group Backs Hatch Proposal," 6. For further discussion of the Hatch vote within the NRLC, see Ann O'Donnell to Charles Rice (July 25, 1981), CRP; Charles Rice to Ann O'Donnell (August 3, 1981), CRP; see also Cuneo, *The Smoke of Satan*, 66–67; Cuneo, "Life Battles," 283; Cassidy, "The Right to Life Movement," 145.

131. "President's Column: Senator Hatch, No!" *A.L.L. About Issues*, January 1982, 1, WC, A.L.L. About Issues Folder.

132. "Guts," 1. For related stories in *The Human Life Review*, see M. J. Sobran, "The Abortion Ethos," *Human Life Review* 3(1977): 19; Ellen Wilson,

"Young and Gay in Academe," *Human Life Review* 3 (Fall 1977): 96; M. J. Sobran, "Bogus Sex: Reflections on Homosexual Claims," *Human Life Review* 3 (Fall 1977): 99–100; Francis Canavan, "ERA: The New Legal Frontier?" *Human Life Review* 4 (Fall 1978): 75; Janet E. Smith, "Abortion as a Feminist Concern," *Human Life Review* 4 (Summer 1978): 70.

133. Bernard Weinraub, "Abortion Curbs Endorsed, 10–7, by Senate Panel," *New York Times*, March 11, 1982, A1.

134. Ibid. On the lead-up to the Senate panel vote, see "Helms Offers New Anti-Abortion Bill," *Chicago Tribune*, March 2, 1982, 3; "Senate Panel OKs Antiabortion Amendment," *Chicago Tribune*, December 17, 1981, A5.

135. On the filibuster and subsequent failed vote, see Robert Pear, "Filibuster Starts Abortion Debate," *New York Times*, August 17, 1982, A18; Robert Pear, "Baker Sets Vote Day After Labor Day on Ending Filibuster on Abortion and School Prayer," *New York Times*, August 21, 1982, 9; Steven Roberts, "Senate Kills Plan to Curb Abortion by a Vote of 47–46," *New York Times*, September 16, 1982, A1. On the new Democratic majority in the House, see Steven Roberts, "Democrats Regain Control in House," *New York Times*, November 4, 1982, A19. On the failure of the Hatch-Eagleton Amendment, see National Committee for a Human Life Amendment, "Human Life Amendment: Major Texts, 1973–2003" 1–2, accessed February 14, 2014, http://www.nchla.org/datasource/idocuments/HLAmajortexts.pdf.

136. *City of Akron v. Akron Reproductive Health Center*, 462 U.S. 416, 458 (1983) (O'Connor, J., dissenting).

137. On the movement's focus on Supreme Court nominations in the post-*Akron I* period, see Richard Davis, *Electing Justice: Fixing the Supreme Court Nomination Process* (New York: Oxford University Press, 2005), 84–85, 109, 111; Cassidy, "The Right to Life Movement," 147.

138. Erik Eckholm, "Anti-Abortion Groups Split on Legal Tactics," *New York Times*, Dec. 5, 2011, A1.

139. James T. McCafferty, "The Perils of Promoting Personhood," *The New Oxford Review* 79 (2012): 24. For further discussion of contemporary conflict about the personhood movement, see Lauren Markoe, "After Mississippi Defeat, What About Personhood?" *Christian Century*, December 13, 2011, 18; Cheryl Wetzstein, "State Abortion Curbs Rose in '11," *Washington Times*, January 9, 2012, A6 (detailing personhood battles in states like Mississippi and Colorado); Steve Siebelius, "What It Means to Be 'Pro-Life,'" *Las Vegas Review Journal*, January 18, 2012, 7B (describing Nevada battle); Annysa Johnson, "Equal Rights for the Unborn Proposed," *Milwaukee Journal Sentinel*, December 27, 2011, 1 (describing Wisconsin campaign); Erik Eckholm, "The Christian Vote: 'Personhood' Issue Hangs On," *New York Times*, December 23, 2011, A22 (explaining that personhood movement was still active in spite of major defeat in Mississippi).

140. McCafferty, "The Perils of Promoting Personhood," 24.

Chapter 3. Women's Rights versus Population Control

1. Jesse Jackson, "Country Preacher," *Chicago Defender*, March 24, 1973, 29. For further discussion of Jackson's involvement with the antiabortion movement, see NRLC Ad Hoc Strategy Meeting Minutes (February 11, 1973), 14, ACCL, Box 4, 1973 National Right to Life Committee Folder 1 (pro-lifer Herbert Ratner reporting that Jackson "wanted to be counted in this Right to Life group"); Jesse Jackson, "How We Respect Life Is Over-Riding Moral Issue," *National Right to Life News*, January 1977, 5, JRS, 1977 National Right to Life Box.

2. Jackson, "Country Preacher," 29. On the number of women of color seeking abortions immediately after the *Roe* decision, see Barbara Campbell, "City Blacks Get Most Abortions: Lead With 47.6%, Though Whites Outnumber Them," *New York Times*, December 6, 1973, 94. Civil-rights leaders demanding "black power" also made this claim in the mid- to late 1960s, as this chapter later explores.

3. "Key Sections from Transcripts of Democrats' Debate in Iowa," *New York Times*, February 13, 1984, B6; see also "Jackson the Orator Has Become Jackson the Politician," *Los Angeles Times*, November 27, 1983, 1.

4. Martha Minow, "1986 Term Foreword: Justice Engendered," *Harvard Law Review* 101 (1987): 86n360.

5. Robin West, "From Choice to Reproductive Justice: De-Constitutionalizing Abortion Rights," *Yale Law Journal* 118 (2009): 1411.

6. Joan Williams, "Gender Wars: Selfless Women in the Republic of Choice," *New York University Law Review* 66 (1991): 1577. For further arguments in this vein, see Rhonda Copelon, "Unpacking Patriarchy: Reproduction, Sexuality, Originalism, and Constitutional Change," in *A Less Than Perfect Union: Alternative Perspectives on the United States Constitution*, ed. Jules Lobel (New York: Monthly Review Press, 1988), 303–334; Catharine MacKinnon, "*Roe v. Wade*: A Study in Male Ideology," in *Abortion, Moral and Legal Perspectives*, eds. Jay L. Garfield and Patricia Hennessey (Amherst: University of Massachusetts Press, 1984), 45–53. Historians have raised similar criticisms in discussing the impact of *Roe* on the relationship between the women's movement and women of color. See Jennifer Nelson, *Women of Color and the Reproductive Rights Movement* (New York: New York University Press, 2003), 171 (describing how threats to *Roe* encouraged "[m]ainstream white activists" to again make "abortion top priority" and made it difficult to "sell [a] broader economic agenda as part of mainstream feminist politics"); Rickie Solinger, *Beggars and Choosers: How the Politics of Choice Shapes Adoption, Abortion, and Welfare in the United States* (New York: Farrar, Straus, and Giroux, 2001), 10 ("In the period immediately following *Roe v. Wade*, unofficial, extra-legislative public policy continued to target women of color in ways that clarified dramatically the limits of the Court's ruling"); Rebecca M. Kluchin, *Fit*

To Be Tied: Sterilization and Reproductive Rights in America, 1950–1980 (Piscataway, NJ: Rutgers University Press, 2009), 120 (explaining how the ACLU prioritized abortion, rather than other reproductive-rights issues, after *Roe*).

7. For scholarship identifying the abortion-rights movement with a particular view of women's rights, see Kristin Luker, *Abortion and the Politics of Motherhood* (Berkeley: University California Press, 1984), 112–113 (explaining that abortion had not always been a central feminist demand but connecting feminism to the "reasons that so many women took up the language of women's rights, and eventually insisted on nothing less than abortion on demand"); Faye D. Ginsburg, *Contested Lives: The Abortion Debate in an American Community* (Berkeley: University of California Press, 1998), 17 (explaining that interactions with second-wave feminism proved foundational for pro-choice activists' mobilization); William N. Eskridge Jr. "Channeling: Identity-Based Social Movements and Public Law," *University of Pennsylvania Law Review* 150 (2001): 455 (narrating "the creation of the pro-choice movement as a branch of the women's movement"). For an example of arguments on the ways in which *Roe* constrained feminists, see West, "From Choice to Reproductive Justice," 1423 ("*Roe v. Wade* and the right it articulates [became] a chapter in a narrative authored, developed, and controlled by the Court, rather than part of a narrative of women's rights authored, developed, and controlled by feminists, progressives, or other women's rights devotees").

8. On the role of race in the anti-vice crusade, see Nicola Kay Beisel, *Imperiled Innocents: Anthony Comstock and Family Reproduction in Victorian America* (Princeton: Princeton University Press, 1997), 10–11, 107 (explaining how anti-immigrant sentiment and concern among the elite about immigrants' increasing political power fueled anti-vice campaigns); see also Nicola Beisel and Tamara Kay, "Abortion, Race, and Gender in Nineteenth Century America," *American Sociological Review* 69 (2004): 498–518.

9. On the use of racial bias by the eugenic movement, see Wendy Kline, *Building a Better Race: Gender, Sexuality, and Eugenics from the Turn of the Century to the Baby Boom* (Berkeley: University of California Press, 2001), 2–17, 32–49; Alexandra M. Stern, *Eugenic Nation: Faults and Frontiers of Better Breeding in Modern America* (Berkeley: University of California Press, 2005), 4–5, 9–10, 85–86. On the rise of a more race-specific policy of reproductive control after World War II, see Rickie Solinger, *Wake Up Little Susie: Single Pregnancy Before* Roe v. Wade (New York: Routledge, 2000), 10, 230, 234; see also generally Johanna Schoen, *Choice and Coercion: Birth Control, Sterilization, and Abortion in Public Health and Welfare* (Chapel Hill: University of North Carolina Press, 2005).

10. Brief as Amicus Curiae for Women for the Unborn, 16, *Roe v. Wade*, 410 U.S. 113 (1973) (Nos. 70–18, 70–40).

11. For a sample of the medical or rights-based arguments made before 1973 by mainstream abortion-legalization organizations, see Meeting Minutes, Planned Parenthood-World Population Board of Directors (May 8, 1969), 10–11, PPFA I, Box 49, Folder 19 (emphasizing that abortion was "a medical procedure" that should be "governed by the same rules as apply to any other medical procedure"); "New Group Will Seek Changes in Abortion Laws," *New York Times*, February 17, 1969, 32 (describing the formation of NARAL and setting forth the resolution passed by the organization stating that "the decision for or against abortion should be made without legal encumbrances, so that women and physicians may be able to exercise their best judgments"); Myra MacPherson, "M.D.s File Abortion Lawsuit," *Washington Post*, September 30, 1969, B1. On the various positions on abortion taken by population-control organizations, see Donald T. Critchlow, *Intended Consequences: Birth Control, Abortion, and the Federal Government in Modern America* (New York: Oxford University Press, 1999), 8, 147, 177–178. For further discussion of the population-control movement, see Simone M. Caron, *Who Chooses? American Reproductive History Since 1850* (Gainesville: University Press of Florida, 2008), 150–151, 153–155, 160–163; Matthew Connelly, *Fatal Misconception: The Struggle to Control World Population* (Cambridge, MA: Harvard University Press, 2008); Donald T. Critchlow, "Birth Control, Population, and Family Planning: An Overview," in *The Politics of Abortion and Birth Control in Historical Perspective*, ed. Donald T. Critchlow (University Park: Penn State University Press, 1996), 1–22.

12. For polls demonstrating the popularity of population-control reforms, see Ernest B. Furgurson, "Zero Population Growth Isn't Zero," *Los Angeles Times*, January 30, 1972, 17 (reporting that 65 percent of Americans believed that population growth was a serious problem). On the involvement of Rockefeller and of the Scaife Foundation in abortion and population politics, see Critchlow, *Intended Consequences*, 27–28, 136, 147, 151. Moore's involvement will be discussed later in the chapter.

13. Hugh Moore to Ruth Proskauer Smith (October 19, 1962), HMP, Box 15, Folder 6. On the use of the term "underdeveloped" country, see Daniel J. Kevles, *In the Name of Eugenics: Genetics and Human Heredity* (Berkeley: University of California Press, 1985), 258. On the priorities of first-generation population controllers, see Connelly, *Fatal Misconception*, 134–151, 168–258; Critchlow, *Intended Consequences*, 3–13, 143–160. For examples of the initiatives pursued by the Population Council, see Jane Brody, "Population Group Offers Care Plan," *New York Times*, April 20, 1971, 36; "Tunisia Puts Hope in Birth Control," *New York Times*, December 27, 1964, 21. AVS was founded in 1929 in order to study the psychological, physical, and sexual effects of compulsory eugenic sterilization. See Kline, *Building a Better Race*, 184; Edward J. Larson, *Sex, Race, and Science: Eugenics in the Deep South* (Baltimore: Johns Hopkins University Press, 1995), 149–152, 161; Ian Dowbiggin, *The Sterilization Movement*

and Global Fertility in the Twentieth Century (New York: Oxford University Press, 2008), 147, 157.

14. John D. Rockefeller III, "On the Origins of the Population Council," *Population and Development Review* 3 (1977): 496, 502.

15. Hugh Moore, "Voluntary Sterilization: Is It an Answer to the Population Bomb?" (December 1959), 14, HMP, Box 20, Folder 5 (citation and quotation omitted). For further discussion of Moore's career in the movement, see Critchlow, *Intended Consequences*, 5, 16, 29–33, 66–68, 229; Elaine Tyler May, *America and the Pill: A History of Promise, Peril, and Liberation* (New York: Basic Books, 2010), 49–52; Connelly, *Fatal Misconception*, 162, 199, 231, 248, 296.

16. Hugh Moore to Bill Draper (August 10, 1965), HMP, Box 1, Folder 19.

17. Ruth Moss, "Population—Our Most Pressing Problem," *Chicago Tribune*, March 2, 1970, B11.

18. John Sibley, "'Wanted' Babies Said to Cause U.S. Population Explosion," *New York Times*, November 14, 1968, 26; Judy Klemesrud, "To Them, Two Children Are Fine, but Three Crowd the World," *New York Times*, January 12, 1971, 30 (a member of ZPG arguing that it did not make a difference "whether the family can support all those children or not").

19. For Ehrlich's personal story: Paul Ehrlich, interview with Mary Ziegler, February 11, 2011. For a sample of Ehrlich's writings on the subject, see Paul Ehrlich, *The Population Bomb* (New York: Ballantine, 1968). On his views and career, see Connelly, *Fatal Misconception*, 258–259, 264, 273; Kluchin, *Fit to Be Tied*, 34, 86–87.

20. Ehrlich, interview. For further discussion of ZPG's activities in the period, see Critchlow, *Intended Consequences*, 90, 135, 156–158; Connelly, *Fatal Misconception*, 248–269; Roy Beck and Leon Kolankiewicz, "The Environmental Movement's Retreat from Advocating United States Population Stabilization (1970–1990): A First Draft of History," in *Environmental Politics and Policy, 1960s–1990s*, ed. Otis Graham (University Park: Penn State University Press, 2000), 123–139.

21. For Senderowitz's individual journey: Judy Senderowitz, interview with Mary Ziegler, February 10, 2010. Senderowitz went on to write extensively on the subject. See Ellen Peck and Judith Senderowitz, *Pronatalism: The Myth of Mom and Apple Pie* (New York: Cromwell, 1974); Judith Kunofsky and Judith Senderowitz, *The One Child Family* (New York: Zero Population Growth, 1976). For further discussion of ZPG's role in abortion politics, see Suzanne Staggenborg, *The Pro-Choice Movement: Organization and Activism in the Abortion Conflict* (New York: Oxford University Press, 1991), 9, 53, 18–19, 162–164.

22. Ehrlich, *The Population Bomb,* 135.

23. Jane Brody, "More Than 100,000 Persons a Year Are Reported Seeking Sterilization as Method of Contraception," *New York Times*, March 22, 1970, 62.

24. Daniel C. Beggs and Henry Copeland, "On the Campus: Some Students Offer Methods for Curbing World Population," *Chicago Tribune*, November 7, 1970, 2. For ZPG's use of these slogans, see Klemesrud, "To Them, Two Children Are Fine," 30; "Looking into The ZPGeneration," *Time Magazine*, February 28, 1977, 71–72.

25. Klemesrud, "To Them, Two Children Are Fine," 30. On Moore's involvement in the founding of Earth Day, see Dowbiggin, *The Sterilization Movement*, 154, 194; Thomas Robertson, *The Malthusian Moment: Global Population Growth and the Birth of American Environmentalism* (Piscataway, NJ: Rutgers University Press, 2012), 152.

26. See "Forum Set on Abortion," *Hartford Courant*, April 9, 1969, 10B; Kit Barrett, "Women's Rights: Where Have All the Shrinking Violets Gone," *Chicago Tribune*, May 17, 1970, SCL4 (describing the participation of Illinois branch of ZPG in a repeal rally); Elaine Johnson, "Abortion Law Repeal Pondered at Parley," *Hartford Courant*, January 17, 1971, 9A (describing participation of state-level ZPG affiliate in abortion repeal discussion).

27. See Staggenborg, *The Pro-Choice Movement*, 19. For individuals' memories of these divisions: Senderowitz, interview; Ehrlich, interview.

28. See "The Abortion Report," *Chicago Tribune*, March 20, 1972, 20. The report stated that "there is little doubt that legal and illegal abortions exert a downward influence on the United States birthrate." *Population and the American Future: The Report of the Commission on Population Growth and the American Future* (New York: New American Library, 1972), 137, 171, 178, 189–190.

29. Laurie Johnston, "Nationwide Drive for Abortion Planned in 3-Day Session Here," *New York Times*, July 20, 1971, 30.

30. Furgurson, "Zero Population Growth," 17. The chapter later discusses the practical attraction of population claims for NARAL, NOW, and Planned Parenthood. On the overlapping membership and leadership of ZPG and NARAL, see Staggenborg, *The Pro-Choice Movement*, 19, 38, 53; James R. Kelly, "Beyond Compromise: *Casey*, Common Ground, and the Pro-Life Movement," in *Abortion Politics in the American States*, eds. Mary C. Segers and Timothy Byrnes (Armonk, NY: M. E. Sharpe, 1995), 211. On bipartisan support for population-control legislation, see Nan Robertson, "Nixon Considers Proposal for a Commission on Domestic Population Problem," *New York Times*, June 11, 1969, 20.

31. The 1971 Virginia Slims American Women's Opinion Poll (New York: Louis Harris and Associates, 1971) (finding that 42 percent of women favored efforts to "strengthen or change women's status in society," while 43 percent opposed those efforts). On the lack of interest in feminist arguments among abortion reformers in the state legislatures, see Caron, *Who Chooses?* 192. For an overview of feminist demands in the period, see Sara M. Evans, "Foreword," in *Feminist Coalitions: Historical Perspectives*

on Second Wave Feminism in the United States, ed. Stephanie Gilmore (Champaign: University of Illinois Press, 2008), vi–x.

32. On the disproportionate rate of abortions in the African-American community in New York following legalization, see Philip Wechsler, "State's Abortion Rate Soaring," *New York Times*, November 25, 1973, 97; Campbell, "City Blacks Get Most Abortions," 94.

33. Planned Parenthood leader William Vogt had been heavily involved in population politics. See "William Vogt, Former Director of Planned Parenthood, Is Dead," *New York Times*, July 12, 1968, 31. For a sample of Vogt's writings on family planning and population control, see William Vogt, *The Road to Survival* (New York: William Sloane Associates, 1948); William Vogt, *People! Challenge to Survival* (New York: William Sloane Associates, 1960). On Moore's role in helping Planned Parenthood, see Larry Lader, *Breeding Ourselves to Death* (New York: Ballantine Books, 1971), 10, 14. On the creation of PP-WP, see Critchlow, *Intended Consequences*, 67–71. William Draper, a leader of the PCC and the population movement, also worked to raise money for PP-WP. See John C. Robbins to William Draper (July 30, 1973), PPFA II, Box 110, Folder 45; John C. Robbins to William Draper (January 10, 1973), PPFA II, Box 110, Folder 45; Western Electric Company, Response to William Draper (August 11, 1967), PPFA II, Box 110, Folder 45; D. Miller of Eastman Kodak to William Draper (August 9, 1965), PPFA II, Box 110, Folder 45.

34. Mary Steichen Calderone, "Illegal Abortion as a Public Health Problem," *American Journal of Public Health* 50 (1960): 951.

35. Harriet Pilpel, "The Right of Abortion," *The Atlantic*, June 1969, 69–71. For further discussion of Pilpel's position on abortion and women's rights, see David J. Garrow, *Liberty and Sexuality: The Right to Privacy and the Making of Roe v. Wade* (Berkeley: University of California Press, 1998), 296; Susan M. Hartmann, *The Other Feminists: Activists in the Liberal Establishment* (New Haven, CT: Yale University Press, 1998), 85–88. On Planned Parenthood's activities in the 1960s, see Connelly, *Fatal Misconception*, 247; Critchlow, *Intended Consequences*, 67–68, 151–155.

36. Morris Kaplan, "Abortion and Sterilization Win Support of Planned Parenthood," *New York Times*, November 14, 1968, 50. For further discussion of the Planned Parenthood endorsement, see Meeting Minutes, Planned Parenthood-World Population Board of Directors (May 8, 1969), 10–11.

37. Meeting Minutes, Planned Parenthood-World Population Board of Directors (May 8, 1969), 11.

38. Kaplan, "Abortion and Sterilization Win Support of Planned Parenthood," 50.

39. On Guttmacher's life, see Garrow, *Liberty and Sexuality*, 270–275. For a discussion of Guttmacher's involvement with the American Eugenics Society, see Frederick Osborn to Dr. Alan Guttmacher (April 21, 1965), PPFA II, Box 104, Folder 25; Frederick Osborn to Dr. Alan Guttmacher

(March 9, 1964), PPFA II, Box 104, Folder 25; Frederick Osborn to Alan Guttmacher (May 20, 1963), PPFA II, Box 104, Folder 25. On Guttmacher's involvement with AVS, see Kluchin, *Fit to Be Tied*, 35; Connelly, *Fatal Misconception*, 207. On Guttmacher's image and reputation: Robin Elliott, interview with Mary Ziegler, August 12, 2011; Robin Elliott, interview with Mary Ziegler, February 12, 2011.

40. "Abortion Reform Termed Fantastic," *Hartford Courant*, March 31, 1970, 16. For further discussion of Guttmacher's attitudes toward population control, see David Dempsey, "Dr. Guttmacher Is the Evangelist of Birth Control," *New York Times*, February 9, 1969, SM32.

41. See "Facts and Figures on Abortion of Interest to All Americans" (1972), PPFA II, Box 93, Folder 84. For Elliott's recollections of these campaigns: Elliott, February interview; Elliott, August interview.

42. On Millstone: Elliott, August interview. For a sample of Millstone's writings on the subject, see, e.g., Dorothy L. Millstone, *Family Planning, Population Problems, and the Secondary School* (New York: Planned Parenthood Federation of America, 1966); Dorothy Millstone, *Family Planning: Today's Choice* (New York: Public Affairs Committee, 1974).

43. "New Group Will Seek Changes in Abortion Laws," 32. For more on the founding of NARAL, see Myra MacPherson, "Abortion Laws: A Call for Repeal," *Washington Post*, February 17, 1969, D1; Lyle Lilliston, "National Group to End Abortion Laws Formed," *Los Angeles Times*, February 18, 1969, E1.

44. Senderowitz, interview. For discussion of Lader's background, see Flora Davis, *Moving the Mountain: The Women's Movement Since 1960* (Champaign: University of Illinois Press, 1999), 164–172, 180; Garrow, *Liberty and Sexuality*, 295, 300, 318–319, 346, 350. For Lader's book on abortion, see Lawrence Lader, *Abortion* (Boston: Beacon Press, 1966).

45. On the divisions between radicals and pragmatists on the NARAL Planning Committee, see Ruth Cusack et al. to the NARAL Board of Directors (September 10, 1969), 2, LLP, Box 8, Folder 20 (describing disagreements about the degree to which NARAL should participate in grassroots protests or endorse abortion referral services); Conni Finnerty et al. to NARAL Board of Directors (August 30, 1969), LLP, Box 8, Folder 20 (supporting efforts to make referral services and grassroots protests a central part of NARAL's work); Lonny Myers, MD, Letter to Board Member (September 11, 1969), 1–4, LLP, Box 8, Folder 20 (detailing position of Myers and her allies in opposing emphasis on certain grassroots protests and referral services); Ruth Cusack, Addendum (September 10, 1969), LLP, Box 8, Folder 20 (siding with Myers in debate about protests and referral services). On Friedan's background, see Betty Friedan, *Life So Far: A Memoir* (New York: Simon and Schuster, 2000), 106–180; Daniel Horowitz, *Betty Friedan and the Making of the Feminine Mystique: The American Left, the Cold War, and Modern Feminism* (Amherst: University of

Massachusetts Press, 2000), 216–252. For the text of the *Feminine Mystique*: Betty Friedan, *The Feminine Mystique* (New York: W. W. Norton, 1963).

46. For a summary of the positions taken by both sides, see Conni Finnerty et al. to NARAL Board of Directors (August 30, 1969), 1; Ruth Cusack et al. to NARAL Board of Directors (September 10, 1969), 1–2.

47. On the September compromise, see Agenda—NARAL Board of Directors Meeting, 2 (September 27, 1969), LLP, Box 8, Folder 20 (listing as priorities for NARAL "the formation in every state of at least one repeal group" and emphasizing that "direct action programs created by NARAL for local groups be executed and sponsored by local groups and not by NARAL"); New Business: General Areas and Specific Motions (n.d., ca. September 1969), LLP, Box 8, Folder 20 (taking the same position on direct NARAL involvement with grassroots protests); NARAL Executive Committee Minutes (September 28, 1969), 1, NRL, Carton 1, 1969 Executive Committee Minutes Folder (outlining as early priorities the drafting of an amicus brief and the "organization of constituent groups," members of which could carry out protests in NARAL's place); NARAL National Board Meeting Minutes (September 27, 1969), 1–2, NRL, Carton 1, NARAL Board Minutes Folder (endorsing the position on direct action protests outlined in the meeting agenda).

48. Lucinda Cisler to NARAL Board of Directors, "Resolution Proposed for Adoption by the NARAL Board of Directors at Its September 27 Meeting" (August 28, 1969), 1, NRL, Carton 1, NARAL Board Minutes Folder.

49. Ibid., 1.

50. NARAL Board of Directors, Meeting Minutes (September 27, 1969), 1.

51. NARAL Executive Committee Meeting Minutes (January 20, 1970), 1, NRL, Carton 1, 1970 Executive Committee Folder.

52. Ibid., 1.

53. See NARAL Executive Committee Meeting Minutes (February 24, 1970), 3, NRL, Carton 1, 1970 Executive Committee Folder (Friedan arguing that NARAL's Mother Day demonstration "should tie into the environment issue because she had found so much respect when she tied the two issues together").

54. NARAL Board of Directors Meeting Minutes (September 28, 1970), 2–3, NRL, Carton 1, NARAL Board Minutes Folder.

55. Lee Gidding to Frances Young (October 26, 1971), NRL, Carton 7, National 1971–1973 Folder. On NARAL's work with ZPG in state campaigns, see Mary Ziegler, "The Framing of a Right to Choose: *Roe v. Wade* and the Changing Debate on Abortion Law," *Law and History Review* 27 (2009): 313–314. On NARAL's joining media sessions with Planned Parenthood and ZPG, see Karen Mulhauser to Participants in St. Louis and Washington ZPG/Planned Parenthood Media Workshops (n.d., ca. 1974), NRL, Carton 9, Zero Population Growth Folder. For the resolution endorsing an increase in funding for population research, see "Resolution

Adopted by the Executive Committee on November 27, 1972" (November 1972), NRL, Carton 1, 1972 Executive Committee Folder.

56. *NARAL Speaker and Debater's Notebook* excerpt (n.d., ca. 1972), Carton 7, 1972 Debating the Opposition Folder.

57. See Ronald Kotulak, "Fears Backlash to Abortion Law Repeal," *Chicago Tribune*, February 16, 1969, 14. For more on divisions about the question of repeal versus reform, see Garrow, *Liberty and Sexuality*, 305, 346, 358; Linda Greenhouse and Reva B. Siegel, "Repeal," in Roe v. Wade: *Voices That Shaped the Abortion Debate before the Supreme Court's Ruling*, eds. Linda Greenhouse and Reva B. Siegel, 2nd ed. (New Haven, CT: Yale Law Library, 2012), 35; Leslie J. Reagan, *Dangerous Pregnancies: Mothers, Disabilities, and Abortion in Modern America* (Berkeley: University of California Press, 2010), 156–169.

58. See, for example, Lucinda Cisler to NARAL Board of Directors, Resolution Proposed for Adoption by the NARAL Board of Directors at Its September 27 Meeting (August 28, 1969), 1. For further discussion of the importance of establishing NARAL's legitimacy and respectability, see NARAL Executive Committee Meeting Minutes (February 24, 1970), 3, NRL, Carton 1, 1970 Executive Committee Folder (Friedan urging her colleagues to adopt an approach that had won her respect); NARAL Executive Committee Meeting Minutes (January 14, 1972), 2, NRL, Carton 1, 1972 Executive Committee Folder (Lonny Myers sharing a presentation that emphasized the respectability of the organizations endorsing repeal while highlighting "the religious composition of the opposition").

59. Draft, NOW Statement of Purpose (October 19, 1966), BFP, Carton 126, Folder 1544; see also Maryann Barasko, *Governing NOW: Grassroots Activism in the National Organization for Women* (Ithaca, NY: Cornell University Press, 2004), 10–15. For individual recollections of the founding of NOW: Karen DeCrow, interview with Mary Ziegler, February 3, 2011; Mary Jean Collins, interview with Mary Ziegler, October 20, 2011.

60. DeCrow, interview.

61. Barasko, *Governing NOW*, 12; see also NOW Board Meeting Agenda (November 20, 1966), 1, BFP, Carton 126, Folder 1544 (listing ideas for task forces on education, employment, political rights and responsibilities, the image of women, and poverty). For the personal stories of individual members: DeCrow, interview; Collins, interview.

62. Minutes of the National Organization for Women Conference (November 18–19, 1967), 2, BFP, Carton 127, Folder 1553. For the text of the proposal debated by NOW members, see NOW Proposed Resolution: "The Right of a Woman to Determine Her Own Reproductive Process" (1967), 1–2, BFP, Carton 127, Folder 1553. For further discussion of the NOW abortion debate, see Staggenborg, *The Pro-Choice Movement*, 20–23; Barasko, *Governing NOW*, 41–42; Greenhouse and Siegel, *Before* Roe v. Wade, 36.

63. Minutes of the National Organization for Women Conference (November 18–19, 1967), 2, 4.

64. See ibid., 5. On the founding and function of WEAL: Christopher Loss, *Between Citizens and the State: The Politics of American Higher Education in the Twentieth Century* (Princeton: Princeton University Press, 2012), 197; Amy Erdman Farrell, *Yours in Sisterhood: "Ms." Magazine and the Promise of Popular Feminism* (Chapel Hill: University of North Carolina Press, 1998), 17; William Henry Chafe, *Women and Equality: Changing Patterns in American Culture* (New York: Oxford University Press, 1977), 97. For a personal recollection of the split between NOW and WEAL: DeCrow, interview.

65. Betty Friedan, "Abortion: A Woman's Civil Right: Keynote Speech before the First National Conference for the Repeal of Abortion Laws" (February 14, 1969), 1, BFP, Box 121, Folder 1467; see also Resolution Adopted in Chicago (1968), BFP, Box 121, Folder 1456. On the NOW Abortion Committee: see Staggenborg, *The Pro-Choice Movement*, 20, 24. For a personal recollection of the early NOW Abortion Committee: Carol Downer, interview with Mary Ziegler, February 7, 2012. For Maginnis and Phelan's writings on abortion: see Pat Maginnis, "Elective Abortion as a Woman's Right," in *The Case for Legalized Abortion Now*, ed. Alan Guttmacher (Pleasant Hill, CA: Diablo Press, 1967), 26–53; Pat Maginnis and Lana Clarke Phelan, *The Abortion Handbook for Responsible Women* (Canoga Park, CA: Weiss, Day, and Lord, 1970).

66. Friedan, "Abortion: A Woman's Civil Right," 1.

67. For a sample of Heide's work on the connection between nursing, public health, and women's rights, see Wilma Scott Heide, *Feminism for the Health of It* (Buffalo, NY: Margaretdaughters, 1975); Wilma Scott Heide, President of NOW, "Statement in Support of Public Law 91–213, 92nd Congress, *An Act to Establish a Commission on Population Growth and the American Future*" (April 15, 1971), WSH, Box 11, Folder 12. For individual recollections of Heide and her career: DeCrow, interview; Collins, interview.

68. Wilma Scott Heide to NOW Board of Directors et al. (December 13, 1970), WSH, Box 14, Folder 7. For Tietze's original letter, see Christopher Tietze to Wilma Scott Heide (November 5, 1970), 1–2, WSH, Box 14, Folder 7.

69. Wilma Scott Heide to Meg Letterman (October 10, 1973), 1, WSH, Box 11, Folder 13. On Heide's testimony before the Rockefeller Commission, see *Statements at Public Hearings of the Commission on Population Growth and the American Future* (Washington, DC: US Government Printing Office, 1974), 7–8. For more on Heide's views on feminism and population growth, see Wilma Scott Heide, "Maude: To See or not to See" (August 17, 1973), 1, NRL, Carton 1, 1974–1975 Executive Committee Minutes Folder.

70. See Wilma Scott Heide to Meg Letterman (October 10, 1973), 1 (describing and celebrating the partnership between the organizations). On the 1971 Conference session, see National Conference Planning Subcommittee to

NOW National Committee, "Proposed Agenda 1971 Conference" (May 18, 1971), 2, BFP, Carton 128, Folder 1583. On NOW's work with the Ford Foundation, see Wilma Scott Heide to NOW Members (February 19, 1972), 5, WSH, Box 12, Folder 14. On the feedback offered by NOW members about the possibility of working with the Population Council, see Handwritten Tally of Responses from Board and Chapters (n.d., ca. 1972), WSH, Box 14, Folder 7.

71. Motion for Leave to File Brief and Brief Amici Curiae on Behalf of Women's Organizations and Named Women, 35, *Roe v. Wade*, 410 U.S. 113 (1973) (Nos. 70–18, 70–40); see also Motion for Leave to File a Brief with Brief as Amici Curiae of Planned Parenthood Federation of America et al., 28–29, *Roe v. Wade*, 410 U.S. 113 (1973) (Nos. 70–18, 70–40).

72. Dr. Joseph Stanton to Friends for the Unborn (August 29, 1978), JRS, Dr. Joseph Stanton Papers; Dr. Joseph Stanton to Patrick Trueman (July 12, 1979), JRS, Dr. Joseph Stanton Papers (arguing that Margaret Sanger's connections to the movements for eugenics and population control should "be made a top research priority" for Americans United for Life).

73. For discussion of the NRLC's relationship with Jesse Jackson, see NRLC Ad Hoc Strategy Meeting Minutes (February 11, 1973), 14. For Barron's recollections of working with Jackson: Thea Rossi Barron, interview with Mary Ziegler, April 23, 2012.

74. See Nelson, *Women of Color*, 7–10, 114, 184–188; Linda Gordon, *The Moral Property of Women: A History of Birth Control Politics in America* (Champaign: University of Illinois Press, 2002), 289–294, 345–347; Rickie Solinger, *Pregnancy and Power: A Short History of Reproductive Politics in America* (New York: New York University Press, 2005), 193–203; Loretta Ross, "African American Women and Abortion," in *Abortion Wars: A Half-Century of Struggle, 1950–2000*, ed. Rickie Solinger (Berkeley: University of California Press, 1998), 183–185.

75. Stokely Carmichael with Ekwueme Michael Thelwell, *Ready for Revolution: The Life and Struggles of Stokely Carmichael (Kwame Ture)* (New York: Scribner's, 2003), 507.

76. Jeffrey O. G. Ogbar, *Black Power: Radical Politics and African American Identity* (Baltimore: Johns Hopkins University Press, 2004), 146.

77. Stokely Carmichael and Charles Hamilton, *Black Power: The Politics of Liberation in America* (New York: Vintage Books, 1967), viii. On the history of black power ideology earlier in the politics of civil rights, see Clayborne Carson, *In Struggle: SNCC and the Black Awakening of the 1960s*, 2nd ed. (Cambridge, MA: Harvard University Press, 1995), 1–9; Christopher B. Strain, *Pure Fire: Self-Defense as Activism in the Civil Rights Era* (Athens: University of Georgia, 2005), 1–8; Lance Hill, *The Deacons for Defense: Armed Resistance and the Civil Rights Movement* (Chapel Hill: University of North Carolina Press, 2004), 1–10; William L. Van Deburg, *New Day in Babylon: The Black Power Movement and American Culture, 1965–1975*, 2nd ed. (Chicago: University of Chicago Press, 1993), 1–11,

29–62; Ogbar, *Black Power*, 1–12; Cedric Johnson, *Revolutionaries to Race Leaders: Black Power and the Making of African American Politics* (Minneapolis: University of Minnesota Press, 2007), xix–xxxvi; Waldo E. Martin, *No Coward Soldiers: Black Cultural Politics in Postwar America* (Cambridge, MA: Harvard University Press, 2005), 1–10. For contemporary press coverage of CORE and black power, see "McKissick Defines 'Black Power,'" *Chicago Defender*, July 11, 1966, 5; "McKissick Cites Positive Black Power," *Chicago Defender*, February 7, 1968, 12. On the founding of the Black Panther Party, see Lawrence Swaim, "An Interview with a Black Panther," *North American Review* 253 (July–August 1968): 27–34; "The Black Panther Ten-Point Program," *North American Review* 253 (July–August 1968): 16–17.

78. See Van Deburg, *New Day in Babylon*, 32–44; Hill, *The Deacons for Defense*, 3, 60, 269–272; Strain, *Pure Fire*, 1–12, 27–30.

79. Carson, *In Struggle*, 3.

80. Jonathan Rieder, *The Word of the Lord Is upon Me: The Righteous Performance of Martin Luther King, Jr.* (Cambridge, MA: Harvard University Press, 2008), 42. For further analysis of the rise of black power politics in the 1960s, see Strain, *Pure Fire*, 78–97, 145–175; Van Deburg, *New Day in Babylon*, 32–43; Donna Jean Murch, *Living for the City: Migration, Education, and the Rise of the Black Panther Party in Oakland, California* (Chapel Hill: University of North Carolina Press, 2010), 1–24.

81. Jackson, "How We Respect Life Is Over-Riding Moral Issue," 5.

82. Dick Gregory, "My Answer to Genocide," *Ebony Magazine*, October 1971, 66. For further discussion of the rise of the black-genocide argument, see Nelson, *Women of Color*, 85–99; Ross, "African American Women and Abortion," 180–182; Critchlow, *Intended Consequences*, 101, 110, 141–143, 188; Leslie J. Reagan, *When Abortion Was a Crime: Women, Medicine, and Law in the United States, 1867–1973* (Berkeley: University of California Press, 1997), 231–232.

83. Shirley Chisholm, "Facing the Abortion Question," in *Black Women in White America: A Documentary History*, ed. Gerda Lerner (New York: Vintage, 1973), 604. On Keemer's involvement, see Eileen Shanahan, "Doctor Leads Group's Challenge to Michigan Anti-Abortion Law," *New York Times*, October 5, 1971, 28.

84. Mary Smith, "Birth Control and the Negro Woman," *Ebony Magazine*, March 1968, 31. For contemporary discussion of attitudes toward birth control and abortion, see William A. Darity and Castellano B. Turner, "Family Planning, Race Consciousness, and the Fear of Race Genocide," *American Journal of Public Health* 62 (1972): 1454; William A. Darity and Castellano B. Turner, "Fears of Genocide Among Black Americans as Related to Age, Sex, and Region," *American Journal of Public Health* 63 (1973): 1029; Margaret Sloan, "Do Blacks Belong in Women's Lib? Yes!" *Chicago Tribune*, June 6, 1971, E12; Leontyne Hunt, "Keep Your Family the Right Size," *Chicago Defender*, February 13, 1965, 9.

85. Larry Lader, Chairman of the Board, to NARAL Board Members et al., "The Damage Done to the Abortion Movement from the Second Hour of TV Report of the Commission on Population Growth and the American Future" (n.d., ca. November 1972), NRL, Carton 7, 1972 Debating the Opposition Folder.

86. See *NARAL Speaker and Debater's Notebook* excerpt, 1–4.

87. See Kluchin, *Fit to Be Tied*, 74, 93, 104, 177–178. For further analysis, see Robert Weisbord, "Birth Control and the Black American: A Matter of Genocide?" *Demography* 10 (November 1973): 571–590; Robert Weisbord, *Birth Control and the Black American* (Westport, CT: Greenwood Press, 1975), 43, 44, 130. On the lack of organized Catholic opposition, see Garrow, *Liberty and Sexuality*, 329; Gene Burns, *The Moral Veto: Framing Contraception, Abortion, and Cultural Pluralism in the United States* (New York: Cambridge University Press, 2005), 173–174, 198.

88. On Bowers and opposition to voluntarism, see Kluchin, *Fit to Be Tied*, 34, 66. On the Alabama sterilization crisis, see "Clinic Defends Sterilization of 2 Girls, 12, 14," *New York Times*, June 28, 1973, 14. The Relf controversy produced a Senate Panel, a well-publicized lawsuit, and a halt to sterilizations funded by the federal government. See Bill Kovach, "Sterilization Consent not Given, Father Tells Kennedy's Panel," *New York Times*, July 11, 1973, 16 (on the Senate panel); "Expand Sterilization Suit," *Chicago Defender*, August 14, 1973, 4 (on the lawsuit); "Sterilization Halt," *Chicago Defender*, August 2, 1973, 17 (on the suspension of federally funded sterilizations). On other reported sterilizations: Jack Slater, "Sterilization: Newest Threat to the Poor," *Ebony Magazine*, October 1973, 150.

89. On the Bucharest conference, see Frederick Jaffe, "Bucharest: The Tests Are Yet to Come," *Family Planning Perspectives* 6 (1974): 213, 214; Connelly, *Fatal Misconception*, 278, 310, 313. On the sterilizations in India, see Kaval Gulhati, "Compulsory Sterilization: The Change in India's Population Policy," *Science*, March 25, 1977, 1300–1305; Henry Kamm, "Indian State Is Leader in Forced Sterilization," *New York Times*, August 13, 1976, 8; Connelly, *Fatal Misconception*, 228–230, 310–323.

90. For Camp's recollections: Sharon Camp, interview with Mary Ziegler, November 6, 2011. For an example of Camp's work in the PCC in the period, see Draper Fund of the *Population Crisis Committee*, "Improving the Status of Women," *Draper Fund Report No. 9*, ed. Sharon Camp (Washington, DC: Population Crisis Committee, 1980), 5.

91. Connelly, *Fatal Misconception*, 334.

92. Marilyn Brant Chandler, "Alternatives to Abortion," *New York Times*, October 23, 1976, 25. On the group's efforts to distance itself from the issue of legal abortion, see "Rate of Illegal Abortions Is Placed at 20 Million a Year Worldwide," *New York Times*, April 30, 1979, B12. For individual recollection of this strategy: Phyllis Piotrow, interview with Mary Ziegler, October 28, 2011. Within a few years, under President Ronald Reagan's Mexico City policy, the PCC would be fighting to maintain family

planning aid to countries that used funds from other sources for abortion services. See Phil Gailey, "Reagan Said to Seek Cutoff if Aid Abroad Goes for Abortions," *New York Times*, June 18, 1984, A1.

93. See Critchlow, *Intended Consequences*, 173–178; Connelly, *Fatal Misconception*, 333–334; Critchlow, "Birth Control, Population, and Family Planning: An Overview," 14–18.

94. On the Tietze study, see Jane E. Brody, "Legal Abortions Up 53% Since Court Ruled in '73," *New York Times*, February 3, 1975, 1. The Council joined other organizations in calling on the Carter Administration to fund alternatives to abortion. See Victor Cohn, "Pregnancy Prevention Plan Proposed," *Washington Post*, July 20, 1977, A3. For examples of the Council's post-*Roe* research, see William Claiborne, "Pregnancy Held Greater Risk Than Pill," *Los Angeles Times*, February 15, 1976, A1; Jane E. Brody, "Researchers Seek New Male Contraceptive," *New York Times*, February 21, 1978, 18.

95. Carol Oppenheim, "Big Zero for Zero Population's Goal," *Chicago Tribune*, December 14, 1978, A1. For discussion of ZPG's focus on the immigration issue in the latter half of the 1970s, see Elena R. Gutierrez, *Fertile Matters: The Politics of Mexican-Origin Women's Reproduction* (Austin: University of Texas Press, 2008), 18–19, 75–79; Derek S. Hoff, *The State and the Stork: The Population Debate and Policy Making in US History* (Chicago: University of Chicago Press, 2012), 180–182.

96. Kay Mills, *This Little Light of Mine: The Life of Fannie Lou Hamer* (Lexington: University Press of Kentucky, 2007), 273 (emphasis in the original). For more on Hamer, see Chana Kai Lee, *For Freedom's Sake: The Life of Fannie Lou Hamer* (Champaign: University of Illinois Press, 1999); Stephen Tuck, *"We Ain't What We Ought to Be": The Black Freedom Struggle from Emancipation to Obama* (Cambridge, MA: Harvard University Press, 2010), 366.

97. Nathan Hare, "Will the Real Black Man Please Stand Up?" *The Black Scholar* 2 (1971): 32. On the tension between white and non-white feminists in the late 1960s and 1970s, see Benita Roth, *Separate Roads to Feminism: Black, Chicana, and White Feminist Movements in America's Second Wave* (New York: Cambridge University Press, 2004), 77–103; Winifred Breines, *The Trouble between Us: An Uneasy History of White and Black Women in the Feminist Movement* (New York: Oxford University Press, 2006), 3–19.

98. See Roth, *Separate Roads to Feminism*, 104. For more on gender hierarchy in the black-power movement, see Ogbar, *Black Power*, 29–32, 92–105; Kimberly Springer, "Black Feminists Respond to Black Power Masculinism," in *The Black Power Movement: Rethinking the Civil Rights Era*, ed. Peniel Joseph (New York: Routledge, 2006), 105–119; Breines, *The Trouble Between Us*, 10–17, 62–63, 71–73.

99. Frances Beal, "Double Jeopardy: To Be Black and Female," in *The Black Woman: An Anthology*, ed. Toni Cade Bambara (New York: Simon and

Schuster, 2005), 108. Beal's essay first appeared in 1970. See Frances Beal, "Double Jeopardy: To Be Black and Female," in *The Black Woman: An Anthology*, ed. Toni Cade Bambara (New York: New American Library, 1970), 90–100.

100. On Kennedy's work, see Diane Schulder and Florynce Kennedy, *Abortion Rap* (New York: McGraw Hill, 1971). On early African-American feminism in SNCC and the Third World Women's Alliance, see Breines, *The Trouble Between Us*, 118–119, 136–139; Kimberly Springer, *Living for the Revolution: Black Feminist Organizations, 1968–1980* (Durham, NC: Duke University Press, 2005), 49–73, 154–158.

101. See Barbara Smith, "Combahee River Collective: A Black Feminist Statement," *Off Our Backs*, June 1979, 6, 8; see also Michelle Wallace, "On the National Black Feminist Organization," in *Feminist Revolution*, ed. Robin Morgan (New York: Random House, 1978), 174–175; Barbara Campbell, "Black Feminists Form Group Here," *New York Times*, August 16, 1973, 36.

102. See Nelson, *Women of Color*, 81; Breines, *The Trouble between Us*, 123; Ross, "African American Women and Abortion," 184.

103. Arlie Scott, Sample Letter to House of Representatives (June 13, 1979), 1, NOW, Box 54, Folder 42.

104. "Still No Agreement on Abortion Funding Cutoff," *Planned Parenthood-World Population Memo* (November 11, 1977), 1, LLP, Box 16, Folder 64. For further evidence of the emphasis put on the harm done to poor women, see "Rape and Incest Victims May Be Denied Abortions under New Regulations," *Planned Parenthood-World Population Washington Memo* February 17, 1978, 1, LLP, Box 16, Folder 64.

105. Judy Klemesrud, "Planned Parenthood's New Head Takes a Fighting Stand," *New York Times*, February 3, 1978, A14. For further examples of similar arguments, especially discussion of the Jimenez case, see Karen De Witt, "Abortion Foes March in Capitol on Anniversary of Legalization," *New York Times*, January 23, 1979, C10; Ellen Frankfort and Frances Kissling, *Rosie: The Investigation of a Wrongful Death* (New York: Dial, 1979). On the influence of the Hyde Amendment in helping feminists reach out to poor, non-white women, see Serena Mayeri, *Reasoning from Race: Feminism, Law, and the Civil Rights Revolution* (Cambridge, MA: Harvard University Press, 2011), 188, 192–194.

106. Nelson, *Women of Color*, 109.

107. Robin Elliott, Denver Strategy Conference Report (October 7–9, 1973), PPFA II, Box 108, Folder 20.

108. On Vaughn's background and career in Planned Parenthood, see "Vaughn Urges Business to Assist the Peace Corps," *New York Times*, February 14, 1968, 12. For discussion of Vaughn's ambassadorial appointment, see "Vaughn Sworn In as Envoy," *New York Times*, June 6, 1969, 29. For discussion of Vaughn's tenure at Planned Parenthood, see Faye Wattleton, *Life on the Line* (New York: Ballantine, 1998), 173–180. For an example

of the projects pursued by the group in the period, see Cass Canfield of Planned Parenthood-World Population to Bea Blair, Executive Director of NARAL (April 12, 1974), 1, NRL, Carton 8, Planned Parenthood 1975–1976 Folder (discussing Planned Parenthood's involvement in sponsoring and shaping the 1974 Bucharest conference).

109. Jack Hood Vaughn, "Abortion: It Has no Place in Politics," *Los Angeles Times*, March 4, 1976, C7.

110. Abortion Rights Strategy '77 Invitation (April 4, 1977), 1, PPFA II, Box 108, Folder 2.

111. See Klemesrud, "Planned Parenthood's New Head," A14. For more on Wattleton's life, see Tom Davis, *Sacred Work: Planned Parenthood and Its Clergy Alliances* (Piscataway, NJ: Rutgers University Press, 2005), 164; "Family Planning's Top Advocate," *Ebony Magazine*, September 1978, 85–86, 88. For an example of Planned Parenthood's arguments about equal justice, women's rights, and abortion in the period, see Adam Clymer, "Senate Vote Forbids Using Federal Funds for Most Abortions," *New York Times*, June 30, 1977, 37.

112. Klemesrud, "Planned Parenthood's New Head," A14.

113. See Garrow, *Liberty and Sexuality*, 393–400, 516–526; see also Marian Faux, *Roe v. Wade: The Untold Story of the Landmark Supreme Court Decision That Made Abortion Legal* (New York: Cooper Square Press, 2001), 232–250; Sarah Weddington, *A Question of Choice* (New York: Penguin, 1992), 5, 51, 64.

114. Mulhauser, interview. For more on Mulhauser's work with NARAL, see "Coat Hangers Used in Abortion Protests," *New York Times*, September 8, 1977, 39; Leslie Bennetts, "For Abortion Group, An 'Aggressive New Campaign,'" *New York Times*, May 1, 1979, C22; Michael Knight, "Drive for Abortion Rights Begins," *New York Times*, January 23, 1980, A12.

115. NARAL Executive Committee Meeting Minutes (April 13, 1975), 1, NRL, Carton 1, 1975 Executive Committee Minutes Folder. For more on the internal discussion on how to defend abortion rights, see NARAL Executive Committee Meeting Minutes (June 21, 1975), 1–2, NRL, Carton 1, 1975 Executive Committee Minutes Folder; NARAL Executive Committee Meeting Minutes (November 21, 1975), 1–2, NRL, Carton 1, 1975 Executive Committee Minutes Folder.

116. Mulhauser, interview.

117. See Joan Zyda, "Abortion Rights Leader Argues for a Free Choice for Women," *Chicago Tribune*, December 9, 1975, B1; see also NARAL Executive Committee Meeting Minutes (April 13, 1975), 1.

118. For an example of Duke's involvement with NARAL in the late 1970s, see Nadine Brozan, "Abortion Rights in Peril, Say Advocates at Conference," *New York Times*, July 20, 1979, A14. For individuals' recollections of NARAL's activities in the period: Ron Fitzsimmons, interview with Mary Ziegler, October 27, 2011; Jane Bovard, interview with Mary Ziegler,

October 18, 2011; Carolyn Buhl, interview with Mary Ziegler, September 25, 2011.

119. See Departments of Labor, Health, Education, and Welfare Appropriations for 1978 Part 7: Testimony Before the Subcommittee of Labor and HEW Appropriations Committee, 95th Congress, 1st Session (1977) 127–139 (Statement of Karen Mulhauser); Departments of Labor and Health, Education, and Welfare and Related Agencies Appropriations, FY 1980, Part 5: Testimony Before the Senate Subcommittee on Labor and HEW Appropriations of the Senate Appropriations Committee, 96th Congress, 1st Session (1979) 277–285 (Statement of Karen Mulhauser). For individuals' recollections of this argumentative strategy: Buhl, interview; Mulhauser, interview.

120. National Abortion Rights League, *Legal Abortion: A Speaker and Debater's Notebook* (Washington, DC: The League, 1978), 7, 29, MRL, Box 2, Folder 5.

121. Laurie Johnston, "NOW Elects Syracuse Lawyer as Head," *New York Times*, May 28, 1974, 29. For further perspective on DeCrow's thinking and leadership, see Laurie Johnston, "NOW Expands List of What It's For and What It's Against," *New York Times*, June 1, 1974, 18; Nadine Brozan, "New President of NOW Prepares Speech for Another New President," *New York Times*, September 6, 1974, 40; Eileen Shanahan, "Lawyer Re-elected President of NOW," *New York Times*, October 27, 1975, 8; Reginald Stuart, "NOW Getting Organized to Fight for Amendment," *New York Times*, April 25, 1977, 57.

122. "Abortion: NOW Action Program" (April 1974), 1, NOW, Box 54, Folder 24; see also "Chronology of Major Events Affecting a Woman's Right to Choose Abortion, 2600 BC to the Present" (October 3, 1978), 1, NOW, Box 54, Folder 42 (describing and endorsing the idea of abortion as a woman's right); Arlie Scott, Sample Letter to House of Representatives (June 13, 1979), 1 (explaining that NOW "opposes any restrictions whatsoever on a woman's right to choose abortion").

123. NOW National Conference '77 (April 22–23, 1977), 25–26, NOW, Box 24, Folder 27. For individuals' recollections of NOW's abortion activities in the period: Collins, interview; DeCrow, interview.

124. "Call to Action for Reproductive Rights" (September 14, 1979), 3, NOW, Box 95, Folder 13; see also NOW, "Chronology of Major Events Affecting a Woman's Right to Choose Abortion, 2600 BC to the Present" (October 3, 1978), 1; "Mother's Day—A Day of Outrage? Protect Your Right to Choose!" (1974), WSH, Box 11, Folder 15.

125. "Excerpts from Transcripts of Democratic Candidates' Debate," *New York Times*, January 16, 1984, B8.

126. For further discussion of Jackson's framing of the abortion issue and women's rights in the 1984 election, see Fay S. Joyce, "Presidential Decision Nears for Jesse Jackson," *New York Times*, September 22, 1983, A1; John Herbers, "1983 March: The Left Revives," *New York Times*, August 29,

1983, A1. On NOW's endorsement of Mondale, see Bernard Weinraub, "NOW, in First Endorsement, Backs Mondale," *New York Times*, December 11, 1983, 1.

127. "Call to Action for Reproductive Rights" (September 14, 1979), 1.

Chapter 4. The Rise of Choice

1. For DeCrow's personal journey: Karen DeCrow, interview with Mary Ziegler, February 3, 2011. For further discussion of her work within NOW, see Laurie Johnston, "NOW Expands List of What It's For and What It's Against," *New York Times*, June 1, 1974, 18; Nadine Brozan, "New President of NOW Prepares Speech for Another New President," *New York Times*, September 6, 1974, 40; Eileen Shanahan, "Lawyer Re-elected President of NOW," *New York Times*, October 27, 1975, 8; Reginald Stuart, "NOW Getting Organized to Fight for Amendment," *New York Times*, April 25, 1977, 57.

2. Marilyn Katz, interview with Mary Ziegler, March 10, 2012.

3. Ibid. For further discussion of Katz's career in reproductive-rights work, see Wendy Kline, *Bodies of Knowledge: Sexuality, Reproduction, and Women's Health in the Second Wave* (Chicago: University of Chicago Press, 2010), 92, 95; Suzanne Staggenborg, *The Pro-Choice Movement: Organization and Activism in the Abortion Conflict* (New York: Oxford University Press, 1991), 111–112, 121; Kathy Rudy, *Beyond Pro-Life and Pro-Choice: Moral Diversity in the Abortion Debate* (Boston: Beacon, 1996), 88.

4. Rickie Solinger, *Beggars and Choosers: How the Politics of Choice Shapes Adoption, Abortion, and Welfare in the United States* (New York: Farrar, Straus, and Giroux, 2001), 5.

5. See Ruth Colker, "An Equal Protection Analysis of United States Reproductive Health Policy: Gender, Race, Age, and Class," *Duke Law Journal* 1991, no. 2 (1991): 324 ("The popularity of the abortion debate is a reflection of the problem of essentialism because this debate chooses one issue . . . and generally ignores the larger and more complex problems relating to reproductive health issues"); Robin West, "From Choice to Reproductive Justice: De-Constitutionalizing Abortion Rights," *Yale Law Journal* 118 (2009): 1411–1412, 1427–1431. Historians have also highlighted the narrowing effect of *Roe* on the agenda of reproductive rights activists. See Jennifer Nelson, *Women of Color and the Reproductive Rights Movement* (New York: New York University Press, 2003), 56, 134 (detailing how women of color and dissenting groups challenged the narrow agenda of certain mainstream groups); Solinger, *Beggars and Choosers*, 2–10; Rebecca M. Kluchin, *Fit to Be Tied: Sterilization and Reproductive Rights in America, 1950–1980* (Piscataway, NJ: Rutgers University Press, 2009), 134, 218.

6. For perspective on the thinking of these activists in the 1970s, see "Position Paper on Abortion Adopted by the National Women's Health Network Board" (June 4, 1978), 1–2, BSP, Carton 3, Folder 142; JoAnne Fischer to Eleanor Smeal (February 13, 1979), BSP, Carton 3, Folder 148; Reproductive Rights National Network Organizational Brochure (n.d., ca. 1980), 1–4, R2N2, Box 1, Abortion Task Force Folder; Chicago Women Organized for Reproductive Choice (WORC), "Some Thoughts on Abortion Strategy—A Beginning Consensus" (n.d., ca. 1981), 1–2, R2N2, Box 1, Abortion Task Force Folder. For further discussion of the emergence of R2N2: Katz, interview; Karen Stamm, interview with Mary Ziegler, March 9, 2012; Meredith Tax, interview with Mary Ziegler, April 10, 2012.

7. On the setbacks suffered by the abortion-rights movement in the period, see Patricia Donovan, "Fertility-Related State Laws Enacted In 1981," *Family Planning Perspectives* 14 (March–April 1982): 63–65; Debra W. Stewart and Jeanne Bell Nicholson, "Abortion Policy in 1978: A Follow-Up Analysis," *Publius* 9 (Winter 1979): 161–167. On defeats suffered by the abortion-rights movement in the Supreme Court in the period, see *Maher v. Roe*, 432 U.S. 464, 470–474 (1977) (upholding a Connecticut law allowing for Medicaid funding for abortion only for first trimester abortions that were "medically necessary"); *Poelker v. Doe*, 432 U.S. 519, 521–525 (1977) (upholding a directive prohibiting abortions in city hospitals); *Beal v. Doe*, 432 U.S. 438, 444–448 (1977) (upholding state regulations prohibiting the Medicaid funding of most abortions); *Planned Parenthood of Central Missouri v. Danforth*, 428 U.S. 52, 66–67 (1976) (upholding an informed-consent restriction).

8. For examples of the new choice-based rhetoric that became prominent in the late 1970s, see NOW Resolution on Reproductive Rights (n.d., ca. 1979), 1, NOW, Box 24, Folder 37 (presenting abortion as an issue centering on women's "freedom to choose"); "Mother's Day—A Day of Outrage? Protect Your Right to Choose!" (1974), WSH, Box 11, Folder 15; "Freedom Is the Right to Choose: Rally for Abortion Rights" (July 1, 1978), RHS, Box 1, Folder 15; NARAL Press Release (June 1978), 1, RHS, Box 11, Folder 15; "The ACLU's Campaign for Choice: The Right of a Woman to Control Her Own Body" (n.d., ca. 1977), RHS, Box 1, Folder 15; Karen Mulhauser, NARAL Fundraising Letter (n.d., ca. 1979), 1, RHS, Box 1, Folder 1; Planned Parenthood Fundraising Letter (n.d., ca. 1979), 1–4, JRS, Dr. Joseph Stanton Papers.

9. For examples of this perspective from the late 1970s, see R2N2, Letter of Introduction to Abortion Task Force Paper (October 2, 1981), R2N2, Box 1, Abortion Task Force Folder; R2N2, Abortion Task Force Paper (1981), 3–4, 7–8, 10–14, R2N2, Box 1, Abortion Task Force Folder; NWHN, "Position Paper on Abortion Adopted by the National Women's Health Network Board" (June 4, 1978), 1–2; JoAnne Fischer to Eleanor Smeal (February 13, 1979), 1–2, BSP, Carton 3, Folder 142; Chicago Women

Organized for Reproductive Choice, "Some Thoughts on Abortion Strategy—A Beginning Consensus" (n.d., ca. 1981), 1–2. On the position taken by these organizations on informed consent regulations and sterilization abuse, see Linda Gordon, *The Moral Property of Women: A History of Birth Control Politics in America* (Champaign: University of Illinois Press, 2002), 342–348; Nelson, *Women of Color*, 6–7, 137–142, 145–160. For examples of the positions taken by mainstream organizations, see NOW Resolution: Sterilization Abuse (n.d., ca. 1978), NOW, Box 24, Folder 37; Planned Parenthood of New York, Public Issues and Action Special Subcommittee Meeting Minutes (February 7, 1977), 1–3, LLP, Box 16, Folder 63; "Sterilization Abuse: A New National Issue," *Washington Memo*, The Alan Guttmacher Institute, 2–3 (December 16, 1977), LLP, Box 16, Folder 16.

10. On pro-life optimism after the election, see Dave Gaetano, "Pro-Life Gains: President, 10 Senators and More," *National Right to Life News*, November 10, 1980, 1, JRS, 1980 National Right to Life News Box; "NRL PAC Proclaims Victories," *National Right to Life News*, November 10, 1980, 12, JRS, 1980 National Right to Life News Box (Dr. John Willke of NRLC explaining that the 1980 election was "a major step forward for the Right to Life Movement"). This chapter later discusses abortion-rights activists' response to the setbacks of the late 1970s and early 1980s.

11. Kate Millett, Notes on Abortion (n.d., ca. 1972), KMP, Box S9.

12. See Edith Evans Asbury, "Women Break Up Abortion Hearing," *New York Times*, February 14, 1969, 42; Susan Brownmiller, "'Sisterhood Is Powerful': A Member of the Women's Liberation Movement Explains What It Is About," *New York Times Magazine*, March 15, 1970, 230. For discussion of the "speak outs" and Stearns' role therein, see Amy Kesselman, "Women Versus Connecticut: Conducting a Statewide Hearing on Abortion," in *Abortion Wars: A Half Century of Struggle, 1950–2000*, ed. Rickie Solinger (Berkeley: University of California Press, 1998), 43; Susan Brownmiller, *In Our Time: Memoir of a Revolution* (New York: Random House, 2000), 110–112, 117. For the decision in *Abele*, see *Abele v. Markle*, 342 F. Supp. 800 (D. Conn. 1972).

13. On the yearly struggle on the scope of Hyde restrictions, see Martin Tolchin, "But Now There Is Pressure of Time and Money to Reach Agreement," *New York Times*, November 27, 1977, 176; Karen DeWitt, "Foes of Abortion Seek to Tighten Restrictions on Medicaid Funds," *New York Times*, March 1, 1979, B20; Martin Tolchin, "Financing Bill and Abortion: Both Sides Emphasize Questions of Conscience," *New York Times*, October 2, 1980, A19.

14. For press coverage of the *Maher* decision, see "Court Rules States May Deny Medicaid for Some Abortions," *New York Times*, June 21, 1977, 69; "Anti-Abortion Forces Gain," *New York Times*, June 26, 1977, 126.

15. "The ACLU's Campaign for Choice: The Right of a Woman to Control Her Own Body" (n.d., ca. 1977), 3. On the impact of the Hyde Amendment on

access to abortion, see James Trussell, Jane Menken, Barbara L. Lindheim, and Barbara Vaughan, "The Impact of Restricting Medicaid Financing for Abortion," *Family Planning Perspectives* 12 (1980): 120. For the decision in *Maher, see Maher v. Roe*, 432 U.S. 464, 470–477 (1977). For the decision in *Poelker, see Poelker v. Doe*, 432 U.S. 519, 521–522 (1977). For the decision in *Beal, see Beal v. Doe*, 432 U.S. 438, 445–448 (1977).

16. NARAL Press Release (June 1978), 1.

17. See Sylvia Hampton and Donna J. Jones, "Involving Significant Others: A Health Rights Advocacy Program Guide" (1979), 1–10, RHS, Box 1, Folder 8.

18. On the formation of CESA, see Nelson, *Women of Color*, 5, 142; Kluchin, *Fit to Be Tied*, 186. For further discussion of CESA's work, see Judy Klemesrud, "Complacency on Abortion: A Warning to Women," *New York Times*, January 23, 1978, A18; Nadine Brozan, "The Volatile Issue of Sterilization Abuse: A Tangle of Accusations and Remedies," *New York Times*, December 9, 1977, B10.

19. Brozan, "The Volatile Issue of Sterilization Abuse," B10.

20. On the relationship between the ERA and abortion strategy, see Serena Mayeri, "A New E.R.A. or a New Era? Amendment Advocacy and the Reconstitution of Feminism," *University of Pennsylvania Law Review* 103 (2009): 1233, 1243–1244; Reva B. Siegel, "Sex Equality Arguments for Reproductive Rights: Their Critical Basis and Evolving Constitutional Protection," *Emory Law Journal* 56 (2007): 828–829. On feminists' prioritization of the ERA, see Laurie Johnston, "NOW Expands List of What It's For and What It's Against," *New York Times*, June 1, 1974, 18 (explaining that NOW's conference "confirmed support for the Equal Rights Amendment"). On the success of the Amendment in early 1973 and its subsequent stalling, see Eileen Shanahan, "Women See Delay on Equal Rights," *New York Times*, June 29, 1974, 30. On the defeat of state equal rights amendments in New York and New Jersey, see Linda Greenhouse, "Defeat of Equal Rights Bills Traced to Women's Votes," *New York Times*, November 6, 1975, 85.

21. Phyllis Schlafly, "ERA Means Abortion and Population Shrinkage," *The Phyllis Schlafly Report*, December 1974, vol. 8, no. 5, sec. 2, PSR. For more on Schlafly's arguments on abortion, see Linda Greenhouse and Reva B. Siegel eds., *Before Roe v. Wade: Voices That Shaped the Abortion Debate before the Supreme Court's Ruling*, 2nd ed. (New Haven: Yale Law Library, 2012), 293 (explaining how ERA opponents used the abortion issue to mobilize cultural conservatives). On Schlafly's tactics in the ERA battle, see Donald T. Critchlow, *Phyllis Schlafly and Grassroots Conservatism: A Woman's Crusade* (Princeton: Princeton University Press, 2005), 220–227. For more on concerns about the connection between the amendment and abortion among ERA proponents, see Mayeri, "New E.R.A.," 1233, 1244–1245; Siegel, "Sex Equality Arguments for Reproductive Rights," 828–829.

22. Toni Carabillo, "Who Really Cares about Housewives?" (n.d., ca. 1975), 2, NOW, Box 192, Folder 32. For further discussion of feminists' ERA-driven campaign for divorce reform, see Mary Ziegler, "The Incomplete Revolution: Feminists and the Legacy of Marital Property Reform," *Michigan Journal of Law and Gender* 19 (2013): 259–289.

23. NOW, "Summary of the July 29, 1977 Meeting on ERA Strategy" (1977), NOW, Box 138, Folder 11. For more on NOW's concerns about homemakers and the ERA, see Gail Falk, Strategy Memorandum (March 28, 1973), 1–3, CEP, Box 22, Folder 47; Press Release, "NOW LDEF and the Women's Law Project Win Grants for the ERA Impact Project" (December 27, 1979), NOW, Box 197, Folder 3; Arlie Scott, Sample Letter to Member of Congress on Displaced Homemaker Legislation (May 1, 1978), NOW, Box 46, Folder 38 (describing NOW's promotion of legislation aiding displaced and impoverished homemakers after divorce). For arguments about the ERA and homemakers made by Phyllis Schlafly and STOP ERA, see Phyllis Schlafly, "The Fraud Called the Equal Rights Amendment," *The Phyllis Schlafly Report*, May 1972, vol. 5, no. 10, sec. 2, PSR; Phyllis Schlafly, "ERA Takes Away Rights from Wives," *The Phyllis Schlafly Report*, November 1973, vol. 7, no. 4, sec. 2, PSR.

24. See NOW, "Summary of the July 29, 1977 Meeting on ERA Strategy," 1 (exploring how to separate the abortion and ERA issues to "split off those religious people who are being used by the anti-ERA right wing"). For more on efforts to separate abortion and the ERA, see "The Truth About the Equal Rights Amendment" (n.d., ca. 1978), 6, ERA, Box 1, Folder 1 (explaining that the ERA would not impact "cases involving a physical function (such as childbearing) of which only one sex (female) is capable"); ERA Brochure (n.d., ca. 1975), ERA, Box 1, Folder 1 (arguing that the ERA would "neither add nor detract from . . . decisions" on abortion); Common Cause, "The Equal Rights Amendment: A Report on the 27th Amendment to the Constitution" (n.d., ca. 1977), 2, ERA, Box 1, Folder 1 (arguing that abortion laws would "not be affected by the Equal Rights Amendment").

25. See Jan Liebman, Abortion Amendment Strategy (n.d., ca. 1974), 1–3, WSH, Box 11, Folder 12.

26. Ann Scott and Jan Liebman to NOW Legislative Task Force Coordinator et al. (September 1, 1974), 1–2, NOW, Box 54, Folder 27. For further discussion of the argumentative strategies used in the abortion funding context, see Religious Coalition for Abortion Rights, "Back to the Beginning: It's Hyde Again" (n.d., ca. 1978), RHS, Box 2, Folder 19 (emphasizing that Hyde was "blatantly discriminatory in its attack on the poor"). For further material on NOW's lobbying strategy, see NOW Abortion Action Program (April 1974), NOW, Box 24, Folder 26; National NOW Right to Choose Lobbying Action (n.d., ca. 1974), NOW, Box 54, Folder 27.

27. On Smeal's election as NOW President, see Anna Quindlen, "NOW President: I Definitely See the Movement Coming of Age," *New York*

Times, September 2, 1977, 36; Ben A. Franklin, "A New President for NOW: Eleanor Marie Cutri Smeal," *New York Times*, April 28, 1977, 18. On Smeal's role in DeCrow's election, see Sara M. Evans, *Tidal Wave: How Women Changed America at Century's End* (New York: Simon and Schuster, 2003), 109–110; Sherrye Henry, *The Deep Divide: Why American Women Resist Equality* (New York: Macmillan, 1994), 259–261.

28. "National NOW Conference Resolutions on Reproductive Rights, 1969–1977" (September 30, 1978), 2, NOW, Box 87, Folder, 47.

29. Arlie Scott to Jean Marshall Clarke (April 25, 1978), 3, NOW, Box 49, Folder 24. On the membership of the NOW Reproductive Rights Task Force in the period, see "Summary of Reproductive Task Force Meetings, April 28 & 29, 1979" (April 1979), 1, NOW, Box 49, Folder 20. For more on Jean Marshall Clark, see Toni Carabillo, Judith Meuli, and June Bundy Csida, *Feminist Chronicles: 1953–1993* (Los Angeles: Women's Graphic, 1993), 81, 86; Martha Sontag Bradley, *Pedestals and Podiums: Utah Women, Religious Authority, and Equal Rights* (Salt Lake City: Signature Books, 2005), 284. For more on Sackman-Reed, see "Gloria Sackman-Reed," in *Feminists Who Changed America, 1963–1975*, ed. Barbara J. Love (Champaign: University of Illinois Press, 2006), 401. For more on Taft, see Wendy Simonds, *Abortion at Work: Ideology and Practice in a Feminist Clinic* (New Brunswick, NJ: Rutgers University Press, 1996), 90, 130; Mark Donald, "Charlotte's Web," *Dallas Observer*, May 18, 1995, accessed April 23, 2014, http://www.dallasobserver.com/1995-05-18/news/charlotte-s-web/. Taft went on to become director of the Abortion Care Network. See Charlotte Taft, "Remembrances of *Roe*: Charlotte Taft" (January 22, 2013), accessed April 21, 2014, http://www.acnsaysstopthewaronwomen.org/blogs/blog/7150154-remembrances-of-roe-charlotte-taft.

30. "NOW Resolution on Sterilization Abuse" (1978), 1, NOW, Box 24, Folder 37. For discussion of the NOW resolution, see Meredith Tax, "NOW Resolution," *CARASA News*, November 2, 1978, 2, MTP, Box 8, CARASA News Folder 1; "NOW vs. Sterilization Guidelines," *CARASA News*, November 2, 1978, 3, MTP, Box 8, CARASA News Folder 1.

31. Judy Klemesrud, "Sterilization Is an Answer for Many," *New York Times*, January 18, 1971, 24.

32. Ibid.; see also "Feminist Marchers Brave Icy Rain," *New York Times*, December 13, 1970, 66.

33. See Nelson, *Women of Color*, 4–6, 133; Kluchin, *Fit to Be Tied*, 149, 185; Rickie Solinger, *Pregnancy and Power: A Short History of Reproductive Health Politics in America* (New York: New York University Press, 2005), 22–23.

34. NOW National Conference Minutes (October 8, 1978), 46, NOW, Box 24, Folder 39. On the position taken by members of New York NOW, see Brozan, "The Volatile Issue of Sterilization Abuse," B10.

35. "Summary of Reproductive Task Force Meetings, April 28 & 29, 1979" (April 1979), 1; see also "Summary of Conference Call Meeting, August 19, 1979" (August 31, 1979), NOW, Box 49, Folder 22.

36. On the abortion-ERA discussion in the states, see Douglas Kneeland, "The Equal Rights Amendment: Missouri Is the Target Now," *New York Times*, February 7, 1975, 37; Eileen Shanahan, "Equal Rights Test Is Near in Illinois," *New York Times*, March 2, 1975, 1; Roy Reed, "In the South: Road to Equal Rights Is Rough and Full of Detours," *New York Times*, March 20, 1975, 51.

37. Karen DeWitt, "Abortion Foes March in Capitol on Anniversary of Legalization," *New York Times*, January 23, 1979, C10. For individual recollections of the strategic reasons for downplaying equality arguments: Nancy Gertner, interview with Mary Ziegler, December 8, 2011. For Gertner's account of NOW's efforts to downplay equality arguments for abortion, see Nancy Gertner, *In Defense of Women: Memoirs of an Unrepentant Advocate* (Boston: Beacon Press, 2011). On the effort to separate the ERA campaign from the effort to protect legal abortion, see Mayeri, "New E.R.A.," 1233, 1244–1245; Siegel, "Sex Equality Arguments for Reproductive Rights," 828–829.

38. On the reluctance of major foundations to fund abortion-rights work in the 1970s, see Susan M. Hartmann, *The Other Feminists: Activists in the Liberal Establishment* (New Haven, CT: Yale University Press, 1998), 168, 172; cf. Flora Davis, *Moving the Mountain: The Women's Movement Since 1960* (Champaign: University of Illinois Press, 1999), 152–153 (explaining that foundations' donations were often earmarked for specific—and relatively uncontroversial—purposes). As Hartmann recognizes, funding constraints also made it difficult for feminists to pursue rights for poor women, both inside and outside the context of abortion. Hartmann, *The Other Feminists*, 172.

39. NARAL Press Release (June 1978), 1.

40. NARAL Fundraising Letter (n.d., ca. 1978), 1, RHS, Box 2, Folder 19. In the period, abortion providers also became politically active to combat new abortion restrictions. See National Abortion Federation Press Release (n.d., ca. 1979), RHS, Box 2, Folder 19. Abortion providers like Missouri activist Sylvia Hampton and her colleagues also worked to infiltrate antiabortion meetings, an activity also carried out by the opposition. See Sylvia Hampton, "Re: Political Action Committee and Workshop Number 2" (June 1981), 1–2, RHS, Box 2, Folder 21; Sylvia Hampton, "Notes of National Right to Life Convention" (June 1981), RHS, Box 2, Folder 21; Mary Meehan and Elizabeth Moore, "NARAL Targets HLA," *National Right to Life News*, February 23, 1981, 1, 21, JRS, 1981 National Right to Life News Box.

41. Leslie Bennetts, "For Pro-Abortion Group, an 'Aggressive New Campaign,'" *New York Times*, May 1, 1979, C22.

42. Mulhauser, NARAL Fundraising Letter (n.d., ca. 1979), 1.

43. Ibid.

44. Richard Phillips, "The Shooting War over 'Choice' or 'Life' Is Beginning Again," *Chicago Tribune*, April 20, 1980, J3. For more on NARAL's new emphasis on choice rhetoric and Impact '80, see Staggenborg, *The Pro-Choice Movement*, 95.

45. Planned Parenthood Fundraising Letter (n.d., ca. 1979), 3.

46. Ibid. On NOW's Sanger campaign, see "Call to Action for Reproductive Rights" (September 14, 1979), NOW, Box 95, Folder 13.

47. "Freedom Is the Right to Choose: Rally for Abortion Rights," 1; see also "Freedom to Choose Is the American Way" (n.d., ca. 1978), RHS, Box 1, Folder 16.

48. "Abortion Rights Action Week: Statement of Purpose" (n.d., ca. 1978), RHS, Box 1, Folder 16. For examples of similar choice-based arguments, see Bennetts, "For Pro-Abortion Group," C22; Knight, "The Shooting War over 'Choice' or 'Life,'" J3.

49. Planned Parenthood of New York, Public Issues and Action Special Subcommittee Meeting Minutes (February 7, 1977), 1–2. For more on Planned Parenthood's position on sterilization regulations, see Nelson, *Women of Color*, 143–145; Kluchin, *Fit to Be Tied*, 137–142, 192.

50. Judy Klemesrud, "Planned Parenthood's New Head Takes a Fighting Stand," *New York Times*, February 3, 1978, A14.

51. Missouri Citizens for Life, "Pro-Life: Defending Fetal Rights" (n.d., ca. 1978), 6, MCL, Box 1, Folder 1.

52. Ibid. For a further example of the graphic images of abortions used by abortion opponents, see John Willke and Barbara Willke, *Handbook on Abortion* (Cincinnati, OH: Hayes Publishing, 1975), 30.

53. Frances Beal, "Double Jeopardy: To Be Black and Female," in *The Black Woman: An Anthology*, ed. Toni Cade Bambara (New York: Simon and Schuster, 2005), 119.

54. See Nelson, *Women of Color*, 2, 6, 8, 77, 179; see also Duchess Harris, "From the Kennedy Commission to the Combahee Collective: Black Feminist Organizing, 1960–1980," in *Sisters in the Struggle: African-American Women in The Civil Rights-Black Power Struggle*, eds. Bettye Collier-Thomas and V. P. Franklin (New York: New York University Press, 2004), 292–293; Loretta Ross, "African American Women and Abortion," in *Abortion Wars: A Half-Century of Struggle, 1950–2000*, ed. Rickie Solinger (Berkeley: University of California Press, 1998), 183–185.

55. Karen Stamm, "The Master's Plan" (March 1981), R2N2, Box 1, Abortion Task Force Folder. On Stamm's background: Stamm, interview. For further discussion of her career, see Nelson, *Women of Color*, 136, 155, 176; Kluchin, *Fit to Be Tied*, 186.

56. Alice Wolfson, interview with Mary Ziegler, November 30, 2011. For further discussion of Wolfson's career, see Anne M. Valk, *Radical Sisters: Second-Wave Feminism and Black Liberation in Washington, D.C.* (Champaign: University of Illinois, 2008), 84–85, 96, 100, 143; Anne M.

Valk, "Fighting for Abortion as a 'Health Right' in Washington, D.C.," in *Feminist Coalitions: Historical Perspectives on Second-Wave Feminism in the United States*, ed. Stephanie Gilmore (Champaign: University of Illinois Press, 2008), 146–150.

57. Wolfson, interview.

58. On feminist health activism and abortion care in the period: see Janet Hadley, *Abortion: Between Freedom and Necessity* (Philadelphia: Temple University Press, 1996), 121; Sheryl Burt Ruzek, *The Women's Health Movement: Feminist Alternatives to Medical Control* (New York: Praeger Publishers, 1978), 60–64, 133, 144–146; Claudia Dreifus, "Introduction," in *Seizing Our Bodies: The Politics of Women's Health*, ed. Claudia Dreifus (New York: Vintage, 1977), xvi–xxviii. On Jane, a pre-1973 underground abortion service, see generally Laura Kaplan, *The Story of Jane: The Legendary Underground Feminist Abortion Service* (Chicago: University of Chicago Press, 1995); Laura Kaplan, "Beyond Safe and Legal: The Lessons of Jane," in *Abortion Wars: A Half Century of Struggle, 1950–2000*, ed. Rickie Solinger (Berkeley: University of California Press, 1998), 40–45. On the experience of feminist women's health activists: Charlotte Taft, interview with Mary Ziegler, May 5, 2011; Claire Keyes, interview with Mary Ziegler, November 17, 2011; Linda Weber, interview with Mary Ziegler, December 7, 2011; Mickey Stern, interview with Mary Ziegler, September 10, 2011; Carolyn Buhl, interview with Mary Ziegler, September 21, 2011; Sally Tatnall, interview with Mary Ziegler, September 12, 2011; Carol Downer, interview with Mary Ziegler, February 7, 2012.

59. For the text of *Our Bodies, Ourselves*, see The Boston Women's Health Collective, *Our Bodies Ourselves: A Book by and for Women* (Boston: New England Free Press, 1971). For analysis of the impact of the volume, see Kathy Davis, *The Making of "Our Bodies, Ourselves": How Feminism Travels across Borders* (Durham, NC: Duke University Press, 2007), 6, 186; Sandra Morgen, *Into Our Own Hands: The Women's Health Movement in the United States, 1969–1990* (Piscataway, NJ: Rutgers University Press, 2002), 24. On Rothman and Downer's contributions to the movement, see Morgen, *Into Our Own Hands*, 8, 21–24; Simonds, *Abortion at Work*, 31; Cynthia Gorney, *Articles of Faith: A Frontline History of the Abortion Wars* (New York: Simon and Schuster, 2000), 208–210.

60. On sales of the pill, see Solinger, *Pregnancy and Power*, 172. For the text of Seaman's work, see Barbara Seaman, *The Doctor's Case against the Pill: 25th Anniversary Updated Edition* (Alameda, CA: Hunter House, 1995). On the importance of Seaman's work, see Morgen, *Into Our Own Hands*, 8–15; Elaine Tyler May, *America and the Pill: A History of Promise, Peril, and Liberation* (New York: Basic Books, 2010), 130–132. On the DES scandal, see Morgen, *Into Our Own Hands*, 10, 30; Davis, *Moving the Mountain*, 238–239.

61. On the early days of NWHN, see "Letter to National Women's Health Network Founders" (February 14, 1976), BSP, Carton 3, Folder 141; Meeting Minutes, National Women's Health Network (August 7–8, 1976), 1–7, BSP, Carton 3, Folder 141; Marian Sandmeier to NWHN Board Members and Friends (November 18, 1976), BSP, Carton 3, Folder 141.

62. On NWHN's mobilization around issues tied to the Hyde Amendment, see Press Release, "NWHN Launching of the Women's Health Network 'One on One Campaign'" (August 1977), BSP, Carton 3, Folder 141; Press Release, NWHN to President Jimmy Carter et al. (August 11, 1977), BSP, Carton 3, Folder 141 (contending that "the right to abortion [had] been continuously undermined since it was guaranteed by the Supreme Court").

63. NWHN, "Position Paper on Abortion Adopted by the National Women's Health Network Board" (June 4, 1978), 1.

64. Ibid.

65. ARM Information Letter (June 1978), BSP, Box 46, Folder 10. On ARM's later suit challenging the tax-exempt status of the Catholic Church and the National Conference of Catholic Bishops, see James Risen and Judy L. Thomas, *Wrath of Angels: The American Abortion War* (New York: Basic Books, 1998), 154; Linda Gordon, *The Moral Property of Women: A History of Birth Control Politics in America* (Champaign: University of Illinois Press, 2002), 147.

66. Mecca Rylance and Tacie Dejanikus, "Pro-Choice/Anti-Choice Dialogue: Cooption or Cooperation?" *Off Our Backs*, March 9, 1979, 5. For further discussion of ARM's activities between 1978 and 1980, see ARM Position Paper on Abortion (n.d., ca. 1978), BSP, Box 46, Folder 10; ARM Annual Board of Directors Meeting (June 20, 1979), BSP, Box 46, Folder 10; Larry Lader to ARM Board Members (January 15, 1980), BSP, Box 46, Folder 10.

67. DeWitt, "Abortion Foes March," C10. For the view of the National Right to Life Committee on the common-ground summit, see Dr. Carolyn Gerster to Friend of Life (n.d., ca. 1979), RHS, Box 2, Folder 21.

68. JoAnne Fischer to Eleanor Smeal (February 13, 1979), 1. For more on the conflict between NOW, NARAL, and NWHN on abortion, see Phyllis West and Carol Blum to JoAnne Fischer (February 14, 1979), BSP, Carton 3, Folder 142; Belita Cowan to Phyllis West and Carol Blum (February 14, 1979), 1, BSP, Carton 3, Folder 142; Belita Cowan to NWHN Board Members Re. NOW Meeting (February 16, 1979), BSP, Carton 3, Folder 142.

69. NWHN Press Release (February 15, 1979), BSP, Carton 3, Folder 142. For more on the response to NWHN's position, see NWHN "Newsalert" (March 1979), BSP, Carton 3, Folder 142.

70. "Call to Action for Reproductive Rights" (September 14, 1979), 3. On the disruption of and disappointment in the parley, see "Birth Control Parley Shaken as Protestors Display Two Fetuses," *New York Times*, February

16, 1979, B7; "NOW Dialogues," *Sisterlife*, May/June 1979, LEP, Box 1, Folder 1.

71. Robin Herman, "After Decision, Focus Turns to Lower Courts and Abortion Politics," *New York Times*, July 1, 1980, A1.

72. Enid Nemy, "Feminists, Set Back, to Stress Politics," *New York Times*, July 7, 1980, B12.

73. On the history of neoliberalism, see Daniel Stedman Jones, *Masters of the Universe: Hayek, Friedman, and the Rise of Neoliberal Politics* (Princeton: Princeton University Press, 2012); David Harvey, *A Brief History of Neoliberalism* (New York: Oxford University Press, 2005); Monica Prasad, *The Politics of Free Markets: The Rise of Neoliberal Economic Policies in Britain, France, Germany, and the United States* (Chicago: University of Chicago Press, 2006).

74. See Jones, *Masters of the Universe*, 1–18; Donald T. Critchlow, *The Conservative Ascendancy: How the GOP Right Made Political History* (Cambridge, MA: Harvard University Press, 2007), 202–204; Prasad, *The Politics of Free Markets*, 37–100.

75. "National Network Builds for Action," *CARASA News*, March 22, 1979, 3, MTP, Box 8, CARASA News Folder 2.

76. On the history of CARASA and R2N2, see Nelson, *Women of Color*, 6, 133–171; Kluchin, *Fit to Be Tied*, 196–220; Gordon, *The Moral Property of Women*, 346–347; Staggenborg, *The Pro-Choice Movement*, 85, 88, 111–126.

77. "Defend Women's Right to Choose—Draft Outline for CARASA" (n.d., ca. 1979), 1, MTP, Box 8, CARASA Folder. On *Women under Attack*, see CARASA, *Women under Attack: Abortion, Sterilization Abuse, and Reproductive Rights* (New York: CARASA, 1979). For more on CARASA's focus on a multi-issue agenda and a more radical understanding of choice, see Notes on Strategy for Steering Committee Meeting (March 18, 1978), MTP, Box 8, CARASA Steering Committee Folder (contending that CARASA had forced other groups to make concessions because of "its people, [its] activism, and clear and consistent politics"); Meredith Tax, "R2N2 Fights Right to Life and Hyde," *CARASA News*, June 1979, 1, MTP, Box 8, CARASA News Folder 2; "Reports from the Triannual Meeting," *CARASA News*, July/August 1979, 1, MTP, Box 8, CARASA News Folder 2.

78. Reproductive Rights National Network Brochure, "Women United to Defend Abortion Rights and End Sterilization Abuse" (n.d., ca. 1980), 2, R2N2, Box 1, Abortion Task Force Folder. On the organization of R2N2 in 1978, see Kline, *Bodies of Knowledge*, 92; Staggenborg, *The Pro-Choice Movement*, 85.

79. Draft, "CARASA: Principles of Unity" (n.d., ca. 1977), MTP, Box 8, CARASA Folder. For more on the consensus set forth by CARASA, see CARASA Conference Committee, "Presentation 1: Current Consensus"

(n.d., ca. 1977), 1–2, MTP, Box 8, CARASA Folder; CARASA, "Outreach Proposal" (December 1, 1977), MTP, Box 8, CARASA Folder.

80. R2N2, Abortion Task Force Paper (1981), 10.

81. On the human life bill, see Joan Beck, "The Pro-Life Groups Turn to Congress on Abortion," *Chicago Tribune*, January 30, 1981, B2; Jon Margolis, "The Abortion Struggle on Capitol Hill," *Chicago Tribune*, March 2, 1981, A2; "Senate OKs New Limit on Abortion," *Chicago Tribune*, May 22, 1981, 1–2. On the Hatch Amendment, see Steven Roberts, "Catholic Bishops for Amendment Allowing States to Ban Abortion," *New York Times*, November 6, 1981, A1; Kenneth A. Briggs, "The Bishops Take a Risk: New Peace Position Sure to Ignite Dissent," *New York Times*, November 23, 1981, B10; "Anti-Abortion Group Backs Hatch Proposal," *New York Times*, December 13, 1981, 39.

82. On antiabortion debate about the strategic costs and benefits of the bill and the amendment, see Michael W. Cuneo, "Life Battles: The Rise of Catholic Militancy within the American Pro-Life Movement," in *Bearing Right: Conservative Catholics in America*, eds. Mary Jo Weaver and R. Scott Appleby (Bloomington: University of Indiana Press, 1995), 275–283; Michael W. Cuneo, *The Smoke of Satan: Conservative and Traditionalist Dissent in Contemporary American Catholicism* (New York: Oxford University Press, 1999), 66–67. On the comparative ease of passing a statute versus ratifying an Article V amendment, see William N. Eskridge Jr. and John A. Ferejohn, *A Republic of Statutes: The New American Constitution* (New Haven, CT: Yale University Press, 2010), 37–38 (describing the achievement of a formal amendment as "politically impossible").

83. Jones, *Masters of the Universe*, 11.

84. Jimmy Carter, "The State of the Union: Annual Message to Congress" (January 16, 1981), accessed April 7, 2014, http://www.presidency.ucsb.edu/ws/?pid=44541. For more on Carter's interest in deregulation, see Kim McQuaid, *Uneasy Partners: Big Business in American Politics, 1945–1990* (Baltimore: Johns Hopkins University Press, 1994), 151–153; W. Carl Biven, *Jimmy Carter's Economy: Policy in an Age of Limits* (Chapel Hill: University of North Carolina Press, 2002), 154–165; Prasad, *The Politics of Free Markets*, 62–63.

85. Marissa Chappell, *The War on Poverty: Family, Poverty, and Politics in Modern America* (Philadelphia: University of Pennsylvania Press, 2010), 199. On the bipartisan support for the Reagan tax cuts, see McQuaid, *Uneasy Partners*, 168–169; Steven F. Hayward, *The Age of Reagan: The Conservative Counterrevolution, 1980–1989* (New York: Random House, 2009), 163–165.

86. Adam Clymer, "Reagan Urges Party to Support Tax Cuts," *New York Times*, June 25, 1978, 27.

87. Daniel Béland and Alex Waddan, *The Politics of Policy Change: Welfare, Medicare, and Social Security Reform in the United States* (Washington,

DC: Georgetown University Press, 2012), 44. On the impact of OBRA, see Chappell, *The War of Welfare*, 204.

88. See ibid., 38–55. On Reagan's successful attack on "big government," see Seth King, "Reagan Urges an Alliance to Defy Big Government," *New York Times*, January 16, 1979, A7; Adam Clymer, "Reagan off to a Fast Start," *New York Times*, November 18, 1979, E4; Morton Kondracke, "The GOP Gets Its Act Together," *New York Times*, July 13, 1980, SM5. On the poll numbers on the threat posed by "big government," see Gallup Politics, "Record High in U.S. Say Big Government Greatest Threat" (December 18, 2013), accessed April 7, 2014, http://www.gallup.com/poll/166535/record-high-say-big-government-greatest-threat.aspx.

89. R2N2 Abortion Task Force Paper Draft (July 20, 1981), 11, R2N2, Box 1, Abortion Task Force Folder. For a somewhat different take on the problems with the *Roe* decision offered by a leading member of R2N2, see Stamm, "The Master's Plan," 1.

90. R2N2 Abortion Task Force Paper Draft, 19. The draft also criticized the place of population controllers in mainstream groups. See "CARASA Proposal on Abortion Rights for R2N2" (n.d., ca. 1981), 1, R2N2, Box 1, Abortion Task Force Folder ("We distinguish ourselves from NOW, NARAL, PP [Planned Parenthood] and others on the abortion issue in that we see abortion as a key part of women's control over reproduction, not as a single issue or as a part of policy of population control"); Reproductive Rights Task Force of the New Haven Feminist Union (n.d., ca. 1981), R2N2, Box 1, Abortion Task Force Folder ("Recently, feminists have been very much on the defensive in our abortion work. . . . We need to find a way of moving beyond what we have, since we are not satisfied with it").

91. Chicago WORC, "Some Thoughts on Abortion Strategy: A Beginning Consensus" (n.d., ca. 1981), 1–2.

92. Midwest R2N2, "Suggestions for Discussion Questions for Midwest R2N2 Meeting, Feb. 21, 1981" (February 1981), 1, R2N2, Box 1, Abortion Task Force Folder; see also Sally Koplin to Midwest R2N2 (February 8, 1981), 1–2, R2N2, Box 1, Abortion Task Force Folder (arguing that there was no use "putting a lot of energy into a single-issue defense—it's like treating one symptom of a disease").

93. "CARASA Proposal on Abortion Rights for R2N2" (n.d., ca. 1981), 1.

94. Ibid., 2.

95. Twin Cities Reproductive Rights Committee, "Some Thoughts on an Abortion Program and the Need for a More Cohesive Network" (n.d., ca. 1981), R2N2, Box 1, Abortion Task Force Folder.

96. "CARASA Proposal on Abortion Rights for R2N2" (n.d., ca. 1981), 1.

97. R2N2 Abortion Task Force Paper (1981), 4, 9, 11.

98. "Women United to Defend Abortion Rights and End Sterilization Abuse" (n.d., ca. 1980), 3.

99. "CARASA Proposal on Abortion Rights for R2N2" (n.d., ca. 1981), 2.

100. R2N2 Abortion Task Force Paper (1981), 7. On the decline and dissolution of R2N2 in the early 1980s, see Staggenborg, *The Pro-Choice Movement*, 121–126, 169; Nelson, *Women of Color*, 139–140.
101. Katz, interview.

Chapter 5. The Popular Reinterpretation of *Roe v. Wade*

1. Richard A. Posner, *The Problematics of Moral and Legal Theory* (Cambridge, MA: Harvard University Press, 1999), 254. For more on the way in which *Roe* froze dialogue about abortion in the states and within social movements, see Cass R. Sunstein, *One Case at a Time: Judicial Minimalism on the Supreme Court*, 2nd ed. (Cambridge, MA: Harvard University Press, 2001), 114–115 (arguing that had the Court not issued so broad and philosophical a ruling in *Roe*, "[i]t would not have caused so much destructive and unnecessary social upheaval, because it would have produced a range of creative compromises well adapted to federal system"); Ruth Bader Ginsburg, "Speaking in a Judicial Voice," *New York University Law Review* 67 (1992): 1205 (contending that *Roe* "invited no dialogue with legislators"); William N, Eskridge Jr., "Some Effects of Identity-Based Social Movements on Constitutional Law in the Twentieth Century," *Michigan Law Review* 100 (2002): 2144 (arguing that antiabortion activists despised the *Roe* decision because it "took the most moral of issues away from family and state decision-making"); Elizabeth Mensch and Alan Freeman, *The Politics of Virtue: Is Abortion Debatable?* 2nd ed. (Durham, NC: Duke University Press, 1995), 109 (claiming that because of the *Roe* decision, "a dialogue that might have really spoken to Americans from within their own seriously considered religious traditions seemed to be lost").
2. Kathleen Hendrix, "Impassioned Argument for Right to Life," *Los Angeles Times*, September 26, 1975, F1.
3. Enid Nemy, "Feminists, Set Back, to Stress Politics," *New York Times*, July 7, 1980, B12. For more on Jefferson's media appearances, see "A Fighter for Right to Life," *Ebony Magazine*, April 1978, 78–88. On Jefferson's background and legacy: see Anthony J. Lauinger, "Focus: Mildred F. Jefferson, M.D.," *National Right to Life News*, January 1977, 5, JRS, 1977 National Right to Life News Box; Dennis Hevesi, "Mildred Jefferson, 84, Anti-Abortion Activist, Is Dead," *New York Times*, October 18, 2010, accessed April 7, 2014, http://www.nytimes.com/2010/10/19/us/19jefferson.html?_r=0; "Mildred Jefferson, Anti-Abortion Activist, Dies at 84," *Los Angeles Times*, October 16, 2010, accessed April 7, 2014, http://latimes-blogs.latimes.com/afterword/2010/10/mildred-jefferson-anti-abortion-activist-dies-at-84.html.
4. Hendrix, "Impassioned Argument," F1.

5. Judy Klemesrud, "Abortion in the Campaign: Methodist Surgeon Leading the Opposition," *New York Magazine*, March 1, 1976, 44.

6. See Hendrix, "Impassioned Argument," F1. For more on Jefferson's medical interpretation of the *Roe* decision, see "Woman Doctor Calls Abortion 'Private Death Contract,'" *New York Times*, March 11, 1974, 18 (arguing that the *Roe* decision gave the woman and doctor a form of "supercitizenship" in making life and death decisions); see also Press Release, "Noted Female Gun in Anti-Abortion Movement Received Honorary Degree at Seattle University" (January 1, 1975), 1, ACCL, 1975 NRLC Board and Executive Committee Folder 2 (stressing that *Roe* "allowed the woman and her doctor to make a private death contract").

7. "A Fighter for the Right to Life," 92. Jefferson had expressed some frustration with the women's movement earlier in the 1970s as well. See Hendrix, "Impassioned Argument," F1; Klemesrud, "Abortion in the Campaign," 44. For more on the feminist summit at the International Women's Year celebration that Jefferson condemned, see Donald T. Critchlow, *Phyllis Schlafly and Grassroots Conservatism: A Woman's Crusade* (Princeton: Princeton University Press, 2005), 245–247; Christina Wolbrecht, *The Politics of Women's Rights: Parties, Positions, and Change* (Princeton: Princeton University Press, 2000), 43–44.

8. Mickey Stern, interview with Mary Ziegler, September 10, 2011. For more on Stern's personal journey: "Mickey Stern," in *Feminists Who Changed America, 1963–1975*, ed. Barbara J. Love (Champaign: University of Illinois Press, 2006), 445. For recollections of the Cleveland Preterm Clinic and the abortion-rights movement in Ohio: Carolyn Buhl, interview with Mary Ziegler, September 21, 2011; Sally Tatnall, interview with Mary Ziegler, September 12, 2011.

9. On the history and operations of the Preterm clinics, see Carolyn E. Joffe, *Doctors of Conscience: The Struggle to Provide Abortion before and after Roe v. Wade* (Boston: Beacon Press, 1995), 18–19, 148; Warren Hern, "Life on the Front Lines," in *Abortion Wars: A Half Century of Struggle, 1950–2000*, ed. Rickie Solinger (Berkeley: University of California Press, 1998), 301, 307.

10. Stern, interview.

11. Lawrence Lader, *Abortion II: Making the Revolution* (Boston: Beacon Press, 1974), 8. For further analysis of Vuitch's work, see David J. Garrow, *Liberty and Sexuality: The Right of Privacy and the Making of Roe v. Wade* (Berkeley: University of California Press, 1998), 318, 382–383; Linda Greenhouse, *Becoming Justice Blackmun: Harry Blackmun's Supreme Court Journey* (New York: Henry Holt, 2005), 75. For the decision in *Vuitch*, see *United States v. Vuitch*, 402 U.S. 62 (1971).

12. Lader, *Abortion II*, 8.

13. For expressions of frustration with reform laws, see Keith Monroe, "How California's Abortion Law Isn't Working," *New York Times*, December 29, 1968, SM21; see also Martin Tolchin, "Doctors Divided on Issue,"

New York Times, February 27, 1967, 1; Robert D. McFadden, "Flaws in Abortion Reform in 8-State Study," *New York Times*, April 13, 1970, 1.

14. Lawrence Lader, "The Scandal of Abortion Laws," *New York Times*, April 25, 1965, SM32. On physicians' campaign to liberalize abortion laws, see Jennifer Nelson, *Women of Color and the Reproductive Rights Movement* (New York: New York University Press, 2003), 10; Leslie J. Reagan, *When Abortion Was a Crime: Women, Medicine, and Law in the United States, 1867–1973* (Berkeley: University of California Press, 1997), 60–71; Kristin Luker, *Abortion and the Politics of Motherhood* (Berkeley: University of California Press, 1984), 31–45.

15. Shirley Chisholm: NARAL Press Release (September 29, 1969), 1, LLP, Box 8, Folder 20.

16. See NARAL Sample Letter to Physician (n.d., ca. December 1969), NRL, Carton 1, 1969 Executive Committee Minutes Folder (arguing that "[a]bortion laws demean a physician by telling him what constitutes good medicine"). For more on NARAL's focus on physician's rights, see NARAL Executive Committee Meeting Minutes (February 24, 1970), 2, NRL, Carton 1, 1970 Executive Committee Minutes Folder (describing a project designed to enlist the support of physicians and to publicize medical arguments for abortion); NARAL Press Release, "Amendments to New Abortion Law Would Endanger Women and Medical Choice" (April 1970), NRL, Carton 1, 1970 Executive Committee Minutes Folder.

17. Eileen Shanahan, "Doctor Leads Group's Challenge to Michigan Anti-Abortion Law," *New York Times*, October 5, 1971, 28. Lader and his colleagues also led a program designed to encourage physicians to perform and advocate for abortions. See John Sibley, "Physicians Urged to Defy City and State Guidelines on Abortion," *New York Times*, June 11, 1970, 18.

18. NARAL Executive Committee Meeting Minutes (December 10, 1971), 1, NRL, Carton 1, 1971 Executive Committee Minutes Folder.

19. NARAL Board of Directors Meeting Minutes (October 4, 1971), 2, NRL, Carton 1, Board Minutes Folder.

20. NARAL Executive Committee Meeting Minutes (November 27, 1972), 1–2, NRL, Carton 1, 1972 Executive Committee Minutes Folder. For more on the medical arguments made by NARAL and Planned Parenthood, see *NARAL Speaker and Debater's Notebook* excerpt (n.d., ca. 1972), Carton 7, 1972 Debating the Opposition Folder (arguing that "[a] physician has a right to practice medicine as he sees fit"); Meeting Minutes, Planned Parenthood-World Population Board of Directors (May 8, 1969), 10–11, PPFA I, Box 49, Folder 19; "New Group Will Seek Changes in Abortion Laws," *New York Times*, February 17, 1969, 32; Myra MacPherson, "M.D.s File Abortion Lawsuit," *Washington Post*, September 30, 1969, B1.

21. *Roe v. Wade*, 410 U.S. 113, 165–166 (1973); see also Outline and Redraft of *Doe v. Bolton* (July 19, 1972), 3, HBP, Box 151, Folder 4.

22. Harry Blackmun to Lewis Powell (December 4, 1972), 2, HBP, Box 151, Folder 4 (explaining that *Roe* and *Doe* stood for the idea that the states could leave the abortion decision to physicians).

23. National Right to Life Committee Board of Directors Meeting Minutes (December 9, 1972), 2, ACCL, Box 4, 1970 National Right to Life Folder.

24. On the relationship between the NRLC and the Catholic Church, see Robert Karrer, "The Formation of Michigan's Anti-Abortion Movement, 1967–74," *Michigan History Review* 22 (1996): 98–100; Ziad W. Munson, *The Making of Pro-Life Activists: How Social Mobilization Works* (Chicago: University of Chicago Press, 2008), 85; Faye D. Ginsburg, *Contested Lives: The Abortion Debate in an American Community* (Berkeley: University of California Press: 1998), 44.

25. Nick Thimmesch, "Right to Life Fights for Human Values," *Chicago Tribune*, June 17, 1973, A6.

26. Ibid.

27. "Woman Doctor Calls Abortion 'Private Death Contract,'" 18; see also Speech Excerpts, Mildred F. Jefferson (June 8, 1973), ACCL, Box 4, June 1973 National Right to Life Convention Folder (contending that "[t]he physician bears the power and the burden of [the] social revolution-policy decision" in *Roe*).

28. Robert M. Byrn, "Abortion on Demand: Whose Morality?" *Notre Dame Law Review* 46 (1970): 16.

29. Robert M. Byrn, "Abortion in Perspective," *Duquesne Law Review* 5 (1966–1967): 128. On the evolution of fetology and its use by the pro-life movement, see Sarah Dubow, *Ourselves Unborn: A History of the Fetus in Modern America* (New York: Oxford University Press, 2010), 3–5, 113–120. For further arguments of this kind by abortion opponents, see A. James Quinn and James A. Griffin, "The Rights of the Unborn," *Jurist* 3 (1971): 577–578; David W. Louisell, "Abortion, The Practice of Medicine and the Due Process of Law," *UCLA Law Review* 16 (1968–1969): 234; Note, "The Unborn Child and the Conception of Biological Life," *Iowa Law Review* 56 (1971): 1003. On the panels at the 1972 NRLC Convention and at earlier events, see Agenda, Third Annual National Right to Life Committee Meeting (June 16–18, 1972), ACCL, Box 4, 1972 National Right to Life Convention Folder; Agenda, National Meeting: Right to Life Movement (July 31–August 2, 1970), ACCL, Box 4, 1970 National Right to Life Meeting Folder (describing a panel on fetology and the "two patients" of physicians dealing with pregnant patients).

30. "Note: The Unborn Child and the Constitutional Conception of Life," 996.

31. Louisell, "The Practice of Medicine," 234.

32. Resolution # 7 (July 10, 1973), ACCL, Box 4, 1973 NRLC Folder 4.

33. On struggles over the top-down management style adopted by Golden and Vanderhoef, see National Right to Life Committee, Inc., Meeting of the Executive Committee (n.d., ca. October 1973), ACCL, Box 4, 1973

NRLC Board and Executive Committee Folder 6 (demanding Golden's resignation because of his supposed "unwillingness . . . to accept the decisions of a majority of the Executive Committee"); Michael Taylor to Edward Golden to the National Right to Life Committee Board of Directors et al., Re: Correct Operational Policies of the NRLC, Inc. (October 24, 1973), 2, ACCL, Box 4, 1973 NRLC Board and Executive Committee Folder 6 (criticizing the "grassroots" organizational style previously endorsed by the Executive Committee). As the chapter later discusses, those leaders endorsing a more informal style of organization left the organization. For studies of homemakers active in the antiabortion movement, see Munson, *The Making of Pro-Life Activists*, 18, 57, 70; Carol J. C. Maxwell, *Pro-Life Activists in America: Meaning, Motivation, and Direct Action* (New York: Cambridge University Press, 2002), 114, 138; Luker, *Abortion*, 128, 139, 145, 176, 204–206. For the personal stories of homemakers involved in major state and national organizations: Randy Engel, interview with Mary Ziegler, August 19, 2011; Pam Manning, interview with Mary Ziegler, August 17, 2011; Garnett Biviano, interview with Mary Ziegler, February 23, 2012; Denise Neary, interview with Mary Ziegler, February 18, 2012.

34. "Conflicts Lead to Forming of New Right to Life Unit," *Catholic Star Herald*, August 30, 1974, 1. For more on disagreements between NRLC leaders, see National Right to Life Committee Board of Directors Meeting Minutes (December 8, 1973), 1–8, ACCL, Box 5, 1973 NRLC Board and Executive Committee Folder 7 (discussing the replacement of Schaller and the organization's internal disagreements); William P. Maloney, "The Owl in the Saguaro: Report to Officers and Board of Directors of the Right to Life Committee of New Mexico" (January 23, 1974), 1–4, ACCL, Box 8, 1974 NRLC Board and Executive Committee Folder 1 (same).

35. Abortion Part 1: Testimony on S. 119 and S. 130 before the Subcommittee on Constitutional Amendments of the Senate Judiciary Committee, 93rd Congress, 2nd Session (1974), 91 (Statement of Senator Jesse Helms). Chapter 1 discusses the Hogan Amendment and alternative constitutional proposals in more depth.

36. Abortion Part 4: Testimony on S. 119 and S. 130 before the Subcommittee on Constitutional Amendments of the Senate Judiciary Committee, 94th Congress, 1st Session (1974), 8–9 (Statement of Dr. Mildred Jefferson).

37. "Noted Female Gun in Anti-Abortion Movement Received Honorary Degree at Seattle University" (January 1, 1975), 2.

38. For Brown's recollections on the subject: Judie Brown, interview with Mary Ziegler, August 4, 2011. For more on Brown's pro-life work, see Judie Brown, *Not My Will but Thine: An Autobiography* (Stafford, VA: American Life League, 2002). For news coverage of Brown's activities in the period, see Laurie Johnston, "Abortion Foes Gain Support As They Intensify Campaign," *New York Times*, October 23, 1977, 1; Royce Rensberger, "March of Dimes Group Declares Genetic Aid Program Will Go

On," *New York Times*, March 15, 1978, A20; "Conservative Group to Monitor TV," *New York Times*, February 3, 1981, C8.

39. See Hendrix, "Impassioned Argument," F1. For a similar interpretation of *Roe*, see "Woman Doctor Calls Abortion 'Private Death Contract,'" 18; Press Release, "Noted Female Gun in Anti-Abortion Movement Received Honorary Degree at Seattle University," 1–2; Family Planning Services and Population Research Amendments of 1973: Testimony before the Subcommittee on Human Resources of the Senate Committee on Labor and Human Welfare, 93rd Congress, 1st Session (1973), 199 (Statement of Randy Engel of the United States Coalition for Life) (arguing that *Roe* "provide[d] that a woman's attending physician shall make the determining decision on abortion").

40. NOW Fundraising Letter (n.d., ca. 1973), WSH, Box 11, Folder 14.

41. NARAL Executive Committee Meeting Minutes (February 5, 1973), NRL, Carton 1, 1973–1974 Executive Committee Folder.

42. NARAL Executive Committee Meeting Minutes (March 26, 1973), NRL, Carton 1, 1973–1974 Executive Committee Folder.

43. Lee Gidding to NARAL Board of Directors et al. (February 7, 1973), 1–2, NRL, Carton 1, 1973–1974 Executive Committee Folder. For individual recollections of this attitude among abortion-rights proponents in the period: Fran Kissling, interview with Mary Ziegler, September 13, 2011; Buhl, interview; Karen Mulhauser, interview with Mary Ziegler, February 4, 2011.

44. NARAL Executive Committee Meeting Minutes (July 12–13, 1974), 2, NRL, Carton 1, 1974 Executive Committee Minutes Folder.

45. Vicki Kaplan to Members of the NARAL Executive Committee et al. (April 1974), 2–3, NRL, Carton 1, 1974 Executive Committee Minutes Folder. In particular, NARAL leaders pointed to thorny legal questions (in areas from inheritance to immigration, voting rights, and tort law) that could theoretically arise if the Constitution recognized fetal personhood.

46. Jan Liebman, Abortion Amendment Strategy (n.d., ca. 1974), 1–3, WSH, Box 11, Folder 12; see also Ann Scott and Jan Liebman to NOW Legislative Task Force Coordinator et al. (September 1, 1974), 1, NOW, Box 54, Folder 27; "Abortion: NOW Action Program" (April 1974), 1, NOW, Box 54, Folder 24.

47. NARAL Board of Directors Meeting Minutes (October 20, 1972), 2, NRL, Carton 1, Board Minutes Folder.

48. "Abortion: NOW Action Program" (April 1974), 1.

49. For examples of the visibility of white, male, conservative pro-lifers in Congress, including Henry Hyde and Jesse Helms, see Marjorie Hunter, "Senate Upholds U.S. Abortion Funds," *New York Times*, April 11, 1975, 28; Arthur Siddons, "'Evil' Hyde: Nice Enough to Be a Jekyll," *Chicago Tribune*, June 19, 1977, 16; Peter Ross Range, "Thunder from the Right: Helms," *New York Times*, February 8, 1981, SM6. Karen Mulhauser,

among other activists, recalls seeing her battle as a defense of women's rights. Mulhauser, interview.

50. On Diamond's personal story: Eugene Diamond, interview with Mary Ziegler, August 10, 2011. For a sample of Diamond's antiabortion work, see Eugene F. Diamond, "The Humanity of the Unborn Child," *Catholic Lawyer* 17 (1971): 174–180; Eugene Diamond to George Huntston Williams (February 4, 1972), CRP. Diamond would go on to write on the benefits of chastity. See Eugene Diamond and Rosemary Diamond, *The Positive Values of Chastity* (Chicago: Franciscan Herald, 1983).

51. For Goltz's recollections of her background: Pat Goltz, interview with Mary Ziegler, February 11, 2011.

52. On the positions taken by Goltz and Feminists for Life in the period, see "Feminists for Life Task Force on Consumer Credit," *Feminists for Life Journal* (1972): 2, FFL; "The Equal Rights Amendment," *Feminists for Life Journal* (1973): 8, FFL. For further analysis of the founding and operations of the organization in the period, see Pat Goltz, Cathy Callaghan, and Cindy Osborne, "Pat Goltz, Cathy Callaghan, and the Founding of Feminists for Life," in *Prolife Feminism: Yesterday and Today*, eds. Mary Krane Derr, Rachel MacNair, and Linda Naranjo-Huebl (New York: Sulzberger and Graham, 1995), 219–224; Abortion Part 3: Testimony on S. 119 and S. 130 before the Subcommittee on Constitutional Amendments of the Senate Judiciary Committee, 93rd Congress, 2nd Session (1974), 107–114 (statement of Pat Goltz of Feminists for Life).

53. Pat Colander, "In Illinois: Legal Abortion Belies Its Boon," *Chicago Tribune*, January 23, 1974, C1.

54. Pat Goltz, "Editorial: A Woman's Right to Control Her Own Body," *Feminists for Life Journal* (Summer 1973): 6, FFL. For the Heffernan editorial, see Gloria Heffernan, "Final Insult: Abortion Exploits Women," *Chicago Tribune*, June 2, 1972, 14, FFL.

55. See George Steven Swan, Untitled Article, *Sisterlife Journal*, 1973, 1–4, FFL.

56. For an example of such arguments made in the pamphlets and materials of antiabortion organizations in the early to mid-1970s, see NRLC Press Release, "Three Pro-Life Women Challenge Girl Scout Program" (July 24, 1973), 2, ACCL, Box 4, 1973 NRLC Folder 4 (describing abortion as a "violent, self-defeating philosophy" for women); "Noted Female Gun in Anti-Abortion Movement Received Honorary Degree at Seattle University" (January 1, 1975), 2 (Mildred Jefferson arguing that abortion was "an insult to women"); Women for the Unborn, Brief as Amicus Curiae for Women for the Unborn, 15–16, *Roe v. Wade*, 410 U.S. 113 (1973) (Nos. 70–18, 70–40) ("As women, we believe the state laws restricting abortions protect both thousands of unborn babies and thousands of mothers"); Brief of Amicus Curiae for Robert Sassone et al., 14–16, 36, *Roe v. Wade*, 410 U.S. 113 (1973) (Nos. 70–18, 70–40) (arguing that abortion harmed women and that "after abortion, many women feel that part of them is

gone"). For examples of similar claims made by the United States Coalition for Life and Women for the Unborn, see Statement of Randy Engel, 198 (arguing that abortion and family planning providers exploited and experimented on poor women); Departments of Labor and Health, Education, and Welfare for Fiscal Year 1975: Testimony before the Subcommittee on the Departments of Labor and Health, Education and Welfare Agencies Appropriations of the Senate Appropriations Committee, 93rd Congress, 2nd Session (1975), 5350 (Statement of Connaught Marshner of the United States Coalition for Life). For the Willkes' arguments to this effect, see Dr. John and Barbara Willke, *Handbook on Abortion* (Cincinnati, OH: Hiltz, 1973), 129–133. Woman-protective arguments later became a much more influential part of movement advocacy. See Reva B. Siegel, "The Right's Reasons: Constitutional Conflict and the Spread of Woman-Protective Antiabortion Argument," *Duke Law Journal* 57 (2008): 1471–1692; Reva B. Siegel, "Dignity and the Politics of Protection: Abortion Restrictions under *Casey/Carhart*," *Yale Law Journal* 117 (2008): 1694–1800.

57. NOW, "Major National Groups Opposed to Abortion" (October 6, 1978), NOW, Box 54, Folder 42. Chapter 6 adds more on Mecklenburg's contributions.

58. William Robbins, "Abortion Foes Look to Ultimate Victory," *New York Times*, June 19, 1977, 24.

59. On Nellie Gray's background, see Dave Jolivet, "At 84, Pro-Life Leader Nellie Gray Marches On," *Catholic News Service*, accessed January 22, 2010, http://www.americancatholic.org/news/report.aspx?id=2135; Denise Grady, "Nellie Gray, Abortion Foe and Leader of Annual March, Dies at 88," *New York Times*, accessed August 15, 2012, http://www.nytimes.com/2012/08/16/us/nellie-gray-anti-abortion-activist-dies-at-88.html?_r=0. On the early positions and actions of March for Life, see Nellie Gray to the National Right to Life Committee Board of Directors (December 8, 1973), ACCL, 1973 NRLC Board and Executive Committee Folder 6; Nellie Gray to the National Right to Life Committee Board of Directors (February 10, 1974), ACCL, Box 8, 1974 NRLC Board and Executive Committee Folder 3.

60. "Planned Parenthood Shifting to a Patriotic Claim," *New York Times*, October 5, 1980, 25. For NOW's focus on women's rights and interpretation of *Roe* in the period, see Arlie Scott, Sample Letter to House of Representatives (June 13, 1979), 1, NOW, Box 54, Folder 42. Chapter 3 adds more on abortion-rights organizations' new emphasis on women's rights.

61. Abortion Part 4: Testimony on Constitutional Amendments Regarding Abortion before the Senate Judiciary Subcommittee on Constitutional Amendments, 94th Congress, 1st Session (1975), 711 (Statement of Betty Friedan).

62. Abortion Part 4: Testimony on Constitutional Amendments Regarding Abortion before the Senate Judiciary Subcommittee on Constitutional

Amendments, 94th Congress, 1st Session (1975), 701 (Statement of Audrey Rowe Colom of the National Women's Political Caucus). On Colom's identity as a Republican feminist, see "Women Score G.O.P. on Site," *New York Times*, September 9, 1975, 23; Eileen Shanahan, "Women's Caucus Plans Rights Drive," *New York Times*, June 30, 1975, 12. On the work of the NWPC, see Wolbrecht, *The Politics of Women's Rights*, 35–36, 41–50; Cynthia Harrison, "Creating a National Feminist Agenda: Coalition-Building in the 1970s," in *Feminist Coalitions: Historical Perspectives on Second Wave Feminism in the United States*, ed. Stephanie Gilmore (Champaign: University of Illinois Press, 2008), 20–33.

63. National Abortion Rights League, *Legal Abortion: A Speaker and Debater's Notebook* (Washington, DC: The League, 1978), 7, MRL, Box 2, Folder 5. On the NARAL Executive Committee meeting, see NARAL Executive Committee Meeting Minutes (April 13, 1975), 1, NRL, Carton 1, 1975 Executive Committee Minutes Folder.

64. NOW Public Service Announcement (January 21, 1976), NOW, Box 30, Folder 8.

65. "Chronology of Major Events Affecting a Woman's Right to Choose Abortion, 2600 BC to the Present" (October 3, 1978), 1, NOW, Box 54, Folder 42.

66. Meeting Minutes, Morning Session, Board of Directors, Planned Parenthood Federation of America (May 1975), 167–168, PPFA II, Box 199, Folder 12.

67. Meeting Minutes, Board of Directors, Planned Parenthood Federation of America (January 30, 1976), 105, PPFA II, Box 199, Folder 7.

68. National Women's Conference, "Proposed National Plan of Action" (November 18–21, 1977), 32, PPFA II, Box 109, Folder 5. On discussion of abortion at the June meeting, see Meeting Minutes, Afternoon Session, Board of Directors, Planned Parenthood Federation of America (June 5, 1976), 118–134, PPFA II, Box 199, Folder 4.

69. National Right to Life Education Committee, Inc., Minutes of the Education Committee Meeting (September 24, 1973), 2, ACCL, Box 4, 1973 NRLC Board and Executive Committee Folder 5.

70. Judith Fink, "Midterm Report of the Intergroup Committee of the National Right to Life Committee" (n.d., ca. 1973), 1, ACCL, Box 4, 1973 Midyear Report Folder 2.

71. Ibid., 2.

72. Judith Fink to Ed Golden et al., "In re Policy Statement of the NRLC Concerning 'Birth Control'" (May 15, 1973), ACCL, Box 4, NRLC 1973 Folder 2.

73. George Dugan, "New Drive to End Abortion Scored," *New York Times*, January 18, 1976, 23. For more on the activities of the Religious Coalition for Abortion Rights in the period, see Suzanne Staggenborg, *The Pro-Choice Movement: Organization and Activism in the Abortion Conflict* (New York: Oxford University Press, 1991), 60, 74–75, 101–105,

182–199; Samuel A. Mills, "Abortion and Religious Freedom: The Religious Coalition for Abortion Rights (RCAR) and the Pro-Choice Movement, 1973–1989," *Journal of Church and State* 33 (1991): 569–594.

74. Chapter 1 further discusses intramovement struggles over contraception. On pro-lifers' struggle to reframe their cause as something more than a Catholic issue, see Daniel K. Williams, *God's Own Party: The Making of the Christian Right*, 2nd ed. (New York: Oxford University Press, 2012), 115–121; Keith Cassidy, "The Right to Life Movement: Sources, Development, and Strategies," in *The Politics of Abortion and Birth Control in Historical Perspective*, ed. Donald T. Critchlow (University Park: Penn State Press, 1996), 140–142; Patricia Miller, *Good Catholics: The Battle over Abortion in the Catholic Church* (Berkeley: University of California Press, 2014), 71–73.

75. See Barry Hankins, *Uneasy in Babylon: Southern Baptist Conservatives and American Culture* (Tuscaloosa: University of Alabama Press, 2002), 171–172; Williams, *God's Own Party*, 117–118. On concerns that abortion was seen to be a Catholic cause, see James Risen and Judy L. Thomas, *Wrath of Angels: The American Abortion Wars* (New York: Basic Books, 1998), 20 (explaining that the pro-life movement remained predominantly Catholic in the late 1960s and early 1970s); Williams, *God's Own Party*, 117–120. On the SBC's position prior to the *Roe* decision, see Southern Baptist Convention, "Resolution on Abortion" (June 1971), accessed April 8, 2014, http://www.sbc.net/resolutions/search/results.asp?query=abortion. For further analysis of the SBC's position, see Southern Baptist Convention, "Resolution on Abortion and Sanctity of Human Life" (June 1974), accessed April 9, 2014, http://www.sbc.net/resolutions/search/results.asp?query=abortion. In 1976, the SBC would reverse its prior stand and condemn all non-therapeutic abortions. See Southern Baptist Convention, "Resolution on Abortion" (June 1976), accessed April 10, 2014, http://www.sbc.net/resolutions/search/results.asp?query=abortion. For discussion of the National Council of Churches' position on abortion, see Tom Davis, *Sacred Work: Planned Parenthood and Its Clergy Alliances* (Piscataway, NJ: Rutgers University Press, 2005), 2–3, 42; Brief as Amicus Curiae on Behalf of the National Council of Churches, *Harris v. McRae*, 448 U.S. 297 (1980) (No. 79–1268).

76. On the wish of ERA proponents to separate the amendment from abortion politics, see Serena Mayeri, "A New E.R.A. or a New Era? Amendment Advocacy and the Reconstitution of Feminism," *University of Pennsylvania Law Review* 103 (2009): 1233, 1243–1244; Reva B. Siegel, "Sex Equality Arguments for Reproductive Rights: Their Critical Basis and Evolving Constitutional Protection," *Emory Law Journal* 56 (2007): 828–829.

77. Judith Fink to Ed Golden et al., "In Re Policy Statement of the NRLC Concerning 'Birth Control'" (May 15, 1973), 2.

78. See David R. Swartz, *The Moral Minority: The Evangelical Left in an Age of Conservatism* (Philadelphia: University of Pennsylvania Press, 2012),

220–226, 233–250 (charting the ambivalence of many progressive evangelicals about pro-life activism); see also Mark Hulsether, *Building a Protestant Left: Christianity and "Crisis" Magazine, 1941–1993* (Knoxville: University of Tennessee Press, 1999), 169–177.

79. Phyllis Schlafly, "ERA Means Abortion and Population Shrinkage," *The Phyllis Schlafly Report*, December 1974, vol. 8, no. 5, sec. 2, PSR. On discussion of gay and lesbian rights within NOW and other feminist organizations in the later 1970s, see Maryann Barasko, *Governing NOW: Grassroots Activism in the National Organization for Women* (Ithaca, NY: Cornell University Press, 2004), 50–81; Sara M. Evans, *Tidal Wave: How Women Changed America at Century's End* (New York: Simon and Schuster, 2003), 51–53, 110. On Schlafly's anti-lesbian rhetoric, see Judy Klemesrud, "Opponent of ERA Confident of Its Defeat," *New York Times*, December 15, 1975, 53; John Herbers, "Equal Rights Amendment Is Mired in Confused and Emotional Debate," *New York Times*, May 28, 1978, 1; Karen DeWitt, "Rights' Foes Celebrate Its Difficulties with a Gala," *New York Times*, March 23, 1979, A18. On DeCrow and other feminists' protest of the 1976 Democratic Party Platform, see Thomas P. Ronan, "Women Stress Feminist Issues in Rally Opposite the Garden," *New York Times*, July 11, 1976, 41.

80. On the backgrounds of ERA opponents, see Val Burris, "Who Opposed the ERA? An Analysis of the Social Bases of Antifeminism" *Social Science Quarterly* 64 (June 1983): 305–317; Kent L. Tedin et al., "Social Background and Political Differences Between Pro- and Anti-ERA Activists," *American Politics Quarterly* 5 (July 1977): 395–404; David W. Brady and Kent L. Tedin, "Ladies in Pink: Religion and Political Ideology in the Anti-ERA Movement," *Social Science Quarterly* 56 (March 1976): 564–575.

81. On the view that McCormack's campaign had identified an important group of swing voters, see Fundraising Letter, "Ellen McCormack for President" (March 8, 1976), 2, JRS, Ellen McCormack Papers; Fran Watson, "Response to President Ford's Statement on Abortion" (February 5, 1976), JRS, Ellen McCormack Papers. On Carter's *Playboy* interview and its impact, see Williams, *God's Own Party*, 81, 126–127; J. Brooks Flippen, *Jimmy Carter, The Politics of Family, and the Rise of the Religious Right* (Athens: University of Georgia Press, 2011), 99–103. For the interview itself, see Robert Scheer, "The Playboy Interview: Jimmy Carter," *Playboy*, November 1976, 66.

82. Leslie Bennetts, "Conservatives Join on Social Concerns," *New York Times*, July 30, 1980, A1. On New Right efforts to recruit pro-lifers, see Nathan J. Muller, "One Issue Groups Educate Congress," *Conservative Digest*, January 1979, 43; Sanford J. Ungar, "New Right Senators: They're Getting Results," *Conservative Digest*, March 26, 1979, 26–27; "Mobilizing the Moral Majority," *Conservative Digest*, August 1979, 14. For more on the campaign to forge a coherent conservative coalition, see Williams, *God's Own Party*, 168–169; Linda Greenhouse and Reva B. Siegel, eds.,

Before Roe v. Wade: *Voices That Shaped the Abortion Debate before the Supreme Court's Ruling*, 2nd ed., (New Haven, CT: Yale Law Library, 2012), 292–296.

83. Francis A. Schaeffer, *How Shall We Then Live? The Rise and Decline of Western Thought and Culture*, 50th Anniversary L'Abri ed. (Wheaton, IL: Crossway Books, 2005), 222–223. *How Shall We Then Live* was first published in 1976. See Francis A. Schaeffer, *How Shall We Then Live? The Rise and Decline of Western Thought and Culture* (Old Tappan, NJ: Fleming H. Revel, 1976). On changing patterns in evangelical turnout, see Jeff Manza and Clem Brooks, *Social Cleavages and Political Change: Voter Alignments and U.S. Party Coalitions* (New York: Oxford University Press, 1999), 97; Jon A. Shields, *The Democratic Virtues of the Christian Right* (Princeton: Princeton University Press, 2009), 120; Corwin Smidt, "Evangelical Voting Patterns: 1978–1988," in *No Longer Exiles*, ed. Michael Cromartie (Washington, DC: Ethics and Public Policy Center, 1993), 85–117.

84. On Schaeffer's influence on Jerry Falwell, see Risen and Thomas, *Wrath of Angels*, 126–129; Williams, *God's Own Party*, 155–156, 173–174. On Schaeffer's influence on LaHaye and other evangelicals, see Sarah Barringer Gordon, *The Spirit of the Law: Religious Voices and the Constitution in Modern America* (Cambridge, MA: Harvard University Press, 2010), 142–152; Robert Wuthnow, *The Restructuring of American Religion: Society and Faith since World War II* (Princeton: Princeton University Press, 1988), 206. For LaHaye's popularization of Schaeffer's argument, see Timothy LaHaye, *The Battle for the Mind* (Old Tappan, NJ: Fleming H. Revell, 1980).

85. Moral Majority, "The ERA: A Satanic Attack upon the Family and the Bible" (n.d., ca. 1979), JFP, Series 3, Box 1, Folder 2.

86. Ibid. (citation and internal quotation omitted).

87. The Moral Majority, ERA Brochure (n.d., ca. 1979), 3, JFP, Series 3, Box 1, Folder 2.

88. Brochure, "What Is the Moral Majority?" (n.d., ca. 1979), MMP, Series 1, Box 1, Folder 1.

89. Dr. Jerry Falwell, "What Is the Moral Majority?" *Moral Majority Capitol Report*, August 1979, 1, MMP, Series 1, Box 1, Folder 1.

90. See Greenhouse and Siegel, *Before* Roe v. Wade, 293–295; Williams, *God's Own Party*, 168–169; Michele McKeegan, *Abortion Politics: Mutiny in the Ranks of the Right* (New York: Free Press, 1992), 21–27.

91. Chapter 6 traces the larger impact of these political changes, studying the reasons for the polarization of the abortion conflict.

92. Proposed Constitutional Amendments on Abortion, Part 1: Testimony before the Subcommittee on Civil and Constitutional Rights of the House Judiciary Committee, 94th Congress, 2nd Session (1976), 14 (Statement of Joseph Witherspoon).

93. See Treasury, Postal Services, and General Government Appropriations, FY 77, Part 3: Testimony before the Subcommittee on Treasury, Postal

Services, and General Government Appropriations of the Senate Appropriations Committee, 94th Congress, 2nd Session (1976), 2971–2972 (Statement of Nellie Gray).

94. Brief of Amicus Curiae for the United States Catholic Conference, 81, *Planned Parenthood of Central Missouri v. Danforth*, 428 U.S. 52 (1976) (Nos. 74-1151, 74-1419).

95. Motion and Brief Amici Curiae for Americans United for Life and Dr. Eugene Diamond, 17, *Bellotti v. Baird*, 443 U.S. 622 (1979) (Nos. 78-329, 78-330). *Bellotti* ultimately struck down the law, emphasizing that it required a minor to get the consent of both parents and did not adequately provide a judicial-bypass option for minors who could convince a court of their maturity. *Bellotti v. Baird*, 443 U.S. 622, 646–650 (1979).

96. See Brief Amicus Curiae for the National Right to Life Committee, 1A, *Williams v. Zbaraz*, 448 U.S. 358 (1980) (Nos. 79-4, 79-5, 79-491). The Court ultimately rejected challenges to both state and federal bans on abortion funding. See *Williams v. Zbaraz*, 448 U.S. 358 (1980); *Harris v. McRae*, 448 U.S. 297 (1980).

97. See Helen Epstein, "Abortion: An Issue That Won't Go Away," *New York Times*, March 30, 1980, SM111. Chapter 2 offers more discussion of Jefferson's failure to secure reelection. On Gerster's early work as NRLC President, see Carolyn Gerster, "From the President's Desk," *National Right to Life News*, January 1979, 11, JRS, 1979 National Right to Life News Box (stressing the importance of rhetoric in the abortion wars); Carolyn Gerster, "From the President's Desk," *National Right to Life News*, March 1979, 9, JRS, 1979 National Right to Life News Box (outlining Gerster's opposition to a common-ground summit); Carolyn Gerster, "From the President's Desk," *National Right to Life News*, June 1979, 7, JRS, 1979 National Right to Life News Box (reciting arguments that life began at conception); Carolyn Gerster, "From the President's Desk," *National Right to Life News*, November 1979, 11, JRS, 1979 National Right to Life News Box (setting forth NRLC agenda for International Year of the Child).

98. Epstein, "Abortion: An Issue That Won't Go Away," SM111.

99. Press Release, Mildred Jefferson, "Statement on IWY Meetings" (July 14, 1977), ACCL, Box 11, 1976, NRLC Folder 2.

100. Ibid.

Chapter 6. Compromise and Polarization

1. See Jeffrey Rosen, *The Most Democratic Branch: How the Courts Serve America* (New York: Oxford University Press, 2006), 91, 101 (contending that "fights over *Roe* have become a proxy for the political battles that social conservatives and liberal pro-choice extremists increasingly despaired of winning in the legislatures"); Cass Sunstein, "Civil Rights Legislation

in the 1990s: Three Civil Rights Fallacies," *California Law Review* 79 (1991): 766–767 (arguing that *Roe* "may well have created the Moral Majority, helped defeat the equal rights amendment, and undermined the women's movement by spurring opposition and demobilizing potential adherents"). For further discussion of various explanations of the way that *Roe* polarized debate, see Donald T. Critchlow, "Birth Control, Population, and Family Planning: An Overview," in *The Politics of Abortion and Birth Control in Historical Perspective*, ed. Donald T. Critchlow (University Park: Penn State University Press, 1996), 5 (arguing that "*Roe* polarized the pro-life and pro-choice forces"); Elizabeth Mensch and Alan Freeman, *The Politics of Virtue: Is Abortion Debatable?* 2nd ed. (Durham, NC: Duke University Press, 1995), 4, 125–137; Sara Dubow, *Ourselves Unborn: A History of the Fetus in Modern America* (New York: Oxford University Press, 2010), 64, 185 (arguing that arguments about fetal rights became more partisan after *Roe*); Daniel K. Williams, *God's Own Party: The Making of the Christian Right*, 2nd ed. (New York: Oxford University Press, 2012), 117 (arguing that *Roe* "shocked the pro-life movement and galvanized it into action"); Leigh Ann Wheeler, *How Sex Became a Civil Liberty* (New York: Oxford University Press, 2012), lx (asserting that *Roe* "inspired the emergence of a powerful antiabortion movement that quickly claimed the moral high ground"); Paul Boyer, "The Evangelical Resurgence in 1970s American Protestantism," in *Rightward Bound: Making America Conservative in the 1970s*, eds. Bruce J. Shulman and Julian E. Zelizer (Cambridge, MA: Harvard University Press, 2008), 36–37; Kristin Luker and Faye Ginsburg offer a related explanation of the post-1973 polarization. By revealing deep social divisions about motherhood and other gender issues, the Supreme Court supposedly fueled a broader conflict about sex roles. See Faye D. Ginsburg, *Contested Lives: The Abortion Debate in an American Community* (Berkeley: University of California Press, 1998), 15; Kristin Luker, *Abortion and the Politics of Motherhood* (Berkeley: University of California Press, 1984), 137, 144.

2. Warren Schaller, interview with Mary Ziegler, February 11, 2011. Chapter 1 further discusses Schaller's time with the NRLC.

3. Mary Meehan, interview with Mary Ziegler, March 20, 2012. For more on Meehan's early work in the movement, see Mary Meehan, "Abortion and 'The Consistency Thing,'" *Human Life Review* 7 (1981): 60–68; Mary Meehan, "Abortion: The Left Has Betrayed the Sanctity of Life," *Progressive*, September 1980, 34; Mary Meehan, "The Other Pro-Lifers," *Commonweal*, January 18, 1980, 13–16.

4. Meehan, interview. Meehan went on to work in several pro-life organizations seeking to build consensus on issues such as nuclear weapons, the death penalty, and war. See "Activists Reminisce: An Oral History of Pro-Lifers for Survival," in *Consistently Opposing Killing: From Abortion to Assisted Suicide, the Death Penalty, and War*, eds. Rachel M. MacNair and Stephen Zunes (Westport, CT: Praeger, 2008), 105–117; Mary Meehan,

"Changing Hearts and Minds," in *Consistently Opposing Killing: From Abortion to Assisted Suicide, the Death Penalty, and War*, eds. Rachel M. MacNair and Stephen Zunes (Westport, CT: Praeger, 2008), 133–147.

5. Mary Ann Kuharski, interview with Mary Ziegler, February 5, 2011. Kuharski later wrote a series of books on parenting Catholic children. See Mary Ann Kuharski, *Raising Catholic Children* (Huntington, IN: Our Sunday Visitor, 1991); Mary Ann Kuharski, *Parenting with Prayer* (Huntington, IN: Our Sunday Visitor, 1993).

6. On the conscious manipulation of the abortion issue by New Right activists, see James Risen and Judy L. Thomas, *Wrath of Angels: The American Abortion War* (New York: Basic Books, 1998), 120–128; Williams, *God's Own Party*, 167–170; Patricia Miller, *Good Catholics: The Battle over Abortion in the Catholic Church* (Berkeley: University of California Press, 2014), 85–87. On the relevance of political party realignment, see Thomas J. Sugrue and John Skrentny, "The White Ethnic Strategy," in *Rightward Bound: Making America Conservative in the 1970s*, eds. Bruce J. Shulman and Julian E. Zelizer (Cambridge, MA: Harvard University Press, 2008), 174–175; Linda Greenhouse and Reva B. Siegel, "Before (and After) *Roe*: New Questions about Backlash," *Yale Law Journal* 120 (2010): 2052–2072; Christina Wolbrecht, *The Politics of Women's Rights: Parties, Positions, and Change* (Princeton: Princeton University Press, 2000), 40–71.

7. "The New Abortion Debate: Decision on Medicaid Funding," *Commonweal*, July 22, 1977, 451–452. For more on antiabortion efforts to seek common ground on other gender issues, see American Citizens Concerned for Life, "ACCL Philosophy and Objectives" (n.d., ca. 1978), ACCL, Box 17, ACCL Philosophy and Objectives Folder; "To Build a Caring Society: The Goals of American Citizens Concerned for Life" (n.d., ca. 1978), ACCL, Box 17, ACCL Philosophy and Objectives Folder; William C. Hunt and Joseph A. Lampe, "Strategy Considerations for ACCL Involvement in Abortion and Related Issues" (n.d., ca. 1977), 1–7, ACCL, Box 18, 1977 Strategy Folder; "Feminists for Life Task Force on Consumer Credit," *Feminists for Life Journal* (1972): 2, FFL; "The Equal Rights Amendment," *Feminists for Life Journal* (1973): 8, FFL.

8. On the polarization of the abortion issue before 1973, see Gene Burns, *The Moral Veto: Framing Abortion, Contraception, and Cultural Pluralism in the United States* (New York: Cambridge University Press, 2005), 225–227; Greenhouse and Siegel, "Before (and After) *Roe v. Wade*," 2046–2071.

9. Juli Loesch, "Are Some Pro-Choice Arguments Anti-Feminist?" (n.d., ca. 1979), LEP, Box 1, Folder 1 (emphasis in the original); see also The Pax Center, "Abortion, Language, and Violence" (n.d., ca. 1978), LEP, Box 1, Folder 1. Loesch would later publish these arguments. See Juli Loesch, "Abortion, Language, and Violence," *Erie Christian Witness* 5 (September–October 1977): 8.

10. Feminists for Life, "Feminists for Life Statement on the Occasion of the Fifth Anniversary of the Supreme Court Decision on Abortion" (January 22, 1978), 1, LEP, Box 1, Folder 1.

11. Life and Equality/Feminists for Life of Missouri Fundraising Letter (January 30, 1975), 1, LEP, Box 1, Folder 1.

12. Life and Equality/Feminists for Life of Missouri Fundraising Letter (n.d., ca. 1978), LEP, Box 1, Folder 1. For more on Feminists for Life and the ERA, see Life and Equality, "Abortion and the Equal Rights Amendment: There Is No Connection" (n.d., ca. 1978), LEP, Box 1, Folder 1; "The Equal Rights Amendment," *Feminists for Life Journal* (1973): 8.

13. On the extension battle and the reasons for the failure of the ERA, see Mary Frances Berry, *Why ERA Failed: Politics, Women's Rights, and the Amending Process of the Constitution* (Bloomington: Indiana University Press, 1988), 70–101; Jane J. Mansbridge, *Why We Lost the ERA* (Chicago: University of Chicago Press, 1986), 2, 43; Donald T. Critchlow, *Phyllis Schlafly and Grassroots Conservatism: A Woman's Crusade* (Princeton: Princeton University Press, 2005), 243–249, 281. For more on the ERA struggle, see Donald G. Mathews and Jane Sherron DeHart, *Sex, Gender, and the Politics of the ERA: A State and the Nation* (New York: Oxford University Press, 1990).

14. See Marjory Mecklenburg and Joseph Lampe to James T. McHugh and Michael Taylor (July 11, 1972), ACCL, Box 4, 1972 National Right to Life Convention Folder. For more on Mecklenburg's influence and views of the early NRLC, see Marjory Mecklenburg to NRLC Executive Committee (August 16, 1973), ACCL, Box 4, 1973 Board and Executive Committee Folder 5; Marjory Mecklenburg to NRLC et al. (May 16, 1973), ACCL, Box 4, 1973 National Right to Life Convention Folder. For discussion of the family planning work of Mecklenburg's husband, Fred, see "Biographical Sketch: Dr. Frederick E. Mecklenburg, M.D." (n.d., ca. 1979), ACCL, Box 20, ACCL Speakers Folder; Fred E. Mecklenburg, "Building Bridges Instead of Walls" (n.d., ca. 1975), ACCL, Box 20, ACCL Speakers Folder; Dr. Fred E. Mecklenburg, "Minnesota Should Seek Sexual Responsibility, Not 'Easier' Abortion" (n.d., ca. 1972), ACCL, Box 20, ACCL Speakers Folder. For the NRLC's early statement of purpose, see Pennsylvanians for Life, National Right to Life Committee Statement of Purpose (n.d., ca. 1972), ACCL, Box 4, 1973 National Right to Life Convention Folder (calling for consideration "of prenatal and maternal health care programs, as well as improvement for social services for those children whose parents are unable care for them"). Marjory Mecklenburg's official early biography described her as the "[w]ife of Fred E. Mecklenburg" and a "[m]other of four children," mentioning only her leadership of pro-life organizations in describing her career. See Pennsylvanians for Life, "Biographies of Persons Attending Convention of National Importance to Right to Life Work" (n.d., ca. 1972), ACCL, Box 4, 1972 National Right to Life Convention Folder. By 1981, by contrast, Mecklenburg had served

as the president of American Citizens Concerned for Life, the vice-chair of Americans United for Life, and the chairman of the National Right to Life Committee, attracting the attention of the Reagan Administration. See Mary Bader Papa, "'Abortion Alternatives' Leader up for U.S. Job," *National Catholic Reporter*, February 27, 1981, 6.

15. Resolution #4 (June 1974), ACCL, Box 8, 1974 NRLC Board and Executive Committee Folder 6. In June 1973, Mecklenburg lost an election to Edward Golden for president of the NRLC by a vote of 22 to 18. At the same time, however, Mecklenburg was reelected to the NRLC Executive Committee, receiving thirty-six votes, the most of any candidate. See NRLC Board of Directors Meeting Minutes (June 8–10, 1973), 11, ACCL, Box 4, 1974 NRLC Board and Executive Folder 1. On the efforts of Mecklenburg and her allies to ensure that the NRLC would endorse or at least remain neutral on contraception, see Judith Fink to Ed Golden et al., "In re Policy Statement of the NRLC Concerning 'Birth Control'" (May 15, 1973), ACCL, Box 4, NRLC 1973 Folder 2. On the position taken by Mecklenburg and her NRLC supporters on sterilization abuse, see Judith Fink to NRLC Executive Committee et al., "Re. Action of NRLC Regarding Girl Scouts, Forced Sterilization, and Approval of 'Euthanasia Committee' by AMA President" (June 1973), ACCL, Box 4, 1973 NRLC Board and Executive Committee Folder 4.

16. Thomas Hilgers, Marjory Mecklenburg, and Gayle Riordan, "Is Abortion the Best We Have to Offer? A Challenge to the Aborting Society," in *Abortion and Social Justice*, eds. Thomas Hilgers and Dennis Horan (New York: Sheed and Ward, 1972), 183. In the mid- to late 1960s, some abortion opponents opposed legalization not only because they viewed abortion as murder but also because they thought it would unleash a wave of sexual promiscuity. See Frank Ayd Jr., "Liberal Abortion Laws," *America*, February 1, 1969, 130–132; Charles Rice, *The Vanishing Right to Live: An Appeal for a Renewed Reverence for Life* (New York: Doubleday, 1969), 120–130.

17. Hilgers, Mecklenburg, and Riordan, "Is Abortion the Best We Have to Offer?" 183.

18. For an example of this perspective, see Mensch and Freeman, *The Politics of Virtue*, 138. On the MCCL's work in the late 1960s and early 1970s, see "Six Testify against Liberalized Abortion," *The Winona Daily News*, April 1, 1969, 13; Gerry Nelson, "House Subcommittee Kills Most Restrictive Abortion Measure," *The Winona Daily News*, March 9, 1971, 5; Gerry Nelson, "Minnesota's Court Delays Abortion Case," *The Fergus Falls Daily Journal*, December 29, 1972, 1.

19. "Schaller Testifies as Head of New Pro-Life Organization," *National Right to Life News* clipping (1974), ACCL, Box 17, 1974 ACCL Folder. For more on Schaller's views, see "Former Pro-Abortion Pastor New 'Right to Life' Executive," *St. Paul Pioneer Press* clipping, August 1, 1973, ACCL, Box 4, 1973 NRLC Folder 4.

20. Fred E. Mecklenburg, "Building Bridges Instead of Walls" (n.d., ca. 1975), 3.

21. Abortion Part 4: Testimony before the Senate Judiciary Committee Subcommittee on Constitutional Amendments, 94th Congress, 1st Session (1975), 657–663 (Statement of Marjory Mecklenburg).

22. School Age Mother and Child Health Act of 1975: Hearing before the Subcommittee on Health of the Senate Committee of Labor and Welfare, 94th Congress, 1st Session (1975), 499 (Statement of Marjory Mecklenburg). For a description of the proposed law, see ibid., 1–2, 10–16. For Planned Parenthood's support of the law, see ibid., 552–581 (Statement of Jack Hood Vaughn of Planned Parenthood) (supporting the Act).

23. See Statement of Marjory Mecklenburg on the School Age Mother and Child Health Act of 1975, 499.

24. On rising illegitimacy, see "Rising Concern over Surge in Illegitimacy," *U.S. News and World Report*, June 26, 1978, 59. On Carter's position, see Steven V. Roberts, "The Epidemic of Teenage Pregnancy," *New York Times*, June 18, 1978, E6. On the heated battle surrounding Medicaid funding restrictions, see James Strong, "Thousands Face Pay Delay in Abortion Fight," *Chicago Tribune*, October 8, 1977, 3; Marjorie Hunter, "Congress Approves an Abortion Accord," *New York Times*, November 17, 1979, 10. On the failure of the 1975 act, see Kristin Luker, *Dubious Conceptions: The Politics of Teenage Pregnancy* (Cambridge, MA: Harvard University Press, 1996), 70–71.

25. For the positions of the ACCL and Planned Parenthood on the Adolescent Health, Services, and Pregnancy Prevention and Care Act of 1978, see Adolescent Health, Services, and Pregnancy Prevention and Care Act of 1978: Hearings before the Senate Committee on Human Resources, 95th Congress, 2nd Session (1978), 192–193 (Statement of Faye Wattleton of the Planned Parenthood Federation of America); ibid., 422–440 (Statement of Marjory Mecklenburg). For more on ACCL's support of the bill, see ACCL, Fundraising Letter (June 5, 1978), ACCL, Box 19, Fundraising Folder.

26. For the differences in views on sexual freedom expressed by R2N2/CARASA and Mecklenburg's followers, compare Hilgers, Mecklenburg, and Riordan, "Is Abortion the Best We Have to Offer?" 179, with Reproductive Rights National Network Brochure, "Women United to Defend Abortion Rights and End Sterilization Abuse" (n.d., ca. 1980), 2, R2N2, Box 1, Abortion Task Force Folder. For more on the idea of meaningful reproductive choice forged by R2N2 and CARASA, see CARASA Conference Committee, "Presentation 1: Current Consensus" (n.d., ca. 1977), 1–2, MTP, Box 8, CARASA Folder. The leaders of CARASA and R2N2 worked to address racial differences in access to reproductive health care, although they had limited success in recruiting women of color. See Jennifer Nelson, *Women of Color and the Reproductive Rights Movement* (New York: New York University Press, 2003), 150–162; 170; Rebecca

M. Kluchin, *Fit to Be Tied: Sterilization and Reproductive Rights in America, 1950–1980* (Piscataway, NJ: Rutgers University Press, 2009), 213. Mecklenburg and her supporters, by contrast, discussed marital status and class but made little mention of race. On the relatively minimal discussion of race among Mecklenburg's followers during debate about the federal Pregnancy Discrimination Act, see Deborah Dinner, "Strange Bedfellows at Work: Neomaternalism in the Making of Sex Discrimination Law," *Washington University Law Review* 91 (2014): 496–503.

27. Deborah Dinner, "The Costs of Reproduction: History and the Legal Construction of Sex Equality," *Harvard Civil Rights-Civil Liberties Review* 46 (2011): 454. For further discussion of the paradigm, see, e.g., ibid., 415–435. For more on the history of the fight against pregnancy discrimination, see Serena Mayeri, *Reasoning from Race: Feminism, Law, and the Civil Rights Revolution* (Cambridge, MA: Harvard University Press, 2011), 120–121; Tracy A. Thomas and Tracy Jean Boisseau, "Introduction: Law, History, and Feminism," in *Feminist Legal History: Essays on Women and Law*, eds. Tracy A. Thomas and Tracy Jean Boisseau (New York: New York University Press, 2011), 11.

28. For the decision on the Equal Protection Clause, see *Geduldig v. Aiello*, 417 U.S. 484, 494, 496–97 & n. 20 (1974). For the decision on Title VII of the Civil Rights Act of 1964, see *General Electric Company v. Gilbert*, 429 U.S. 125, 138–140, 146 (1976). For contemporary reaction to *Geduldig* and *Gilbert*, see Warren Weaver, Jr., "Court Says States Can Bar Job Benefits in Pregnancy," *New York Times*, June 18, 1974, 81; Lesley Oelsner, "Supreme Court Rules Employers May Refuse Pregnancy Sick Pay," *New York Times*, December 8, 1976, 53.

29. On the founding of the CEDAPW, see Dinner, "The Costs of Reproduction," 469–470. For discussion of the founding of the coalition, see Patricia Beyea, Susan Deller Ross, and Marjorie M. Smith, "Pregnancy Discrimination Is Alive and Well—Temporarily!" *Notes from the Women's Rights Project* (ACLU Rights Project, New York, NY), (February 15, 1977), 1, 3, TEP, Series I, Box 11, Folder 162; Peggy Simpson, "Pregnant Workers Have a Tough Ally," *Parade*, May 20, 1979, 31, WEAL, Box 4, Folder 9. For more on the coalition and its influence, see Robert H. Blank, *Fetal Protection in the Workplace: Women's Rights, Business Interests, and the Unborn* (New York: Columbia University Press, 1993), 38–39; Dorothy Sue Cobble, *The Other Women's Movement: Workplace Justice and Social Rights in Modern America* (Princeton: Princeton University Press, 2004), 217.

30. For Ginsburg and Deller Ross's editorial, see Ruth Bader Ginsburg and Susan Deller Ross, "Pregnancy and Discrimination," *New York Times*, January 22, 1977, A33. For discussion of Ginsburg's career, see Fred Strebeigh, *Equal: Women Reshape American Law* (New York: W. W. Norton, 2009), 13–25, 41–77; Flora Davis, *Moving the Mountain: The Women's Movement Since 1960* (Champaign: University of Illinois Press, 1999), 402–406;

Christine Stansell, *The Feminist Promise: 1792 to the Present* (New York: Random House, 2010), 303–306. For more on Ginsburg's thinking on pregnancy discrimination in the period, see Neil Siegel and Reva B. Siegel, "'Struck' by Stereotype: Ruth Bader Ginsburg on Pregnancy Discrimination as Sex Discrimination," *Duke Law Journal* 59 (2009): 771–798. On Susan Deller Ross, see Strebeigh, *Equal*, 14, 93, 114–116, 137–138, 195, 344; William N. Eskridge Jr. and John A. Ferejohn, *A Republic of Statutes: The New American Constitution* (New Haven, CT: Yale University Press, 2010), 31–32, 55–56. For the result in key equal-protection cases litigated by Ginsburg, see *Reed v. Reed*, 404 U.S. 71 (1971); *Struck v. Secretary of Defense*, 460 F.2d 1372 (9th Cir. 1971), vacated and remanded for consideration of mootness by *Struck v. Secretary of Defense*, 409 U.S. 1071, 1071 (1972); *Frontiero v. Richardson*, 411 U.S. 677 (1973).

31. Legislation to Ban Sex Discrimination on the Basis of Pregnancy: Testimony before the Subcommittee on Employment Opportunities of the House Committee on Labor and Education, 95th Congress, 1st Session (1977), 11 (Statement of Wendy Webster Williams).

32. Legislation to Ban Sex Discrimination on the Basis of Pregnancy: Testimony before the Subcommittee on Employment Opportunities of the House Committee on Labor and Education, 95th Congress, 1st Session (1977), 31–32 (Statement of Susan Deller Ross).

33. See Dinner, "Strange Bedfellows at Work," 503–505. For examples of arguments of this kind, see Discrimination on the Basis of Pregnancy: Testimony before the Subcommittee on Labor of the Senate Committee on Human Resources, 95th Congress, 1st Session (1977), 452 (Statement of Letty Cottin Pogrebin); Women's Equity Action League, "What Constitutes Sex Discrimination in Insurance," WEAL, Box 10, Folder 19.

34. See Discrimination on the Basis of Pregnancy: Testimony before the Subcommittee on Labor of the Senate Committee on Human Resources, 95th Congress, 1st Session (1977), 432–441 (Statement of Jacqueline Nolan-Haley of American Citizens Concerned for Life); Statement of Wendy Webster Williams, 19.

35. ACCL Press Release, "Pro-Life Group Says General Electric Co. 'Encourages Abortion' in *Gilbert* Case" (March 15, 1977), 1, ACCL, Box 19, Fundraising Folder.

36. ACCL Press Release on Pregnancy Discrimination (April 29, 1977), 1, ACCL, Box 19, Fundraising Folder.

37. On the Beard Amendment, see Martin Tolchin, "A House Panel Bars Curb on Abortions in Women's Aid Bill," *New York Times*, February 3, 1978, A11. On the Eagleton Amendment, see "Senate Votes Pregnancy Benefits in Disability Plans for Workers," *New York Times*, September 17, 1977, 8. For more on Beard and Eagleton's proposals, see Legislative History of the Pregnancy Discrimination Act of 1978, Pub. L. 95–555, prepared for the Senate Committee on Labor and Human Resources, 96th Congress (1979), 112–113.

38. See Legislation to Prohibit Sex Discrimination on the Basis of Pregnancy Part 2: Testimony before the House Subcommittee on Employment Opportunities of the Committee on Education and Labor, 95th Congress, 1st Session (1977), 66 (Statement of Dr. Dorothy Czarnecki of American Citizens Concerned for Life).

39. Ibid. For more on the ACCL's work on pregnancy discrimination, see Marjory Mecklenburg to Representative James Tonry (March 8, 1978), 1, ACCL, Box 19, Fundraising Folder (explaining that the ACCL supported the PDA "as a pro-life bill with or without an abortion amendment").

40. Congressional Record—Senate: Proceedings and Debates of the 95th Congress 1st Session, vol. 123, pt. 16 (1977), 29657 (Statement of Thomas Eagleton).

41. Congressional Record—House: Proceedings and Debates of the 95th Congress 2nd Session, vol. 124, pt. 17 (1978), 38574 (Statement of Ronald Sarasin).

42. Sample Fundraising Letter (n.d., ca. 1979), ACCL, Box 19, Fundraising Folder. On the ACCL's participation in mainstream antiabortion efforts, see "Some Accomplishments of ACCL" (n.d., ca. 1979), 1, ACCL, Box 18, ACCL Philosophy and Objectives Folder (explaining that ACCL members had assisted Representative Henry Hyde's election campaign, had testified in favor of abortion restrictions in Akron, Ohio, and had worked with the Edelin prosecution). On ACCL's views of the strategic advantages of seeking common ground, see William C. Hunt and Joseph A. Lampe, "Strategy Considerations for ACCL Involvement in Abortion and Related Issues" (n.d., ca. 1977), 5 (stressing the importance of "build[ing] good will even among opponents and the uncommitted" and of "[a]chieving a reputation for competence and credibility"); American Citizens Concerned for Life, "No Vehicle Quite Like Ours" (n.d., ca. 1977), ACCL, Box 18, ACCL Philosophy and Objectives Folder (explaining that the organization sought to work in "broad coalitions").

43. Marjory E. Mecklenburg et al., "The Adolescent Family Life Program as a Prevention Measure," Public Health Report 98 (1983): 26. On reports of an increase in adolescent pregnancy, see Nadine Brozan, "More Teenagers Are Pregnant despite Rise in Contraception," New York Times, March 12, 1981, A1. For more on panic about adolescent pregnancy in the early 1980s, see Luker, Dubious Conceptions, 78–80; Kristin Luker, When Sex Goes to School: Warring Views on Sex—and Sex Education—Since the 1960s (New York: W. W. Norton, 2006), 222; Jeffrey Moran, Teaching Sex: The Shaping of Adolescence in the Twentieth Century (Cambridge, MA: Harvard University Press, 2000), 179–183.

44. Robert Pear, "Reagan Family-Planning Aide Quits," New York Times, February 27, 1985, A17. On Mecklenburg's role in supposedly promoting the squeal rule, see Steve Chapple and David Talbot, Burning Desires: Sex in America—A Report from the Field (New York: Doubleday, 1989), 143. The Reagan Administration first proposed the squeal rule in 1982, and in

February 1983, a federal district court held that the policy was unlawful. See "U.S. Plans to Appeal Ruling on Teenager Birth Control," *New York Times*, February 17, 1983, A21. When an appeals court affirmed this ruling, the Reagan Administration gave up on the squeal rule. See Marjorie Hunter, "Court Blocks Rule on Notice by Family Planning Clinics," *New York Times*, July 9, 1983, 5 (on the first of four appeals court decisions ruling against the squeal rule); "U.S. Drops Efforts for Notice of Child's Birth Control Use," *New York Times*, December 1, 1983, B13. On AFLA and Mecklenburg's role in shaping it, see Janice M. Irvine, *Talk about Sex: The Battles over Sex Education in the United States* (Berkeley: University of California Press, 2002), 88–97. On the scandals surrounding Mecklenburg's service and resignation, see, e.g., ibid., 96; Pear, "Reagan Family-Planning Aide Quits," A17.

45. NRLC Board Meeting Minutes (September 20–21, 1975), ACCL, Box 10, 1975 NRLC Folder 5.

46. See Judie Brown to Recipients of First Class Mailing (October 17, 1977), ACCL, Box 11, 1977 NRLC Folder 7 (describing a resolution opposing the ERA passed at the June 1977 meeting of the NRLC Board of Directors).

47. See "Protestant Unit Hits Abortion," *Washington Post*, July 11, 1975, C5. On local groups, see Karen Elliot House, "Evangelicals: New Political Force?" *Wall Street Journal*, October 8, 1976, 8 (on the Christian Freedom Foundation); Laurie Johnston, "Abortion Foes Gain Support as They Intensify Campaign," *New York Times*, October 23, 1977, 1 (on Christians for Life). On Christian Voice, see Williams, *God's Own Party*, 164–170; Sara Diamond, *Spiritual Warfare: The Politics of the Christian Right* (Montreal: Black Rose Press, 1990), 61–71.

48. For the decisions in *Maher, Beal,* and *Poelker,* cases on the constitutionality of bans on abortion funding, see *Maher v. Roe,* 432 U.S. 464 (1977); *Poelker v. Doe,* 432 U.S. 519 (1977); *Beal v. Doe,* 432 U.S. 438 (1977). For Schlafly's arguments about abortion funding and the ERA, see Phyllis Schlafly, "ERA Means Abortion and Population Shrinkage," *The Phyllis Schlafly Report,* December 1974, vol. 8, no. 5, sec. 2, PSR; Phyllis Schlafly, "What Really Happened in Houston," *The Phyllis Schlafly Report,* December 1977, vol. 11, no. 5, sec. 2, PSR. On Schlafly's arguments about the state ERA litigation in Hawaii and Massachusetts, see Critchlow, *Phyllis Schlafly and Grassroots Conservatism,* 225.

49. On antiabortion perceptions of the Minnesota and Missouri fights, see Janet Grant, "Pro-Life Missouri Women Elected IWY Delegates," *National Right to Life News,* July 1977, 1, 7, JRS, 1977 National Right to Life News Box; "Orchestration by IWY," *National Right to Life News,* July 1977, 8, JRS, 1977 National Right to Life News Box. On pro-life perceptions that the ERA would strengthen abortion rights, see Janet Grant, "Women Fight for Voice in State IWY Meetings," *National Right to Life News,* June 1977, 4, JRS, 1977 National Right to Life News Box; "Orchestration by IWY," 3. For additional discussion of the supposed discrimination against

antiabortion women, see "The Pictures the Press Didn't Print," *The Phyllis Schlafly Report*, June 1976, vol. 9, no. 11, sec. 2, PSR; "Federal Financing for a Foolish Festival for Frustrated Feminists," *The Phyllis Schlafly Report*, May 1977, vol. 10, no. 10, sec. 2, PSR; Schlafly, "What Really Happened in Houston," 1. On pro-life women's influence on at least some state IWY conferences, see Marjorie J. Spruill, "Gender and America's Right Turn," in *Rightward Bound: Making America Conservative in the 1970s*, eds. Bruce J. Shulman and Julian E. Zelizer (Cambridge, MA: Harvard University Press, 2008), 81–85.

50. Grant, "Women Fight for Voice," 4. For White's view, see Ray White to Board of Directors (December 10, 1975), ACCL, Box 10, 1975 NRLC Board and Executive Committee Folder 5. For Willke's argument, see John Willke to NRLC Board of Directors et al., Re: IWY (May 17, 1977), ACCL, 1977 NRLC Folder 3.

51. On the financial troubles facing the NRLC, see NRLC Board of Directors Meeting Minutes (December 8, 1973), 2, ACCL, Box 4, 1973 Board and Executive Folder 9 (arguing that expenses for the organization should no longer exceed one-third of the funds available to the organization); Connie Paige, *The Right to Lifers: Who They Are, How They Operate, Where They Get Their Money* (New York: Summit Books, 1983), 87. For individuals' recollections of the subject: Judie Brown, interview with Mary Ziegler, August 4, 2011; Schaller, interview. On the financial struggles of the Society for a Christian Commonwealth, see Cyrus Brewster Jr., Society for a Christian Commonwealth Fundraising Letter (August 1976), WC, Society for a Christian Commonwealth Folder (explaining that the organization no longer had the funds to publish *Triumph*); L. Brent Bozell, Fundraising Letter (February 25, 1977), WC, Society for a Christian Commonwealth Folder. For a related discussion of the financial difficulties of antiabortion groups, see "CAC Head Sees Human Life Amendment," *The Presbyterian Journal*, October 16, 1978, WC, Christian Action Council Folder (explaining that organization leaders had not drawn a formal salary). On the wealth accumulated by the Moral Majority and Christian Voice, see Maxwell Glen, "The Electronic Ministers Listen to the Gospel According to the Candidates," *The National Journal*, December 22, 1979, 2142–2145; Joel Kotkin, "Ready on the Right: Christian Soldiers Are on the March," *Washington Post*, August 25, 1979, A10; Dan Gilgoff, *The Jesus Machine: How James Dobson, Focus on the Family, and Evangelical America Are Winning the Culture War* (New York: St. Martin's, 2008), 82–83.

52. Nathaniel Sheppard Jr., "Group Fighting Abortion Planning to Step Up Its Drive," *New York Times*, July 3, 1978, 20. On LAPAC's influence in the 1978 elections, see John Herbers, "Anti-Abortionists' Impact Is Felt in Elections across the Nation," *New York Times*, June 1, 1978, A1; Douglas Kneeland, "Clark Defeat in Iowa Laid to Abortion," *New York Times*, November 13, 1978, A18.

53. Resolutions (October 7, 1977), ACCL, Box 11, 1977 Folder 4 (describing resolutions passed by the NRLC Board of Directors at its June 1977 Convention).

54. "Hot Air Balloon," *The National Right to Life News*, January 1978, 3, JRS, 1978 National Right to Life News Box; "Thousands in States Mark January 22," *The National Right to Life News*, March 1977, 1, 4, JRS, 1977 National Right to Life News Box (describing the use of religious rhetoric in major state and national March for Life rallies).

55. On Nixon's use of the abortion issue, see Robert Mason, *Richard Nixon and the Quest for a New Majority* (University of North Carolina: Chapel Hill, 2003), 153; Donald T. Critchlow, *The Conservative Ascendancy: How the GOP Right Made Political History* (Cambridge, MA: Harvard University Press, 2007), 136–137. On the prominence and decline of anti-abortion Democrats, see William V. D'Antonio, Steven A. Tuch, and John Kenneth White, "Catholicism, Abortion, and the Emergence of the 'Culture Wars' in the U.S. Congress, 1971–2006," in *Catholics and Politics: The Dynamic Tension Between Faith and Power*, eds. Kristin E. Heyer et al. (Washington, DC: Georgetown University Press, 2008), 130–147; Carol J. C. Maxwell, *Pro-Life Activists in America: Meaning, Motivation, and Direct Action* (New York: Cambridge University Press, 2002), 35–37. For Hatfield's speech at the NRLC Convention, see "News from Senator Mark Hatfield" (June 9, 1973), 1–4, ACCL, Box 4, 1973 National Right to Life Convention Folder 1. For Gephardt and Eagleton's positions, see Thomas Eagleton to Sylvia Hampton (October 19, 1981), RHS, Box 1, Folder 9; Richard Gephardt to Sylvia Hampton (August 6, 1981), RHS, Box 1, Folder 9. On Javits and other abortion-rights Republicans, see Rickie Solinger, *Beggars and Choosers: How the Politics of Choice Shapes Adoption, Abortion, and Welfare in the United States* (New York: Farrar, Straus, and Giroux, 2001), 13; David J. Garrow, *Liberty and Sexuality: The Right of Privacy and the Making of* Roe v. Wade (Berkeley: University of California Press, 1998), 311.

56. Richard L. Madden, "GOP Panel Backs Anti-Abortion Plank," *New York Times*, August 11, 1976, 14.

57. Christopher Lydon, "Abortion Plank Is Fought by Republican Feminists," *New York Times*, August 18, 1976, 23.

58. For discussion of the failed efforts of Republican feminists, see "Republican Feminists Prepare to Fight for Conversion Delegates," *New York Times*, February 19, 1976, 25; Eileen Shanahan, "G.O.P. Feminists Angry At Party," *New York Times*, July 28, 1976, 9; Lydon, "Abortion Plank," 23. For discussion of the reasons for the Democratic Party's movement toward the abortion-rights side in 1976, see Scott H. Ainsworth and Thad A. Hall, *Abortion Politics in Congress: Strategic Incrementalism and Policy Change* (New York: Cambridge University Press, 2011), 60–74; David Karol, *Party Position Change in American Politics: Coalition Management* (New York: Cambridge University Press, 2009), 67–72; Wolbrecht,

The Politics of Women's Rights, 18, 75, 227. For details on the competing platforms, see Richard L. Madden, "2 Party Platforms Show Sharp Contrast on Issues," *New York Times*, August 18, 1976, 1. On the Democratic Party platform, see David S. Rosenbaum, "Democrats Adopt a Platform Aimed at Uniting Party," *New York Times*, June 16, 1976, 1

59. On the 1980 Democratic platform, see David E. Rosenbaum, "Platform Drafters Back Carter Stands," *New York Times*, June 25, 1980, A1. On the Republican platform: Warren Weaver Jr., "Republicans Also Back Proposed Amendment to Prohibit Abortions," *New York Times*, July 9, 1980, A1.

60. John Herbers, "Sweeping Right to Life Goals Set as Movement Gains New Power," *New York Times*, November 27, 1978, A1. For Gerster's comments, see John Herbers, "Convention Speech Stirs Foes on Abortion," *New York Times*, June 24, 1979, 16. On the Democratic Party's retreat from antiabortion positions, see Ainsworth and Hall, *Abortion Politics in Congress*, 60–74; Karol, *Party Position Change*, 67–72; Wolbrecht, *The Politics of Women's Rights*, 18, 75, 227.

61. On the 1980 platform, see Warren Weaver Jr., "Republicans Also Back," A1; Adam Clymer, "The Conservatives' Message: G.O.P. Platform Waves 'Banner of Bold Colors,'" *New York Times*, July 16, 1980, A1; Robert Strauss, "The Platform: Just What Reagan Wanted and So Richly Deserved," *New York Times*, July 20, 1980, E21. On Faucher's assessment of the Congress of 1980, see "Right to Life Committee Plans Drive for Anti-Abortion Amendment," *New York Times*, June 30, 1980, A17. For similar evaluations of the political landscape of 1980, see "Can the Pro-Life Movement Really Win?" *Action Line*, January 22, 1981, 1, WC, Action Line Folder (complaining about "the failure of the Democratic Party to keep a minority of abortion activists from dominating its direction and policy"); "New Pro-Life Faces in the Senate," *National Right to Life News*, December 1976, 1, JRS, 1976 National Right to Life News Box.

62. Harold M. Schmeck Jr., "Health Agency Report Proposes Limits on Fetal Experiments," *New York Times*, July 16, 1973, 12.

63. For more on the controversy surrounding fetal experimentation in the period, see Dubow, *Ourselves Unborn*, 72–75. For contemporary discussion, see Richard E. Behrman, "The Importance of Fetal Research," *New York Times*, June 9, 1974, 209; Maggie Scarf, "The Fetus as Guinea Pig," *New York Times*, October 19, 1975, 236; Harold M. Schmeck Jr., "Senate Adopts Bill to Aid People in Medical Studies," *New York Times*, May 31, 1976, 14.

64. On Kennedy's fight against the Bartlett Amendment, see Marjorie Hunter, "Senate Upholds U.S. Abortion Funds," *New York Times*, April 11, 1975, 28. On Kennedy's later efforts in favor of abortion funding, see David E. Rosenbaum, "Conferees Vote Ban on Medicaid Fund for Abortions," *New York Times*, September 16, 1976, 1; David E. Rosenbaum, "Congress Approves Curb on Abortions, But Veto Is Likely," *New York Times*,

September 18, 1976, 1. On Kennedy's position on abortion earlier in the
1970s, see NARAL, "Senator Edward Kennedy" (n.d., ca. 1972), NRL,
Carton 1, 1974–1975 Executive Committee Minutes Folder (relating Kennedy's pre-1973 opposition to "abortion on demand").

65. "What Price Research?" *New York Times*, May 6, 1973, 252.

66. Fetal Tissue Research, 1974: Testimony before the Subcommittee on
Health of the Senate Committee on Labor and Public Welfare, 93rd Congress, 2nd Session (1974), 2 (Statement of Senator Edward Kennedy).

67. Chapters 3 and 4 further examine the sterilization-abuse scandal. On reac-
tion to the Tuskegee Experiment, see Jean Heller, "Syphilis Victims in U.S.
Study Went Untreated for 40 Years," *New York Times*, July 26, 1972, 1;
James T. Wooten, "Study of '32 Syphilis Study Recalls Diagnosis," *New
York Times*, July 27, 1972, 18. For more on the study, see James How-
ard Jones, *Bad Blood: The Tuskegee Syphilis Experiment* (New York: Simon and Schuster, 1993); Susan M. Reverby, *Examining Tuskegee: The
Infamous Syphilis Study and Its Legacy* (Chapel Hill: University of North
Carolina Press, 2009). On Kennedy's view of fetal experimentation and
patients' rights, see David J. Rothman, *Strangers at the Bedside: A History
of How Law and Bioethics Transformed Medical Decision Making* (New
York: Basic Books, 1991), 183–184. As early as 1973, Kennedy favored
the establishment of a national commission that would protect human
subjects of scientific research and set guidelines on fetal research. See Harold M. Schmeck Jr., "Panel on Fetuses Passed in Senate," *New York Times*,
September 17, 1973, 34. Ultimately, Congress instead created a commission with a more limited, two-year mandate. See Harold M. Schmeck Jr.,
"Conferees Agree to Ban Research on Live Fetus," *New York Times*, June
8, 1974, 1.

68. Fetal Tissue Research, 1974: Testimony before the Subcommittee on
Health of the Senate Committee on Labor and Public Welfare, 93rd Congress, 2nd Session (1974), 103 (Statement of Andre Hellegers).

69. Ibid., 49 (Statement of Richard Behrman).

70. On Kennedy's preference for a permanent commission, see Schmeck,
"Conferees Agree to Ban," 1. For Behrman's position on women's ability
to give informed consent after abortion, see Statement of Richard Behrman, 109. On Hellegers, see Statement of Andre Hellegers, 95–96.

71. See Jan Liebman, Abortion Amendment Strategy (n.d., ca. 1974), 2, WSH,
Box 11, Folder 12. The fetal research issue was equally absent in NOW's
other lobbying materials on a fetal-protective amendment. See Ann Scott
and Jan Liebman to NOW Legislative Task Force Coordinator et al. (September 1, 1974), 1, NOW, Box 54, Folder 27.

72. See Susan M. Hartmann, *The Other Feminists: Activists in the Liberal
Establishment* (New Haven: Yale University Press, 1998), 5, 68–73. For
more on the ACLU's treatment of women's rights issues in the late 1960s
and early 1970s, see Samuel Walker, *In Defense of American Liberties: A
History of the ACLU*, 2nd ed. (Carbondale: Southern Illinois University

Press, 1999), 304–307, 320, 352, 358; Sarah Azaransky, *The Dream Is Freedom: Pauli Murray and American Democratic Faith* (New York: Oxford University Press, 2011), 59–88.

73. ACLU, "Policy 316a: Internal Organization," ACLU, Box 23, Folder 6.

74. See "Minutes of Special Board Committee on the Role of Women Within the ACLU, November 10, 1972" (November 22, 1972), 1–3, ACLU, Box 103, Folder 12; see also "Summary of Discussion at October 27, 1972 Meeting of Special Board Committee on Role of Women Within the ACLU" (November 3, 1972), 1–5, ACLU, Box 103, Folder 12; Hartmann, *The Other Feminists*, 68–73.

75. On the achievements of fetal researchers, see Diana S. Hart, "Fetal Research and Antiabortion Politics: Holding Science Hostage," *Family Planning Perspectives* 7 (March–April 1975): 73–75; Ronald Michael Green, *The Human Embryo Research Debates: Bioethical Research in the Vortex of Controversy* (New York: Oxford University Press, 2001), 8; Gary Reback, Note, "Fetal Experimentation: Moral, Legal, and Medical Implications," *Stanford Law Review* 26 (1974): 1191–1196. On the impact of *Roe* on fetal research, see Hart, "Fetal Research," 73.

76. See John D. Lantos, *The Lazarus Case: Life-and-Death Issues in Neonatal Intensive Care* (Baltimore: Johns Hopkins University Press, 2001), 15; John D. Lantos and William L. Meadow, *Neonatal Bioethics: The Moral Challenges of Medical Innovation* (Baltimore: Johns Hopkins University Press, 2006), 36–41, 154–156; Judith Rooks, *Midwifery and Childbirth in America* (Philadelphia: Temple University Press, 1997), 56–58.

77. Daniel Callahan, "Abortion and Medical Ethics," *Annals of American Academy of Political and Social Science* 437 (May 1978): 116. On technology and the changing image of the fetus, see Janelle S. Taylor, *The Public Life of the Sonogram: Technology, Consumption, and the Politics of Reproduction* (Ithaca, NY: Cornell University Press, 2008), 4, 27, 32, 39; Lisa Meryn Mitchell, *Baby's First Picture: Ultrasound and the Politics of Fetal Subjects* (Toronto: University of Toronto Press, 2001), 25–37.

78. ACLU Privacy Committee Meeting Minutes (June 16, 1975), 1, 3, ACLU, Box 112, Folder 8.

79. In 1973, over 80 percent of all abortions occurred in the first trimester, when there was no real chance of fetal survival. See Institute of Medicine, *Legalized Abortion and the Public Health* (Washington, DC: National Academy of Sciences, 1975), 22; see also Centers for Disease Control, *Abortion Surveillance: 1973* (Atlanta: United States Department of Health, Education, and Public Welfare, 1975). According to the Centers for Disease Control, approximately 18 percent of all abortions in 1972 were performed at or after thirteen weeks. David A. Grimes, "Second-Trimester Abortions in the United States," *Family Planning Perspectives* 16, no. 6 (1984): 261. By 1981, the rate of abortions after thirteen weeks had declined to 10 percent. Ibid. For the study, see Centers for Disease Control, *Abortion Surveillance, 1981* (Atlanta: United States Department

of Health, Education, and Public Welfare, 1985). For more on changing patterns of late-term abortion, see Stanley Henshaw, Jacqueline Derrosh Forrest, and Elaine Blaine, "Abortion Services in the United States, 1981–1982," *Family Planning Perspectives* 16 (March–April 1984): 125. On conventional definitions of abortion in the period, see Nancy K. Rhoden, "New Neonatal Dilemma: Live Births from Late Abortions," *Georgetown Law Journal* 72 (1983–1984): 1452 (summarizing period understandings that abortion involved fetal killing); see also Centers for Disease Control, *Abortion Surveillance: Annual Surveillance 1977* (Washington, DC: United States Department of Health, Education, and Public Welfare, 1979), 7.

80. On the rate of live births after a prostaglandin abortion, see David C. Nathan, "The Unwanted Child: Caring for the Fetus Born Alive After Abortion," *The Hastings Center Report* 6 (October 1976): 14 (estimating 22 live births per 1,000 prostaglandin abortions); W. Cates and D. A. Grimes, "Morbidity and Mortality of Abortion in the United States," in *Abortion and Sterilization*, ed. Jane Hodgson (Waltham, MA: Academic Press, 1981), 156, 164 (finding a 3 percent rate of live births); W. K. Lee and M. S. Baggish, "Live Birth as a Complication of Second Trimester Abortion Induced with Intra-Amniotic Prostaglandin," *Advances in Planned Parenthood* 13 (1978): 7–10 (finding a live-birth rate of 7 percent); P. G. Stubblefield et al., "Laminaria Augmentation of Intraamniotic PGF2 for Midtrimester Pregnancy Termination," *Prostaglandins* 10 (1975): 421. On the rate of live births after and consequences associated with a saline abortion, see Rhoden, "New Neonatal Dilemma," 1457–1458. On the uncertainty surrounding the proper definition of and data concerning live birth in the period, see Grimes, "Second Trimester Abortions in the United States," 263–264; G. Stroh and A. R. Hinman, "Reported Live Births Following Induced Abortion: Two and One Half Years' Experience in Upstate New York," *American Journal of Obstetrics and Gynecology* 126 (1976): 83.

81. Privacy Committee Meeting Minutes (October 13, 1976), 1–3, ACLU, Box 112, Folder 9.

82. See Barbara Kaiser to the ACLU Privacy Committee, "Fetal Viability" (November 30, 1976), 2, ACLU, Box 112, Folder 9.

83. Ibid., 1–4 ("[I]f the fetus should be born alive, it would be incumbent upon the doctors to keep it alive").

84. The National Institutes of Health, *Prevention of Embryonic, Fetal, and Perinatal Disease*, eds. R. L. Brent and M. I. Harris (Washington, DC: National Institutes of Health, 1976), 356.

85. See "Weinberger Moves to End Ban on Fetal Research," *New York Times*, July 30, 1975, 11. For further discussion of the federal government's resolution of the fetal research issue in the 1970s, see Dubow, *Ourselves Unborn*, 79; Bonnie Steinbock, *Life before Birth: The Moral and Legal Status of Embryos and Fetuses* (New York: Oxford University Press, 1992), 188–191. For reporting on the subject, see Harold M. Schmeck, "National

Board Would End Ban on Live Fetal Study," *New York Times*, April 28, 1975, 61.

86. Compare *Roe v. Wade*, 410 U.S. 113, 165 (1973) (explaining when the State can act in "promoting its interest in the potentiality of human life") with Barbara Kaiser to the ACLU Privacy Committee, "Fetal Viability" (November 30, 1976), 1–4.

87. On the expense of care for very premature infants in the 1970s, see David M. Cutler and Ellen Meara, "The Medical Costs of Young and Old: A Forty Year Perspective," in *Frontiers in the Economics of Aging*, ed. David A. Wise (Chicago: University of Chicago Press, 1998), 237; Suzanne Wymelenberg, *Science and Babies: Private Decisions, Public Dilemmas* (Washington, DC: National Academy Press, 1990), 100. On the rise of D&E procedures, see Rhoden, "New Neonatal Dilemma," 1459–1460. The Supreme Court itself recognized that D&E abortion precluded live birth. *Planned Parenthood Association of Kansas City, Missouri v. Ashcroft*, 103 S. Ct. 2517, 2521 n.7 (1983). On the advantages of D&E abortions, see "Dilation and Evacuation," in *Second Trimester Abortion*, eds. G. Berger, W. Brenner, and L. Keith (Littleton, MA: PSG Publishing, 1981), 128.

88. For Loesch Wiley's recollections: Juli Loesch Wiley, e-mail interview with Mary Ziegler, April 1, 2012. For more on the conflict surrounding Loesch Wiley's group, Pro-Lifers for Survival, see Tacie Dejanikus, "Abortion and Coalition Politics: Whose Survival?" *Off Our Backs*, April 1981, 2, 25; Suzanne Staggenborg, *The Pro-Choice Movement: Organization and Activism in the Abortion Conflict* (New York: Oxford University Press, 1991), 199; David R. Swartz, *The Moral Minority: The Evangelical Left in an Age of Conservatism* (Philadelphia: University of Pennsylvania Press, 2012), 244.

89. Ad Hoc Committee in Defense of Life, "Court Blockbusters," *Lifeletter* #11, July 12, 1977, 2, WC, Lifeletter Folder. For more on anti-feminist rhetoric within the antiabortion movement and aligned groups, see "A Fighter for Right to Life," *Ebony Magazine*, April 1978, 78, 92 (Mildred Jefferson of the NRLC condemning the agenda and aspirations of second-wave feminists); Judy Klemesrud, "Equal Rights Plan and Abortion Opposed by 15,000 at Rally," *New York Times*, November 20, 1977, 32; Elizabeth Moore, "Witnesses Say Feminist Faction Suppressed Others," *National Right to Life News*, October 1977, 5, JRS, 1977 National Right to Life News Box.

90. Larry Lader, "Abortion Opponents' Tactics," *New York Times*, January 11, 1978, 19.

91. "Summary of Reproductive Task Force Meetings, April 28 & 29, 1979" (April 1979), 1, NOW, Box 49, Folder 20.

92. "Planned Parenthood Shifting to a Patriotic Theme," *New York Times*, October 5, 1980, 25; see also Planned Parenthood Fundraising Letter (n.d., ca. 1979), 1–4, JRS, Dr. Joseph Stanton Papers.

93. "Call to Action for Reproductive Rights" (September 14, 1979), 2, NOW, Box 95, Folder 13. For CARASA and R2N2's arguments in this vein, see "Women United to Defend Abortion Rights and End Sterilization Abuse" (n.d., ca. 1980), 3, R2N2, Box 1, Abortion Task Force Folder; "CARASA Proposal on Abortion Rights for R2N2" (n.d., ca. 1981), 2, R2N2, Box 1, Abortion Task Force Folder; R2N2 Abortion Task Force Paper (1981), 7, R2N2, Box 1, Abortion Task Force Folder.

94. On the importance of countering the momentum of the antiabortion movement and the New Right in electoral politics, see Linda Greenhouse, "Abortion Rights Group Expects Hard Times," *New York Times*, February 16, 1981, B6 (describing conclusion of NARAL annual meeting that the partnership between pro-lifers and the political right had become "an effective coalition"); Leslie Bennetts, "For Pro-Abortion Group, An 'Aggressive New Campaign,'" *New York Times*, May 1, 1979, C22 (describing NARAL's "sense of urgency about the 1980 elections"). For an example of efforts to present the opposition as anti-sex or anti-birth control, see Statement by Eleanor Smeal (January 22, 1979), 2, NOW, Box 96, Folder 21 ("The campaign against abortion is becoming a campaign against contraception"). For an example of arguments that the antiabortion movement was actually anti-sex, see "Women United to Defend Abortion Rights and End Sterilization Abuse" (n.d., ca. 1980), 3.

95. On pro-life voters' preference for the Democratic Party into the 1980s, see Karol, *Party Position Change*, 57, 62–63; Greg D. Adams, "Abortion: Evidence of an Issue Evolution," *American Journal of Political Science* 41 (1997): 723, 730–731. On increasing feminist influence at the Democratic National Convention, see Lisa Young, *Feminists and Party Politics* (Toronto: UBC Press, 2000), 43–49, 93–96; Wolbrecht, *The Politics of Women Rights*, 204–221.

96. Bennetts, "For Pro-Abortion Group, an 'Aggressive New Campaign,'" C22.

97. Michael Knight, "Drive for Abortion Rights Begins," *New York Times*, January 23, 1980, A12.

98. Douglas E. Kneeland, "Clark Defeat in Iowa Laid to Abortion Issue," *New York Times*, November 13, 1978, A18; see also John Herbers, "Anti-Abortionists Impact Is Felt in Elections Across the Nation," *New York Times*, June 20, 1978, NJ19 ("The anti-abortion movement . . . has been showing a surprising impact in recent months").

99. John Herbers, "Ultraconservative Evangelicals a Surging New Force in Politics," *New York Times*, August 17, 1980, 1. For more on the contributions of evangelicals, see Darren Dochuk, *From Bible Belt to Sun Belt: Plain-Folk Religion, Grassroots Politics, and the Rise of Evangelical Conservatism* (New York: W. W. Norton, 2011), 361–400; Laura Kalman, *Right Star Rising: A New Politics, 1974–1980* (New York: W. W. Norton, 2010), 250–255, 350–358; Williams, *God's Own Party*, 193–208.

100. On the divisions within the new conservative coalition, see Herbers, "Ultraconservative Evangelicals," 1; see also E. J. Dionne, "Poll Finds Evangelicals Not United Voting Bloc," *New York Times*, September 7, 1980, 34. On Faucher's electoral strategy, see Memorandum, "Political Action Committees: Workshop #2 Political Action Strategy" (June 1981), 1–2, RHS, Box 2, Folder 17. On Faucher's views on the Culver election and the importance of the intensity of voter preference, see ibid., 2.

101. Karen Mulhauser, NARAL Fundraising Letter (n.d., ca. 1979), RHS, Box 2, Folder 19; see also Planned Parenthood Fundraising Letter (n.d., ca. 1979), 1–4.

102. Maryann Barasko, *Governing NOW: Grassroots Activism in the National Organization for Women* (Ithaca, NY: Cornell University Press, 2004), 73.

103. Steven V. Roberts, "Balance of Power in Favor of Abortion," *New York Times*, September 20, 1982, B10. On the expulsion of antiabortion activists: see Laurie Johnston, "NOW Elects Syracuse Lawyer as Head," *New York Times*, May 28, 1974, 29 (Karen DeCrow of NOW explaining: "You can be a NOW member and be against abortion if you don't speak for NOW, but I don't think you can be a feminist and be against the right of a woman to choose abortion"). For activists' recollections of the formation of CARASA: Karen Stamm, interview with Mary Ziegler, March 9, 2012.

104. Meehan, interview.

105. Ibid. For other recollections of the struggle to find common ground: Pat Goltz, interview with Mary Ziegler, March 15, 2011; Kuharski, interview; Wiley, interview; Joseph Lampe, interview with Mary Ziegler, February 9, 2011.

106. Kuharski, interview.

107. Schaller, interview; Wiley, e-mail interview. Later in her career, Loesch Wiley joined Operation Rescue, a controversial direct-action organization. Ultimately, concerned that Operation Rescue marginalized women, Loesch Wiley quit, focusing again on efforts to seek common ground. See Risen and Thomas, *Wrath of Angels*, 264–265, 280, 296.

108. Phyllis Schlafly, interview with Mary Ziegler, November 8, 2010.

109. For the Willkes' volume, see Dr. John and Barbara Willke, *Why Can't We Love Them Both: Questions and Answers on Abortion* (Cincinnati: Hayes Publishing Co., 1997).

Conclusion

1. Lori Moore, "Representative Todd Akin: The Statement and Reaction," *New York Times*, August 20, 2012, accessed April 1, 2014, http://www.nytimes.com/2012/08/21/us/politics/rep-todd-akin-legitimate-rape-statement-and-reaction.html. For more on Akin's comments, see Patrick Marley, "Abortion Has Become Eye of Political Storm," *Milwaukee Journal*

Sentinel, August 28, 2012, 1; Kim Geiger, "The Nation: GOP Left Dispirited After Akin's Gaffe," *Los Angeles Times*, August 28, 2012, 6; Kevin McDermott, "Comments Damage Akin: Poll Shows He Now Trails McCaskill in Race for Senate," *St. Louis Post-Dispatch*, August 26, 2012, A1.

2. "Interview with RNC Chairman Reince Priebus," *Erin Burnett out Front*, August 20, 2012.

3. Jonathan Weisman and John Eligon, "GOP Trying to Oust Akin from the Race for Rape Remarks," *New York Times*, August 20, 2012, accessed April 15, 2014, http://www.nytimes.com/2012/08/21/us/politics/republicans-decry-todd-akins-rape-remarks.html?pagewanted=all.

4. On the Democratic claims about a "war on women," see Stephanie McCrummen, "A War on Women? Not to Them," *Washington Post*, August 28, 2012, A1. For more on requests that Akin drop out of the race, see Bill Lambrecht, "Akin Is Feeling More GOP Heat to Exit Missouri Senate Race," *St. Louis Post-Dispatch*, August 29, 2012, A1; David Espo, "Republicans' Distractions Harmful, Romney Concedes," *Tulsa World News*, August 27, 2012, A10. On absolutist support for Akin, see Ben Johnson, "Todd Akin to Stay in Senate Race; Pro-Life Groups Applaud Decision," *Life Site News*, August 30, 2012, accessed April 13, 2014, http://www.lifesitenews.com/news/breaking-todd-akin-to-stay-in-senate-race-pro-life-groups-applaud-decision; Ben Johnson, "Pro-Family, Tea Party Leaders Coalesce Around Todd Akin," *Life Site News*, August 23, 2012, accessed April 13, 2014, http://www.lifesitenews.com/news/pro-family-tea-party-leaders-coalesce-around-todd-akin. Akin ultimately decided to stay in the Senate race, but he lost his bid to the incumbent, Senator Claire McCaskill (D-MO). See Sean Sullivan, "Democrat Claire McCaskill Defeats Republican Todd Akin in Missouri Senate Race," *Washington Post*, November 6, 2012, accessed April 14, 2014, http://www.washingtonpost.com/blogs/the-fix/wp/2012/11/06/democrat-claire-mccaskill-defeats-republican-todd-akin-in-missouri-senate-race/.

5. Sara Terzo, "The Racist Underpinnings of the Abortion Movement," *Life Site News*, March 26, 2013, accessed April 16, 2014, http://www.lifesite-news.com/news/the-racist-underpinnings-of-the-abortion-movement/. For discussion of efforts to defund Planned Parenthood, see Kathleen Hennessey, "House Republicans See Timely Target in Planned Parenthood," *Los Angeles Times*, February 11, 2011, 21; Bruce Alpert, "House Votes to Defund Planned Parenthood," *New Orleans Times Picayune*, February 19, 2011, Section A; Erik Eckholm, "Budget Feud Ropes in Planned Parenthood," *New York Times*, February 18, 2011, A16.

6. For the Supreme Court's decision on DOMA, see *United States v. Windsor*, 570 U.S. _, 133 S. Ct. 2675 (2013). In the wake of *Windsor*, many federal lower courts, including several courts of appeal, have struck down bans on same-sex marriage. See *Baskin v. Bogin*, 766 F.3d 648 (7th Cir. 2014); *Bostic v. Schaeffer*, 760 F.3d 452 (4th Cir. 2014); *Latta v. Otter*, _ F.3d _ (9th Cir. 2014); *Kitchen v. Herbert*, 755 F.3d 1193 (10th Cir. 2014).

On the Court's decision not to resolve the marriage issue, see Paul Waldman, "A Loud Fight's Quiet End," *Washington Post*, October 7, 2014; "States Issue First Marriage Licenses After Supreme Court Declines Appeal," *Washington Post*, October 6, 2014. For discussion of the history of the movement for marriage equality, see Michael J. Klarman, *From the Closet to the Altar: Courts, Backlash, and the Struggle for Same-Sex Marriage* (New York: Oxford University Press, 2013); George Chauncey, *Why Marriage? The History Shaping Today's Debate over Gay Equality* (New York: Basic Books, 2004); Ellen Ann Anderson, *Out of the Closets and into the Courts: Legal Opportunity Structure and Gay Rights Litigation* (Ann Arbor: University of Michigan Press, 2005).

7. Robert P. George, "Gay Marriage, Democracy, and the Courts," *Wall St. Journal*, August 3, 2009, A11. On *Roe* and the backlash that might accompany a ruling in favor of marriage equality, see Michael J. Klarman, "The Court of Popular Opinion," *Los Angeles Times*, August 15, 2010, 31; Christopher Capozzola, "Suing for Equality," *Gay and Lesbian Review*, May 1, 2011, 41; Eric J. Segall, "Beware a Gay Rights Backlash," *Los Angeles Times*, May 15, 2012, 13. For explanations of why the Court declined to hear cases on marriage equality, see Charles Lane, "A Quiet Triumph for Gay Marriage," *Washington Post*, October 9, 2014; Adam Liptak, "In Surprise, Justices Give Victory to Gay Marriage," *New York Times*, October 7, 2014, 3; Adam Winkler, "Why the Supreme Court Waited on Marriage Equality," *The Huffington Post*, October 6, 2014, accessed October 27, 2014, http://www.huffingtonpost.com/adam-winkler/why-the-supreme-court-wai_b_5939678.html.

8. Cf. Linda Greenhouse and Reva B. Siegel, "Before (and After) *Roe v. Wade*: New Questions about Backlash," *Yale Law Journal* 120 (2010): 2033 ("Understanding the dynamics of conflict before *Roe* changes the questions that we might ask of the record after *Roe*").

9. On the rising violence against abortion providers and abortion clinics in the 1980s and 1990s, see James Risen and Judy L. Thomas, *Wrath of Angels: The American Abortion War* (New York: Basic Books, 1998), 74–76, 339–371; Suzanne Staggenborg, *The Pro-Choice Movement: Organization and Activism in the Abortion Conflict* (New York: Oxford University Press, 1991), 130–132; Donald T. Critchlow, *Intended Consequences: Birth Control, Abortion, and the Federal Government in Modern America* (New York: Oxford University Press, 1999), 215–222. For statistics on clinic violence in the 1980s and 1990s, see Wendy Simonds, *Abortion at Work: Ideology and Practice in a Feminist Clinic* (New Brunswick, NJ: Rutgers University Press, 1996), 7–9.

10. For more on clinic violence, see Mary C. Segers, "The Pro-Choice Movement After *Casey*: Preserving Access," in *Abortion Politics in American States*, eds. Mary C. Segers and Timothy A. Byrnes (Armonk, NY: M. E. Sharpe, 1995), 233–235; Raymond Tatalovich, *The Politics of Abortion in the United States and Canada: A Comparative Study* (Armonk, NY: M. E.

Sharpe, 1997), 229. For the history of the rescue movement, see Risen and Thomas, *Wrath of Angels*, 285–303; Joshua C. Wilson, *The Street Politics of Abortion: Speech, Violence, and America's Culture Wars* (Stanford: Stanford University Press, 2013), 3, 48, 81–82; Carol J. C. Maxwell, *Pro-Life Activists in America: Meaning, Motivation, and Direct Action* (New York: Cambridge University Press, 2002), 52–82. On the decrease in the number of physicians providing abortions, see Lori Freedman, *Willing and Unable: Doctors' Constraints in Abortion Care* (Nashville: Vanderbilt University Press, 2010), 9–19, 21–33. For a sample of efforts made by providers' organizations in the period, see The National Coalition of Abortion Providers Strategic Plan (2000), NCAP, Box 3, Strategic Plan Folder; NCAP Press Release, "Abortion Providers Acknowledge Terminating Potential Human Life" (November 19, 1992), NCAP, Box 3, Newsletters Folder; National Abortion Federation Strategic Plan 1996–2000, CKP, Box 1, National Abortion Federation 2000 Folder.

11. On abortion and the politicization of the Supreme Court nomination process, see John Anthony Maltese, *The Selling of Supreme Court Nominees* (Baltimore: Johns Hopkins University Press, 1998), 1–7; Richard Davis, *Electing Justice: Fixing the Supreme Court Nominations Process* (New York: Oxford University Press, 2005), 84–86, 106–111. For O'Connor's dissent in the Akron case, *City of Akron v. Akron Reproductive Health Center*, 462 U.S. 416, 458 (O'Connor, J., dissenting).

12. For a sample of scholarship on the possible relationship between abortion law and assisted reproductive technologies, see Radhika Rao, "Equal Liberty: Assisted Reproductive Technology and Reproductive Equality," *George Washington Law Review* 76 (2008): 1465–1487; John Robertson, "Assisting Reproduction, Choosing Genes, and the Scope of Reproductive Freedom," *George Washington Law Review* 76 (2008): 1490–1513. On the expanding use of assisted reproductive technologies, see Centers for Disease Control, "Assisted Reproductive Technologies," accessed April 14, 2014, http://www.cdc.gov/art/.

13. *Planned Parenthood of Southeastern Pennsylvania v. Casey*, 505 U.S. 833, 853 (1992) (plurality decision). For discussion of the lead-up to *Casey*, see Linda Greenhouse, "Top Court Could Overturn *Roe* without Saying So," *New York Times*, January 24, 1992, A12; "The Looming Abortion Showdown," *New York Times*, December 18, 1991, A28.

14. For *Casey*'s account of the undue-burden standard, see *Planned Parenthood of Southeastern Pennsylvania v. Casey*, 876–877. For examples of scholarly analysis of *Casey*, see David D. Meyer, "The Paradox of Family Privacy," *Vanderbilt Law Review* 53 (2000): 538–539 (noting that the "undue burden" test is extremely deferential because it "turn[s] more frankly on the Court's assessment of . . . 'reasonableness'"); Linda J. Wharton, Susan Frietsche, and Kathryn Kolbert, "Preserving the Core of *Roe*: Reflections on *Planned Parenthood v. Casey*," *Yale Journal of Law and Feminism* 18 (2006): 353 (arguing that in the aftermath of *Casey*,

lower court decisions "manipulat[ed] the undue burden standard in an incremental undermining of *Roe*").

15. *Gonzales v. Carhart*, 550 U.S. 124, 159 (2007). For analysis of the *Carhart* opinion, see Khiara M. Bridges, "Capturing the Judiciary: *Carhart* and the Undue Burden Standard," *Washington and Lee Law Review* 67 (2010): 955–984; Maya Manian, "The Irrational Woman: Informed Consent and Abortion Decision-Making," *Duke Journal of Law and Gender* 16 (2009): 254–262; Reva B. Siegel, "Dignity and the Politics of Protection: Abortion Restrictions under *Casey/Carhart*," *Yale Law Journal* 117 (2008): 1707–1735.

16. On the *Casey* template, see Neal Devins, "How *Planned Parenthood v. Casey* (Pretty Much) Settled the Abortion Wars," *Yale Law Journal* 118 (2009): 1323–1341. For examples of state laws that test the boundaries of *Casey*, see Guttmacher Institute, "State Policies in Brief: Requirements for Ultrasound" (April 1, 2014), accessed April 14, 2014, https://www.guttmacher.org/statecenter/spibs/spib_RFU.pdf; Guttmacher Institute, "Monthly State Updates: Major Developments for 2014" (April 1, 2014), accessed April 14, 2014, http://www.guttmacher.org/statecenter/updates/index.html?utm_source=feedburnerutm_medium=feedutm_campaign=Feed%3A+Guttmacher+(New+from+the+Guttmacher+Institute. For Justice Ginsburg's dissent in *Carhart*, see *Gonzales v. Carhart*, 550 U.S. 124, 169–191 (2007) (Ginsburg, J., dissenting).

17. On the contemporary conflict between absolutists and incrementalists, see Erik Eckholm, "Anti-Abortion Groups Split on Legal Tactics," *New York Times*, December 5, 2011, A1; James T. McCafferty, "The Perils of Promoting Personhood," *The New Oxford Review* 79 (2012): 24; Cheryl Wetzstein, "State Abortion Curbs Rose in '11," *Washington Times*, January 9, 2012, A6 (detailing personhood battles in states like Mississippi and Colorado); Steve Siebelius, "What It Means to Be 'Pro-Life,'" *Las Vegas Review Journal*, January 18, 2012, 7B.

18. *Planned Parenthood of Southeastern Pennsylvania v. Casey*, 1000 (Scalia, J., dissenting) (emphasis in the original). For other arguments about the damage done by the *Roe* decision to popular perceptions of the legitimacy of the Supreme Court, see William N. Eskridge Jr. and John A. Ferejohn, *A Republic of Statutes: The New American Constitution* (New Haven, CT: Yale University Press, 2010), 242 (arguing that pro-lifers opposed *Roe* because it "represented arrogant judicial legislation"); William N. Eskridge Jr., "Channeling: Identity-Based Social Movements and Public Law," *University of Pennsylvania Law Review* 150 (2001): 489 (claiming that in the aftermath of *Roe*, "pro-life advocates also maintained that the nationalization of the issue violated precepts of federalism"); cf. Jack M. Balkin, "'Wrong the Day It Was Decided': *Lochner* and Constitutional Historicism," *Boston University Law Review* 85 (2005): 688 (noting that *Roe* "has become the central and fraught symbol of the Supreme Court's legitimacy and authority to interpret the Constitution"); Thomas M. Keck, "The Neoconservative

Assault on the Courts: How Worried Should We Be?" in *Confronting the New Conservatism: The Rise of the Right in America*, ed. Michael Thompson (New York: New York University Press, 2007), 165; Nancy MacLean, "Guardians of Privilege," in *Debating the Conservative Movement: 1945 to Present*, eds. Donald T. Critchlow and Nancy MacLean (Lanham, MD: Rowman and Littlefield, 2009), 156; Paul Boyer, "The Evangelical Resurgence in 1970s American Protestantism," in *Rightward Bound: Making America Conservative in the 1970s*, eds. Bruce J. Shulman and Julian E. Zelizer (Cambridge, MA: Harvard University Press, 2008), 36–37.

19. Klarman, *From the Closet to the Altar*, x.

20. Ibid., 204; see also Michael J. Klarman, *From Jim Crow to Civil Rights: The Supreme Court and the Struggle for Racial Equality* (New York: Oxford University Press, 2004), 465.

21. See Klarman, *From Jim Crow to Civil Rights*, 409, 465 (describing the empowerment of extremists as a feature of backlash); Elizabeth Mensch and Alan Freeman, *The Politics of Virtue: Is Abortion Debatable?* 2nd ed. (Durham, NC: Duke University Press, 1995), 127, 135; Jeffrey Rosen, *The Most Democratic Branch: How the Courts Serve America* (New York: Oxford University Press, 2006), 91. For Rosenberg's argument, see Gerald N. Rosenberg, *The Hollow Hope: Can Courts Bring about Social Change?* 2nd ed. (Chicago: University of Chicago Press, 2008), 173–199; Gerald Rosenberg, "Courting Disaster: Looking for Change in All the Wrong Places," *Drake Law Review* 54 (2006): 810–812.

22. See Martha Minow, "1986 Term Foreword: Justice Engendered," *Harvard Law Review* 101 (1987): 86 n.360; Robin West, "From Choice to Reproductive Justice: De-Constitutionalizing Abortion Rights," *Yale Law Journal* 118 (2009): 1411; Joan Williams, "Gender Wars: Selfless Women in the Republic of Choice," *New York University Law Review* 66 (1991): 1577. For further arguments in this vein, see Rhonda Copelon, "Unpacking Patriarchy: Reproduction, Sexuality, Originalism, and Constitutional Change," in *A Less than Perfect Union: Alternative Perspectives on the United States Constitution*, ed. Jules Lobel (New York: Monthly Review Press, 1988), 303–334; Catharine MacKinnon, "*Roe v. Wade*: A Study in Male Ideology," in *Abortion, Moral and Legal Perspectives*, eds. Jay L. Garfield and Patricia Hennessey (Amherst: University of Massachusetts Press, 1984), 45–53. Historians have raised similar criticisms in discussing the impact of *Roe* on the relationship between the women's movement and women of color. See Jennifer Nelson, *Women of Color and the Reproductive Rights Movement* (New York: New York University Press, 2003), 171; Rickie Solinger, *Beggars and Choosers: How the Politics of Choice Shapes Adoption, Abortion, and Welfare in the United States* (New York: Farrar, Straus, and Giroux, 2001), 10.

23. William N. Eskridge, Jr. "Pluralism and Distrust: How Courts Can Support Democracy by Lowering the Stakes of Politics," *Yale Law Journal* 114 (2005): 1312. Other scholars and advocates have argued that *Roe*

short-circuited a productive and creative debate about the meaning of abortion rights. See Richard A. Posner, *The Problematics of Moral and Legal Theory* (Cambridge, MA: Harvard University Press, 1999), 254. For more on the way in which *Roe* froze dialogue about abortion in the states and within social movements, see Cass R. Sunstein, *One Case at a Time: Judicial Minimalism on the Supreme Court*, 2nd ed. (Cambridge, MA: Harvard University Press, 2001), 114–115; Ruth Bader Ginsburg, "Speaking in a Judicial Voice," *New York University Law Review* 67 (1992): 1205; Mensch and Freeman, *The Politics of Virtue*, 109; George, "Gay Marriage, Democracy, and the Courts," A11.

24. For understandings of *Roe* as a decision related to sexual liberation, see Brian Heffernan to the ACLU Due Process Committee (March 19, 1975), ACLU, Box 108, Folder 2 (describing an existing constitutional right to privacy that would cover sexual intimacy); COYOTE Press Release, "Prostitution and the Constitution" (1974), COYOTE, Carton 1, Folder 26 (contending that sexual freedom enjoyed protection because of "the individual's right to control his or her own body without unreasonable interference from the state"); Marilyn Haft, "Hustling for Rights," *Civil Liberties Review* (Winter 1974), 8–26. On the hookers' balls, see Samantha Majic, *Sex Work Politics: From Protest to Service Provision* (Philadelphia: University of Pennsylvania Press, 2014), 3; Stephanie Gilmore, "Strange Bedfellows: Building Feminist Coalitions around Sex Work in the 1970s," in *No Permanent Waves: Recasting Histories of U.S. Feminism*, ed. Nancy A. Hewitt (Piscataway, NJ: Rutgers University Press, 2010), 246–273. On the ACLU Sexual Privacy Project and the coalition it helped to create, see ACLU Due Process Committee Minutes (March 7, 1974), 3–8, ACLU, Box 108, Folder 2 (describing early debate on rights for prostitutes); ACLU Due Process Committee Meeting Minutes (March 19, 1975), 1–4, ACLU, Box 108, Folder 2 (discussing new policies on prostitution and gay rights); Brian Heffernan to ACLU Due Process Committee, "Revision of Proposed Policy on Rights of Homosexuals" (March 19, 1975), 1–2, ACLU, Box 108, Folder 2 (discussing new campaign against sexual-orientation discrimination).

25. For examples of these arguments, see The National Coalition of Abortion Providers Strategic Plan (2000), 3 (calling for a different approach than the one adopted by groups that "focus attention and fund raising on protecting the *right* to abortion") (emphasis in the original); NCAP Strategic Plan Overview (April 2005), 6, NCAP, Box 3, Strategic Plan Folder (emphasizing arguments that "[a]bortion [is] not a problem, rather the solution to the problem" and calling for "support for women dealing with the complex issues of pregnancy").

26. Kristin Luker, *Abortion and the Politics of Motherhood* (Berkeley: University of California Press, 1984), 193.

27. Faye D. Ginsburg, *Contested Lives: The Abortion Debate in an American Community* (Berkeley: University of California Press: 1998), 216.

28. Ibid., 15.

29. Ibid., 220.

30. Luker, *Abortion*, 244. For further expressions of this view, see Donald T. Critchlow, "Birth Control, Population, and Family Planning: An Overview," in *The Politics of Abortion and Birth Control in Historical Perspective*, ed. Donald T. Critchlow (University Park: Penn State University Press, 1996), 5; Klarman, *From Jim Crow to Civil Rights*, 465.

31. Reva B. Siegel, "Reasoning from the Body: A Historical Perspective on Abortion Regulation and Equal Protection," *Stanford Law Review* 44 (1992): 379. For additional arguments in this vein: Susan Frelich Appleton, "Doctors, Patients, and the Constitution: A Theoretical Analysis of the Physician's Role in 'Private' Reproductive Decisions," *Washington University Law Quarterly* 63 (1985): 231 ("[E]ven when [abortion] laws do not limit access, they demean women by perpetuating stereotypes of women as a special class of medical patients in need of governmental protection"); Sylvia A. Law, "Rethinking Sex and the Constitution," *University of Pennsylvania Law Review* 132 (1984): 1035 (arguing that abortion legislation "reinforces the cultural stereotype that motherhood is women's destiny, . . . express[es] disapprobation for abortion, [and] regard[s] the woman as a 'mother-machine'").

32. See Laurence H. Tribe, *Abortion: The Clash of Absolutes* (New York: W. W. Norton, 1992), 234 (explaining that "opposition to abortion rights may in large part be about sexual morality"). For further discussion of the polarization of gender issues after *Roe*, see Donald T. Critchlow, *The Conservative Ascendancy: How the GOP Right Made Political History* (Cambridge, MA: Harvard University Press, 2007), 134–136; Daniel K. Williams, *God's Own Party: The Making of the Christian Right*, 2nd ed. (New York: Oxford University Press, 2012), 117; Leigh Ann Wheeler, *How Sex Became a Civil Liberty* (New York: Oxford University Press, 2012), lx.

33. For examples of contemporary, dissenting, left-leaning abortion-rights organizations, see All Our Lives, "Mission," accessed April 14, 2014, http://www.allourlives.org/about-us/mission/; Consistent Life: Voices for Peace and Life, accessed April 12, 2014, http://www.consistent-life.org/.

34. Ginsburg, "Speaking in a Judicial Voice," 1199–1200. For more on efforts to reframe abortion rights, see Law, "Rethinking Sex," 1030–1035; Siegel, "Reasoning from the Body," 351–380; Eileen McDonagh, "The Next Step after *Roe*: Using Fundamental Rights, Equal Protection Analysis to Nullify State-Level Abortion Legislation," *Emory Law Journal* 56 (2007): 1174–1175, 1180–1181; Cary Franklin, "The Anti-Stereotyping Principle in Constitutional Sex Discrimination Law," *New York University Law Review* 85 (2010): 141–160; Jennifer Hendricks, "Body and Soul: Equality, Pregnancy and the Unitary Right to Abortion," *Harvard Civil Rights-Civil Liberties Law Review* 45 (2010): 331. For Scalia's view, see *Planned Parenthood of Southeastern Pennsylvania v. Casey*, 995–1001 (Scalia, J., dissenting).

35. Tribe, *The Clash of Absolutes*, 135.

36. See Ruth Bader Ginsburg, "Some Thoughts on Autonomy and Equality in Relation to *Roe v. Wade*," *North Carolina Law Review* 63 (1985): 379–386; Ginsburg, "Speaking in a Judicial Voice," 1199–1200; Tribe, *The Clash of Absolutes*, 75, 105–108, 212, 256.

37. Cass R. Sunstein, "If People Would Be Outraged by Their Rulings, Should Judges Care?" *Stanford Law Review* 60 (2007): 183. For further perspective on Sunstein's theory of minimalism, see Cass R. Sunstein, "Burkean Minimalism," *Michigan Law Review* 105 (2006): 353–405; Cass R. Sunstein, "Problems with Minimalism," *Stanford Law Review* 58 (2006): 1899–1918. On Sunstein's many-minds theory, see Cass R. Sunstein, *A Constitution of Many Minds: Why the Founding Document Doesn't Mean What It Meant Before* (Princeton: Princeton University Press, 2009), 2–15; Cass R. Sunstein, *Infotopia: How Many Minds Produce Knowledge* (New York: Oxford University Press, 2006), 49–51.

38. Sunstein, *One Case at a Time*, 114.

39. Cass R. Sunstein, "Concurring in the Judgment," in *What Roe v. Wade Should Have Said: The Nation's Top Legal Experts Rewrite America's Most Controversial Decision*, ed. Jack M. Balkin (New York: New York University Press, 2005), 248.

40. Eskridge and Ferejohn, *A Republic of Statutes*, 378, 380, 387.

41. Ibid., 242; see also Eskridge, "Channeling: Identity-Based Social Movements and Public Law," 465.

42. See Richard A. Posner, *Law, Pragmatism, and Democracy* (Cambridge, MA: Harvard University Press, 2003), 123–126; see also Richard A. Posner, *Sex and Reason* (Cambridge, MA: Harvard University Press, 1992), 80.

43. An important body of work argues that some of the changes defining the current abortion struggle actually arose before *Roe*. See Gene Burns, *The Moral Veto: Framing Abortion, Contraception, and Cultural Pluralism in the United States* (New York: Cambridge University Press, 2005), 225–227; Greenhouse and Siegel, "Before (and after) *Roe v. Wade*," 2046–2071. This book establishes that the now-familiar polarization of abortion politics emerged neither immediately after nor primarily because of the *Roe* decision.

Acknowledgments

To thank everyone who contributed to this book would require another chapter at least, but first credit goes to my family. My father, Robert Ziegler, taught me to value stories others had forgotten. In fighting through a life-threatening illness at the time of this writing, he reminded me never to give up. My husband, Dan Tadesse, has contributed almost as much to this book as I have, and it would not have come nearly so far without his belief in me. I could not ask for a better partner. My mother, Louise Ziegler, has read countless drafts, and her critical eye and gracious spirit have brought to life the story in this book.

For intellectual guidance, my colleagues at Florida State University and Saint Louis University have been tremendous. Kenneth Mack has been a mentor and an inspiration since my first legal history course in law school. Working with and learning from Reva Siegel helped me to conceive of this project and make it infinitely more rich. Martha Minow opened my eyes to the relationship between constitutional law and history. Many other wonderful people have shared comments on the ideas advanced in the book, including Susan Appleton, Sarah Barringer-Gordon, Felice Batlan, Caitlin Borgmann, Al Brophy, Beth Burkstrand-Reid, Courtney Cahill, Kristin Collins, Joel Goldstein, Linda Gordon, Ken Kersch, Regina Kunzel, Sophia Lee, Maya Manian, Cilla Smith, Kara Swanson, Steve Teles, Tracy Thomas, and Anders Walker. By allowing me to share the ideas for the book on Legal History Blog, Tomiko Brown-Nagin, Dan Ernst, and Karen Tani brought me into dialogue with other scholars wrestling with the same questions.

Serena Mayeri and Deborah Dinner read the entire manuscript, and their warm support and keen insight steered it through its final stages. Throughout work on the project, Serena has been unfailingly giving and matchless in her ability to see deeper questions I might have missed. Donald Critchlow brought to bear his own deep knowledge of reproductive history in reading parts of the manuscript. Sara Dubow, Daniel K. Williams, and I have been following parallel paths for years, and I cannot thank them enough for their willingness to read parts of this work.

I thank my editor at Harvard University Press, Elizabeth Knoll, for her insight, wit, and kindness. Others at Harvard University Press, including Susan Wallace Boehmer, Joy Deng, and Matthew Higgins, have been unfailingly helpful.

Many archivists have gone out of their way to help me locate primary sources. Kat Klepfer, Mary McCormick, Katrina Miller, and the library staff at Florida State have done more than I could have asked to keep the project on track. In awarding me a Mary Lily Research Grant, the Sally Bingham Center at Duke University provided valuable support. I am indebted to the archivists at the Andover-Harvard Theological Library, Francis A. Countway Medical Library, and Schlesinger Library at Harvard University, Brandeis University, the Concordia Seminary of the Lutheran Church Missouri Synod, the Gerald Ford Presidential Library and Museum, Liberty University, the Library of Congress, the Montana Historical Society Research Center Archives, North Dakota State University, the Rockefeller Archive at Rockefeller University, the Ronald Reagan Presidential Library and Museum, the Seeley G. Mudd Manuscript Library at Princeton University, the State Historical Society of North Dakota, the Sophia Smith Collection at Smith College, the Sterling Memorial Library at Yale University, the University of Missouri-St. Louis, and the Wilcox Collection at the University of Kansas. Judie Brown, Jane Gilroy, Margie Montgomery, Charles Rice, Judith Senderowitz, and Charlotte Taft were kind enough to give me access to their personal papers and writings.

Finally, this book would never have come into being without the help and generosity of those activists on either side of the abortion question who shared their journeys with me. All of them never failed to surprise me with their kindness, their openness, and their complexity. They gave me their time, their trust, and their stories without expecting anything in return. More than anything, they challenged me to rethink the world of abortion politics and my preconceptions about those who made that world. This book belongs to them.

Index

women's liberation, 6–8, 231

women's movement: legal abortion and, 230–231; population control and, 4–6, 95–127, 231, 237; pro-life movement and, 14–15

women's rights: abortion battles and, 173–175, 194, 234–237; abortion-rights movement and, 95–127; arguments about, 14–15, 231–234; compromise and, 189–193; fertility control, 17, 98–101, 113–114, 127–131, 173, 190; fetal rights and, 35, 202–212;

interpretation of *Roe v. Wade,* 169–183, 219–220, 233–234, 239–240; legal abortion and, 230–231; politics and, 95–127, 212–218; population control and, 4–6, 95–127, 231, 237; pro-life movement and, 175–178; reproductive freedom and, 175, 182–183, 192–198, 210–211, 226

Wynn v. Scott, 66

Zero Population Growth, Inc. (ZPG), 6–8, 100–103, 108, 112, 117–119